This volume is dedicated, with admiration and appreciation, to
Di Brooks, Nina Karsov and Colin Smith.

…iant book, full of humanity … A glittering triumph of well-researched
…ship, first-rate writing, and a powerful conviction of integrity,
…ion, courage and patriotism.' – *Jeremy Black*

…st biographies are thoroughly contextual and this one is no exception.
…rative is rich in observation and explanation, yet still enticingly easy
… Its subject comes across as someone quite remarkable for his
…d, adaptive, yet utterly self-effacing courage.' – *Neville Brown*

…splendid book, Julian Lewis gets into the mind-set of a modest young
…frican airman – six times decorated for gallantry in battle – who was
…risk his life repeatedly for causes he thought just, and for an Empire he
…worth serving.' – *M.R.D. Foot*

…ewis has brought back to life the quiet-man-of-the-air, "Kink"
… – an extraordinary figure whose short life spanned service in the
…ar, the Allied expedition against the nascent Soviet Union and
…q, before ending tragically in pursuit of the World Air Speed Record.
…fine piece of historical detective work.' – *Peter Hennessy*

…"Kink" Kinkead was an astonishing British Empire hero, and in
…wis he has found the ideal biographer who combines a complete
…f the sources with a novelist's observational eye. Kinkead died as he
…a preternatural courage attempting to extend the bounds of human
…nt. At long last, he has a biography worthy of his extraordinary
….' – *Andrew Roberts*

Racing Ace

Racing Ace

The Fights and Flights of
'Kink' Kinkead
DSO, DSC★, DFC★

JULIAN LEWIS

Pen & Sword
AVIATION

First published in Great Britain in 2011 by
PEN & SWORD AVIATION
An imprint of
Pen & Sword Books Ltd
47 Church Street
Barnsley
South Yorkshire
S70 2AS

ISBN 978-1-84884-216-8

A CIP catalogue record for this book is
available from the British Library.

Typeset by Concept, Huddersfield, West Yorkshire
Printed and bound in Great Britain by the MPG Books Group

Pen & Sword Books Ltd incorporates the imprints of Pen & Sword Aviation,
Pen & Sword Maritime, Pen & Sword Military, Wharncliffe Local History,
Pen & Sword Select, Pen & Sword Military Classics, Leo Cooper, Remember When,
Seaforth Publishing and Frontline Publishing.

For a complete list of Pen & Sword titles please contact
PEN & SWORD BOOKS LIMITED
47 Church Street, Barnsley, South Yorkshire, S70 2AS, England
E-mail: enquiries@pen-and-sword.co.uk
Website: www.pen-and-sword.co.uk

Contents

List of Plates

58. The engine salvaged.
59. Fawley Church, 16 March 1928.
60. Kink's grave at Fawley.
61. Cranwell's Kinkead Trophy, still awarded annually.
62. Members of the Kinkead-Weekes family visit the Kinkead Room in the original hangar at Calshot Activities Centre: Paul (great-nephew), Mark (nephew) and Roddy (great-nephew).

Photograph credits

List of Maps

Acknowledgements

Many people have contributed in different ways to the revival of interest in Kink Kinkead. They include (with apologies for any inadvertent omissions): Chris Applegarth and Ian Shields of 47 Squadron; Paul Baillie, for material on Edgar Fulford; Anne and David Baker, daughter and grandson of Sir Geoffrey Salmond; Hazel and the late Maurice Baker, for material on Charlie Etherington; Nigel Barker; BBC South Television; David Barnes; John Barrass, Bruce Castle, Pete Cochrane and Peter Dixon of 30 Squadron RAF; Tony Barrington-Hill; Paul Beaver; Nicola Bennett of ancestor.co.za; John Blake; Godfrey Bloom; Cliff Bowen; Di Bentley; Di and Ray Brooks; Alan and Margaret Brown and John Thompson of the New Forest Aviation Group; Jean Buckberry, formerly College Librarian and Archivist, RAF Cranwell; Ron Buckingham; Matthew Butson and Sarah McDonald of Getty Images; Phil and Robin Clabburn; Mike Collins; Pamela Combes; Sebastian Cox and staff at the Air Historical Branch; Charles Curry and the late Brian Down of the *Lymington Times*; Churchwardens and Council of All Saints, Fawley; Sue Dallibar and Professor Paul Hardaker of the Met Office; Andrew Dawrant, Linda Harding and Fred Marsh of the Royal Aero Club; Peter Devitt, Peter Elliott, Keith Ifould, Andrew Renwick, Ajay Srivastava and Ian Thirsk of the RAF Museum; Vic Doggrell; Frank Dorber for material on Rowan Daly, Edgar Fulford and William Burns Thomson; Les Downer; Maldwin Drummond; Jack Dunning; Peter East, Jez Gale and Chris Yandell of the *Southern Daily Echo*; Dave Etheridge; Jonathan Falconer; Bob Franklin; Lee and Stan Freeman; Rosie Gavzey; Muriel Gemmel; Mark Gorringe, formerly of XI (Tornado) Squadron, RAF Leeming; Penny Grinbeek; Gregory Grylls; Stuart Harding; the late Vic Hodgkinson; House of Commons Library; Dave Harrison; Kate Hill; Brett Holman; John Hutton; Ben Irving; Rev. Barry James; Jeff Jefford, for maps; ACM Sir Richard Johns, former Chief of Air Staff; Alan and Kathy Jones, Steve Alcock, Peter Dimmick, Dave Hatchard and Dave Whatley at Solent Sky Museum; Sophie Jones and Karena Smith, formerly of ITN; Nina Karsov; Major J.L. Keene, Director, National Museum of Military History, Johannesburg, for the note from Dr Staz; Patrick Kempe; Tony Kerpel; Bill Kincaid; Peter Kincaid; Mark and Joan Kinkead-Weekes; the late Noel (Bobby) Kinkead-Weekes; Paul and Ruma Kinkead-Weekes; Roddy Kinkead-Weekes; Sue Kinkead-Weekes; Tim Kinkead-Weekes; David Kirkpatrick; Brian Lamb and Phil Quill, former and current Directors of

Calshot Activities Centre; Judy Le Grange, Curator of Jeppe High School for Boys' Museum and Archive; Stuart Leslie and the late Jack Bruce; Keith Mans and Brian Riddle of the Royal Aeronautical Society; Ann McCarthy and Helen Morgan of the University of Melbourne, and Kevin Molloy of the State Library of Victoria, for material on L.P. Coombes; Alexis McEvoy, Alan Rice, Ken Thornber and Ewart Wooldridge of Hampshire County Council; Sue McMahon, Librarian, Worthing Reference Library, and Ron Iden, West Sussex Record Office, for material on Thompson Kinkead; Air Cdre Gordon McRobbie; Meridian Television; Hon Ralph and Ailsa Montagu; Eric Morris; Graham Mottram, Moira Gittos, Jan Keohane, Thomas Langham and Sue Wilson of the Fleet Air Arm Museum, Yeovilton; Brian and Brenda Mudge; Clare Murley and Graham Parkes of Fawley Historians; Heather Nelson; Michael Oakey of *Aeroplane* magazine; Frank Olynyk and Christopher Shores, for sharing their unparalleled knowledge of Great War Combat Reports; Rev. Gary Philbrick; Garfield Porter; Tony Pritchard; Gary and Jeri Radder, for material on Marion Aten; Norman and the late Marion Richardson; Andy Ridley; Léonie Rosenstiel, widow of Arthur Orrmont; Melanie Rolfe; Gill Rushton; Paul Sanger-Davies; John Shelton; Colin Smith; John Smith, for Felixstowe photographs; Frank Souness; Southampton Air Training Corps; William Spencer, Hugh Alexander and other staff at The National Archives UK; 30 Squadron RAF; 47 Squadron RAF; 201 Squadron RAF; AVM Ian Stewart; Lesley Stewart; Richard Stovin-Bradford; Gisela Stuart; Roderick Suddaby, Simon Offord and David Bell of the Imperial War Museum; Jessica Talmage; Leonard Taylor; Philip Taylor; Steve and Wendy Taylor; Penny Tennant-Thomas; Mark Thackeray; Brad Thompson, publisher of the new edition of *Last Train Over Rostov Bridge*; Sir Neil Thorne; Colin van Geffen, for maps and for material from his own research; Fiona Vandersluys; Ruth Vernon; Jake Waterson, past winner of the Kinkead Trophy; Brother Martin Whiteford, Archivist for the Marist Brothers, Southern African Province; Jacky Williams; Henry Wilson, Pamela Covey, Katie Eaton, Matt Jones, Noel Sadler and Jon Wilkinson of Pen & Sword Books, whose support for the project made publication possible; and Stephen Wood.

Permission from The National Archives to reproduce Crown Copyright material is gratefully acknowledged, as is that from Oxford University Press to republish extracts from the Official History, *The War in the Air*, by H.A. Jones. Norman Franks, John Shelton and Christopher Shores also kindly gave permission for quotations from their books, listed among the sources, to be used. Copyright holders for other works quoted, whom it has not been possible to locate so long after publication, are invited to contact the author for full acknowledgement, if possible, in the future.

JL

Preface

by Graham Mottram
Director, Fleet Air Arm Museum,
Yeovilton

When national pride is a principle almost discouraged in today's society, it is difficult to imagine the pride in the British Empire which existed a century ago. It was a pride which inspired many thousands of young men from across the Empire and Commonwealth to flock to join the armed forces in the war against the Triple Alliance. Probably the best-known of this migration were the Australians and New Zealanders, who proudly made up the ANZACS and who suffered dreadfully in the slaughter and debacle of the Dardanelles.

Less well-known were the young men from the Dominion of South Africa, and one of these had his first experience of war flying over the Dardanelles – Sam or 'Kink' Kinkead, the subject of this book. Military flying was still in its infancy, equipment was unreliable and tactics were sketchy. Survival needed both talent and luck. Kink was lucky to begin his operational career in the Dardanelles because, although his aircraft had their performance diminished by the climate, it was an area of low operational risk and new pilots could build up their experience in comparative safety. Many of the Army's Royal Flying Corps' high-loss periods can be put down to rushing 'green' pilots into very dangerous circumstances. Kink, however, had put his novitiate behind him when he was transferred to the Western Front.

There he put his talent to lethal use, rapidly becoming one of the Royal Naval Air Service's most capable and deadly fighter pilots. Much has been written about the unreliability of fighter pilot scores in both World Wars; but the most reliable modern research still attributes Kink with more than thirty victories, and history records his survival over a long period in fighting squadrons. His roll of gallantry decorations places Kink high in the lists of Great War aces.

Racing Ace will correct the relative anonymity in which this brilliant but modest pilot has been cloaked since his premature death, again flying in the service of the 'mother country', in 1928. Dr Lewis has done a remarkable job in assembling that information which remains about the man himself, and –

especially where it is lacking, particularly for Kink's early service – in describing the context in which he flew. The book thus gives the reader detailed insights into, and a condensed history of, much of the Great War and of the little-known Allied support in 1919 for the White Russians after the Bolshevik Revolution. Kink's luck did not desert him in South Russia, despite the total collapse of the Allied expedition and a desperate escape to a friendly port.

And when Kink's luck did run out, as he attempted to capture the World Air Speed Record following a consummate performance in the 1927 Schneider Trophy team, all that remains of the somewhat limited inquiry – even by the standards of the day – into the cause of his death has been unearthed. Not by the hagiography of a biased author, but through the words of the contemporaries who admired him in life and mourned him in death, Samuel Marcus Kinkead emerges as a brilliant pilot and an exemplary man.

Introduction

Finding a Family

The telephone at the house in Ramsgate rang several times before it was answered: 'Mark Kinkead-Weekes,' said a deep, melodious voice. 'Forgive me for calling out of the blue. My name's Julian Lewis; I'm the MP for part of the New Forest, near Southampton, and I gather you're a nephew of the late Flight Lieutenant Kinkead.' 'Oh, yes – Kink – in fact, I am actually named after him.' 'Well, he is buried in my constituency, and we want to honour his memory, in March, on the 70th anniversary of his death. We really hope that the family would be willing to take part . . .'

The events leading up to that call began, as so often happens, purely by chance. In the summer of 1995, as a would-be parliamentarian in search of a seat, I knew the odds were against me. My Party had lost its way and was heading for defeat. Not many new Conservative MPs would emerge after the next election – there were, in the event, a mere thirty-two – and, if I were to be one of them, in-depth research in likely seats would be vital. Thus, I found myself criss-crossing the newly-created New Forest East constituency by motorcycle. It was a visit to the great Esso plant at Fawley on Southampton Water which led me to the lovely Norman church of All Saints, just opposite the refinery headquarters.

In the churchyard, my eye was caught by two rows of military graves – unexpected in a calm civilian environment, but actually most appropriate: for where else should those who die in the skies above their country finally be laid to rest? Two young Hurricane pilots lie there, alongside the crews of two bombers lost as they fought their way home. One of these was a Whitley V of 77 Squadron, struggling back from a raid on Bordeaux at 3.30am on 15 August 1940. It was brought down by the cable of a barrage balloon intended for the Luftwaffe. The Wireless Operator, Sergeant John Burrow from Blackburn, was just 20. The inscription on his headstone reads: 'Into the mosaic of victory we lay this priceless piece – our son'. I promised myself that, in the unlikely event of winning the New Forest East nomination, I would quote that noble sentence in my Maiden Speech.

Guarding the front row of the military plot are a few Celtic crosses. They mark the graves of peacetime casualties from RAF Calshot – the famous seaplane base set up, where the Solent meets Southampton Water, by the Royal Naval Air Service in 1913. The most prominent bears the following legend:

IN MEMORY OF
FLIGHT LIEUTENANT
SAMUEL MARCUS KINKEAD
D.S.O., D.S.C., D.F.C.
WHO, ON THE 12TH MARCH 1928
WHILE FLYING AT CALSHOT, GAVE
HIS LIFE IN AN ATTEMPT TO BREAK
THE WORLD'S SPEED RECORD.

For a Flight Lieutenant to have such decorations was surely remarkable. For him to have died in such circumstances was surely extraordinary. The 70th anniversary of his death was fairly close at hand: it gave me an incentive to investigate.

Although familiar with the period, I am no historian of the Great War. My field is Strategic Studies, centring on British military planning at the start of the Cold War and the case for nuclear deterrence throughout and beyond it. Yet, the more I heard about Kink, the more it seemed unjust that his tale had been forgotten. A number of people soon volunteered to help. One was Gregory Grylls, a South African researcher who, like me twenty years earlier, spent much of his time working on archives at the Public Record Office in Kew. He obtained details of Kink's medals and citations from the *London Gazette*. Altogether there were half a dozen: Kink won the Distinguished Service Cross twice with the RNAS and then the Distinguished Flying Cross twice in 1918 after the formation of the RAF. No sooner had the Great War ended, than he volunteered to fight the Bolsheviks as part of the Allied Intervention Force in South Russia. There he was awarded an immediate DSO in the field, as well as a Mention in Despatches at the end of the campaign.

With so many ex-Servicemen and women living in the New Forest and on the Waterside, it is not surprising that the local Aviation Group is thriving. Alan Brown, its tireless Secretary, is a former expert RAF parachutist. He took a break from organising exhibitions and chronicling the New Forest Airfields to pay a visit to the Fleet Air Arm Museum at Yeovilton. Sure enough, his hunch paid off: two large albums of photographs had been deposited there – one from Kink's career as a Great War ace, the other from his time as a Schneider Trophy pilot the year before he died.

By the end of 1997, as a newly-elected MP, I could take plans forward to commemorate the 70th anniversary. RAF Cranwell told me of the existence of the Kinkead Trophy – awarded annually in his memory to the best young graduate from the Flying Training programme. The College also has a fine portrait, by George Harcourt RA, of Kink with the sea at his back: it was commissioned as part of the Kinkead Memorial and hangs in the York House Officers' Mess, where it is 'regarded as one of the College's most valuable possessions'. The original version of this painting was unveiled by Sir Hugh Trenchard in November 1928, and still dominates the staircase of the RAF Club, Piccadilly.

Local councillors and local authorities were becoming seriously interested. Hampshire County Council protects and promotes the military history of the area. It restored and preserved the three main hangars at the Calshot site after the air station closed in 1961. It was decided to rename these hangars – which now house fine sporting facilities for young people – to reflect their role in the history of aviation. They became the Sopwith Hangar, the Schneider Hangar and the Sunderland Hangar. With the keen support of local County Councillor Alexis McEvoy and Heritage Committee Chairman Alan Rice, it was proposed to name the main conference room in the main hangar in honour of Flight Lieutenant Kinkead – a move endorsed at Westminster by more than 100 Members of Parliament.

The question remained: how to find the family of an unmarried junior officer almost seventy years after his death at the age of 31? My first attempt failed utterly. Thinking the 'Kinkead' surname (spelt the Irish way) would be un-common in England, I approached Directory Enquiries. British Telecom quickly disabused me. There were thirty-eight Kinkeads in the London area alone. 'May I have about half a dozen numbers to try?' I asked. 'You need to tell me in which area they would be living,' came the response. 'How can I do that when this chap died seventy years ago? Just let me have a few numbers to start with.' 'No – sorry – not permitted under Data Protection rules. That would be what is called "fishing for information".' Chastened, I thought again. Kink had been born in South Africa. His surname would be more of a rarity in the land where he grew up. I called the International Operator and found him to be a man after my own heart. Either he had not heard about Data Protection, or (more likely) he quickly caught the Kinkead 'bug' which has done so much to enthuse people about his story – the story of a real-life 'Biggles' with a very sad ending. Together we worked our way through the directories of the main South African cities. There were two 'Kinkeads' and a 'Kinkead-Weekes'. I thanked him warmly but forgot to take his name. It was probably just as well: I should not want him to fall foul of his employers!

I dialled the first of the 'Kinkeads': there was no reply. My colleague, Colin Smith, was calling the 'Kinkead-Weekes' from the adjacent room. I heard him introduce himself and explain his slightly bizarre enquiry: '... So we were wondering if you are in any way connected with Flight Lieutenant Kinkead? Oh, you are ...' and he began quickly taking down the details.

Kink, it emerged, was one of four children, only one of whom, a sister, had married. She had three sons – one remained in South Africa and became a senior naval officer. He had recently died but, his daughter told us, the other two nephews were alive and well and living in England. Thus it was that I found myself calling Mark Kinkead-Weekes, in Ramsgate, in early 1998. It turned out that there would have been a much easier way of finding the family.

Mark is a former Professor of English and American Literature and Pro-Vice-Chancellor of Kent University. As such he is listed in *Who's Who*. Out of curiosity, I checked how many Kinkeads had entries in that volume: he was the only one; so I could have found him at the first attempt – though, given the number of Kinkeads in the country, there would have been no reason to suppose that this sole entry was the actual one required.

With the anniversary drawing near, the pace was increasing. The head of the Air Historical Branch at the Ministry of Defence, Sebastian Cox, was another enthusiast, as was Brian Lamb, the Director of the Calshot Activities Centre. We wanted to unveil a portrait of the airman as a centrepiece for the future permanent display which Brian and I were planning for the proposed Kinkead Room. Seb arranged for the RAF to make a fine photographic print from the Cranwell portrait and to have it mounted and framed, provided that the public purse was duly reimbursed. The result was spectacular.

At the heart of Britain's role in the Schneider Trophy races looms the legendary figure of Reginald Mitchell. His seaplanes, which secured the Trophy permanently with three successive victories, were the forerunners of the Spitfire. Indeed, *The First of the Few*, starring Leslie Howard and David Niven, focuses on the 1927 Venice competition in which Kink participated and – although other key characters are fictionalised – there is a reference to his death and the effect that it had on the great aircraft designer.

Squadron Leader Alan Jones is the founder of the R.J. Mitchell Memorial Museum, now known as 'Solent Sky'. It houses, among other Supermarine aircraft, a Spitfire, a small flying boat, and one of the two surviving seaplanes (N248) from the final Schneider contests. Alan arranged for a contingent of Southampton Air Cadets to provide the guard of honour at the Memorial Service. The RAF agreed to send an Air Vice-Marshal, Ian Stewart, to represent the Chief of Air Staff and unveil the portrait. They also sent a contingent from Cranwell, bringing with them the Kinkead Trophy which features a silver model of the Supermarine S5 Kink was flying when he died. There was one other contribution which they were planning to make as well . . .

Fawley Church is about 3 miles from Calshot: the route between them running parallel to the course on Southampton Water where Kink tackled the record in 1928. Mark Kinkead-Weekes, his elder brother Noel and other family members travelled to the Waterside on 11 March. Noel (known as Bobby) had also been an airman. As a pilot in the Second World War, he crash-landed – instead of baling out – to save a trapped crew member, when their bomber was hit over enemy territory. There had been some advance publicity for the Memorial Service in the *Lymington Times* and a large feature with photographs that very day in the *Southern Daily Echo*. Yet, there was no way of knowing what the turnout at the church would be. At dinner, the night before the service, I told the family that I hoped they would not be disappointed if only forty or fifty people came. 'We just think it's marvellous that Kink is being remembered, at last, so long after his death,' was their reply. In fact, we need not have worried: the publicity had worked and the beautiful little church was packed with approximately 300 people, ranging from Scouts and Guides to bemedalled military veterans. A deeply moving service had been planned by Reverend Gary Philbrick in conjunction with the Kinkead-Weekes family, and an illustrated programme printed as a souvenir. Afterwards, prayers were said at the graveside, and then all eyes turned skyward as, precisely at the stroke of 3 o'clock, a Tornado F3 jet fighter, crewed by two Flight Lieutenants from RAF Leeming, swooped low over the cemetery dipping its wings in honour of Samuel Kinkead.

★　★　★

Speaking to the local team from Meridian Television, Mark described his gallant uncle as one of a group of young men who were 'the astronauts of their day'. For me, a particularly poignant moment was when a lady approached me saying: 'When we moved here twenty-five years ago, I saw this gravestone and its inscription and I asked the vicar of the day what was the story behind it – but he couldn't tell me. Isn't it a shame to have waited so long to find out about this very brave man?' 'Well,' I responded, 'sadly, *he* has all the time in the world.'

After the solemnity of the service and the excitement of the fly-past, two more events remained. The visitors, dignitaries and congregation reassembled at Calshot – in the hangar from which Kink flew – for the naming of the Kinkead Room, the unveiling of his portrait and an impressive memorial plaque, the presentation of the Kinkead Trophy to that year's winner from Cranwell, and the customary speeches and reminiscences from all concerned. While the assembly enjoyed refreshments and examined an exhibition about the Schneider Trophy contests, thoughtfully supplied by Alan Jones and his Museum colleagues, the Kinkead family and a few others embarked on HSL102 – a wartime Air-Sea Rescue launch. Lovingly restored by Phil Clabburn and his team, she had been built at Hythe by the British Power Boat Company, founded by Hubert Scott-Paine who with Noel Pemberton-Billing had set up the Supermarine Aircraft Company itself. The High Speed Launch made her way gently out into the Solent. By 5.15pm, the time of the fatal flight, she had reached the vicinity of the old Calshot Light – where seaplane N221 had carried Kink to oblivion at more than 300 miles per hour. A floating wreath of poppies marked the final act of remembrance as the boat headed back to the shore.

Chapter One

An End and a Beginning

The telegram to Mrs Kinkead, out in Johannesburg, contained the news dreaded by the parents of every airman. It was 4 September 1917:

> Deeply regret Lieutenant T.C. Kinkead Flying Corps killed aeroplane accident Shoreham-by-Sea. Army Council express their sympathy.

It had happened just before 9 o'clock the previous morning, and this was the second cable to be sent. The first, from 3 Training Squadron at Shoreham, went to Royal Flying Corps Headquarters just two hours after the crash. Thompson Calder Kinkead – popularly known as 'Toss' – had been flying a Maurice Farman Shorthorn biplane, with a 70hp Renault engine, when it side-slipped to disaster. Unusually, given the frequency of training accidents, this young man's death was fully covered in the press – perhaps because he had travelled so far to enlist; perhaps because of the speed and clarity of the accident inquiry, which took place the next day; and perhaps because of the evidence given about the skill and misfortune of the pilot.

Toss was stated in *The Times* to have shown 'splendid control over the machine'. The *West Sussex Gazette* called him 'a learner of great promise, although Monday's was only his second flight alone'; and the *Sussex Daily News* ran the headline 'Unlucky Young Airman' as it set out in depth what had actually happened. RFC Captain Samuel Saunderson told the Coroner that Second Lieutenant Kinkead had completed nearly four hours' instruction under dual control and made his first solo flight early on 3 September. He was fully competent to fly alone and was keen to go up a second time, which he did at 8.45am. The wreckage of the training biplane had been examined since the accident. There was no evidence of structural failure, nor any sign that the engine had been faulty.

A second witness, Flight Commander Thomas Stewart, had watched Kinkead's first solo take-off and landing, while waiting to go up with another trainee. He thought that Toss, who was not one of his pupils, had put up 'quite a good show'. Later, at 2,000 feet over Worthing, Stewart saw the biplane again. It was 1,000 feet above him and, initially, he assumed that the pilot was also an instructor. In fact, it was Toss. He spiralled down until level with Stewart and began a series of vertical banks, first to the right and then to the left, descending another 1,000 feet. With hindsight, Stewart felt that Toss had been 'over-confident for a beginner'. He ought not to have made a spiral

1

descent of this sort on only his second solo flight, 'but it was very well done' – which was why the instructor was sure that the person flying the biplane had to be 'an experienced pilot'. Indeed, the spiral was successfully carried out and 'had nothing to do with the accident'.

As Toss straightened out and began heading towards the aerodrome, Stewart was shocked to see the machine continuing to go down. Realising that the engine must have failed, the instructor altered course at once towards the stricken biplane. Toss was clearly looking for a suitable place for an emergency landing; but, when he reached a height of about 250 feet, 'he appeared to lose his "flying speed" and nosedived' out of view. Diving to only 50 feet, Stewart desperately sought somewhere to land; but that was impossible. People were running towards the wreckage, where Toss lay still. He had come down in a field adjoining the Ivy Arch Nursery, on the north side of the railway. First on the scene was Harry Pattenden, a nursery-hand, who had heard the sound of an engine close overhead, then the thud of the impact. He lifted the machine which was lying on the aviator's body, while others pulled him out. There was nothing to be done. Thompson Kinkead was 24 when he died. He had been at 3 Training Squadron just over a fortnight.

Stewart, who had raced back to Shoreham for medical help, told the Coroner what the RFC's own investigation had concluded:

It was unlucky, because [Kinkead] was making an excellent descent, and even when the engine failed at 1,000 feet, he kept his head and looked out for a landing place. Had he been a couple of miles nearer Shoreham, over open fields, he would have landed all right. A Military Court of Inquiry, composed of flying officers of the RFC, who were all experts, had been held since the fatality, and the conclusion arrived at, after visiting the scene, and considering the evidence, was that the accident was due to the pilot 'stalling' his machine while endeavouring to make a forced landing on difficult and unfavourable country, this in turn being probably due to engine failure.

Prior to the nurseryman's evidence, Stewart had stated his view of the cause of the tragedy. To descend as he did, first by a spiral and then by banking, Toss

would have throttled down his engine, and then tried to open it again; but as the machine had come down from such a height in one stretch, the engine would probably choke or 'fail to mix' properly, or it might have got cold. [Kinkead], as most beginners did, might have pushed the aero-lever forward quickly instead of gradually as he should have done, with the result that the engine failed to respond in the crisis. He was then too low down to glide to more open country, being only about 1,000 feet high ... Unfortunately, [he] was over a very bad place to land in, because of the trees, glasshouses and market-gardens. He probably saw ahead of him a meadow which would afford him a safe landing, and tried to lift to reach it, with the result that he 'stalled' the machine or lost his 'flying speed', and

2

the glide – diverted from its course and [with] no engine at work – ended in a quiver, and a sudden crash to earth nose-downwards.

It seemed that the engine could not have been completely dead, as Pattenden had heard it at very low level. Furthermore, a member of the jury who saw the accident commented that, as the biplane came down, Toss had managed to lift it sufficiently to clear some trees just before the impact. Stewart thought that the engine could well have been spluttering, but that this all pointed to a stall with fatal consequences. Toss had, in fact, died instantly from a spinal fracture near his neck, perhaps after being thrown out of the biplane before it landed on top of him.

One mystery was not cleared up by the Coroner – indeed, it was never raised. Why was a man whose personnel file showed him to have been passed 'fit for Observer' but 'unfit for Pilot', when his eyesight was examined in July, flying solo in September? Toss had been passed as fit for military service when medically assessed in Johannesburg in March 1917; but, even then, it had been noted that he suffered from astigmatism in both eyes. His oath of attestation for a Short Service Commission for the duration of the war was made on 20 April, and his appointment to the RFC approved on 26 May. The July examination described Toss as a 'concealed hypermetrope'. Hyper-metropia is far-sightedness – not necessarily a problem for aerial observers, but a definite one for would-be pilots. The word 'concealed' refers to an under-lying condition which might emerge only during an eye test. Yet, Thompson Kinkead was not going to let faulty eyesight prevent him becoming a combat pilot. If he did cut a few corners, he may not have been alone: one of the greatest of all British aces, 'Mick' Mannock VC, was thought to have deceived his medical examiner by pretending to see with a sightless eye.

Well-practised procedures had to be followed when a fatal accident occurred. On the day of Toss's death, a 'Committee of Adjustment', consisting of a Captain and two Second Lieutenants, assembled at Shoreham Aerodrome to 'take an inventory of the personal effects of the deceased, which were found in his quarters', to check his cash, settle his bills, and secure receipts and under-takings from his next of kin. Toss had named his elder sister, Vida Weekes, who was married to an Army officer and lived in London, as the first point of contact; but it was his younger brother, Samuel, who made the sad journey to Shoreham on 6 September, to collect his property and sign off the inventory. This poignant list – including '1 Pair Spectacles and Case' – remains in Thompson Kinkead's file to this day.

* * *

Although the press described Toss as South African, he had been born in 1893 during a return visit to Ballykelly, from which his Irish Protestant father – also named Samuel – originated. However, his two elder sisters and younger brother were all born in South Africa, to which Samuel senior and their Scottish mother, Helen Calder, had emigrated in 1889. After the long sea passage to Cape Town, they undertook a gruelling 1,000-mile journey by wagon to Johannesburg, earning the status of 'pioneers' and pitching their tent, according to legend, close to that of the Cullinans. Sadly, only one of the two families found its fortune in diamonds.

Helen was a formidable character who kept a gun hidden in her skirts for protection on the trek. Her husband was just 45 when he died suddenly from influenza in June 1903, and their youngest child – named after his father, but known as 'Babs' – was only 6. Samuel's will, drawn up the previous month, described him as an 'estate agent'; but he mainly bought and sold property on his own behalf. For a while his enterprise prospered, but he was under financial pressure at the time of his passing. Helen was left with four children whom she managed to support by opening a boarding-house. Vida, the eldest, met and married Alfred Weekes – always known as 'Bill' – an assayer for a gold company, who came to South Africa because of a lung problem in about 1910. She was then 20; her sister Nora was 18.

Both Kinkead boys attended the Marist Brothers College in Johannesburg, Toss serving for more than six years in its Cadet Force and rising to the rank of Sergeant. In civil life he trained in accountancy, but did not stress this when applying to become an Officer Cadet in March 1917. He described his former employment simply as 'Secretarial work'. His application form also listed two years with the Transvaal Scottish Defence Force and a year's Active Service with the 4th South African Horse in the German East Africa campaign. Babs, of course, was still at school when the Great War began: on 21 January 1913, a month before his 16th birthday, he had entered Jeppestown High School, where he quickly made his mark.

Originally founded by the Anglican Church for the children of mineworkers, St Michael's College evolved into a grammar school after surviving financial crises and periods of closure in the 1890s and during the Boer War. Reopened in 1903, it acquired new buildings in 1909 from the proceeds of land donated by members of the Jeppe family who remained closely involved with its long-term welfare. Its Latin motto, translated as 'For the Brave Nothing is Too Difficult', would be burnished in two world wars – not least by Samuel Kinkead in the first, and the equally remarkable Reverend Cecil Pugh in the second. One would win six awards for gallantry in the air; the other a posthumous George Cross for lowering himself, with no chance of escape, into the hold of a sinking troopship to pray with men who were hopelessly trapped. Even the Headmaster of Jeppe High School, J.H.A. Payne, volunteered for the front line and lost his life on active service in 1917. In June of that year, he set out the ethos of the school in a letter to its magazine:

> During the fifteen months spent in German East Africa my thoughts were constantly with the School, and my greatest pleasure was the meeting in all units and at every post of masters or Old Boys who are serving at the front. I must admit to having feared that the absence of so many would sap vitality from some branches of the School life ... To my intense delight, however, I found on my return that the School had not suffered even

4

temporarily in vigour; on the contrary, there is an atmosphere of moral obligation which has spurred those who were compelled to remain behind to great effort ... In these times, each individual's first and final consideration must be his duty to the Empire, and just as men must be prepared to make sacrifices, so also must institutions ... At the reception given to those on leave and during my brief stay in Johannesburg, I met many Old Boys and was delighted in their general keenness to return to the front ... Probably no large institution is entirely free from shirkers; at any time we must own to a few – thank goodness only a few ... Perhaps it is a failing in the Schoolmaster to feel compelled to criticise, but I can assure you, Mr Editor, that strongly as I feel about a few who have failed, I am rejoiced in the splendid response of the many.

Having recovered from his wounds, the Headmaster succumbed to a fever. James Payne was 44 when he died.

One Jeppe High School pupil who had no intention of shirking was Babs Kinkead. Between his arrival in January 1913 and his departure in December 1914, he represented the school in cricket, athletics and the Football XI, as well as captaining his House football team. By the end of his first year, he was also listed as one of half a dozen Troop Sergeants in the School Cadets. Theirs was no easy task, as the December 1913 school magazine wryly remarked:

Things in the Cadet world have been in a very unsettled state for some time past. Without uniforms, arms, drill-book or parade ground, it is little wonder that our military ardour has been in danger of cooling ... Under the new scheme, all schoolboys of 17 or over come under the Defence Act and are consequently lost to the Cadets. The drill, too, is to be changed from Infantry to a special SA Cadet Drill, on the lines of Mounted Infantry Drill. These changes have necessitated a complete reorganisation of the Corps, which has been divided up into two Squadrons of three Troops each ... The band under Bugler Stokkeland, consists of six buglers and five drummers who are only waiting for instruments on which to demonstrate their skill.

Throughout his career, Samuel Kinkead – whose 'Babs' nickname gave way to 'Kink' on transition from South Africa to England – combined qualities of courage and leadership with an unwillingness to engage in any form of self-promotion. His unassuming nature, while exasperating to the biographer, endeared him to his comrades. It is not fanciful to see early signs of this in his school career, whether as an 'Acting NCO' in the Cadets or as a sturdy, but not flashy, member of a range of school sports teams. Periodically, as the Great War unfolded, reports of Kink's adventures, and some misadventures, filtered back to Jeppe. A year after he left, the magazine reported:

'Babs' Kinkead is flying vigorously. We have just heard that he fell 1,000 feet recently, but escaped with the temporary loss of consciousness and a few teeth.

5

In June 1916, its readers learned that:

> Flight Lieutenant S. Kinkead has been in hospital owing to an accident. He was only just able to get back to the British lines before his engine failed,

and an update twelve months later recorded his posting to RNAS Cranwell:

> 'Babs' Kinkead is instructing budding airmen at Sleaford, Lincolnshire, a very large flying centre. As a result of his 18 months' flying in Gallipoli, Salonika and Mitylene, he contracted 'Mediterranean Fever'. Hence his present occupation, which, however, is an extremely strenuous one.

Few records remain of Kink's personal experiences in this, his first, military campaign. It is known that, before leaving South Africa in 1915, he was an apprentice civil engineer but there is no indication of exactly when or why he decided to become an airman. Dr L. Staz, a childhood friend who became a distinguished ophthalmologist, recalled:

> We all lived around the St Andrew's Presbyterian Church, Commissioner Street, Fairview [the Kinkead family home was at 69 Browning Street] ...
> 'Babs' Kinkead used to perform tricks for us on his bicycle – pulling the front wheel away from the ground and twisting the handlebars in circles. No doubt such tricks enabled him to become a Schneider Trophy pilot!

After turning 18 on 26 February, Kink made his way to England to enlist. He was commissioned as a 'Temporary Probationary Flight Sub-Lieutenant' in the Royal Naval Air Service on 11 September 1915 and sent to the Naval School at Portsmouth twenty-four hours later. His Service number was 37453, and by 8 October his course had been set. He was posted to the Naval Flying School at Eastbourne for two months. During that time he flew six aeroplane types – a Maurice Farman, a Henri Farman, a Bleriot and a Caudron (all with 80hp engines), as well as a 90hp Curtiss and 70hp BE2C. On 1 December, near the end of his training, his Confidential Report predicted: 'He is a keen young officer who should develop well. Will be ready for his appointment.' Within days he was selected for service in the Dardanelles with 2 Wing RNAS.

Previously known as 2 Squadron – the name was changed in June 1915 – this unit had been formed at Eastchurch, on the Isle of Sheppey, the previous October. Its first Commanding Officer, Louis Gerrard, was a Royal Marine who had been one of the first four British naval aviators. Gerrard held definite views about pioneer airmen. They tended to be, he recalled, 'very quiet people', like Wilbur Wright who visited Eastchurch and 'listened intently to everything *we* (mere children in aviation) had to say, but scarcely ever spoke':

> A very high proportion of our early pilots were of this quiet type. Introverts, I suppose you might call them. They liked doing things by themselves and not having to talk about them and impress people. The Extrovert, who is a bit of an exhibitionist, wants a lot of people around to

say: 'How wonderful!' You can distinguish the two types while extremely young. The latter will show you everything – of them are our actors, actresses and politicians. The former include many thinkers, scientists and explorers. They say his friends had great difficulty in persuading Newton to publish his work. I spent an evening with Shackleton, the Polar explorer. He never spoke unless spoken to. I found it hard to believe when quiet little [Albert] Ball became one of the notable VCs of the war. I flew down about 100 miles (a considerable distance for those days) to ask him about it. He said: 'It's quite simple. You dive and come up underneath him, put your gun like that, and fire.' Simple for him, perhaps!

Kink conformed to this pattern, writing nothing about himself unless his duties required it. No letters home, if composed, have survived. All who knew him have long gone, and the record of his career is uneven. Kink fought in four theatres, organised an expedition, competed in an air race and attacked a world air speed record. His personal role can sometimes be discerned in detail, from public archives, private memoirs and, in the last two cases, the press. But what should be done where only glimpses survive – as at the Dardanelles, in Iraq and on the Cape Flight expedition? The obvious answer would be not to tell his tale at all. Yet, there is an alternative: Kink's campaigns and endeavours are of intrinsic interest, particularly those which are scarcely remembered. By recounting them now, we can gauge his experiences and use his career as a window on his times.

★ ★ ★

British naval aviation had an inauspicious beginning. Its first machine was neither an aeroplane nor a seaplane, but an airship – dubbed 'The Mayfly' – which took two years to build. She never flew and was wrecked in September 1911 while being taken from her shed to her mooring mast. Gerrard's reputation had a narrow escape. His duties included being Meteorologist to the airship, even though he knew nothing whatever about the subject:

> It was my horrible responsibility to name the date and time for the launch. If quite a mild gust of wind struck her when partly out of her shed, she would break in two. I had to issue a weather forecast every night (the local green-keeper was useful). She did in fact break her back at the second launching, but, fortunately for me, by then I had gone off to learn to fly heavier-than-air craft.

Ironically, it was his assumed weather-forecasting skills which helped him make the transition:

> I never had any confidence in airships, what I knew of meteorology convinced me that their life was ephemeral, and when the Navy called for volunteers for aeroplanes, my name was easily first in. The knowledge of aeronautics it was thought I possessed (!) accounted for my being among the four officers selected from over 300 applicants.

Two of the four, Gerrard himself and Charles Rumney Samson, were destined to command Nos. 2 and 3 Wings respectively during the Dardanelles Campaign. Samson, the most senior, made a strong impression on Gerrard:

> He came to us from the Persian Gulf where he had been hunting pirates. Doubtless his fierce pointed beard helped to inspire terror in the wrong-doer. There was a rumour he got sunstroke in the Gulf. They say a man grows like his dog. Maybe Samson absorbed something from his pirates.

His was the first unit to go to the Dardanelles, a desperate endeavour which has been often analysed. It was, according to Gerrard,

> a typical 'Winston Churchill sideshow' (he loved giving a prod where the enemy least expected it). It's all very well if you have sufficient forces to pour in after your initial success. Mere surprise achieves nothing if you are going to be pushed into the sea soon afterwards. Although the campaign was a failure, it was extremely interesting from our point of view. We could see the whole war in five minutes! And we dabbled in everything: bombing, reconnaissance, photography, fighting, and anti-submarine work.

The background to the campaign lay in secret negotiations between the Turks and the Germans which had led to a deal just days before war broke out. Its consequences were soon felt. The German battle-cruiser *Goeben* and its attendant light cruiser *Breslau* were allowed to pass through the Dardanelles to Constantinople, where they were, theoretically, purchased by the Turks, though still manned by the Germans. Turkey, supposedly neutral, began to assemble large forces in Palestine in October 1914, posing a threat to Egypt and the Suez Canal. By the time the Turkish Fleet began bombarding Russian ports from the Black Sea on 27 October, a British naval squadron was concentrated at Tenedos in the Aegean, near the Gallipoli peninsula. The Allies delivered an ultimatum at Constantinople on 30 October, and war was declared the following day.

The Royal Navy's first contribution, a ten-minute bombardment of forts guarding the Dardanelles, caused just enough damage to show the Turks that their defences ought to be strengthened. Two months later, the British were requested by their Russian allies to relieve the pressure on them by taking action against Turkey. On 13 January 1915, the British Government authorised a naval expedition to bombard the Peninsula, force the Straits and ultimately capture Constantinople. An official account of the campaign sums up how it came to be regarded:

> It was just before 10 o'clock on the morning of 19 February 1915 that the first shot, fired by *Cornwallis* at Fort Orkanie, heralded the opening of the unparalleled operations which were destined to attain such vast proportions, to consume so much resource and tragic effort, and to end with so glorious a failure.

The seaplane carrier *Ark Royal* had arrived from England two days earlier. As the battleships went into action, her aircraft acted as their eyes and ears – reporting the fall of shot, the damage done and the targets yet to be hit. Their role, at this stage, was of limited value – not least because of the unreliability of wireless communications. Where they proved more productive was in identifying minefields laid in the Straits. Yet, this failed to prevent the loss of one French and two British battleships on 18 March, when they were struck by mines sown the previous night, after aerial reconnaissance had finished.

General Sir Ian Hamilton's appointment in command of Allied forces in the Eastern Mediterranean on 11 March came at a time when the process now known as 'mission creep' was well under way:

> it had become increasingly apparent that, even if the Navy succeeded in forcing the Dardanelles, the provision of military forces would be necessary to occupy the Peninsula ... After the failure of 18 March, it came to be realised that the object of the campaign could only be attained by the strong co-operation of the Army and then only by landing troops in strength.

Naval bombardment against fortifications had proved less effective than anticipated, and the warships had shown themselves to be totally vulnerable. It took until the third week in April to assemble an assault force. In the meantime, the first RNAS unit – under Samson – had arrived in theatre:

> On 24 March the advance party of 3 Aeroplane Squadron of the Naval Air Service, which had left Dunkirk at the end of February, arrived at Tenedos ... Some days later the balance of the personnel and equipment arrived. The Squadron now consisted of eleven pilots, three observers, four ground officers and 100 men. The aeroplanes, which numbered eighteen, were of six varieties: eight Henri Farmans, two BE2Cs, two BE2s, two Sopwith Tabloids, one Breguet and three Maurice Farmans.

Establishing the airbase meant that the *Ark Royal* could be deployed further afield to cover areas which land-based aircraft might be unable to reach.

> The first aeroplane flight was made on 28 March and from now on the machines of 3 Squadron were over the Peninsula at every opportunity which the trying weather afforded. Systematically the officers plotted the enemy positions; they controlled the ships' fire against enemy batteries, especially those in the difficult country on the Asiatic side. They photographed the landing beaches and the ground in the area and wrote descriptions of the beaches as they appeared from the air; they corrected the inaccurate maps; and they dropped bombs on the batteries and camps.

The assault on Gallipoli began before dawn on 25 April. RNAS personnel were involved in supplying and manning eleven Maxim guns on the forecastle of the collier *River Clyde* from which it was intended to land many of the troops. On the right- and left-hand beaches of Cape Helles the troops went ashore with little loss, but the assault force in the centre met with disaster as Turkish fire focused on the *River Clyde* and the bridge of boats over which the troops were meant to pass. Only after nightfall did they manage to land. Samson's squadron was heavily engaged throughout:

> The first aeroplanes were over the coast at dawn with orders to spot for the ships covering the landing onto any Turkish batteries that were firing. As soon as the Turks opened fire, the aeroplanes had no difficulty in picking up targets and soon urgent wireless signals were being sent down ... They co-operated also with the artillery ashore by Very light, as the batteries, in the beginning, were unable to take in wireless signals. The aeroplanes, also, bombed guns and camps, took photographs of the important inland positions and reconnoitred the whole peninsula ... These reports gave Sir Ian Hamilton very detailed information of the rapid movements of the Turkish troops to counter him.

It was all in vain, of course. The land campaign on Gallipoli soon proved to be as impenetrable a stalemate as the Western Front. Attempts to break the deadlock failed repeatedly. A week before 2 Wing left Dunkirk for the Dardanelles on 13 August, 20,000 men were quietly landed at Suvla Bay, behind the Turkish front line, where complete tactical surprise was achieved. The official account refers to 'various delays ... in pressing forward', such that 'the initial advance fell far short of what it was hoped to achieve'. Cyril Falls describes the operation more starkly:

> The Suvla affair started perfectly. The leading troops were put ashore without resistance to speak of. The build-up was not interfered with. Yet there was a fantastic lack of any sense of urgency from the corps command downwards. At a time when there were in fact 1,500 Turks to hold up two divisions, the generals talked of landing artillery to bombard the enemy's defences. The Turks actually did everything possible to help by botching the movement of reinforcements ... Two vices of the original [Gallipoli] landing were reproduced: the troops did not know enough about what they had to do, and Hamilton intervened too late. Some of the scenes, troops making tea, bathing in the sea, lying in the sun, were reminiscent rather of an August bank holiday than of one of the most vital military operations of modern times ... Mustapha Kemal ... again played the part of a great fighting man. One Turkish charge drove back the British at Suvla; another, a tremendous affair with fearful loss on both sides, recovered the Anzac heights.

A shortcut to victory had become another lethal quagmire. The land campaign foundered, just as the naval effort had failed. On 25 May the German submarine *U-21* had torpedoed the battleship *Triumph*, followed by the *Majestic* two days later. These disasters led to the withdrawal of the large bombarding ships and the *Ark Royal* too could no longer operate in unprotected waters. She remained at Kephalo Bay, on the island of Imbros – becoming, in effect, a

10

depot ship while her aircraft operated from the island base. Kephalo Point on Imbros was the site of a new landing ground chosen by Colonel F.H. Sykes, who had been appointed over Samson's head in July to command the RNAS in the Eastern Mediterranean. Samson, returning reinvigorated from leave in Egypt,

> found my crowd on a narrow little beast of an aerodrome on the edge of a cliff. I immediately hunted around for a new aerodrome, and found a possible site about half a mile away. It was covered with scrub and rocks, and on first sight it looked a long job to clear it; but I had seen from the air how Turks dug trenches, so I went to GHQ and persuaded them to let me have some Turkish prisoners. They gave me seventy. At first they were closely guarded; but after we got to know them and gave them cigarettes each day, they used to work like Trojans. I told off one of my sailors to be in charge, and they worshipped him. They used to troop off each night to their cage as happy as tinkers, generally carrying the guards' rifles. I had some of these Turks as working party for the rest of the campaign. They took a great interest in the aeroplanes, and seemed delighted to watch the bombs being placed on the carriages. In fact, in time I really believe they considered themselves members of the Squadron.

The airfield was nearing completion by the end of August when 2 Wing arrived, bringing with it twenty-two aeroplanes, sixteen pilots and 200 other personnel. According to the official narrative:

> These reinforcements which added greatly to the assistance which the air could give to the sea and land forces, also gave the air service the first real opportunity to strike, by bombing, its own direct blow at the enemy. Nothing, perhaps, caused the Turk more uneasiness than the vulnerability of his communications to the Peninsula. From Constantinople supplies and reinforcements might go by sea through the Marmara or by the Thracian Railway to Uzun Keupri and thence by road through Kejhan and Bulair. The sea route was virtually closed after April by British sub-marines and rarely did the Turk try to move transports across ... In all, during 1915, seventy attacks were made by the various types of aircraft on enemy war vessels, transports, tugs, lighters and sailing craft; two large steamers and one tug were hit and damaged, and one lighter and six dhows wrecked by bombs. By the menace of submarine and aircraft attack, the enemy was thus compelled to rely mainly on his overland route. The road between Uzun Keupri and Bulair was bombed on several occasions by aeroplanes, but although large craters were often made they were soon filled in and offered no obstacle to the pack animals or bullock carts which formed the bulk of the transport.

In his memoirs, Samson claimed not to mind that Colonel Sykes had been sent out from England and 'installed as Chief of the Air Force' in the

Dardanelles. What troubled him was the shortage of resources to throw into the fight. He was scathing about purely organisational changes:

> My Squadron was called [i.e. renamed] No. 3 Wing and Gerrard's No. 2 Wing – grand-sounding titles which no doubt looked fine on paper, but we didn't get expanded either by pilots or aeroplanes; in fact, in October, after two months of the Wing business, I find that between us we had only twenty-five pilots and forty-four aeroplanes of all sorts; about eight of these were useless for war.

While welcoming the arrival of Gerrard and his men, the irascible Commanding Officer of 3 Wing at first 'thought them a bit of a nuisance' as, with one or two exceptions, they were all young pilots. Sometimes his veterans were asked 'to do their work over again', but even he admitted that they soon settled in very well. Kink, at this time, had yet to arrive. He was posted to the Dardanelles on 9 December and it is highly probable that he travelled there in the company of another new recruit to the Royal Naval Air Service, who has left a vivid account of his experiences. At the outbreak of war, Donald Bremner had volunteered to serve on a steam yacht which was offered to the Admiralty for the duration. After about a year, the members of her crew were invited to apply for commissions in any branch of the services. Bremner chose the RNAS. He was interviewed by Captain Francis Scarlett RN, who held a key post overseeing the work of the RNAS on behalf of the Board of Admiralty. Having learnt navigation at Portsmouth and aviation at Chingford, Bremner was chosen to fly a Bristol Scout; but, at 6 feet 3 inches, he had to remove the cushion from its seat in order to squeeze into the cockpit. At 5 feet 7 inches, Kink had no such problem; but, to Bremner, this discomfort was a small price to pay for the pleasure of piloting what he regarded as the best machine he ever flew – though lacking much in the way of effective armament.

Bremner spent a wet and windy month at Dover in November 1915, familiarising himself with the Bristol Scout, before he was drafted with several other pilots 'to lend a hand' at Gallipoli. Great changes were afoot by the time he and Kink arrived. In October, Sir Ian Hamilton had been recalled. General Sir Charles Monro, his successor, promptly recommended evacuation of the Peninsula. It was to prove by far the most successful aspect of the entire campaign:

> This skilfully handled operation began during the middle of December, just as [Bremner] and his companions were on their way to join the campaign. Crossing France, they travelled south in a packed civilian train, sleeping on the floor. Reaching Marseilles the pilots embarked on a ship for Malta. When they arrived the senior naval officer said he had no idea why they were there and advised them to book into a hotel for the night. The following morning, there being no apparent urgency, [Bremner] decided to visit a hospital where he knew a doctor ... There had been such a rush on leaving England that he had only had time to complete the first stage of his

series of typhoid injections. After his medical friend in Malta had finished with him, he strolled back to the hotel where, to his astonishment, he was told that a ship, with the other pilots aboard, was already leaving for their destination, an aerodrome on the island of Imbros. Rushing to the quay, he managed to leap aboard as the vessel was pulling away.

First came the withdrawal from Suvla Bay and Anzac Cove, completed without loss by dawn on 20 December. Before the end of the month, Monro was ordered to evacuate the Helles area too, and this was achieved by 9 January 1916. The timing could not have been better for Bremner. Flying with an observer late in the afternoon of 8 January, he had to touch down on an emergency landing ground near Cape Helles after being attacked by a Fokker monoplane. If they had been forced down the following day, they would have fallen into the hands of the Turks. As it was, they were prevented from setting fire to their machine, as this might have given the enemy the impression that stores were being burned prior to an evacuation:

> For eight hours they sat on W beach ... As soon as darkness fell, troops marched in a continuous column eight abreast onto a low pier and were marshalled into large barges moored on either side. They were then ferried out to waiting ships which took the men away to safety ... Long before daybreak all the men had gone, leaving the beaches strewn with the tangled debris of war. [Bremner] and his companion were taken off at 1.00am and embarked on SS *Partridge*, one of the last two ships to leave the area, and sailed back to Imbros.

Wars – as Winston Churchill famously said in 1940 – are not won by evacuations, but those from Gallipoli could certainly have ended in catastrophe. That they did not was largely due to the almost total air supremacy enjoyed by the Allies. The Official History explains this in relation to the withdrawal from Suvla and Anzac:

> By constant patrol, the two aeroplane Wings prevented any hostile aircraft from flying over these two beaches during the whole week which preceded our coming away.

The same applied to the final evacuation from Helles:

> Throughout this operation the aeroplanes were on patrol and again allowed no enemy to pass. A recent arrival of six Bristol Scouts, fitted with Lewis guns, had put a weapon in their hands which ensured their ability to do this last service for those below. The pilots and observers eased their spirits by a continuous bombing of the Turkish troops. They did not work without losses ... It is a point of some interest that the last days of the campaign should be reserved for the only flying losses which the enemy air service inflicted.

Between 6 and 12 January, five airmen had been killed and a sixth made prisoner, following the recent arrival of three Fokker monoplanes. As we have seen, Bremner and his observer only narrowly avoided being added to their number. There is a snapshot of one of the victims in Kink's personal photograph album, together with a note that he had been killed by the German ace Hans-Joachim Buddecke. Flight Sub-Lieutenant James Bolas was 23 when he died. Not only did Kink know the victim but, according to Gerrard, he also encountered the victor:

> There was not much in the way of fighting till a section of Richthofen's Circus [presumably a loose description of former Western Front pilots] arrived. They laid about us, and the situation was getting awkward, but the Nieuports had arrived and were in process of being erected.
>
> Young Kinkead made his first flight over the lines in one. Too late, he saw a machine diving on him out of the sun. He pulled the stick right back until he stood on his tail and fired a burst. He told me he did not quite know what happened then, but after some time he got her right side up, flying level, and there in front of him was the Circus machine! He pressed the trigger and shot him down!
>
> It was their leader, Buddecke. (He recovered from his wounds, returned to the Western Front and was shot down again immediately, this time finally.) All this happened practically over their aerodrome. It made them windy, and it was little trouble sending the rest of them home.

Gerrard, in 1947, was recalling a combat in 1916. It is easy to condense events retrospectively. RNAS Operations Reports for the Dardanelles mention Kink twice. First, on the evening of 11 August, when he accompanied four bombers on a raid against an enemy aerodrome at Maswakli, near the Bulgarian city of Xanthi:

> Whilst carrying out these operations, one bombing machine was attacked by a perfectly new Fokker. Flight Sub-Lieutenant Kinkead, in a Bristol Scout, engaged him from behind, firing three trays. The Fokker nosedived about 2,000 feet and made off in the direction of Xanthi. The apparent immunity from damage, although attacked at close quarters, raises the presumption that the vital parts are arm[our]ed. Beyond a hit in the cowling of the Bristol Scout, no damage was inflicted on our machines.

This, clearly, had nothing to do with the episode described by his Squadron Commander, as the Fokker managed to escape. The second reference is to a fight on 28 August when three enemy aircraft appeared over Thasos Aerodrome and were confronted by three from the Allied detachment based there. After a chase, one was brought down by Flight Sub-Lieutenant G.K. Blandy who – together with Kink, Bremner, five other pilots and two observers – comprised A Squadron of 2 Wing, based on the island:

> Flight Sub-Lieutenant Kinkead, in a Bristol Scout, attacked a second machine at 7,000 feet above the mouth of the [River] Nestos, closing up from a range of 150 yards. He was then attacked by a third machine from the starboard side, which he eventually got behind and attacked. The

14

hostile machine then dived and was driven to land on rough ground 2 miles north-east of Zinelli.

This could conceivably be the fight referred to by Gerrard, but it seems unlikely. By August 1916, far from making his first flight over the lines, Kink was nearing the end of his tour of duty in the Aegean. Gerrard was clear that he was flying one of the Nieuports which had just arrived, whereas the RNAS report has him flying a Bristol Scout on 28 August. According to his list of victories, Buddecke was definitely back on the Western Front by 6 September, which makes it extremely unlikely that he encountered Kink on 28 August over Macedonia. Buddecke was certainly a formidable opponent, being only the third German fighter pilot to receive the coveted *Pour le Mérite*. The award was made in April 1916 following his string of successes in the Dardanelles. However, contrary to Gerrard's account, he survived his next posting to the Western Front and a further one to Turkey, before falling victim to the guns of 3 (Naval) Squadron over France in March 1918. Hans-Joachim Buddecke was 27 when he died.

It was only natural that distinguished airmen like Gerrard, when casting back over thirty years – with the Second World War in between – tended to 'telescope' their memories in this way. Kink probably did score the victory which Gerrard attributed to him, despite the minor discrepancies in his story caused by the passage of time. The same can be seen in the memoirs of Wing Commander Arthur Longmore, another of the first four naval pilots, who formed 1 Squadron RNAS at Gosport in October 1914, just as Gerrard was creating 2 Squadron at Eastchurch. Writing in 1946, Longmore paid tribute to one of Kink's lesser-known comrades in A Squadron of 2 Wing on Thasos:

[A] most interesting character was an observer, Jones, who was a hunch-back and weighed only 6 stone. He first came to the aerodrome at St Pol in some sort of uniform, acting as chauffeur to Sarel, the British Consul. He begged to be taken up for an operational flight and I sent him off with an experienced pilot on the Zeebrugge Coast reconnaissance. On his return, I asked what he had seen and I got from him a most detailed report of what was inside Ostend and Zeebrugge harbours. No, he had not been using field-glasses; it was just that he had abnormal vision, perhaps nature's compensation for his other physical deficiencies. I lost no time in getting him commissioned and appointed as an observer to my Squadron, where he served for a few months before leaving for the Dardanelles. I heard of him later as the one observer who really was a captain of an air-craft; for, if the pilot did not fly sufficiently close to the objective he wanted to observe, or attempted to turn back too soon when things were getting hot, Jones, from the passenger seat behind the pilot, would produce a spanner, and with this, held in close proximity to the pilot's head, would enforce his wishes. This unsung hero was later lost in a seaplane during operations against submarines in the Adriatic, but what a glorious few months for this brave little fellow who served his country so very actively.

In fact, far from serving for just a 'glorious few months', Second Lieutenant W.B. Jones survived until the last year of the war. The only son of a former Bishop of St David's, he was educated at Harrow and Oxford, and commissioned into the Royal Marines in September 1914. Mentioned in Despatches in 1916, he was promoted to Flight Observer at the end of that year, but drowned on an Active Service patrol on 7 January 1918. William Jones was 28 when he died.

★ ★ ★

Withdrawal from Gallipoli did not mark the end of hostilities in the region. Bulgaria had been traditionally at odds with the Ottoman Empire but overcame this after a series of Balkan conflicts caused great resentment at Serbian, Greek and Romanian control of territory it viewed as its own. Courted both by the Allies and by the Central Powers, Bulgaria threw in its lot with the latter by declaring war against Serbia in October 1915. This was, arguably, another evil outcome of the patent failure on Gallipoli. Despite the resultant Allied declaration of war on Bulgaria, it was Serbia's situation which rapidly became desperate. In addition, the loyalties of Greece were divided, with a pro-German King and a pro-British Prime Minister. In October 1915, the French and the British landed at Salonika and a new battlefront was created in Macedonia. This was the arena in which the Royal Naval Air Service in the Aegean was now expected to participate. Once again, it was a sideshow – but a sideshow on a very considerable scale.

While the Gallipoli Campaign was still under way, Wing Commander Samson had been allowed a fairly free hand:

> Colonel Sykes and his staff didn't worry me at all, but left me to go on in my own routine as usual, the only thing being that we had to send in reports to him as well as to the usual people; in fact, as far as my Wing was concerned, they might not have been there at all. His staff started to try to build up an aeroplane repair section; but no-one ever saw any result, although they had quite a large party who were reported to be carrying out mystic rites over a Voisin they had in a hangar.

Samson was pleased when the Nieuport Scouts arrived, even though – like the Bristols – they were poorly armed with Lewis guns which could 'only shoot upwards at an angle of 45 degrees'. The Allies took a long time to develop adequate armament for fighter pilots. This led some of them to improvise quite dangerously:

> At the beginning of 1915, Lieutenant Garros of the French Aviation Service accomplished this by means of a special propeller fitted with suitable plates, so that those bullets that would otherwise have struck the propeller were deflected ... [But this] resulted in such a reduction of speed and performance of the machine that this system was not adopted ... It was found that the propeller would stand up to its work with a

16

considerable number of holes in it and several pilots considered that the advantage to be obtained by having the gun in this position was worth the addition to the already great risks of flying ... Although officers were willing to take this risk, it was not desirable for them to do so ... Every effort was therefore made to produce a device for so regulating the action of the gun ... that firing only occurred at such times as the propeller would not be hit. But it was not until the spring of 1916 that this was satis-factorily accomplished.

One snapshot of Kink in the cockpit of his Bristol Scout shows a stripped Lewis gun mounted to fire through an unprotected airscrew. Evidently, he thought this to be a risk worth taking. Throughout 1915, a shortage of guns for the number of aircraft available had led to them being transferred from machine to machine according to need. Not until the spring of 1916 did the British produce an aeroplane armed with a Vickers machine gun, fixed to fire through the arc of the propeller, but synchronised to do so without striking its blades. This was the Sopwith 1½ Strutter, a light, fast two-seater, later described as 'probably the finest fighting machine in the world of its day ... [which] largely contributed to overcoming the Fokker menace'. No such machines were available to Samson and his men: aerial fighting was not their primary task, but bombing soon became one – in addition to reconnaissance, mapping and spotting for artillery. Samson tried to be an innovator, some of his schemes working better than others:

For a long time we had been constructing a real father of a bomb, using an old 26-gallon petrol tank. We made a streamline tail to it, and fitted on a head which contained a fuse constructed out of a Very light pistol with a cartridge in the barrel. As an extra detonator, a 20lb bomb was incor-porated, the idea being that the explosion of this would disperse the burning petrol and paraffin with which we filled the main body ... I may say that, in addition to everything, some bright brain made and attached a most efficient whistle to the tail of the bomb, the idea being that the sound of its descent would be more terrifying to the Turks. Trials made with a dummy bomb fitted with the whistle certainly gave good results, as the bomb emitted a most piercing shriek as it fell. When all was ready the bomb was fitted to a Henri [Farman], and we all took to the air to watch the hoped-for conflagration ... It went off all right when it hit; but only a tiny little fire resulted, the 20lb bomb having no doubt blown the liquid all over the scene before any of it except a small residue had ignited. It was rather disappointing; but Helles reported that the bomb made a most satisfactory noise as it hurtled through space.

From such unpromising beginnings, highly effective weapons were developed – one of the principal activities throughout 1916, for example, being devastating incendiary raids against Bulgarian crops. Samson was a prickly character but a doughty warrior and no-one took more pride than he in the achievements of his men, even if inadvertent:

> One day one of my pilots let go a 100lb bomb at some Turks he saw in a gulley . . . He made a rotten bad shot, and to his horror saw the bomb burst in the Turks' foremost trench at a point where the front lines were only about 20 yards apart. He came back and reported to me that he thought he must have killed some of our own people. At the instant he reported, I received a message from Anzac to say: 'One of your aeroplanes bombed Turks' trench; bits of Turks seen in the air, remainder of occupants got onto parapet, where we killed a lot with machine guns; please repeat bombing.' I didn't reply that it was a fluke, and that it was only by the mercy of the Lord that the bomb hadn't hit the Anzacs. No. 3 [Wing] lived on this reputation for accuracy for a long time.

Until late 1915, only one Victoria Cross had been awarded to the RNAS, when Flight Sub-Lieutenant Rex Warneford in a tiny monoplane successfully bombed Zeppelin LZ 37 in mid-air over Bruges on 7 June. The next VC was for an exploit less obviously spectacular but equally courageous. Samson had organised a series of attacks aiming to disrupt railway communications from Constantinople. Repeated attempts were made to damage the Maritza Bridge near Adrianople, Turkish encampments were bombed and, between 13 November and 1 December, a dozen attacks were made at Ferejik – a vital junction on the Salonika–Constantinople line. It was on 19 November that Squadron Commander Richard Bell Davies won his Victoria Cross by rescuing Flight Sub-Lieutenant Gilbert Smylie, who had been forced down in enemy territory when his engine was disabled by ground-fire. By landing to pick up Smylie, Davies

> ran a deadly risk of crashing; in addition, he was fired at the whole time. Smylie was just as gallant. Immediately he had landed he set fire to his aeroplane; then, seeing Davies was going to attempt to land, he went close up to his aeroplane and detonated a bomb which was still on it by firing at the fuse with his pistol. He feared that if he didn't explode the bomb it might go off in the fire and damage Davies's aeroplane. He then took off his flying coat and left a scribbled message in his pocket to say: 'Please return my coat, which I have had to leave, to No. 3 Wing.'

Smylie was rewarded with his freedom and the Distinguished Service Cross. Davies's *sangfroid* was also extraordinary, reporting the entire raid in the following concise terms:

> Dropped three 20lb bombs at Northern [Ferejik] Station. 1st burst short. 2nd burst on edge of line opposite train of coaches. 3rd burst over. No movement observable in or near town. One locomotive steaming north from Ferejik. Returning, saw H5 burning in marshes. Picked up pilot.
>
> (Signed) R.B. Davies

Between 28 March and 29 December 1915, Samson's wing had spent 2,600 hours in the air, with a maximum of eleven pilots and an average of seven. It was now felt that 2 Wing would suffice to cover the Helles evacuation and support the effort in Macedonia. Therefore, 3 Wing was disbanded; some of its personnel, including Smylie, transferred to Gerrard's; others, including Davies and Samson himself, headed home for a very well-earned rest. The Official History summed up the RNAS contribution to the Dardanelles campaign in eloquent terms:

> Never again in the war were seaplanes compelled to work so much over the land, nor aeroplanes so much over the sea. Too soon the young Service had to bear on its wings a load of responsibility on which, at times, depended the fortunes of the enterprise ... The difficulties which the Service had to overcome to keep its machines in the air called forth every ounce of ingenuity and patience of which the ground personnel were capable. Sand and dust, often driven along in clouds by a hot stinging wind, choked the engines and added enormously to the task of the mechanics ... The summer heat warped and weakened the woodwork of the aeroplanes and seaplanes. That the aeroplanes had to operate from an island base robbed their all-too-short effective working life of many hours. It was calculated that an average of half an hour was so wasted on every flight. It added, too, an almost certain risk of the loss of the aeroplane if the pilot were compelled to alight on the sea ... The Dardanelles formed a section of a vast front, every stretch of which cried out for the new air weapon. That enough material was found to ensure continuous air superiority over the Peninsula was, perhaps, even more than might have been hoped.

* * *

After the evacuation of Gallipoli, British forces in the Eastern Mediterranean were reorganised. A strong naval squadron was stationed at Imbros to attack Turkish troops withdrawing from the Peninsula, as well as bombarding other coastal sites. France had been given formal command in the Mediterranean in August 1914, but changes were made as the war developed. In particular, the Dardanelles ceased to be a French responsibility once Turkey became a belligerent. In December 1915 and March 1916, Allied naval conferences in Paris and Malta led to an increased British role in the Eastern Mediterranean. This would now include the Turkish coast in Asia Minor, where it was hoped to tie down enemy forces and prevent their deployment to other battlefronts. In addition, the Straits had still to be watched, the blockade maintained, enemy submarines suppressed, lines of communication interrupted, and the Allies supported on the Macedonian Front.

It was nevertheless decided that a single wing should suffice, following the evacuation of Gallipoli – hence the disbanding of 3 Wing and the return to England of Colonel Sykes and his staff. Instead, Wing Captain Scarlett

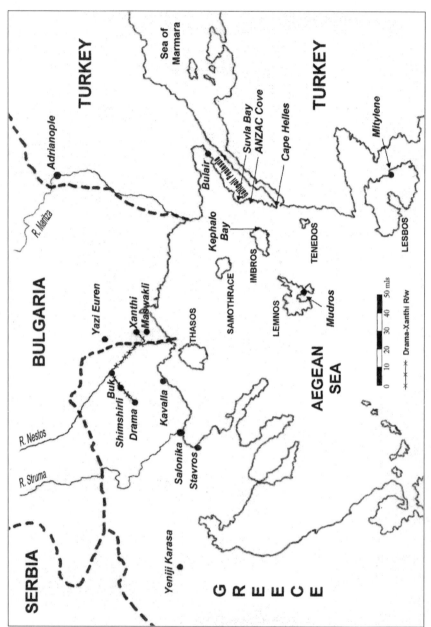

Dardanelles and Aegean theatre, 1916. (*Jeff Jefford*)

assumed overall control of the RNAS in the Mediterranean and sought to redeploy it in accordance with its remaining tasks. Not all his recommendations were accepted, but the Admiralty agreed that 2 Wing should consist of one unit of fighters, one unit of reconnaissance aeroplanes and two units of bombers. To keep up the pressure on Turkey, a detachment, known as B Squadron, was sent from Imbros to Mitylene, off the Turkish coast; while in April, an aerodrome was selected on the island of Thasos for operations against the Bulgarians in Macedonia. At the end of May, A Squadron – a mixed group of fighters and bombers, and including Bremner, Jones and Kink – arrived at Thasos to work alongside a similar French detachment. D Squadron, originally at Mudros on the island of Lemnos, was later transferred to Stavros on the Greek mainland, also to support the Salonika force, and C Squadron remained on Imbros, as the closest base covering Gallipoli, the Straits and – at a stretch – Constantinople itself.

What is striking about all these detachments and deployments is the high level of responsibility laid upon the shoulders of very small numbers of very young men. The military stereotype, in popular culture, which emerges from the Great War, is that of vast armies rigidly following inflexible orders without scope for initiative. In the sideshows, at least, that did not apply to pioneer air fighters. Kink's early military career undoubtedly equipped him for self-reliance, independent action and the assumption of leadership in far-flung theatres. The flavour of his work can be gauged, despite the absence of day-by-day unit records, from the printed RNAS Operations Reports which have been preserved. Occasionally these give quite graphic accounts of particular events and individual airmen; but, for the most part, they set out a pattern of general military activity as it was assessed at the time. Given the very small numbers of pilots and observers operating from Thasos, it is a certainty that Kink was involved in most of these operations. Thus, we learn that, on 1 June 1916:

> Camps between Xanthi and the Nestos River were bombed by British and French machines from Thasos. ... During the week ending 9 June, constant attacks were made by British and French Flights on hostile camps. The seaplane station at Gereviz, on Lake Boru, was bombed and petrol store destroyed. On 8 June, attacks were made with incendiary bombs upon the crops, with fair success ... During the week ending 16 June, French and English Flights effected enormous damage with incendiary bombs to large tracts of crops. During the week ending 30 June, continued operations with French aeroplanes were carried out. Xanthi was twice bombed, first at night, when fifty-five bombs were dropped, besides sixteen on Yeniji Karasa, an important military centre, and second, by day, when forty-seven bombs were distributed over the town and railway. The destruction of crops was continued, large tracts being set on fire.

The attacks on crops in southern Bulgaria continued throughout July and were believed to have had 'a most demoralising effect on the enemy'. Far from avoiding areas which put up resistance, those which mounted the heaviest anti-aircraft fire were 'singled out for special attention, with the result that our machines now fly over these places with little or no opposition'. Where crops had not already been burned by British and French incendiary bombs, regiments of soldiers were observed hurriedly harvesting what they could. This was a useful diversion of manpower and probably had a tangible effect on Bulgarian morale, but the verdict of the Official History was one of doubt 'whether the results obtained justified the use of aircraft for such a purpose'.

In any event, the work of A Squadron had to be refocused in August, when a Bulgarian offensive took control of Macedonia east of the River Struma. Enemy aircraft were based at Xanthi Aerodrome, and a duel developed with raids by each side on the air bases of the other. Pressure on the city of Xanthi, ceded to Bulgaria in 1912, had resulted in the enemy's military headquarters being removed to Yazi Euren in the mountains to the north, and aircraft formerly concentrated at Xanthi Aerodrome had been dispersed to locations where the hangars could be better concealed:

> At Maswakli, 2 miles south of Xanthi, six hangars and a shed were observed, where two days previously there had only been two hangars. The growth of this aerodrome has been watched with interest, and being now considered ripe for destruction, it has been attacked twice during the week. On the evening of 11 August, four machines dropped thirty ... bombs on the aerodrome, three of which fell between the hangars, four on the wood, and the remainder on the landing ground about 70 yards from the hangars.

This was the raid, already referred to, when Kink rescued one of the bombers from a new-type Fokker which managed to escape despite being attacked by his Bristol Scout at close range. When the enemy headquarters was moved to Yazi Euren, that too was raided in mid-August. Later in the month, the railway station at Drama – Greek since 1913, but occupied by the enemy – was successfully attacked, a large fire being seen to break out. Yet, the initiative was not all in one direction: it was as a result of three enemy aircraft appearing over Thasos on 28 August that Kink and Blandy each scored a victory. The fact that both enemy aircraft were forced to land, rather than being destroyed, may illustrate the limited effectiveness of the guns available to the British pilots. On 16 September, in the course of a series of attacks on transport and troops on road and rail, a Bulgarian command centre was discovered in a wood on the road between Drama and the Bulgarian-occupied seaport of Kavalla. A Squadron obliterated it with two 112lb bombs.

Such a systematic programme of harassment and destruction could not go unanswered. On 11 October, it was reported: 'The enemy air service in southern Bulgaria has recently been reinforced and is making serious endeavours to wrest from us the supremacy of the air.' The following day, in order to test the strength of the enemy, a raid was mounted against Maswakli Aerodrome by one Henri Farman, one Nieuport two-seater, and two escorting Scouts. Flight Sub-Lieutenant B.A. Millard, who failed to return, was last seen engaging an Albatros Scout. His Nieuport Scout was later spotted, apparently undamaged, in a field. Of the pilot there was no sign. However, in an act of courtesy which was not untypical, his fate was made clear the following day:

> An enemy machine dropped a message bag containing a letter from Flight Sub-Lieutenant Millard giving some further details of his action. He attacked an Aviatik and succeeded in wounding the observer in the leg. The Nieuport Scout's engine, which had previously 'cut out', then stopped entirely, and the pilot was obliged to land in a field about 4 miles south-west of Maswakli. He started to effect the necessary repairs and had completed one half when he was captured. The engine trouble was not due to enemy fire, only one bullet having hit the cowl. The letter stated that Flight Sub-Lieutenant Millard was in good health and being well treated, and was to be sent inland on the succeeding day.

Something similar happened when Blandy's two-seater was shot down near Drama on 23 October. Forty-eight hours later, 'a message was dropped by a hostile machine stating that both pilot and observer had been made prisoners, the former being wounded in the leg, but doing well'.

A Squadron's main strategic role, at this time, was to render the Xanthi–Drama railway useless to the enemy for supplying its forces on the Struma Front. Bridges constituted by far its most vulnerable points and that crossing the River Nestos at Buk was successfully attacked and its second span completely demolished. This achievement by Flight Sub-Lieutenant L.C. Shoppee in a Henri Farman on 15 October was repeated on 30 October when he and another bomber pilot destroyed the two centre spans of the bridge at Shimshirli, halfway between Buk and Drama. Such raids were invariably carried out under the protection of escorting Scouts and it is thus highly probable that Kink derived much valuable experience from taking part in them.

It was at this time that one more call was made on the limited resources of 2 Wing in the Aegean. Romania had entered the war on the Allied side at the end of August but soon found herself under great pressure. The Germans, realising the weakness of the Romanian Air Service, sent a Squadron of bombers to Bulgaria for an offensive against Bucharest and other key centres. Relentless attacks forced the Romanians to appeal to the Allies for help and no fewer than nine 2 Wing pilots were despatched on 25 October and 21 November. Several of these feature prominently in Kink's photographs from Imbros and Thasos, including Flight Lieutenants A.F.F. Jacob and C.E. Brisley, the latter having been the commander of C Squadron on Imbros. Arthur Jacob's experience, on this extremely long journey, found its way into the RNAS Operations Reports, and illustrates the hazards which he and his comrades endured:

> After leaving Imbros at 10.30, good weather prevailed for the first two hours and good time was made to the Bulgarian coast ... Passing westward of Adrianople much activity was observed ... The weather became

rapidly worse on the Balkan mountains, and during a thunderstorm, enveloped in a large cloud, the pilot lost control. He fell from 9,000 to 1,000 feet, at which height he emerged from the cloud upside down, regaining control at 500 feet. He considers he must have been upside down several times, as not only did he feel his belt tighten, but various things fell out of the machine. His compass was now useless. The petrol in his front tank was almost finished, and pressure in the back tank faulty. The pilot consequently decided to land, which he did successfully, and repaired the defects with his engine running. A party of Bulgarians opened fire as he was taxiing off, and [the] pilot charged them, firing a few rounds from his gun, whereupon all fell flat, and he was able to get away. While he was following down the course of a small river, in the hope of striking the Danube, a party of thirty Bulgarians on a barge fired at the machine with rifles. The pilot turned back and emptied a tray of ammunition at them, and then dived within a few feet, causing them all to jump into the water. Most of the last two hours' flying was done at about 50 feet owing to bad visibility. The pilot, having flown for more than six hours, continually losing his way, decided to land. He found that he was about 20 miles north of Ismail, in Russia, and at length reached Bucharest on 30 October.

It is hard not to empathise with Jacob's reaction to being fired at from the river, after all he had endured. Nor did he forget to speak highly of the engine of his Nieuport – 'the excellent condition of which he attributes to Chief Petty Officer J.E. Clarke'. Nevertheless, none of these gallant efforts saved Bucharest from capture by the Germans in December 1916.

★   ★   ★

The chronological record set out in RNAS Operations Reports, though enlivened occasionally by stories such as Jacob's, cannot convey an authentic picture of what it was like to be based on Thasos during the time Kink was there. For that, we need to examine the evocative snapshots compiled in his albums and to return to the interviews given by Donald Bremner, whom we last saw being taken off Gallipoli on the night of 8/9 January 1916. Bremner served with Kink on the same two Aegean bases. Imbros he described as 'a bleak, forbidding place, lacking many of the amenities available on a home station':

Although the flying officers ate in a stone-built mess, they lived and slept in aeroplane packing cases, 10 × 7 feet; each 'hut' afforded an area large enough for two camp beds. The interior walls were lined with tarred paper. A familiar feature was a scratching sound from behind the paper. Pinpointing the exact location, a slit would be made with a penknife, revealing a 6-inch centipede which was then extracted wriggling on the tip of the blade. A strip of sticky paper effected an immediate repair to the hole.

When the pilots and observers were not fighting centipedes, their main duty until the evacuation of the Peninsula was spotting the fall of shot for the 15-inch gun monitors afloat nearby:

> Executing figures of eight between the naval monitors and their targets on the peninsula, the aircrew corrected the ship's line and angle of fire by wireless messages. Flying at no more than 50 knots, they remained above the range of rifle fire from the ground.

This work continued, though at a reduced tempo, once the Allies had withdrawn – the monitors now 'lobbing shells from their moorings in the harbour a couple of times a week'. Bremner's last mission from Imbros was on 29 May. The next morning he took off in his Bristol Scout, together with a Nieuport and three Henri Farmans, to join forces with the French on Thasos. This he found much more isolated than Imbros:

> It was a very difficult aerodrome to approach because it was on a piece of land which rather jutted out into the sea. You flew into the hill and made a sharp turn and landed ... It was quite difficult really ... The French were very nice people, very fine pilots and they were very helpful to me because they flew Nieuports and knew everything that was to be known about them. I had trouble with my engine, and they were beautiful mechanics ... None of the French were pukka service people. Their Adjutant was a man called Prezler who was one of the chief artists for *La Vie Parisienne*, and their Chief Pilot was a man called Constantini, who was a very famous motor racing driver and always used to call me 'le grand pilot du petit Bristol', and he always introduced himself by smacking his chest and saying 'Constantini, pilot du Nieuport, très bon pilot, moi'.

By now, Samson's incendiary techniques had been perfected. Tinsmiths from the offshore monitors would supply bomb-shaped containers to Bremner, A Squadron's Armament Officer. These were converted with petrol and Very cartridges into an effective crop-burning weapon:

> I fitted a bomb rack just behind the engine under the fuselage. No bomb sights, or anything like that. There was a hole in the floor of the fuselage and I used to squint down through that ... when I could see the target I let the bombs go. Sometimes I pulled the machine up too much and the bombs bounced off my axle. But it didn't seem to do any damage.

Although enemy aircraft occasionally caused problems, there was a more insidious threat to be faced. In the first half of September, an Operations Report referred in passing to 'a shortage of pilots owing to malaria'. Bremner explained – all too graphically – why this situation came about:

> Living conditions were much more primitive than on Imbros. At one side of the aerodrome was an olive grove and the shade of an olive tree is a very overrated thing. We lived in tents, with a tented mess, and I think the

worst disadvantage we had to put up with was the flies. If you were eating jam you had to wave your hand over the jam all the way from the plate to your mouth to make sure you weren't eating flies. Our latrines were the most primitive things, all open round the seat and the flies used to crawl all over your bottom as you were sitting there – most unpleasant. The only time to use lavatories was just before lunch. As soon as the gong went, the flies left the latrines and went to the mess tent.

Having contracted both dysentery and malaria, Bremner was hospitalised at Stavros before being sent home. In this respect, too, his experience mirrored Kink's. Early in November, Kink was admitted to hospital in Malta suffering from malaria. There he remained for more than a month, until repatriated to England and briefly admitted to Haslar Hospital two days before Christmas. Not until 6 February 1917 was he judged fit to return to duty. A week later, after more than three months' sick leave, Kink was posted to the RNAS Central Training Establishment, opened at Cranwell near Grantham the previous April. There he spent three weeks re-qualifying, before being taken onto the staff as a Flying Instructor. At the end of June, he gained special promotion to Acting Flight Lieutenant, remaining in post until September. A grainy snapshot in his personal album records a visit by his elder brother. Toss looks solemn; Kink relaxed. Within weeks one would be dead – and the other on his way to the bloodiest battlefields of the Western Front.

Chapter 2

Glory Days – The Western Front

On 19 September 1917, Kink was posted to a unit synonymous with the history of naval aviation: 1 Squadron RNAS had been formed at Fort Grange, Gosport, on 16 October 1914 with just four Bristol biplanes and seven pilots. Led by Squadron Commander Arthur Longmore, they operated from Newcastle mounting coastal patrols to detect enemy warships in the North Sea. By the end of 1914, the Squadron had established separate Flights at Gosport and at Dover, rotating with 2 Squadron – under Gerrard – in manning the stations. With the failure of each side's attempt to outflank the other on the Continent and the emergence of static front lines, it became practicable to establish a coastal base at Dunkirk. From there 3 Squadron – under Samson – undertook major bombing raids on Zeebrugge and Ostend in February 1915; but, before the end of the month, that unit was despatched to the Dardanelles and 1 Squadron arrived at St Pol to replace it. The pilots specialised not only in attacking enemy troops and positions, but also in mounting raids on submarine bases and airship stations. It was on one of these that, in the early hours of 7 June, Flight Sub-Lieutenant Warneford won his VC for bringing down LZ 37, the first Zeppelin to be destroyed in the air.

June 1915 was also the month when Nos. 1, 2 and 3 Squadrons were re-designated as 1, 2 and 3 Wings RNAS, as the Naval Air Stations passed from the direct control of the Air Department of the Admiralty to that of the senior naval officers in the areas where they were located. Thus, the Dover-Dunkirk Group came under the Admiral in command of the Dover Patrol. It was decided to return 1 Wing to Dover and replace it with 2 Wing, led by Gerrard; but only a fortnight later, on 2 August, 1 Wing found itself back at Dunkirk. This was because 2 Wing was being sent to reinforce Samson in the Dardanelles, where Kink joined it in December 1915. Meanwhile, the Squadron in which he would later make his name on the Western Front continued to develop.

By March 1916, 1 Wing consisted of four permanent Flights: No. 1 for reconnaissance (Nieuport two-seaters); No. 2 for aerial combat and anti-Zeppelin work (Nieuport single-seaters); No. 3 for wireless telegraphy spotting (Nieuport two-seaters); and No. 4 for night spotting (BE2Cs). There was also a fifth Flight, of Caudrons, for bombing and anti-submarine patrolling. The reconnaissance, fighting and anti-Zeppelin Nieuports in Nos. 1 and 2 Flights were grouped into A Squadron, together with the Bombing Flight, temporarily attached. The W/T spotting and night spotting Flights (Nos. 3 and 4) were grouped into B Squadron. As will be seen, A Squadron eventually became 1 (Naval) Squadron; and, at this early stage, its personnel included Flight Sub-Lieutenants Stanley Dallas and Richard Minifie – two Australians who, like Kink, were to become outstanding aces.

With the arrival in France of 4 and 5 Wings in the spring of 1916, 1 Wing could concentrate on fighting, patrolling, spotting, photography, reconnaissance, and protection of the Fleet. Dallas was beginning to build his reputation as a formidable aerial fighter, destroying several enemy aeroplanes and seaplanes. By the summer, both sides were raiding each other's aerodromes, the protection of which became a major concern. According to the Squadron History

it was arranged at a discussion between the French and British air commanders that defensive patrols to protect Dunkirk from hostile aircraft should be shared by the French Squadron at Furnes and the RNAS at Dunkirk. These patrols had barely commenced when the French Squadron was called away to the Verdun sector, and the RNAS assumed the sole responsibility for the air defence of the Dunkirk area with effect from 5 June. To facilitate this defence, A Squadron, consisting of two Flights of Nieuport Scouts under Squadron Commander F.K. Haskins, was detached from No. 1 Wing and on 10 June took up quarters at the Furnes Aerodrome which had been placed at its disposal by the French. This Squadron was the first homogenous fighting unit of the Naval Air Service.

On 22 June 1916, the Squadron received its first Sopwith Triplane (110hp Clerget engine), a machine with a better performance than any of its predecessors:

Arriving at 7.45pm, it was at 8.00pm sent up in pursuit of an enemy aircraft reported over Oost-Dunkirk, and reached a height of 12,000 feet in thirteen minutes.

With effect from 3 July, A Squadron changed its designation and became known as the Detached Squadron:

During the month the Squadron carried out 110 Fighter Patrols over the Nieuport-Dixmude-Ypres-Middelkerke-Ostend area, and in addition provided forty-five escorts to British and French reconnaissance, spotting, and photographic machines.

Yet, although Dallas and other pilots in the unit continued to add to their scores, the number of aerial combats in the Belgian coastal region diminished because of the Germans' need to concentrate their machines near the terrible fighting on the Somme. Enemy activity in the coastal area did not resume until the second half of October.

On 6 December 1916, the Detached Squadron was designated 1 Squadron RNAS. At an Air Board meeting just five days later, Major-General Sir Hugh Trenchard – in command of the Royal Flying Corps on the Continent – stated that more help from the RNAS was vital to maintain supremacy in the air: 8 Squadron RNAS had been attached to the RFC on 26 October 1916, and Trenchard asked the Admiralty to provide another four. This was agreed and the first to be transferred was 1 Squadron – now equipped with sixteen Sopwith Triplanes. It arrived at Chipilly from Furnes on 15 February 1917, where it formed part of 14th (Army) Wing of IV Brigade RFC. To avoid confusion with a similarly-numbered RFC Squadron, it became known as 1 (Naval) Squadron. By the end of the month, Dallas had been promoted to Flight Commander and second-in-command, under Haskins.

When the Battle of Arras was fought, between 9 April and 4 May, 1 (Naval) Squadron found itself transferred to 13th (Army) Wing of III Brigade RFC, operating with the Third Army. The Squadron moved from Chipilly to La Bellevue Aerodrome on 11 April. It was now in the thick of the fighting and, between 22 April and 5 May, ninety-five Offensive Patrols were carried out; 175 enemy aircraft were engaged, four of which were confirmed destroyed with twelve more sent down out of control. During May 1917, combats with the enemy were a daily occurrence, but on 1 June the Squadron was transferred again – this time to Bailleul Aerodrome as part of 11th Wing of II Brigade RFC which was working with the Second Army. The area covered by the Squadron had two patrol sub-divisions: the northern being Bailleul-Ypres-Moorslede-Menin and the southern, Bailleul-Armentières-Lomme-Halluin. 'Offensive Patrols', to seek out the enemy and bring him to combat, were maintained daily, both before and during the Battle of Messines which began on 7 June, and 'Special Missions' were carried out to try to intercept enemy aircraft which had been reported. On 14 June, the last day of that battle, Stanley Dallas succeeded Francis Haskins in command of the Squadron.

Only three weeks later came a severe blow. Six Triplanes, led by Flight Commander Cyril Eyre, set out on 7 July as escorts for two photo-reconnaissance aircraft of 45 Squadron. The formation was ambushed by about eighteen Germans, and although two of these were shot down, three of the six Triplanes, including Eyre's, failed to return. Already there had been a lack of reinforcements where pilots were concerned and a lack of spare parts for the Triplanes. Not until 28 August would the Squadron return to its former establishment of eighteen machines, by the transfer of three Triplanes from 10 (Naval) Squadron – which, by then, was being re-equipped with Sopwith Camels.

★   ★   ★

Such was the Squadron to which Kink was sent in September 1917, but what was the strategic situation? He had already been involved at the tail-end of a failed expedition: now he would be plunged into the attritional stalemate which had provoked the Dardanelles fiasco in the first place. Almost a century after the appalling losses on the Western Front, historians still debate whether alternatives existed. Some blame political intrigue and poor generalship, others emphasise technology – with the battlefield dominated by interlocking fields of fire. This ensured that slowly advancing troops would be mown down by machine guns before making any worthwhile inroads into the enemy's trenches. Minor advances, occasionally achieved, were usually reversed by counter-attacks or simply absorbed into a new static confrontation a short distance from the original one. *Forgotten Victory* is a recent study of the Western Front battles which rightly draws attention to the Hundred Days' campaign in which the Allied coalition won a sequence of decisive victories between mid-July and early November 1918. Its author, Gary Sheffield, regrets the extent to which this British success has been disregarded:

> The burden of fighting the German Army fell mainly to the French and Russians in the first two and a half years of the war, but in 1918 it was the turn of the BEF. Between them, the French, Americans and Belgians took 196,700 prisoners and 3,775 guns between 18 July and the end of the war. With a smaller Army than the French, Haig's forces captured 188,700 prisoners and 2,840 guns in the same period. This was, by far, the greatest military victory in British history.

Dr Sheffield's thesis is less palatable, however, in suggesting that the catastrophic offensives prior to 1918 were needed to enable Allied generals to learn the lessons they eventually applied at the end of the war. One should not have to waste the lives of legions of soldiers in relentless repetition of unsuccessful tactics. Time and again, those tactics failed to break the stalemate or failed to be exploited when occasionally they achieved surprise. After the catastrophe on the Somme in 1916, there was no reason to believe that a breakthrough could be made and exploited with the available technology. Yet, this was attempted, not once, but twice in 1917. First came the Battle of Arras which Dr Sheffield describes as 'the second of the three great attritional offensives waged by the British Army in 1916–17'. On the first day of the attack, 9 April, the British Third Army took 5,600 prisoners and the Canadians – who captured most of Vimy Ridge – a further 3,400. This is described as the 'greatest success' of the British Expeditionary Force 'since the beginning of trench warfare'. Yet, the British advance soon ran out of steam, as German reinforcements arrived, and the British Fifth Army had little to show for the heavy losses it sustained. Further major efforts on 23 April and 3 May, partly intended to tie down forces which might otherwise be used against the French, simply added to the butchery on both sides.

At the same time, Russia was in revolution – albeit not yet a Bolshevik one – while unrestricted submarine warfare and the diplomatic disaster of the Zimmerman telegram had goaded the United States into entering the war on 6 April. Did Britain and France really have to squander so many lives so fruitlessly after this date? Why risk the colossal price of failure when the balance of forces was shifting so dramatically? As will be seen, the German leadership fully understood the significance of American belligerency. They therefore gambled everything, in the spring of 1918, to exploit the collapse of Russia before the United States could make a real difference. It was folly for the British and French to wear themselves out in 1917, given that the balance of forces would change in their favour once the Americans arrived. Claiming that the Germans could stand the rate of attrition less than the British was no justification at the time, and is equally indefensible now.

After the Arras offensives of April and May, came the unprecedented use of giant subterranean mines. Nineteen of them were exploded under Messines Ridge on 7 June, with a force that could be felt on the far side of the English Channel. Though surprise was achieved, strategic gain was once again lacking. Nevertheless, on the last day of July, the crowning effort of the BEF in 1917 was made. The Third Battle of Ypres would endure until 10 November and imprint itself on the British psyche to an extent matched only by the Somme disaster the previous year. The focus was on the Passchendaele–Staden Ridge, and the main thrust was delivered by General Sir Hubert Gough's Fifth Army along a 7½-mile front. The flanks were defended by the British Second Army on the right and the French First Army on the left. Having overrun some of the outer German defences on the first day, the British Commander-in-Chief, Sir Douglas Haig, then discovered that the weather was an even more formidable opponent than the enemy. The Official History of the air war quotes his despatch as follows:

The low-lying, clayey soil, torn by shells and sodden with rain, turned to a succession of vast muddy pools. The valleys of the chalked and overflowing streams were speedily transformed into long stretches of bog, impassable except for a few well-defined tracks, which became marks for the enemy's artillery ... To leave these tracks was to risk death by drowning ... In these conditions operations of any magnitude became impossible, and the resumption of our offensive was necessarily postponed until a period of fine weather should allow the ground to recover.

The second phase of the attack, known as the Battle of Langemarck, lasted from 16–18 August and naturally lacked any element of surprise. The Germans showed no sign of giving way. Next came the Battle of the Menin Road Ridge, beginning on 20 September – the day after Kink was posted to 1 (Naval) Squadron – and lasting for five days. Its aim was to capture objectives at a distance of between 1,000 yards and 1 mile. This was largely achieved and no fewer than twenty-six British Squadrons, including 1 (Naval) Squadron, managed to mount continuous two-hour patrols in support of the ground forces. The weather had prevented British airmen from discovering German troop concentrations ready to counter-attack during the Battle of Langemarck; but this time 'there were eight specific instances on the front of the Second Army of the breaking-up, by the artillery, of attempted counter-attacks, as a result of information sent down from the air ... These facts may appear colourless in comparison with other forms of air activity, but they represent, nevertheless, a substantial contribution by the air service towards the success of the battle.'

The pattern was the same in the fourth phase, known as the Battle of Polygon Wood. It took place from 26 September to 3 October, with the objective of securing a jumping-off place from which to attack the main Passchendaele Ridge: 'Once again the infantry achieved a tactical success ... The feature of the day's fighting was the defeat of the numerous enemy counter-attacks, due, in part, to the warnings given by the air observers.' The next assault was planned for 4 October, and persevered with despite a great deterioration in the weather. Originally it was hoped that success at Ypres would drive the Germans away from the Channel Ports, and an amphibious force to help achieve this had also been assembled. The reality, in the words of the Official History, was very different:

The British line had now been advanced along the main ridge for 9,000 yards ... The year was already far spent and the prospect of driving the enemy from the Belgian coast had long since disappeared. The continuous delays in the advance as a result of the weather and its effect on the state of the ground, had given the enemy time, after each attack, to bring up reinforcements and to reorganise his defences. Although General Head-quarters now recognised that the major objectives of the Flanders operations were impossible of attainment, they were still anxious to con-tinue the operations with a view to the capture of the remainder of the Passchendaele Ridge before winter set in. The weather was entirely unfavourable but there were hopes that it would improve, hopes based on the somewhat slender foundation that the abnormal rainfall of the summer presaged a normal, perhaps even a dry, autumn.

Instead of remaining a means to an end, the offensive had become an end in itself. At 5.20am on 9 October, after two days of continuous heavy rain, the attack was renewed on a 6-mile front. Haig had decided that Passchendaele must be captured, so captured it would be. The cycle was repeated on 12 October in the hope of helping to prevent German forces being switched to meet the impending French offensive on the River Aisne. Some ground was gained east of Poelcapelle and on the southern edge of Houthulst Forest on 22 October, fighter pilots doing everything they could to attack German infantry in trenches and shell holes, on the roads and in villages. And so it went on and on – a little progress here, a forced withdrawal there, and the final taking of Passchendaele Village on 6 November by the Canadians who, with British assistance, extended their gains on the main ridge four days later.

Passchendaele was, according to the official air historian, 'the most sombre and bloodiest of all the battlefields of the war'. One of the pilots who lived through it and later reached the highest rank in the RAF was Lord Douglas of Kirtleside who, as Sholto Douglas, commanded 84 Squadron's SE5 fighters when he returned to the Western Front in September 1917. He, too, regarded Third Ypres as 'the most terrible of all the battles' of the Great War:

> The Somme of the year before had been bad enough, and after that it was felt that the lesson of the futility of mass attacks must surely have been learnt. But it was not learnt, and less than a year later our Army was called upon to embark on an offensive that in so many ways was even more terrible than the Somme ... [Passchendaele] was the beginning of what was to become for those on the ground a long and indescribable misery ... all the drainage systems were smashed in the opening bombardment, and eventually the whole area became clogged with mud. Over this devastated area, which had been reduced to the state of a quagmire, attack after attack was launched ... For communication there were only the rough tracks which wound their way almost aimlessly across the mire, and wandering off them led to drowning. The Germans welcomed the rain as 'our strongest ally'.

Douglas was well aware that, as an airman, he had much greater control over his fate in battle than a soldier or sailor. Fighting on land or at sea he regarded as largely a question of luck 'whether one came through with a whole skin or fell by the wayside ... it was purely a matter of chance whether a bullet or a shell hit you or the man standing next to you'. In aerial combat, however, if you could think a split second faster and shoot a shade straighter than your opponent, 'then 99 times out of 100' you would emerge victorious:

> In common with most people, I did not particularly mind being beaten by a better man in a fair fight; but I did object strongly to the imposition of any flukes ... I felt that if I were killed in the air it would be very largely because of my own stupidity or lack of skill.

These differences were actually less applicable to Passchendaele, because many of the pilots were tasked to carry out low-level attacks against enemy concentrations on the ground:

> In this job there was very little fighting in the air, and since we were flying at heights of only 200 or 300 feet we were supposed to be able to see plenty of what was going on below us. What I saw was nothing short of horrifying. The ground over which our infantry and light artillery were fighting was one vast sea of churned-up muck and mud, and everywhere, lip to lip, there were shell-holes full of water. These low-flying attacks that we had to make, for which most of my young pilots were quite untrained, were a wretched and dangerous business, and also pretty useless. It was very difficult for us to pick out our targets in the morass because everything on the ground, including the troops, was the same colour as that dreadful mud ... it was quite obvious to anyone viewing from the air this dreadful battleground ... that any chance of a major advance or a breakthrough was quite out of the question.

As Douglas's memoirs make clear, it was not just fashionable post-war opinion which came to damn the strategy of attritional offensives. The ordering of more and more attacks in such an 'appalling morass' was seen at the time, by him and his comrades, as 'the grossest of blunders'. They recognised the need to relieve pressure on the French by keeping the Germans fully stretched:

> But as I watched from the air what was happening on the ground there were presented to me some terrible questions. Why did we have to press on so blindly day after day and week after week in this one desolate area and under such dreadful conditions? Why was there not some variety in our strategy and tactics? The questions that I asked then are the questions that have continued to be asked ever since; and the answers to them have never ceased to be most painful ones.

*   *   *

Toss Kinkead had died without an enemy in sight, barely a fortnight before Kink arrived in the midst of the Passchendaele slaughter. At 20, he was already a veteran of one theatre and a seasoned flying instructor – with an added twist of personal tragedy to absorb. No-one can know if this fuelled his determination: certainly it did not hold him back. For the first few days, air-to-air combat had to wait. As in the case of Douglas, Kink's first task was to support the infantry. We have seen how the Battle of Polygon Wood was meant to secure a springboard from which the assault on Passchendaele Ridge could be mounted. The Official History relates how 'low-flying fighting pilots, from an average height of 300 feet attacked troops and batteries'. They had been given tactical maps which divided the terrain into sections allotted to specific airmen, and which identified the most probable enemy assembly points and routes of approach. Many aspects of Kink's career were to feature his propensity for low flying, and this was no exception:

WORK CARRIED OUT BY GROUND PATROLS OF 11th WING,
RFC – 26 September 1917
8.50am: Flight Lieutenant Kinkead, Naval Squadron No. 1, fired 450 rounds from 100 feet into troops in shell-holes and machine-gun positions north of Zandvoorde and at transport and guns on the road going south-east at 28 Q 3a 9.4. Men scattered on both occasions.
11.50am: Flight Lieutenant Kinkead, Naval Squadron No. 1, at 500 feet attacked troops near Moorslede, who ran, and some fell. Also attacked a hostile kite balloon at the same place which did not catch fire. 450 rounds fired in all.

Tethered observation balloons were particularly dangerous targets, relying not only on patrolling fighters, but also on ground-fire from anti-aircraft and machine guns sited specially to render hazardous any close-range attack. Yet, experience showed that only from about 50 yards – or even less – would tracer and incendiary ammunition be likely to set a balloon ablaze. Douglas noted another factor mitigating against successful balloon strikes during the conditions of late 1917:

> If it was raining or the atmosphere was moist it was almost impossible to set fire to the balloon ... We found that the most effective method was to dive steeply to a point about half a mile away from the balloon and level with it, and then to flatten out and go straight for it with all the added speed that we had picked up in the dive. At a range of 200 yards we would take a sighting shot with our Vickers machine gun, and at 50 yards we would open up with the Lewis gun. We would carry straight on to within 20 yards of the balloon, firing all the time, and then hop over it and zoom away.

One can only admire the cold courage of balloon observers, slung in a tethered open basket, hundreds of feet above the battlefield, and utterly vulnerable to any passing fighter which braved the ring of anti-aircraft guns. At the first sign of attack, however, they could at least try to save their lives by using the parachutes with which they alone were supplied. Extraordinary as it seems – even in terms of the simple arithmetic involved in saving pilots for the fight – not until very late in the war was any serious consideration given to developing a system for use by British pilots or observers. The historian of the parachute gives two explanations, one of which was as bizarre as it was inhumane:

> The virtual indifference which greeted ... the first parachute drop from an aircraft in Britain (at Hendon in May 1914), was to be reflected in a lack of concern for pilot safety throughout World War One ... There was simply not the will to push ahead and produce the right type. Why? There were two reasons. First, it was widely and insensitively thought that pilots with parachutes might abandon their aircraft too easily ... Secondly, because parachutes fell some way short of perfection in design and adaptability, they were considered unsuitable for aircraft use ... With drive and encouragement from those in positions of power, parachutes could undoubtedly have been provided for all who needed them.

When, many years later, Sholto Douglas learned that a belief that pilots would jump prematurely had hindered parachute development, and when he recalled the agonising and terrifying deaths of so many young men, he voiced his anger at 'such a contemptible decision'. Two days before the end of the war, Douglas first saw an enemy pilot escape by parachute. After a slow start, the Germans had given some of their airmen the prospect of survival.

The success of individual pilots in the Great War is inevitably measured by the number of air-to-air combats in which they were victorious. In the context of long periods of stagnation on the ground and infrequent clashes at sea – apart from the deeply despised U-boat campaign – the gladiatorial aspect of aerial duels was bound to catch the imagination of the public. Britain had a deliberate policy of not lionising her aces; but the press had a job to do, and the steady stream of decorations awarded to RNAS and RFC personnel made it easy to build up the reputation of selected recipients. What emerges from the history of 1 (Naval) Squadron, and its successor, 201 Squadron RAF, is the extent to which much of its most dangerous work involved the enemy on the ground. Standing Orders issued by the Headquarters of 13th Wing, attached to III Brigade RFC on Third Army front, were also promulgated to 11th Wing, attached to II Brigade RFC on Second Army front – which included 1 (Naval) Squadron in September 1917. On 24 September, just two days before the Polygon Wood offensive, instructions were given to all Squadrons that 'in future, no machines will fire into trenches from low altitudes, unless expressly ordered to do so. It is considered that the risk of [RFC] casualties occurring is not justified by the amount of good done unless a particularly good target presents itself, such as a large body of troops in the open.' Time and again, throughout the Passchendaele battles, the German Spring Offensive of March 1918, and the Hundred Days' campaign, Kink and his comrades were fully engaged in air-to-ground combat of the very type normally forbidden. Many courageous pilots were lost on such operations, with little acknowledgement of their sacrifice, in this extremely hazardous but unglamorous form of fighting.

The task of reconstructing the combat career of a Western Front fighter ace is fraught with difficulties. Some pilots were credited with tallies which painstaking research later called into question. Seldom are the records consecutive or complete in any one series of files. In Kink's case it is possible to assemble a fairly full picture on the basis of 1 (Naval) Squadron's Daily Reports of Operations and Squadron Record Books, as well as more scattered collections of individual reports – 'Combats in the Air' – held in these volumes and in the War Diaries of the RFC Brigades to which the Squadron was attached. No researcher in this field should fail to acknowledge the meticulous work of Christopher Shores, Norman Franks, Russell Guest and their associates, including Frank Olynyk in the United States. *Above the Trenches*, based on twenty years' research and published in 1990, is an encyclopaedic compilation of the available data. Yet, even this data is inevitably to some extent deficient. As the authors explain:

> In the RFC, RNAS, and later in the RAF, Squadrons wrote out Combat Reports for each pilot following an engagement, and these were sent to the Wing Headquarters, to which the Squadrons were attached. The Wing Commander allowed or disallowed each claim made in these reports, but then passed them on up to Brigade Headquarters . . . and it was possible to have a claim disallowed by a Wing, only to be allowed by Brigade, or for a claim disallowed by both to appear in the [RFC Headquarters] Communiqué. The main weakness of the system lay in the lack of any centralised review process, which meant that two or more patrols from different units involved in the same fight, would each tend to claim all the German aircraft seen spinning down . . . Naturally, the passage of time has reduced the number of Combat Reports and Squadron records that have

survived. Some Wings (11th, for example) kept most of the copies of Combat Reports submitted by all the units operating under their command ... But other Wings, Brigades and Squadrons retained none at all.

Claims were generally judged to fall into one of three categories: shot down and destroyed; sent down 'out of control', which meant 'probably destroyed' but not actually seen to crash; or 'driven down' and forced to land, as a result of damage which might, in fact, be fairly simple to repair. An additional complication was that most of the combats took place over German-occupied territory, given the offensive nature of Trenchard's strategy and the much more reactive attitude of the German Air Service. It was much easier for the latter to confirm the fate of downed aircraft than for the Allied Air Forces to do so.

Kink's first combat on the Western Front clearly illustrates these problems:

SQUADRON RECORD BOOK – 1 October 1917
10.10am – 11.05am: 2 scouts attacked by Flight Lieutenant Kinkead, 1 dived vertically for 1,000 feet and was then lost sight of.

This particular fight has not found its way onto any list of Kink's victories subsequently compiled. Yet there are just as good grounds for regarding it as an 'out of control' victory as many others which have been counted towards his total. Any biography of a fighter ace must try to compile his overall score, and this has been attempted in Appendix I; but the terse contents of Combat Reports and Squadron Record Books usually do less than justice to the moves and manoeuvres of whirling dogfights, in which split-second decisions meant the difference between life and death. Nor do such accounts generally make exciting reading unless enlarged upon by witnesses and set in the context of a wider battle.

Here are the reports of Kink's first four accredited victories on the Western Front, as the battles of 'Third Ypres' ground to their conclusion:

COMBATS IN THE AIR – 17 October 1917
No. 76
At 11.45am at 14,000 feet over Comines Flight Lieutenant Kinkead attacked a two-seater DFW. Pilot attacked from just above and behind, and fired 200 rounds, getting within point-blank range. The EA [enemy aircraft] did not reply but fell completely out of control, falling over and over like a dead leaf. Pilot watched it down to within a short distance of the ground where it was lost to sight.

COMBATS IN THE AIR – 18 October 1917
No. 78
At 10.30am at 16,000 feet east of Poelcapelle, Flight Lieutenant Kinkead and Flight Sub-Lieutenant J.H. Forman attacked a two-seater DFW at point-blank range, firing in all 400 rounds, observing tracers entering the tail and fuselage. The observer replied but after a few bursts he stopped

firing, being apparently hit. The machine then stalled, side-slipped and fell completely out of control for several thousand feet until lost in the clouds.

COMBATS IN THE AIR – 24 October 1917
No. 84
1.30pm: Flight Lieutenant Kinkead sighted a two-seater EA near Comines at 15,000 feet. Pilot attacked from above and fired 300 rounds into him at point-blank range. The EA turned to attack but Flight Lieutenant Kinkead again got in a burst and the EA turned over and dived vertically for 2,000 feet when the left-hand planes came off and pilot followed him down and saw him crash between Comines and Wervicq. Pilot also later attacked a two-seater EA, one of a group of seven, but pilot ran out of ammunition. Two Gothas were in this group.

COMBATS IN THE AIR – 29 October 1917
No. 87
At 5.15pm, in the semi-darkness at 2,000 feet near Gheluvelt, Flight Lieutenant S.M. Kinkead attacked an EA scout at close range. It zoomed up into the clouds but came out again and was attacked with a burst of 50 rounds at 15 yards range. The scout dived vertically, going down in the same position until out of sight.

In each case, the enemy aircraft was dealt with at extremely close range. The term 'point-blank' consistently features in descriptions of Kink's combats. Not for him the premature joining of battle before success could be assured. His method was to bide his time and make every bullet count. Years later, in Iraq, the Great War ace Ira 'Taffy' Jones would see Kink's patience in action. Four victories in a fortnight might have been attributed to the intensity of the fighting over Passchendaele; but the belated ending of the offensive did not affect the trend Kink had now established.

On 2 November, 1 (Naval) Squadron reverted to RNAS control, when it was temporarily attached to 4 Wing at Middle Aerodrome near Dunkirk – where it relocated two days later. Between 9 November and 6 December, its Triplanes were replaced by Sopwith Camels – a change needed to match the latest heavily-armed German machines. In the four days from 12–15 November, Kink had five significant encounters with enemy aircraft, including a giant Gotha bomber, a mile out to sea off Westende. That fight was inconclusive, but three of the others were decisive:

COMBATS IN THE AIR – 12 November 1917
No. 91
3.45pm: I attacked a new type scout with Flight Sub-Lieutenant Forman about [sic] Dixmude at 9,000 feet, from above and behind. We drove him west (himself looping and side-slipping) firing on him at opportune times. He then turned east and began to climb, but we again attacked from above and, when at 4,000 feet, he suddenly appeared to be on fire – ending up in

a vertical nosedive. We watched him until out of sight still on fire. The mist was so thick that I could not see the ground.

COMBATS IN THE AIR – 15 November 1917
No. 95

... When NE of Dixmude, in company with four other Camels, I dived on seven Albatros Scouts from 13,000 feet. I selected one and fired a good burst into him. The EA fell over and over and crashed near some shattered buildings near Beerst at 1.00pm. I then sighted an EA firing at a DH5 and drove him off. I then fired a burst into another EA but he dived away and got free. Then I saw another scout and attacked him and shot him down out of control just N of Dixmude. A French pilot was close by me all the time in this encounter. Time: 1.15pm.

The 15 November victories marked Kink's transition from Triplane to Camel. On his first combat mission in the brand-new machine, he had downed two Albatros Scouts in a quarter of an hour. The Albatros and the Halberstadt fighters were largely responsible for the relatively short deployment of the popular Sopwith Triplane and its replacement by the F1 Camel. The German machines carried the twin synchronised machine guns which later became inseparable from the image of the Great War fighter ace, portrayed in films about the Western Front. They were matched for the first time by the Camel, whose predecessors, the Sopwith Pups and Triplanes, were fitted with only a single synchronised Vickers machine gun. Aviation historian Jack Bruce described the Camel as 'wilful, neurotic and savagely unforgiving to some; agile, exhilarating and enthusiastically responsive to others'. Initial flying tests had quickly established its extraordinary manoeuvrability. According to Chaz Bowyer:

A combination of the rotary engine's torque qualities [actually, its gyroscopic effect] and the built-in masses' concentration centrally, gave the F1 turning capabilities unmatched by any previous design. Controls were highly sensitive and responded instantly to a pilot's lightest touch, giving the illusion that the aircraft virtually 'thought' of the next movement of its controls as fast as its master. It was a feature warmly welcomed by later pilots in the fighting zones, but one which betokened potential disaster for any student pilot unfamiliar with such rapid responses in any aircraft handled previously.

When the Triplane appeared over the front in early 1917, with its outstanding rate of climb, the Germans had rushed to develop their own. Now, the aerial arms race had brought forth the Camel and Kink would become one of its foremost exponents.

A short spell of bad weather soon gave way to another clutch of victories. As well as its regular Offensive Patrols, 1 (Naval) Squadron was undertaking Special Missions to investigate reports of enemy machines. On 4 December, in the late afternoon, Kink attacked a DFW two-seater, south-east of Dixmude, sending it down out of control. Two days later, he joined a 'Special Early Mission', led by Flight Commander Minifie, who had already accumulated eighteen of the twenty-one victories he would achieve before becoming a prisoner of war the following March. The other three members of the patrol were all gifted air fighters. Flight Sub-Lieutenant James Forman, from Canada, had already downed four German aircraft – two of them in conjunction with Kink. Flight Sub-Lieutenant Max Findlay, a Scotsman brought up in Canada, had also downed four; and Flight Sub-Lieutenant Stanley Rosevear – another Canadian – had accounted for eight since opening his score in August 1917. The accepted qualification for status as an ace was five aerial victories; and it is instructive to record just one mission's work by this formidable group of an Australian, two Canadians, an émigré Scot and a South African:

DAILY REPORT OF OPERATIONS – 6 December 1917
Flight Lieutenant Kinkead fired 200 rounds into a two-seater over the Foret d'Houthulst. Machine dived vertically and was lost to sight in the uncertain light ... Flight Commander Minifie fired all his ammunition into the enemy trenches at Nieuport and Dixmude from a height of 200 feet. Flight Sub-Lieutenant Findlay fired 500 rounds into the hangars at Ghistelles Aerodrome, at a train coming out of St Pierre Capelle and into the enemy trenches. Flight Sub-Lieutenant Rosevear attacked a two-seater with 200 rounds at point-blank range. The EA fell over and plunged vertically down out of sight ... Flight Sub-Lieutenant Forman attacked a Gotha with lights on – returning from a raid over Dunkirk – 2 miles out to sea off Westende. He got right on its tail and fired 200 rounds from about 70 yards; coming up under its tail he got into the eddy caused by the retreating EA and his machine was turned over. When he had righted his machine the hostile aeroplane could not be found. Flight Sub-Lieutenant Rosevear fired 100 rounds at a 'Flaming Onion' battery from 1,000 feet east of Nieuport.

All this occurred in a 2½-hour period at dawn. Minifie, Rosevear and Findlay returned between 7.15 and 7.25am, only to go out again in mid-morning and, in Minifie's case, in the afternoon as well. Kink, who returned at 8.45am, was back in the air just over an hour later. At 10.10am, south-east of Passchendaele he attacked an enemy scout, sending it down out of control for his second victory of the day. All these young men were, it is true, more the masters of their fate than the soldiers below them. Yet, the relentless schedule of raids and patrols required an extraordinary mixture of shrewdness, skill and resilience. At least the RNAS had enabled Kink to learn his trade in the Aegean and hone his skills at Cranwell. France and Flanders offered few second chances to inexperienced pilots.

Many successful aces – Kink among them – combined daring and determination with a calm personality. Headstrong characters might cheat death repeatedly, but would usually come to grief after taking one risk too many. Von

Richthofen was probably the most calculating of them all and, for that reason, has his fair share of detractors. Ira 'Taffy' Jones, a fiery and much-decorated Welshman, came through the conflict with thirty-seven victories and a contempt for von Richthofen and his *modus operandi*. He reserved his admiration for Werner Voss who died at the age of 20, in September 1917, in heroic lone combat with seven British airmen – including James McCudden, who was one of the best. In his memoirs, published in the dark days of 1938, Jones took pleasure in claiming that 'Germany's greatest air-fighter had Jewish blood' – though this has subsequently been disputed. In his opinion, 'Voss, a Semite, [was] her greatest air warrior . . . He was an individualist to the core, and time after time he attacked, single-handed, British formations, fighting with supernatural courage like a man inspired, and leaving behind a trail of havoc and death.' Von Richthofen, in his view, did not meet this standard: 'Unlike Voss, who would fight anybody, anywhere, the Baron carefully picked out his victims and having succeeded would hurry back to his aerodrome to acclaim his merit.'

While it is easy to share Jones's admiration for the daring of a Werner Voss or an Edward 'Mick' Mannock (whose biography he wrote), the Great War was primarily a process of industrialised mass slaughter, the like of which had never before been seen. Von Richthofen's calculated ruthlessness better fitted the temper of the times. Of course, the belligerents needed heroes to inspire them, but acts of courage seldom made much difference in the face of modern technology. A ship might be saved, like the *Lion* at Jutland, by a dying man's sense of duty; but there were few shortcuts on the Western Front, where individual valour was subsumed in the anonymity of mass slaughter. Even in the air, lone-wolf tactics gradually gave place to concerted action in formation and close-support work with the troops.

The dozen new Camels of 1 (Naval) Squadron crossed the Channel on 10 December 1917, when the Squadron transferred to Dover. It was still attached to 4 Wing RNAS and it was still on duty, though flying was cut to a minimum to allow as many pilots as possible to go on leave. Until 23 January, only local cross-country and test flights were carried out; but on three occasions the Squadron undertook war flying over the United Kingdom. On 24 January, four aircraft searched, without success, for hostile bombers. These were the Gothas – heavily armed twin-engine biplanes with a wingspan of 75 feet. Their production had begun in the autumn of 1916, when the limitations and vulnerability of Zeppelins were becoming clear. Each Gotha could carry a bomb-load of about 1,000lb, when flying at 10,000 feet on a night raid. Its three machine guns – one of which could fire through a 'tunnel' to attack fighters coming up under the tail – made it dangerous to approach. The bombers were far more lethal than the raiding airships and, as will be seen, they were to play a central part in the creation of the Royal Air Force as a separate Service. Tackling them in the dark, with primitive equipment, was particularly hazardous for fighter pilots.

On the night of 28 January, the Squadron was alerted to a Gotha force bombing the capital. Forman, Kink and Flight Commander Cyril Ridley set out to try to intercept them. Ridley had to turn back because of engine trouble, but Kink reached London and sighted one of the raiders. Heavy anti-aircraft fire prevented him from getting close enough to attack until bad visibility shielded the bomber both from the gunners and from the pursuing fighter. The next night, Ridley led another attempt to intervene after six enemy bombers were seen heading inland. The Camels gave chase but, by the time they gained sufficient height, the Gothas had disappeared.

Two days before 1 (Naval) Squadron returned to France on 16 February, it was transferred from 4 Wing to 1 Wing RNAS. Thirteen Camels led by Dallas flew from Dover to its new base at Téteghem, near Dunkirk. The Squadron would remain there from 16 February until 27 March, when it was again attached to the RFC. During those six weeks, its work consisted of patrolling the coast, protecting spotter aircraft, and preventing enemy machines from helping shore batteries target Royal Navy vessels. It also carried out Special Missions whenever enemy aircraft were discovered. Thus, Rosevear took on five hostile aeroplanes on 19 February, shooting one down near the Ypres-Comines Canal. Kink's own contribution in his first tour with the Squadron was now publicly recognised. The award of his Distinguished Service Cross was promulgated in the *London Gazette* on 22 February:

> In recognition of the conspicuous gallantry and skill displayed by him in the face of the enemy in aerial combats, notably on the following occasions: On 24 October 1917, he brought down an enemy machine, and immediately afterwards encountered and drove off a group of seven hostile aeroplanes. On 4 December 1917, he brought down an enemy two-seater machine completely out of control. By his skill and determination in attacking enemy machines he has always shown a fine example to other pilots.

For very sensible reasons, Great War pilots were encouraged to be concise and objective in their Combat Reports. This creates a problem for biographers whose narrative can become, all too easily, a string of repetitive short accounts conveying little of the atmosphere in which the airmen operated. Sometimes, such accounts managed to incorporate a touch of humour – 'I attacked an enemy balloon south of Armentières. The balloon went up in flames, and the observer went down in parachute', ran a typical report by Sydney 'Timbertoes' Carlin, who already held a DCM and an MC when he joined the Royal Flying Corps after losing a leg as an infantryman. Reconnaissance reports, however, had to be more descriptive, and one drawn up by Squadron Commander Dallas gives a graphic account of a 'Low Flying Special Mission' which he and Kink undertook early on 26 February:

> I left the ground at 5.10am intending to have a general look round over the lines in the moonlight with Flight Lieutenant S.M. Kinkead DSC. We missed each other and I then proceeded up the coast climbing to 7,000 feet. I turned inland halfway between Ostend and Zeebrugge and went towards Bruges which place was quite easy to locate. I was throttled down,

so that I could just maintain my height ... West-south-west of Bruges a large shed or building was rather brilliantly illuminated and made a most conspicuous target. Snelleghem Aerodrome was lighted up as if for night flying but no machines were observed landing. Throttled right down, I lost height and crossed the coast east of Ostend at just above 1,000 feet, and was evidently not heard because nothing was fired at me. A small boat of the drifter type was observed close to Ostend flashing a blue light. Fifty rounds were fired at this vessel from 800 feet but no results were observed. A 'Flaming Onion' battery, evidently roused by seeing tracers flying about, replied with two badly placed shots some hundreds of yards away.

Flight Lieutenant Kinkead went as far as Zeebrugge Mole and observed a large vessel proceeding up coast from Ostend and four trains, with steam up, in the station at Ostend. He also observed AA fire on the Dutch frontier, probably German machines being engaged. No doubt Snelleghem Aerodrome was awaiting their return. Flight Lieutenant Kinkead then proceeded inland, leaving Bruges on his left, and made towards Roulers climbing and looking out for good targets and aerodromes. He observed a big fire south of Roulers by about 4 miles – probably a [munitions] dump or the result of bombing machines. Fires in the trenches were quite distinct and both the enemy's and our fires were shielded from each other. This was a most interesting tour and the absence of AA and searchlights would denote that a pilot with a good knowledge of the coast could, with precaution, sneak up on his target and undertake almost any low bombing on a bright moonlit night without being very much molested.

The Squadron soon settled down to its usual mixture of Offensive Patrols and Special Missions. Typically, Kink would be flying once in the morning and once in the afternoon, generally with four or five other Camels. On 8 March, for example, he had two indecisive encounters. In the first, his Flight of five engaged six enemy Triplanes at 17,000 feet between Menin and Roulers, during a High Offensive Patrol from 10.30am to 12.30pm. At 3.15pm Kink and Forman went up on a Special Mission, initially attacking an Albatros Scout, then a formation of them, and finally another group of five enemy aircraft. The Daily Record of Operations referred to 'Flight Lieutenant Kinkead flying through the centre of the formation':

In each case the whole formation was driven down east. Enemy aircraft showed no disposition to fight and dived as soon as they were turned upon. The above incident is very interesting and looks as if the formation was either one of new pilots, or of a very nervous disposition. These two pilots did good work and attacked single-handed a formation each, being above them the whole time.

Shortly before 3.00pm on 10 March, Kink, Rosevear, Forman and Findlay took off from Téteghem to intercept three enemy scouts and three two-seaters. They caught them over Menin, Rosevear and Findlay accounting for two of the fighters, and Kink sending down a two-seater completely out of control.

1 (Naval) Squadron pilots were steadily registering victories, but always had to be alert for new enemy tricks. On 12 March, Ridley and Flight Commander Herbert Rowley managed to bring down a kite balloon; but, on descending to establish its exact location, Ridley had to make a forced landing. This led him to discover that the balloon 'had inside the basket a dummy man filled with straw – probably a decoy for pilots to shoot at and on which the AA guns were ranged in great numbers'. The following day, Rosevear destroyed an Albatros Scout and Minifie shot down two more. Kink had not been on that patrol, but was part of a Flight of five Camels which tackled seven Albatros Scouts on 16 March, downing three of them without loss.

Dallas was succeeded as OC 1 (Naval) Squadron by Major Charles Booker on 18 March, on leaving to take command of 40 Squadron RFC. British-born but brought up in Australia until 1911, Booker had joined the RNAS direct from Bedford Grammar School in September 1915. His career at 8 (Naval) Squadron had been outstanding, with twenty-three victories already to his credit – almost all of them in Sopwith Triplanes. The Squadron remained heavily engaged, with Rowley and Kink shooting down two out of three Albatros Scouts encountered over Nieuport on 21 March. Early the next afternoon, Ridley, Kink, Forman and two others went out on a Special Mission in support of a photographic aircraft. At 18,000 feet, they intercepted eleven enemy aircraft and immediately went into action:

DAILY REPORT OF OPERATIONS – 22 March 1918
... Flight Commander Ridley attacked one of them at point-blank range and EA was last seen turned on its back. Pilot was then attacked by another EA so was unable to observe results. He drove another of them east over the Floods. Flight Sub-Lieutenant Forman attacked two Albatros – one near Slype and another near Schoore – both indecisively. Flight Sub-Lieutenant Guard fired 200 rounds at one, following him down from 13,000 feet to 5,000 feet where he dived away east ... Flight Lieutenant Kinkead attacked an Albatros Scout which was engaged with a French Caudron, firing 100 rounds at point-blank range. Pilot was then attacked by another machine but succeeded in outmanoeuvring him. He was again attacked by several EA but succeeded in beating them off, firing at them as opportunities occurred. Two more Albatros Scouts were encountered by this pilot over Slype and were engaged indecisively ... Throughout the patrol enemy AA was exceptionally active.

When the citation for Kink's award of a Bar to his DSC was published in the *London Gazette* on 26 April, this encounter was singled out. His second gallantry decoration had been conferred:

For the skill and courage displayed by him as a pilot. On 22 March 1918, he attacked and drove down out of control an Albatros Scout which was attacking a French machine. He has brought down many other enemy machines. He is an exceptionally good pilot, and a clever and plucky

44

fighter, and has performed very fine work, both on Offensive Patrols and on Low Flying missions.

Yet, even as he was gaining this distinction, dramatic changes were under way – both in the structure of British military aviation and in the overall strategic balance.

★   ★   ★

Just as unrestricted submarine warfare profoundly affected American attitudes to the conflict, the German bombing offensive against England galvanised British attitudes towards air power in 1917. Daylight attacks by Gothas on the south-eastern counties had begun in May 1917, but the decisive event was the 13 June raid on London which killed 162 and wounded another 432 civilians. As the Official Historian noted, this level of casualties 'exceeded those inflicted in the County of London area by all of the Zeppelin attacks which had been made up to that time'. It was therefore decided that there should be a large increase in the number of RFC and RNAS Squadrons. The expansion was intended primarily for bombing, but Haig feared a diversion of national resources to a role of secondary importance. The Cabinet approved the increase on 2 July 1917.

In February 1916, a Joint War Air Committee had been set up under Lord Derby but, when this failed very quickly, an Air Board had replaced it. This too lacked executive authority, though achieving some improvement in the rate of aircraft production; so, on 11 July 1917, the War Cabinet turned for help to Lieutenant-General Jan Christian Smuts. He was asked to examine the arrangements for Home Defence against air-raids, and also for the overall organisation and direction of aerial operations. In theory, the Prime Minister was charged jointly with undertaking the task, but 'Mr Lloyd George had only lent his name . . . The whole matter would be dealt with by Lieutenant-General Smuts'.

Smuts had come to England in March 1917, fresh from campaigning in German East Africa, to attend an Imperial Conference. Invited by Lloyd George to join the War Cabinet, he accepted on condition that he would be concerned with military but not with political matters. From his rooms at the Savoy Hotel, he witnessed the 13 June attack and, when it ended, made a tour of the areas which had been bombed. Smuts found that, while damage was limited, morale had been badly shaken. This psychological factor could not be ignored, so he overcame his reluctance to be drawn into controversy and agreed to the War Cabinet's request to review the issues of air defence and overall organisation. The General's detachment from British politics and Service affairs stood him in good stead and his views, according to the Official Historian, 'commanded a wide respect':

> Those who came to confer with him were convinced that his one concern was to find an unprejudiced solution of the problem, and they believed

45

that he would not make up his mind until after he had heard, and carefully weighed, every aspect.

Smuts' first report – on the air defence of the London area – was presented on 19 July, and his second report was placed before the War Cabinet on 17 August 1917:

> It is the most important paper in the history of the creation of the Royal Air Force ... The view was expressed ... that the time was approaching when aircraft would cease to be merely ancillary to naval and military operations, and would be used for independent operations: 'Nobody that witnessed the attack on London on 7 July could have any doubt on that point ... the day may not be far off when aerial operations, with their devastation of enemy lands and destruction of industrial and populous centres on a vast scale, may become the principal operations of war to which the older forms of military and naval operations may become secondary and subordinate.'

Smuts realised that the expansion of Squadrons approved by the War Cabinet would yield a surplus of aeroplanes after the needs of the Army and Royal Navy had been met. Therefore, the creation of an Air Staff to plan and direct *independent* operations would become a matter of urgency:

> [T]o secure the advantages of this new factor ... we must create a new directing organisation, a new Ministry and Air Staff which could properly handle the instrument of offence and equip it with the best brains at our disposal.

On 24 August the War Cabinet met and decided to accept, in principle, the recommendation that 'a separate Service for the air' should be formed and that a committee, under General Smuts, should be appointed 'to investigate the details of amalgamation' and prepare draft legislation for submission to Parliament. The resultant Air Organisation Committee duly drafted a Bill to establish an Air Ministry and prepared plans setting out the composition and duties of a future Air Council. However, when the War Cabinet met on 15 October 1917 – the day before Parliament returned from the summer recess – doubts were expressed about the wisdom of such radical changes in the midst of a war. Parliament was not in a mood to tolerate procrastination, and made its feelings known. Consequently, the Bill was approved by the War Cabinet on 6 November and received Royal Assent at the end of the month. Lord Rothermere became the first Secretary of State for the Air Force (a title changed in March 1919 to Secretary of State for Air) and Trenchard was withdrawn from France to become the first Chief of Air Staff. He was succeeded in command of the RFC in France by Major-General John Maitland Salmond on 18 January 1918, only to resign as CAS in April following 'grave differences of view' with the Secretary of State. Rothermere did not long outlast him, resigning on 25 April. This was the climax of a spate of clashes and disputes –

though the career of Trenchard, in particular, was far from over. Early in the new year, the King had approved the title 'Royal Air Force' for the new Service. When it came into existence on 1 April, one minor effect was that members of the RNAS exchanged their naval titles for the military ones hitherto used by the RFC. Only in August 1919 would new ranks specific to the RAF be announced – by which time Kink would be in the throes of a different campaign as dangerous and desperate as that which he fought in March 1918.

★ ★ ★

Another result of the reorganisation was that 1 Wing RNAS and 1 (Naval) Squadron within it were redesignated as 61 Wing and 201 Squadron RAF, with effect from 1 April. No sooner had the Squadron moved from Téteghem to Sainte-Marie-Cappel, near St Omer, on 27 March, than it became caught up in the crisis of the German Spring Offensive launched six days earlier. So great was the danger that the Vice-Admiral of the Dover Patrol offered to put the Squadron, once again, at the disposal of the Commander-in-Chief. Thus, on 28 March, it moved to Fienvillers, near Amiens. With sixteen Camels, it was now attached to 13th Wing of III Brigade RFC/RAF in support of the British Third Army. This was the first of eight different aerodromes from which 201 Squadron would operate, with the ebb and flow of battle, until the Armistice. Apart from brief attachments to 11th Wing and II Brigade, in support of Second Army in late July, and crucially, to 22nd Wing and V Brigade, in support of Fourth Army in early August, the rest of 201 Squadron's war would be with 13th Wing. In contrast to 1917, when nothing changed except the death toll, the final year of the Great War saw British fortunes alternate between extreme peril and decisive victory.

During the winter of 1917–18, the Germans knew that a window of opportunity briefly existed. With the Bolsheviks in control, Russia was out of the fight. German troops could be transferred wholesale to the Western Front. The United States, though now in the war, had yet to deploy in force. General Ludendorff, in overall charge in the West, could also make use of vast stocks of captured war material, including at least 4,000 Russian and 2,000 Italian artillery pieces. The British Government, appalled at the losses of 1917, was unsympathetic to Haig's pleas for reinforcements and, although the General Staff felt that a German offensive was clearly to be expected, no-one knew where the blow would fall.

Before he left for England, Trenchard drew up a paper stressing that the most important task for his airmen was to detect signs of an impending attack and to report them at once to the Army. The Germans were free to choose where to concentrate and when to strike. According to the Official Historian, at least three major plans were prepared before, on 21 January, Ludendorff made his choice – the 'Michael Attack' – on both sides of St Quentin:

> At the outset, the main offensive was against the Third Army with the object of smashing the Arras bastion and striking towards the coast. Such

action would separate the bulk of the British Army from the French and crowd it up with its back to the sea ... The main direction of the attack was changed after a few days, largely as a result of the resistance of part of the British Third Army and the depth of the German advance against the Fifth Army. Amiens then became the main objective.

Haig knew that he could afford to give ground in front of Amiens, where there was room to manoeuvre, but not further north where the Channel Ports would be at risk. In the event, disaster at Amiens was only narrowly averted. German aerial activity was slight in advance of the offensive, and the British had no inkling of the enemy Squadrons, totalling 730 aircraft – including 326 single-seaters – in the area of the British Third and Fifth Armies. Here the British could muster 579 aircraft, including 261 single-seater fighters. This would be the first battle on the Western Front where the German Air Service outnumbered its British counterpart.

Intelligence from captured prisoners and aerial observation led to a warning on the night of 20 March to expect an attack in the morning. Although this should have helped the defenders, heavy fog shielded the German infantry and put paid to elaborate schemes of signals and crossfire designed to check any advance. Over the next three days, Fifth Army was forced back to the Somme and there was a serious prospect of the Germans breaking through at the junction of Third and Fifth Armies between Péronne and the Bapaume-Cambrai Road. The Commander-in-Chief issued a special Order of the Day to all ranks on Sunday, 24 March:

> We are again at a crisis in the war. The enemy has collected on this front every available division and is aiming at the destruction of the British Army ... I feel that everyone in the Army, fully realising how much depends on the exertion and steadfastness of each one of us, will do his utmost to prevent the enemy from attaining his object.

The crisis intensified on 25 March, with the RFC heavily engaged: 'Very low flying is essential. All risks to be taken', Salmond instructed his airmen. The following day, nearly a quarter of a million rounds were fired from the air at German troops; and the situation on Third Army front was stabilised, to some extent, by the Australians and New Zealanders. The fate of Amiens still hung in the balance and it was agreed on 26 March that General Ferdinand Foch would be appointed to co-ordinate all the Allied Armies on the Western Front. On the morning of 28 March, the German assault north of the Somme was repulsed at Arras with heavy casualties. What had worked a week earlier with the help of the fog, now failed disastrously without it. South of the Somme, British and French troops were again forced back, Sir Hubert Gough and the Staff of his Fifth Army were sacked, and General Sir Henry Rawlinson was put in command with his Fourth Army – which had hitherto been held in reserve. For another week the battle raged, but the line held. The German thrust on the Somme had been blocked.

Still, Ludendorff was not finished. He knew that the British line north of the La Bassée Canal had been rendered vulnerable by the withdrawal of troops to counter the offensive on the Somme. For three days from 9 April, intense German pressure was desperately resisted in the absence of reinforcements; and, on the morning of 12 April, Sir Douglas Haig issued his famous call to hold every position to the last man:

To all ranks of the British Army. Three weeks ago today the enemy began his terrific attacks against us on a 50-mile front. His objects are to separate us from the French, to take the Channel Ports, and destroy the British Army. In spite of throwing already 106 divisions into the battle, and enduring the most reckless sacrifice of human life, he has, as yet, made little progress towards his goals. We owe this to the determined fighting and self-sacrifice of our troops. Words fail me to express the admiration which I feel for the splendid resistance offered by all ranks of our Army under the most trying circumstances. Many amongst us now are tired. To those I would say that victory will belong to the side which holds out the longest. The French Army is moving rapidly and in great force to our support. There is no other course open to us but to fight it out. Every position must be held to the last man; there must be no retirement. With our backs to the wall, and believing in the justice of our cause, each one of us must fight on to the end. The safety of our homes and the freedom of mankind depend alike upon the conduct of each one of us at this critical moment.

On that day – the climax of the whole German offensive – newly-designated RAF Squadrons flew more hours, dropped more bombs and took more photographs than on any day since the outbreak of war. The statistics listed by the Official Historian deserve to be recorded:

Hours flown, by all Royal Air Force Squadrons on the Western Front, 3,240; bombs dropped, 2,548; photographs taken, 3,358; rounds fired, 114,904. Figures of flying hours are available for a few individual Squadrons. No. 201 (Camel) Squadron, with sixteen effective pilots, flew eighty-nine hours ... Composite figures show that the I Brigade, with 287 pilots, flew 798 hours; the II, with 170 pilots, 351 hours; the III, with 200 pilots, 623 hours; the V, with 209 pilots, 675 hours; and the IX, with (approximately) 200 pilots, 538 hours. Many individual pilots did between six and seven hours flying. All figures quoted are as made up in the field and are from 4.00pm on 11 April to 4.00pm on the 12th.

This still did not mark the end of the German effort. Throughout April, battles raged near the River Lys, though it was over the Somme on 21 April that Manfred von Richthofen met his fate. For once, the cult of personality built up around the German aces exacted a heavy price: the impact of his death on national morale was severe. By the end of the month, the Germans were

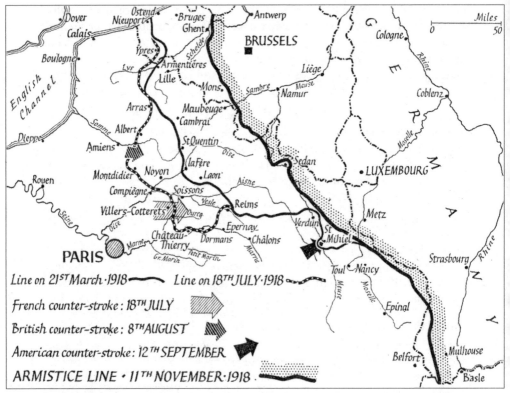

Western Front offensives, 1918. (*Corelli Barnett*)

losing heavily in the Ypres Salient and, although the British yielded up territory bought at such terrible cost in 1917, they fought the Germans to a standstill. The main effort against the British began at 1.00am on 27 May, when the Germans opened one of the greatest artillery bombardments of the war. They had secretly concentrated 1,000 heavy guns on a sector of the front near Rheims, where tired British troops from five depleted divisions had exchanged places with the French. At 3.40am, German infantry attacked and, by the end of the day, had penetrated to a depth of 12 miles. This became known as the Battle of the Aisne and, once again, the British held firm until the French could return. By contrast, Foch was not taken by surprise when the Germans launched yet another offensive at 3.30am on Sunday, 9 June. They penetrated 6 miles, as the French deliberately gave way before counter-attacking two days later. This was termed the Battle of the Matz and, once again, no breakthrough resulted.

The scene was now set for Germany's last, desperate throw of the dice. In September 1914, her invading forces had been thwarted at the River Marne in what the historian Cyril Falls described as 'one of the vital battles of history', when they had 'come within an inch of bringing off a set plan of great length and ending it with the annihilation of their foes', but then 'lamentably failed'. Now, in 1918, the Germans were back on the Marne, threatening Paris. After a four-hour bombardment, they surged across the river at 4.00am on 15 July, encountering stiff resistance from American forces before falling victim to a French counter-attack. Falls regarded the Second Battle of the Marne as being 'as much a turning point' as the First. The bridgehead over the river was abandoned and the Germans began to retreat.

★   ★   ★

Against the titanic clash of forces on the ground, combats in the air were far less important than direct support of the troops and, above all, observation of the enemy. Yet, the sky over the battlefield had still to be controlled and, for once, the German Air Service was on the offensive. Encounters between large formations could be expected, and one of them at the beginning of April – in which a quarter of the enemy force was destroyed without loss – illustrates the intensity of the conflict. By then, as we have seen, 1 (Naval) Squadron had relocated to Fienvillers and been re-designated as 201 Squadron. Since the RAF was less than a week old, the continued use of RNAS ranks in the combined Combat Report is understandable:

COMBATS IN THE AIR – 6 April 1918
No. 128
Fourteen of our machines while on an Offensive Patrol met a formation of about twelve EA – Triplanes – over Bouchoir at 1.15pm. A hot fight ensued for about fifteen minutes during which the following combats took place. Flight Commander Rosevear fired on two ... he then got on the tail of another which was going straight through the mist at 3,500 feet. He fired a burst at point-blank range and EA stalled and dived out of control ... Pilot followed it down to 2,000 feet and saw it crash in a ploughed field. Flight Sub-Lieutenant Spence got close to another of the formation and fired about seventy-five rounds into it ... Pilot watched him going down out of control for 1,500 to 2,000 feet ... Another Triplane then came across the nose of his machine about 2,000 feet below. Flight Sub-Lieutenant Spence closed on his tail and fired about 100 rounds at very close range. EA went down out of control and crashed in a large field. Flight Lieutenant Kinkead fired on three of the formation. Two went into spins and recovered, and the third floated on its back and then fell into a spin completely out of control. Pilot followed its descent until lost in the clouds. Flight Sub-Lieutenant Wallace ... attacked one that was man-oeuvring to get on the tail of one of our machines, firing a burst into it at close range. EA turned on its side and went down in a vertical nosedive apparently out of control ... Flight Sub-Lieutenant Bright observed the EA attacked by Flight Lieutenant Kinkead still going down completely out of control when quite close to the ground. Owing to the number of machines involved and also owing to the clouds it was difficult for the

pilots to observe results with certainty; but two EA were seen to crash and one was without doubt completely out of control. The other two were most likely completely out of control but it is impossible to say definitely.

Kink and his comrades were now in the forefront of the desperate German offensive against the Third Army. Their main line of patrol was between Arras and Albert, but this was often extended to Lens in the north and Villers-Bretonneux, Moreuil and Bouchoir in the south. Some had narrow escapes, notably when Findlay – on an evening patrol, also on 6 April – decided to tackle four enemy Triplanes. As he did so, another four attacked him from above and he was soon surrounded by enemy machines. After a fierce fight, he was forced into a spin, only to find himself still under attack when coming out of it. With two enemy aircraft on his tail and a third attacking at right angles, Findley was forced practically to ground level in his badly damaged machine:

COMBATS IN THE AIR – 6 April 1918
No. 130
... He then stunted as much as possible, but one of the EA put a barrage up in front of him, which riddled the cockpit and put the engine out of action. Practically all the control wires had by this time been shot away, so rendered useless; pilot being then within 45–65 feet off the ground had no time to attempt a proper landing. Machine crashed badly between our first and second line trenches. Pilot was unable to salve any of the machine or instruments as the enemy commenced shelling it at once.

In signing off this Combat Report, Squadron Commander Booker commented on Findlay's 'very fine performance', given that 'all the Triplanes appeared to belong to Richthofen's Circus and were handled extremely well'. Not everyone was as fortunate. On 8 April, Ridley shot down a kite balloon in flames, but then for eleven days bad weather prevented operational flying. It resumed on 20 April and, two days later, Rosevear destroyed one of seven Pfalz Scouts which he attacked near Hangard. On 21 March, when the German offensive began, he had brought down three Albatros Scouts in rapid succession over Nieuport; but, on 25 April, ten minutes into a test flight, he crashed his Sopwith Camel at the aerodrome and was killed instantly. He had received a Bar to his DSC a week earlier, and was credited with two dozen aerial victories. Stanley Rosevear was 22 when he died.

Kink had been recommended for promotion to Flight Commander on 17 April. He immediately began leading his men on Offensive Patrols and Special Missions, securing both shared and individual victories. The Squadron History notes that twice during the month escorts were provided for bombing missions as well:

The first Offensive Patrol for the protection of No. 57 Squadron was carried out on 15 May when a formation of fourteen Camels led by Captain Kinkead escorted five DH4s of No. 57 Squadron on a bombing raid over Bapaume. One hostile machine only was encountered and driven off. During the afternoon seventeen Camels, led by Captains Ridley and Kinkead, observed a large formation of enemy aeroplanes attacking some Bristol Fighters east of Albert. During a general engagement in which at least thirty of the enemy took part, three were driven down out of control by Captain Kinkead and Lieutenants R.C.B. Brading and H.L. Wallace and at least twelve indecisive combats took place. All the pilots remarked on the fine performance put up by the Bristol Fighters. On 20 May, fourteen machines again escorted six DH4s of No. 57 Squadron to Bapaume. On this occasion no hostile aeroplanes were encountered.

The Squadron History also notes that, during May 1918, 201 Squadron took part in approximately 112 individual combats, resulting in eight enemy aircraft destroyed and sixteen more driven down out of control. Eight of these twenty-four victories belonged to Kink, individually or jointly with others. One outstanding result came on 30 May, when – having already shot down a Pfalz Scout in the morning – he led fourteen Camel pilots against a similar number of Albatros Scouts just before 8.00pm. No fewer than five of the Germans were shot down completely out of control over Achiet-le-Grand. Among the victors were Findlay and Kink, whose own report stated:

COMBATS IN THE AIR – 30 May 1918
No. 191
... I picked out one and fired a burst; it went down in a nosedive and recovered. I then attacked a second one at fairly close range, firing long bursts. EA stalled, hung for several seconds, turned over on its back and then nosedived. I could not see EA crash on account of the other EA ...
I observed a very small biplane with square wings and a very small tail. It apparently had a stationary engine, and appeared to be exceptionally fast.

This is a fairly typical example of Kink's tendency to point out, first, whether a potential victim managed to get away; secondly, whether any doubt remained about a claimed victory; and, thirdly, whether any useful details could be gleaned from the fight, particularly in respect of the performance of new enemy machines. The only loss to the Squadron was one Sopwith Camel written off when landing back at base. Its pilot, Lieutenant George Gates, was luckily unhurt. He was in the early stages of a career which would achieve more than a dozen victories in 1918, mostly in August and September. Having wrecked his own machine on this occasion, Gates soon made amends – filing this modestly-worded account on 16 June:

COMBATS IN THE AIR – 16 June 1918
No. 210
While on Offensive Patrol, I observed an enemy two-seater, south-east of Villers-Bretonneux, about 12,000 feet, at 7.45pm. I at once attacked it, firing 300 rounds, the last 50 at point-blank range. EA suddenly folded up

in the air and went down in flames. After pulling out of my dive, I noticed that the main spar of my left-hand lower plane was broken.

Major Booker felt it necessary to expand on this, pointing out that, before the end of the combat, Gates had been 'practically on top of the enemy machine' and that it was not certain whether his main spar had been damaged by actual contact with the other aircraft or in pulling out of the dive: 'It was a very fine performance on his part to get back to the aerodrome and land safely.' Gates was also one of half a dozen Camel pilots used as part of a sophisticated diversionary operation in conjunction with ground forces. With a feint attack scheduled for 2.00am on 20 June, 201 Squadron was detailed to bomb the German airfield at Bancourt at 7.00pm the previous evening. Kink was not on this mission – he had returned from a fortnight's home leave only on 17 June – but almost all the rest of the Squadron took part. Guarded by an escort of SE5s from 60 Squadron, as well as the remainder of their 201 Squadron comrades, an attack Flight of six Camels scattered a total of twenty-four small bombs from 500 feet or less over hangars and approach roads. Given the limited payload of the Flight, and the diversionary nature of the mission, the results were gratifying. Once relieved of their bombs, the attackers rapidly descended and

shot up all the hangars with machine-gun fire, the Nissen huts believed to be officers' quarters, and various sheds and huts, over 3,000 rounds being fired. A Hannoveraner two-seater, which was on the aerodrome outside a hangar, was set on fire. Bombs were seen bursting amongst the sheds and men were seen running for cover.

Although the Squadron History states that Offensive Patrols were then continued without decisive results until 16 July, records do exist of victories by Reginald Brading on 28 June and Cyril Ridley on both 30 June and 4 July. Kink was involved in a clash with ten Fokker biplanes on 2 July and with two formations of fifteen each on 3 and 4 July – each time 'indecisively', either because the enemy aircraft dived away or because the results of his efforts could not be observed in the midst of a whirling dogfight. While leading his Flight north-east of Albert on the evening of 17 July, Kink encountered a two-seater and engaged in a duel: 'I saw the observer disappear in his cockpit when in the act of shooting at me, and this EA dived away east with his propeller stopped'; but it was not until 19 July that he was credited with another victory. This was in co-operation with a young member of his Flight to whose efforts he had previously drawn attention.

Lieutenant Robert Orr, from Malham in Yorkshire, would be shot down in flames on the crucial day of the counter-offensive which led to victory on the Western Front – 8 August 1918. He features on no list of Great War 'aces', though he spared no effort and shunned no risk in attacking the enemy and, especially, their closely-guarded kite balloons. During the mêlée with fifteen Fokkers on 3 July, Kink noted – after reporting his own inconclusive attacks on

54

four of them – that 'Lieutenant Orr made several dives, firing at various ranges. One EA turned on its back and afterwards dived vertically, but pilot was unable to observe what happened to it afterwards.' Yet, Orr was not credited with this possible victory, as conditions made the outcome too difficult to see. Orr's efforts were again referred to by Kink, his Flight Commander, on 4 July, and the Squadron Record Book states that, on 16 July, he 'attacked an enemy KB, east of Albert, driving it down apparently damaged'. But it was not until 19 July that Orr definitely met with success when, together with Kink and Gates, he attacked and destroyed two enemy balloons east and south-east of Albert. Gates and Orr claimed the first one close to Fricourt; but Kink was having difficulty with the second. Typically, he made a point of emphasising his comrade's contribution:

COMBATS IN THE AIR – 19 July 1918
No. 235
I attacked an enemy kite balloon south-east of Albert, near Bray, with Lieutenant Orr. KB was hauled down and observer jumped out. I fired about 100 rounds into KB, but did not observe any flame. On turning round, I observed KB in flames with Lieutenant Orr just beside it. Height 2,000 feet. Time 12.22pm. I also observed Lieutenant Gates bring down another balloon in flames. Lieutenant Orr's machine was apparently hit and was forced to land about 2 miles behind our lines west of Aveluy Wood. Pilot and machine were apparently OK.

Orr's Camel had indeed been hit by anti-aircraft fire and, though he successfully landed between the Allied front and reserve lines, it was seriously damaged by incoming shells. At the end of the month, he reported a further possible victory, and this time was credited with it. South-west of Armentières at 8.50pm, together with Booker, Orr intercepted a large formation of Fokker biplanes. As usual, he waded in:

COMBATS IN THE AIR – 31 July 1918
No. 238
I ... attacked this formation, engaging three machines in succession, one of which turned over on its back and fell away apparently out of control, but I was unable to watch him owing to one of the others attacking and hitting my machine, shooting one of the elevator controls and damaging the machine.

During another dogfight on the following day, 1 August, Orr 'sent one EA down in a flat spin, partly on its back, but did not observe what happened to it finally'. He was killed a week later, on the most important date in the history of his Squadron. Robert Orr was 21 when he died. He lies in the Heath Cemetery, Harbonnières.

Kink, for his part, had three further victories before that climactic day. After four days of bombing raids on a ground target – Warneton Dump – Kink tackled four Fokker biplanes, on the morning of 29 July, sending one of them down in a flat spin apparently quite out of control. At 10.15am on 30 July, he put 100 rounds into the last of three enemy aircraft engaged in succession. It was seen spinning out of control by Bristol Fighter crews of 88 Squadron, who were also involved in the fight. Finally, at 8.30pm on 1 August, he brought down yet another Fokker south-east of Dickebusch Pond from a height of 12,000 feet.

Kink's star was in the ascendant. Even before his four victories in July, the award of a third gallantry medal had been announced. It was the newly-instituted Distinguished Flying Cross – equivalent to the DSCs and Military Crosses formerly awarded respectively to RNAS and RFC pilots. Findlay, Forman and Kink were all listed as recipients in the *London Gazette* of 2 July, although Kink's citation did not appear until 3 August:

> A skilful and gallant leader, who has attacked enemy formations superior in numbers with marked success. In a recent engagement, his patrol flew to the assistance of some of our machines which were greatly out-numbered by the enemy, and succeeded in accounting for three enemy machines and scattered the remainder.

Kink had come into his own on the Western Front and emerged in a pivotal role in a Squadron of formidably determined pilots. He and they had won their spurs in aerial combat, but were now to be tested as never before in tackling their enemies on the ground.

★   ★   ★

In the month leading up to the final sequence of Allied offensives, 201 Squadron was relocated no fewer than three times. Since 12 April, it had been based at Nœux-lès-Auxi, west of Arras, after just a fortnight at Fienvillers. Between 20 July and 6 August it was, once again, at Sainte-Marie-Cappel as part of 11th Wing, within II Brigade RAF, in support of Second Army; and between 6 August and 14 August, it was at Poulainville, north of Amiens, within 22nd Wing of V Brigade RAF, in support of Fourth Army, before returning to Nœux and III Brigade. Although the attachment to 22nd Wing lasted for a mere eight days, those days witnessed momentous events. As the Squadron History notes:

> On arrival in the battle area, the following special instructions were issued by the Officer Commanding 22nd Wing to No. 201 Squadron: 'It is most important that the presence of your Squadron on this Front should be kept <u>SECRET</u> as long as possible. In view of this you will take the fol-lowing precautions: (1) Squadron markings will be changed temporarily. They will be the same as those of No. 65 Squadron, the only Camel Squadron at present working on this Front. One vertical stripe in front and one vertical stripe behind the national markings. (2) Machines will always be kept inside the hangars and not lined up on the aerodrome until

immediately before a patrol leaves the ground. (3) Pilots will not fly over or near the lines without orders from me.'

It had been agreed on 23 July by the French and British Army Commanders that the offensive should begin on 10 August. However, on 28 July, Foch wrote to Haig suggesting that the date be brought forward, given the rate at which the Germans were retreating from the Marne. This time, Haig would be in overall command and, for once, secrecy was both made a priority and achieved. The Germans had no idea that Allied Forces were being concentrated on a 25-mile front from Courcelles to Albert, let alone that they would be unleashed at 4.20am on 8 August.

Three days before the attack, unusually detailed Operation Orders were drafted for 201 Squadron and all other units in V Brigade. Brigadier General L.E.O. Charlton, the Commanding Officer, had drawn them up in order that all pilots and observers 'should be fully informed of the general plan' – on the afternoon of 'Y'-Day, hours before the offensive began – so as to give them 'a wider appreciation of the course of events as they unfold' and to render their actions and reports more valuable:

The strategical objective of the attack is the disengagement of the city of Amiens, which will permit the full use of the important railway systems with which it is connected . . . The battle is designed to be a one-day battle and the ultimate objective, the blue line in the maps, is to be reached in three stages . . . It is very important to realise that the first stage will be conducted on the basis of former attacks wherein the infantry move forward under a creeping barrage. The remaining stages, however, will approximate to open warfare conditions, owing to the fact that our guns cannot reach far enough forward from their old platforms and will be in constant process of moving forward to new positions. In the two first stages, therefore, the battlefield will present entirely different aspects from the air and in the second, the open warfare, stage the tasks of pilots will be more complicated, particularly as regards discrimination between the opposing forces . . . Unless greatest care is exercised, a danger will exist of our own troops being mistaken for the enemy in the open warfare stage of the battle. Pilots must therefore identify, beyond a doubt, ground targets consisting of personnel before engaging them. Similarly, machines flying low on the way out will notice batches of prisoners stationary or moving, and under guard of a few men only. Care must be taken to identify them as such and refrain from molesting them.

The entire focus of action in the air was to assist the troops to be successful on the ground on 'Z'-Day. Given the vital role of armour in any breakthrough:

Single guns in the open, so placed to destroy our tanks, must be engaged and the crews destroyed. Machine-gunning will be the best method of offence in this respect and the importance of the occasion cannot be

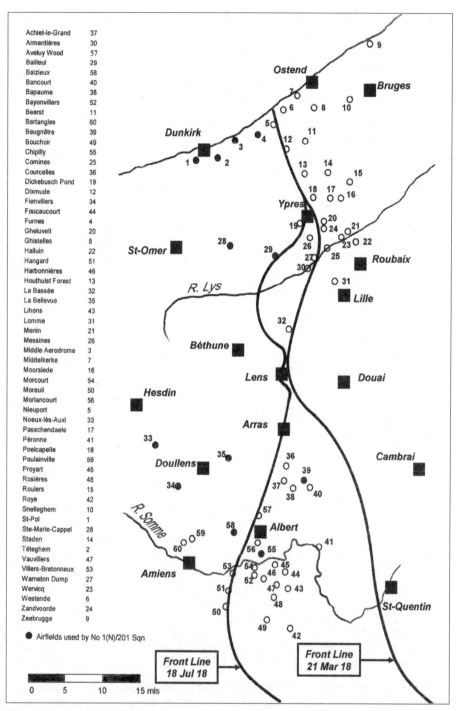

Achiet-le-Grand	37		
Armentières	30		
Aveluy Wood	57		
Bailleul	29		
Baizieux	58		
Bancourt	40		
Bapaume	38		
Bayonvillers	52		
Beerst	11		
Bertangles	60		
Beugnâtre	39		
Bouchoir	49		
Chipilly	55		
Comines	25		
Courcelles	36		
Dickebusch Pond	19		
Dixmude	12		
Fienvillers	34		
Foucaucourt	44		
Furnes	4		
Gheluvelt	20		
Ghistelles	8		
Halluin	22		
Hangard	51		
Harbonnières	46		
Houthulst Forest	13		
La Bassée	32		
La Bellevue	35		
Lihons	43		
Lomme	31		
Menin	21		
Messines	26		
Middle Aerodrome	3		
Middelkerke	7		
Moorslede	16		
Morcourt	54		
Moreuil	50		
Morlancourt	56		
Nieuport	5		
Noeux-lès-Auxi	33		
Passchendaele	17		
Péronne	41		
Poelcapelle	18		
Poulainville	59		
Proyart	45		
Rosières	48		
Roulers	15		
Roye	42		
Snelleghem	10		
St-Pol	1		
Ste-Marie-Cappel	28		
Staden	14		
Téteghem	2		
Vauvillers	47		
Villers-Bretonneux	53		
Warneton Dump	27		
Wervicq	23		
Westende	6		
Zandvoorde	24		
Zeebrugge	9		

● Airfields used by No 1(N)/201 Sqn

0 5 10 15 mls

Front Line 18 Jul 18

Front Line 21 Mar 18

Western Front airfields. (Jeff Jefford)

58

over-emphasised ... Unless retiring in panic order, the enemy's infantry will mostly be encountered in 'worm' formation, proceeding sinuously according to the slightest inequalities of ground. This is ascertained from experience and from captured documents and should be carefully noted. If our men are here and there, and are obviously held up, it will be the duty of Scout pilots to endeavour to assist them by ascertaining the cause and taking action accordingly ... As a matter of interest, No. 9 Squadron will be dropping ammunition by parachute on the 3rd and Anzac Corps front and No. 6 Squadron will be serving the advanced cavalry in the same way. No. 8 Squadron is co-operating with tanks ... Particular care is required in message-writing, which proved a weakness during the former Battle of Amiens. These weaknesses consisted in illegibility, omitting essentials i.e. time, place, etc., and in using scraps of paper.

Whereas it was the task of the infantry to reach the designated 'blue line', and of the cavalry, artillery and tanks to assist the troops to achieve this, the task of the RAF was wider – not only to help the infantry directly, but also help the cavalry, artillery and tanks in their efforts to support the troops. Referring to Charlton's memorandum, Sholto Douglas noted approvingly, in his memoirs:

just before the attack, all Squadron commanders were able to brief their air crews about what was going to happen; and I was able to tell my own pilots ... something of the plan of the battle that was to be fought. Of this unusual advantage the official air historian has said: 'This appears to be one of the few occasions, so far as can be judged from the official records, when a formal considered attempt was made to take the pilots and observers into the confidence of the General Staff.'

On 6 August, Major Douglas himself signed off Operation Order No. 311 to the Squadrons comprising 22nd Wing:

The 3rd Corps, Australian Corps and Canadian Corps are to execute an attack on a front extending from 1,000 yards south of Morlancourt to a point 2,000 yards south-west of Hangard, where the Roye–Amiens Road crosses the German front line. The Cavalry Corps will also participate in the attack, passing through the Canadian Corps when the line has been sufficiently broken ... This Wing will devote itself almost entirely to low-flying attacks on hostile troops, transport, gun teams, ammunition wagons, balloons on the ground and, last but not least, anti-tank guns. All machines will carry 20lb bombs, and a full load of ammunition.

Eight of the nine Squadrons – including 201 Squadron – forming 22nd Wing would 'send out their machines in pairs at intervals of half an hour from Z + 20 minutes', and pilots 'must try and obtain as much information as possible about the ground situation'. Squadron Commanders would be responsible for ensuring that such information was passed on as soon as possible after the pilots had landed. Nothing would be left to chance or overlooked:

> Nos 23, 48, 65, 84, 201 and 209 Squadrons will report direct to Captain Adams, Wing Intelligence Officer, who will establish a report centre at 22nd Wing Headquarters. Pilots will report to him in person, immediately on landing. Squadron Commanders will make suitable arrangements for transport of pilots ... Squadron Commanders must impress on all pilots, the importance of obtaining information as to the ground situation, and of seeing that this information reaches the proper quarters ... There will be an advanced landing ground on the old Drill Ground just south of Amiens. This will only be used in great emergency by this Wing.

In the Allied counter-offensive, air-to-air combat would be an entirely secondary activity; but that did not mean that Kink and his comrades would not have to reckon with it, as increasingly desperate German pilots sought to prevent them carrying out their mission. This was, as Major-General Salmond put it in an eve-of-battle message, to 'give the Boche the biggest hammering they have had in their lives'.

★   ★   ★

Within a few minutes of the opening of the bombardment at 4.20am, the tanks, other armoured vehicles and infantry advanced into the same type of heavy ground mist as had aided the Germans on 21 March. Complete surprise was achieved and, by nightfall, British troops had penetrated some 7 miles. As well as Ludendorff's famous description of 8 August as the 'black day' of the German Army, the Official Historian draws attention to the use of the word 'catastrophe' in the title of the official German account of the battle – *Schlachten des Weltskrieges 1914–1918: die Katastrophe des 8. August 1918* – which summarises it in the starkest terms:

> When darkness came on 8 August over the battlefield of the Second Army, the heaviest defeat suffered by the German Army since the beginning of the war had become an accomplished fact ... Almost everywhere it was obvious that German soldiers had surrendered to the enemy, arms and equipment had been thrown away, trench mortars, machine guns and guns had been abandoned, and men had sought safety in flight.

What helped the infantry naturally hindered the airmen at first. The Official History states that aeroplanes could not enter fully into the battle until after 9.00am but that, as the mist cleared, 'great confusion within the German lines' was revealed and 'exceptional targets' were offered to the low-flying single-seater pilots. The role of 201 Squadron is set out in gripping detail in the Squadron Record Book. Eighteen of its pilots flew that day and eight of them were shot down: Orr was killed, four became prisoners of war, and three made it back to the Squadron. Several pilots who fought in this decisive battle were new to the Squadron and, indeed, to the Western Front. Of those not shot down, most went out twice or three times on 'Low Flying Patrols' – as ground attacks were described – but Captain Brading and Lieutenant Burns completed four missions during the day, while Kink alone completed five.

Regardless of the mist, Kink and Burns went up at 5.30am as the first pair of pilots in the rota system ordered by Douglas. Their target was Morcourt, just to the east of the advancing Allied artillery barrage. At 5.45am, each dropped four 25lb bombs from 300 feet, then returned to the attack firing 1,500 rounds between them into hedges and moving objects as well as diving to attack the 'Flaming Onion' anti-aircraft batteries. So poor was the visibility that they could not find Poulainville, landing instead at a French aerodrome from which they returned to base shortly after 8.00am. Lieutenants Orr and Baker had duly ascended at 6.00am, half an hour after Kink and Burns. Orr was last seen directly above the Allied barrage, then falling in flames to crash east of Villers-Bretonneux. Baker fired 150 rounds into a machine-gun nest, scattering the crew, before he too ran into thick mist, lost direction and had to put down on a French aerodrome.

The mist was proving impossible to deal with, so the third pair, Lieutenants Riddell and Hambrook did not start out till 8.30am. Hambrook bombed a moving transport column and fought a duel with machine-gunners on the ground; but, after thirty-five minutes, he saw Riddell's machine going down to crash after being hit by ground-fire. Next up were Captain Brading and Lieutenant Foggo at 9.00am, and Lieutenant McLaughlin and Second Lieutenant Cox at 9.30am. Brading and Foggo bombed and strafed German troops in a valley east of Morcourt, the former dropping his bombs from only 50 feet and having his machine riddled by machine-gun fire so badly that it had to be replaced: 'All along the valley were enemy machine guns which [the] pilots shot up.' The aircraft were keeping in the closest of contact with Allied ground forces – for example, when McLaughlin 'shot up three machine-gun emplacements just in front of our tanks from 100 feet' south of Morcourt. 'The Huns left the emplacements and scattered', the Record Book stated – and so it went on, with growing intensity throughout the morning.

The half-hour gaps between missions were soon abandoned. From 9.30 until 10.25am, pilots went up in pairs every ten to fifteen minutes. Lieutenant MacKay 'shot up masses of men . . . who were running about panic-stricken'. Captain de Wilde bombed an enemy dump, machine-gunned a troop train and reported British cavalry about to capture enemy kite balloons. His partner, Lieutenant Hemmens, failed to return. Lieutenants Gates and Misener tackled three ammunition trains between Harbonnières and Vauvillers at 10.25am. Gates's bombs set the first two trains alight, whilst Misener's destroyed the third: 'The explosions were quite audible in the air above the noise of the engines. All three trains burnt violently.' Gates then took on horse-drawn transport vehicles and Misener, diving down to 50 feet drove off enemy troops attacking an aircraft which had landed between the lines. They returned safely, despite serious damage to their machines. Lieutenants Wood and Hill bombed and strafed an enemy aerodrome, both reporting Germans in retreat 'all along the front', with enemy infantry 'hurrying eastward in disorder'.

By 10.40am Kink and Burns were back in the air, followed by Brading and Foggo, and Hambrook and Baker, in rapid succession. What happened next formed the basis of the citation for Kink's fourth and last Great War gallantry award – the Bar to his DFC. Gazetted on 2 November 1918, it reads:

> On a recent date, this officer engaged a large party of troops in a wood. The engagement lasted for an hour, but so persistent was his attack that the enemy broke and dispersed. During this attack he was harassed by six hostile Scouts. Later on he shot down an enemy two-seater in our lines. A bold and daring airman.

According to the Squadron Record Book, Kink first 'dropped four 25lb bombs on [the] rear of a train which was burning between La Flaque and Harbonnières; they burst ... among enemy infantry'. He then attacked an enemy two-seater, forcing it down, before engaging the troops in the wood, just north of Proyart: 'They at first replied with machine guns, but later took panic and ran in all directions. Six Fokker biplanes then attacked Captain Kinkead from above and he dived west.' This incident shows the difficulties of trying to establish aerial victory scores. The citation explicitly states that the enemy two-seater was 'shot down ... in our lines'. The Squadron Record Book states that it 'glided to [the] ground' and refers to Combat Report No. 239. In Combat Report No. 240 – clearly referring to the same engagement – Kink states:

> While on a Low Flying Patrol, I engaged an enemy two-seater near Foucaucourt at 11.05am at a height of about 800 feet. I at once attacked it, firing 100 rounds from close range, and EA glided down and I saw it on the ground near La Flaque. Our cavalry were then not far away.

This seems a clear case of an aircraft having been 'driven down', though not 'out of control' – which is precisely what Kink's Combat Report claimed. Nevertheless, someone at a higher level wrote the word 'Indecisive' (which seems inexplicable), while someone else evidently thought it well worth including when recommending him for the Bar to his DFC. That was almost certainly Major Booker, who signed off Kink's report as his Commanding Officer. Of course, it is conceivable that the citation was referring to another two-seater which Kink might indeed have shot down after attacking the troops in the wood, as the citation stated, rather than before, as set out in the Squadron Record Book. As we shall see, he was yet to achieve four more victories on the Western Front: two on 10 August and two on 13 August; but in none of these cases was his victim seen to land rather than to crash or descend out of control.

Three of the eight 201 Squadron pilots shot down making ground attacks on 8 August had extremely narrow escapes. Lieutenants Baker, McLaughlin and

MacKay had set out at 10.55, 11.20 and 11.35am respectively. Baker had bombed railway sidings and fired 600 rounds into an infantry column before his Camel was hit in the petrol tank by an explosive bullet. He managed to land, and patch up the machine sufficiently to bring it back at 4.30pm. McLaughlin bombed an ammunition dump before firing at a body of troops 'causing great panic', but was then attacked from above by eight Fokker biplanes:

> He evaded them for about five minutes but they eventually drove him down to within 50 feet of the ground. The controls of the machine were shot away, and a bullet pierced the petrol tank. The machine burst into flames and went down out of control at Harbonnières just in front of our advancing tanks. Pilot, who had escaped injury, jumped out and made his way back to the aerodrome.

Even more perilous was MacKay's experience after bombing Fricourt and attacking an infantry formation. Spotting a Fokker biplane above him, he fired at long range but was then ambushed by four others:

> His machine was riddled with bullets and, the engine being also hit, he was forced to land 300 yards behind the enemy's lines ... He then made a dash for it until he met one of our tanks into which he climbed; but, learning it was about to go into action, he got out and made another dash west, coming under heavy machine-gun fire from the ground and enemy machines. Fortunately, he escaped being hit and made his way back to his aerodrome.

Kink, meanwhile, together with his remaining comrades, continued to mount raid after raid against the enemy. What repeatedly emerges from the records is his sheer persistence in attacking ground troops for very long periods, no matter how great their numbers. This, above all, had won him his second DFC – though he did not know it at the time – and it was to win him an even higher award in a very different theatre, just over a year later. Somehow he had found a technique enabling him to do this for long periods and survive. Others were not so fortunate.

On 9 August, 201 Squadron lost two more pilots forever: Lieutenants M.S. Misener and R. Stone. Misener had put up a formidable performance the day before, as has been seen, bombing a train and an aerodrome as well as tackling enemy troops and cavalry. Returning early with wing trouble from a morning patrol, he went out again at 5.00pm and did not come back. Stone was on his first day with 201. He was one of four 203 Squadron pilots, roused in the middle of the night and sent to replace 201 Squadron's losses. After an hour's practice learning the country, he returned at 12.25pm and was thrown straight into the battle. Attacked by Fokker biplanes, Stone was seen to go down in a spin, turning over at 200 feet and crashing onto the road just north of Rosières. Milburn Misener was 21 when he died and Richard Stone was 19.

63

At the same time as Stone was being ambushed, Kink – on a separate Low Flying Patrol – was engaged in a repeat performance of his exploits of the previous day:

SQUADRON RECORD BOOK – 9 August 1918
Captain Kinkead dropped four 25lb bombs from 200 feet on troops in [a] wood just east of Vauvillers with good effect, killing a great number of the enemy. [He] then observed infantry retreating from Vauvillers and engaged them with machine-gun fire. He was then attacked by five Fokker biplanes which dived west. He afterwards returned and engaged the same infantry firing all his ammunition, causing panic and probably killing many of them. He was constantly attacked by Fokker biplanes.

By the third day of the campaign, the element of surprise, resulting from the concentration of Allied aircraft on the battlefront, had long gone. The Squadron records increasingly show major dogfights between large formations of opposing aircraft. At 9.00am on 10 August, having previously driven off one Fokker which was in pursuit of a Camel, Kink encountered another near Foucaucourt and hit it with fifty rounds:

COMBATS IN THE AIR – 10 August 1918
No. 246
... EA turned over and went into a slow flat spin apparently quite out of control, but I was unable to follow it down owing to the number of Fokkers above, eight of which came down on me. I retired west and observed twelve more Fokkers above and was driven well west of our lines.

Despite a note by Major Booker confirming that 'Lieutenant Sykes observed the EA attacked by Captain Kinkead turn over on its back and go down', the same hand which had written 'Indecisive' on his 8 August Combat Report did so again on this one. Most historians have rightly taken no notice. It would appear that, at this particular time, only aircraft seen to crash were being credited by some headquarters. In any event, no doubt arose about his second victory of the day, at about 4.15pm near Rosières, when Kink was one of a seven-strong group which attacked fifteen Fokker biplanes. These were most probably the lethal Fokker DVIIs, in service since the summer.

The Lieutenant to whom Booker referred as witnessing Kink's earlier fight was Ronald Sykes who had enlisted in the RNAS in April 1917, at the age of 18. Within days of joining 9 (Naval) Squadron in September 1917, Sykes was shot down behind enemy lines but evaded capture. Later transferred to 203 Squadron, he had two victories to his credit when the urgent call came to reinforce 201 Squadron on the Somme. Like Stone, after a short familiarisation flight, he was pitched into battle on his first day. In the afternoon of 9 August, he bombed a munitions dump near Rosières, setting it ablaze, and discharged hundreds of rounds at enemy troops nearby. On 12 August, while flying with other members of the Squadron including Brading, Kink and de Wilde, Sykes shot down a Fokker biplane 'quite out of control'. Eventually he would win a DFC, before serving in North Russia and surviving imprisonment in Moscow by the Bolsheviks.

Ronald Sykes lived to record detailed interviews for the Imperial War Museum. Yet, as is so often the case, dramatic accounts – though probably authentic – are not easy to reconcile with the archives. His service on Kink's Flight lasted from 9 until 26 August, when both Kink and Henry de Wilde were posted from 201 Squadron back to the United Kingdom. Clearly, Sykes formed a very high opinion of his Flight Commander and it is worth repeating his account of two examples of Kink's skill, even though they cannot be verified from the Squadron Record Book and Combat Reports, which are particularly comprehensive throughout this short period. It is taken from *Dog-Fight: Aerial Tactics of the Aces of World War I* by Norman Franks, one of the compilers of *Above the Trenches*, with whom Sykes corresponded more than fifty years later:

I was flying in my place at the right rear of Kink's close formation on an HOP [High Offensive Patrol] at 16,000 feet on 11 August. A lone Fokker DVII came down in a long, gentle dive and picked on me. As he closed, he began to fire and I looked to Kink for orders. He waved for me to fly straight and keep formation, which I did very reluctantly as the *kak-kak-kak* behind was loud and clear. Fortunately, I had great confidence in Kinkead's judgement. When the Fokker was quite close to my tail, Kink yanked his Camel into a sharp climbing turn and half-rolled back over my head and confronted the Fokker head-on, firing as he did so. I made my Camel split-arse as only a Camel could, and pulled up and fired the burst which I felt entitled to, as the Fokker peeled off, and so did the other three Camels. The Fokker went fluttering down to the ground. Kink told me back at the airfield that the Fokker's aim was very low and from Kink's viewpoint he could see tracer bullets passing down well under my tail; and he thought we could coax the German pilot down within striking distance. He would have signalled me to turn, if the German's aim had been more accurate! ...

On 12 August 1918, the [DH9] day-bombers expected a lot of opposition due to the ground battle, so they asked for an escort and were allotted one Flight of five Camels from 201 Squadron led by Captain S.M. Kinkead. After the raid was over, the DH9s were heading for home with noses down and throttles wide open ... The Camels were behind and above them in a 'vee' formation, staying up at 12,000 feet, for behind the Camels was a formation of ten Fokker DVIIs and closing in from the north was another formation of twelve Fokkers. To the south we could also see another twelve German fighters, at our height, on a course to converge with us ... For the Camels, the direct course home was still open, and the bombers were now all far ahead, nearing the security of the lines. So the five Camel pilots headed for home too ... The lines came into sight below, as a solitary Fokker DVII dived from the group on our right and came directly under us, obviously asking for a fight. I was in the right, rear

Camel, and at my Flight Commander's signal I peeled off and dived for the German's tail. I immediately found I had taken on a most skilful enemy who could anticipate my every manoeuvre, and I could not get him in my sights. Finally I pulled up into a near climbing turn towards my Flight above but, as I did so, down came Captain Kinkead, and he flashed past me onto the tail of the Fokker. I half-rolled over and went down to protect my leader's tail, and as I gave a quick glance astern I saw a general dog-fight was on with the three remaining Camels staying up in circling matches among a lot of Fokkers.

Kinkead and his German, with me just above them, kept together, circling, half-rolling, diving; I had a real bird's-eye view of the deadly aerial combat between two of the most skilful of pilots, beginning at about 11,000 feet and ending at ground level. I do not think either of them ever got their gun sights lined up on each other on their way down, owing to their extraordinarily clever flying. I know that the German easily evaded the few attacks I made, so I kept [to] my duty of protecting my leader's tail, for during rearward glances I could see, at first, many circling Fokkers above us.

Later, as we circled for a time and dived lower, I could not see other aeroplanes above. There were only a few Germans and Kinkead with the Fokker in front. Kinkead pulled hard back on his stick and for a second got his guns to bear on the Fokker's rudder, which was hit and put out of action. The German levelled up and crash-landed unhurt not far from Bayonvillers, among Australian troops. Kinkead and I landed at our field at Bertangles [*sic*] and Kinkead returned by road to the scene.

The German pilot had asked the Australians to give his gold cigarette case to Kinkead (before he had been driven away) whose machine number was taken as being that of the winner and duly reported by the Aussies who had been excited spectators of the fight. The cigarette case was handed over and used by Kinkead. The Aussies said the German had told them he had no idea that he had reached the lines or he would not have given such a futile demonstration to his Squadron of trainee pilots by asking for a fight in his decidedly chivalrous manner.

It is hard for the modern historian to know what to make of this fascinating tale. Certainly it is a modest one, with Sykes keen to minimise his own role while exalting the skill of his Flight Commander. Yet, it is a fact that the records show Kink making no claims for either 11 or 12 August. What they do show is Sykes shooting down one of sixteen Fokker biplanes 'at very close range' on 12 August and Kink claiming two at 11.05am and 11.10am the following day. The first of these 'nosedived and then fell completely out of control on its back near Lihons'. The second was seen 'to crash near Rosières ... [on] our side of the lines'. With regard to the former, Sykes reported that he had 'dived on a large formation of Fokkers which were attacking DH4s over Lihons at 13,000 feet' and 'observed Captain Kinkead fire at a Fokker which went down quite out of control at 11.05am'. Sykes then attacked 'one of the EA, firing a long burst, but EA pulled out and turned sharply ... apparently not hit'. Could this be the machine with which Kink then had his dramatic duel – not on 12 August, as Sykes may have mistakenly noted, but twenty-four hours later? There is one piece of evidence, apart from the convincing detail of Sykes's own account, in favour of this. The Squadron Record Book for 13 August shows that, after Kink's double victory in the morning, he and Sykes were among thirteen pilots who went out on an Offensive Patrol at 6.30pm on the same day:

> A large formation of EA were observed well east of the lines, too far over to be engaged. Captain Kinkead had [a] forced landing south of Amiens with engine trouble. Lieutenant Sykes had [a] forced landing at Bayonvillers with engine trouble. Machines and pilots OK and returning as soon as possible.

If Kink and Sykes had wanted to inspect the result of a victory in the way Sykes later described, they might well have found it convenient to do so by suffering a little imaginary engine trouble at the end of the day's flying, in order to make the trip. As for the earlier victory, attributed to Kink by Sykes on 11 August – in which he states that he too 'fired the burst which [he] felt entitled to' – could this be Sykes's own victory of 12 August for which Kink generously made no claim? Such an explanation would tally both with Sykes's own command of detail, albeit displaced by him from 12 and 13 August to 11 and 12 August. It would also tally with Kink's legendary tendency to be self-effacing and sup-portive of his team. And it would explain why, half a century later, Ronald Sykes was keen to do justice to the skill and courage of his Flight leader. It was not unusual for an ace to help a newcomer claim a victory – and, if the set-piece duel which Sykes described actually happened, an accurate Combat Report of it would hardly have been welcome at Brigade Headquarters.

Yet, something which had happened on 13 August in the morning casts doubt on Kink taking time in the evening to investigate a downed opponent. By now, the gallant Charles Booker was fretting at his exclusion from the conflict. It was important for the Commanding Officer to stand back and keep overall control of what the Squadron was doing, but Booker decided that he could go out on Special Missions. On 10 August, Lieutenant C.L. Wood had failed to return from his second patrol of the day, when seven 201 pilots attacked ten Fokker biplanes, downing one. Booker took off at 6.00pm to intercept a Rumpler two-seater: it recovered from his attack and managed to escape. He tried again the following evening when a Hannover two-seater was spotted, but could not catch it in time. On 13 August, as we have seen, Kink scored his final two Great War victories – the last of all perhaps being the confrontation and duel which Sykes later described. However, Booker had taken off at 10.30am on a local flight to show a new pilot the lines. According to the Squadron Record Book:

They were attacked by Fokkers west of Rosières at 11.00am. Second Lieutenant Fowles spun down and evaded them, returning with his machine much shot about. Major Booker failed to return and was last seen during this engagement.

The effect on the Squadron is described in a contemporary account, reproduced in *Above the Trenches*:

He left the aerodrome at about 10.30am ... and took a new pilot up with him to show him the new line. Just at this time there happened to be about sixty Fokker biplanes on the lines, and he was immediately attacked by ten of them. His first thoughts went to his new pilot, and he successfully drove five Fokkers from his tail, enabling him to cross the line. He then dealt with the remaining five, shot three down and was himself driven down by the remaining two. He died a gallant death, the bravest of all. By his death the Squadron has sustained a great loss, and I cannot tell you how much we all miss him. He took over our Squadron in March, not an easy task at the time, and since then his work has been incomparable.

Charles Booker was 21 when he died.

Kink was now one of the most senior figures in the Squadron and, from Booker's death until Major C.M. Leman succeeded him on 18 August, Kink was Acting OC 201 Squadron. New pilots were arriving by the day and Kink's year on the Western Front was about to end. On 14 August, the Squadron returned to Nœux – rejoining 13th Wing of III Brigade RAF, in support of Third Army. The Squadron History records that 'until the end of August the main work ... consisted of low flying practice, local flights learning the country, practice in bomb-dropping, fighting and formation flying. A few offensive and balloon patrols were carried out but no decisive results obtained.' It also records the move on 19 September from Nœux to Baizieux, about 12 miles north-east of Amiens, in preparation for the final offensives: they began on 27 September and culminated in the capture of the Hindenburg Line.

By the end of September, 201 Squadron teamed up with 148 American Squadron for joint Offensive Patrols. On 8 October, the British Third and Fourth Armies began the second and final phase of the British assault. During the first three days of this battle, 194 25lb bombs were dropped and nearly 7,000 rounds of small-arms ammunition fired. The enemy continued to retreat, but the Squadron enjoyed a brief respite in the third week of October before resuming Low Flying and Offensive Patrols on 21 October. From then on, 'the retiring Army were followed up and harassed with bombs and machine-gun fire unceasingly until 11 November, the day on which the Armistice was signed'.

Kink had come through an extraordinary and prolonged ordeal. He had brought down at least thirty aircraft in addition to a few victories in the Aegean theatre. He had proved himself not only a brilliant fighter pilot, but also a lethal exponent of low-flying attacks on enemy ground forces – and, in less than a year, he had been decorated four times for gallantry. Kink was 'struck off' the strength of 201 Squadron on 26 August 1918, returning to the United Kingdom for a fortnight's leave before joining the Grand Fleet School of Aerial Fighting and Gunnery, East Fortune, on 14 September as an aerial fighting instructor. There he remained until November when the School was transferred to Leuchars in Fife.

One of the few tales about Kink to be passed down through his family was a story that he flew under the Forth Bridge. The fact that his Service Record independently shows him to have served nearby, at Leuchars, tends to confirm this belief. Fortunately, such an escapade – if it happened – did not prevent him remaining in the massively reduced post-war Royal Air Force. Though he continued to operate as an Acting Captain/Flight Lieutenant, Kink's permanent rank was only that of a Flying Officer. In June 1919, after nine months on Home Establishment, he found the lure of Active Service irresistible. On successive days he was posted to 29 Group and 47 Squadron RAF. His new enemies would be those revolutionary forces which had taken Russia out of the Great War, and which had given the Germans their last chance for victory on the Western Front.

Chapter Three

Russia – The Squadron Records

Although decorated four times for gallantry on the Western Front, Kink was awarded his Distinguished Service Order for bravery in the field during a very different conflict. From the static horror of the trenches, he made the transition to the fast-moving brutality of the Russian Civil War. The citation appeared in the *London Gazette* at the beginning of April 1920, just after the final withdrawal of British Forces from Russian territory in the aftermath of a failed Intervention. This is what it said:

> On 12 October 1919, near Kotluban, this officer led a formation of Camel machines and attacked the Cavalry Division of Dumenko. By skilful tactics in low flying he dispersed this force, which had turned the left flank of the Caucasian Army, and threatened to jeopardise the whole defence of Tsaritsyn. Flying Officer Kinkead has carried out similar attacks on enemy troops, batteries, camps and transport with great success and at considerable personal risk.

The award had actually been presented to him on 28 October by the head of the British Military Mission to South Russia, General Herbert Holman. The report recommending it explained that Kink had driven from the field of battle a 'crack enemy Cavalry Division', despite having a cylinder of his engine shot through from the ground. This was hardly surprising given the account of the action in his Squadron's War Diary:

> Captains Kinkead and Burns Thomson raided troops in Kotluban region and, after disposing of eight 20lb bombs, they dived to within 10 feet of the ground and machine-gunned a large force of enemy cavalry about to attack. The whole force rapidly retreated with many casualties and great panic. Captain Kinkead's machine and engine were hit with rifle fire. 1,400 rounds of SAA [small-arms ammunition] fired.

What was this unit to which Kink belonged? Until the end of September, it had been known as '47 Squadron RAF'. Now it had the curious title of 'A Squadron, RAF Training Mission, South Russia' – though, by the middle of October, this had been revised to 'A Detachment, RAF Training Mission'. And what sort of training consisted of preventing by force of arms the envelopment, by thousands of Bolshevik horsemen, of a key city in the front line of a vicious civil war? The events leading to this outcome had unfolded as the Great War drew to its close.

⋆ ⋆ ⋆

The last major Russian offensive had been launched against Germany in 1916, while the British and French bled on the Somme and at Verdun. By the end of the year, the Tsar's Army had suffered more than a million casualties. Mass desertions followed, as did the abdication of Nicholas II in March 1917. Attempts by the new Provisional Government to remain in the war paved the way for the Communist coup in the autumn. Its success should have ended all hope among the Allies that a separate Russo-German peace could be avoided. Yet, even in early 1918, the British continued to clutch at straws – despite the fact that huge numbers of German troops had already been transferred from the Eastern to the Western Front. Indeed, because German peace terms were so harsh, the Bolsheviks briefly considered continuing to fight; but in March they capitulated and signed the Treaty of Brest-Litovsk.

Vast quantities of military hardware, supplied to the failing Russian government by the Western Allies, had been stored in the Arctic ports of Murmansk and Archangel. The British were worried what would happen to it and the Royal Navy feared that Russian warships at Murmansk – and even the port itself – could fall into German hands. This is not the place to consider how local factors gradually led to the piecemeal growth of British military involvement; but the modern term 'mission creep' inevitably comes to mind. With the defeat of the Spring Offensive and the Allied victory in November, Lloyd George had little appetite for Intervention. Although he authorised a deployment to North Russia in March 1918, and although the Allied governments all agreed to help the counter-revolutionary forces, the Prime Minister remained a reluctant participant.

By the end of August 1918, with several thousand British troops in Murmansk and Archangel, the situation had escalated to crisis point: a Bolshevik mob stormed the British Embassy in Petrograd. The Naval Attaché, Captain Francis Cromie – a gallant submariner – confronted the intruders and was murdered. The War Cabinet was divided, with the Minister of Munitions, Winston Churchill, at the head of the anti-Bolshevik faction. So virulent was his hatred and fear of the revolutionaries, that on 10 November – the day before the Armistice with Germany – he told his colleagues: 'We might have to build up the German Army, as it was important to get Germany on her legs again for fear of the spread of Bolshevism.' Churchill's biographer, Sir Martin Gilbert, notes that by the end of the year more than 180,000 foreign troops were within the borders of the former Russian Empire, including the British, Americans, Japanese, French, Czechs, Serbs, Greeks and Italians. Looking to them for support were more than 300,000 men in the counter-revolutionary White Armies:

> On all fronts the British, whose initial concern was to keep Russia as an
> active ally in the war against Germany, had been drawn into a civil war

between the Bolshevik and anti-Bolshevik Russians. The arms which they had sent to be used against Germany had been handed over to the anti-Bolshevik Russians, for use against the poorly armed Bolshevik forces. British troops, sent only to guard those arms, were being involved in the civil war, not only as advisers, but also as participants. Churchill had not been responsible for any of these decisions. But he had approved them.

Lloyd George won Cabinet agreement that British aid should be limited to guaranteeing the independence from Russia of adjoining states in the Baltic and the Caucasus; but then he took a step which greatly increased the tensions within his Government. The 1918 General Election had seen him returned to office at the head of a three-party coalition. Regardless of their wide divergence on how to handle the Bolsheviks, the Prime Minister appointed Churchill as Secretary of State for War and Air in January 1919. The decision, in principle, to evacuate British forces from the North Russian ports was taken in Cabinet on 4 March, although its implementation would not actually occur until several months later. By way of compensation, General Anton Denikin – commander of the White Forces in South Russia – was offered a British Military Mission of up to 2,000 instructors and technical assistants. 'This Military Mission is to be formed of officers and men who volunteer specially for service in Russia and not by men of the regular volunteer Army ordered to proceed there,' wrote Churchill to Lloyd George on 8 March, in confirmation of what they had agreed.

On 15 April, the first British ship bringing supplies to Denikin completed unloading at the Black Sea port of Novorossiysk. During the next four weeks, the totals of heavy guns and ammunition landed exceeded 450 and 10,000 tons respectively. The head of the Military Mission, General Sir Charles Briggs, was replaced on Churchill's initiative by General Holman who had a less pessimistic view of the fighting abilities of Denikin's White Forces. A small, but potent component of the military aid supplied to Denikin was 47 Squadron RAF.

★　★　★

According to a semi-official history of the Squadron published in 1923, its aircraft were thoroughly overhauled once its operations against Bulgarian forces in Macedonia ended. After several false starts and diversions, 47 Squadron found itself based in Salonika, in February 1919, 'sitting, Micawber-like, waiting for something to turn up'. The decision to support Denikin led to its selection for embarkation to Novorossiysk. The first batch of officers and men left on 16 April, and the first shipment of aircraft, stores and transport set out eight days later.

Appointed in command, with effect from 13 June, was the famous Canadian fighter pilot, Major Raymond Collishaw, the third-highest scoring Allied 'ace' of the Great War. Collishaw had been given quite a free hand to recruit experienced volunteers for attachment to the Squadron, in addition to the personnel deployed – some of them very reluctantly – from Salonika. Among these men were Kink and a young American, Marion ('Bunny') Aten, who had passed himself off as a Canadian to enlist in the Royal Flying Corps. Unlike Kink, both Collishaw and Aten lived to write detailed accounts based, to a greater or lesser extent, on their memories of the adventures of 47 Squadron in South Russia. Also available are the weekly or monthly summaries and daily War Diaries which record, usually in stilted and rather formulaic terms, details of the principal activities of the unit from late June 1919 until the end of January 1920, when the three offensive Flights and the Squadron head-quarters personnel were in almost continuous retreat as the White Armies were routed.

Collishaw had originally been earmarked for a possible attempt to cross the Atlantic, from Newfoundland to Britain, in a four-engined Handley-Page bomber; but, he was told, premature publicity had 'scotched the project'. Instead he was offered the chance of taking 47 Squadron to South Russia: 'I now was a career RAF officer; what I had thus far heard about the Bolshies led me to believe that they were a thoroughly bad lot, and I accepted without hesitation.'

Squadron headquarters were quickly set up at Ekaterinodar, on the railway line 60 miles to the north-east of Novorossiysk. In temporary command was Captain Sydney Frogley, pending the actual handover of the Squadron to Collishaw on 11 July. It was equipped with DH9 and DH9A ('Ninak') two-seater bomber/reconnaissance biplanes, which would eventually comprise A and C Flights, and later with the Sopwith Camel fighters of B Flight which Kink was destined to lead. This was a war of movement, with individual Flights being detached to separate battlefronts and operating from temporary forward bases with almost compete autonomy. The railway network was essential for campaigning over such vast distances and with such constantly changing front lines: 47 Squadron therefore operated by means of highly-equipped special trains designed to enable each Flight, as well as the headquarters, to keep pace with the fluctuating fortunes of the Red and White Armies. As Collishaw later explained: 'The plan was that the trains could be pulled into sidings and the aircraft could then be unloaded and could fly from makeshift aerodromes.' Without them,

> it would have been almost impossible for us to have operated, for it would have been quite out of the question for units of the Squadron to have shifted from one part of the country to another by road. Each train consisted of about fifty wagons and carriages. Two large passenger sleeping coaches served as officers' quarters and a third one, with most of its partitions removed, did duty as a mess and ante-room. There were two smaller sleeping coaches, one of them accommodating a mess and quarters for the NCOs and the other being fitted out as a sick bay. The remainder of the train was made up of enclosed goods wagons or freight cars, as we call them in Canada, and flat trucks. The men were

comfortably housed in goods wagons that had bunks and other facilities built into them, and other wagons housed workshops, kitchens and a bakery, and carried equipment, stores, fuel and other material. When the unit was on the move, its aircraft would, if feasible, fly from point to point, rendezvousing with the train. If because of weather or other conditions this was unfeasible, the aircraft were partially dismantled and loaded aboard the flat-bed trucks to travel with the train.

Ekaterinodar – later Krasnodar – was the capital of Kuban Province, and there for much of the time Holman's Military Mission to Denikin was based, as was its subordinate RAF Mission under Lieutenant-Colonel Arthur Clinton Maund. Collishaw regarded both Holman and Maund as 'extremely capable', but the latter was detested by Marion Aten who made no secret of the fact in the accounts he later wrote.

One of the formations under Denikin was the Caucasian Army led by Baron Peter Wrangel – probably the most capable and talented of the White generals. It was in support of his offensive against the city of Tsaritsyn on the Volga (destined to become famous, in another bloody conflict, as Stalingrad) that 47 Squadron was first sent to the front. Collishaw, having arrived at Novorossiysk on 8 June, via Boulogne, Brindisi, the Dardanelles and Constantinople, had to spend a month there organising incoming military assets before taking direct control at Ekaterinodar. In the meantime, under Frogley's direction, C Flight was heavily engaged, mounting eight bombing raids on and around Tsaritsyn in the week to 28 June. Almost 3,000lb of bombs were dropped and over 5,000 rounds of ammunition fired. The city fell to Wrangel at the end of the month, but the Squadron still had much to do to assemble more aircraft, improve the delivery of rations to the men, and establish better means of communication between forward-based aircraft and the main aerodrome at Ekaterinodar. 'Telegrams apparently never reach their destination, and letters can only be sent by the ration trucks which occupy five or more days on a journey,' Frogley reported. What was clearly needed was a 'halfway aerodrome' between the headquarters and the front.

With the arrival of Collishaw in July, Frogley departed for the forward base where a newly-constituted C Flight was replacing the original C Flight on the Volga Front. This base was alongside the railway at Beketovka station, near Tsaritsyn. It had been identified as the 'only suitable place for [a forward] aerodrome' after a survey by an officer of 47 Squadron together with its Russian liaison officer, Lieutenant Grigorieff. Even then, raids had to be mounted at distances of up to 175 miles. Wherever possible, reconnaissance work was combined with attacks on ground targets and, in the course of a raid at Kamyshin, one of the bombers was confronted by a Nieuport Scout. After about five minutes of manoeuvring, the observer – Lieutenant H.E. Simmons – fired a burst of fifty rounds sending the fighter into a fatal dive. Versatility was the order of the day, with pilots encouraged to seize any chance to attack. Even if the purpose of a mission was reconnaissance, Collishaw insisted that no opportunity be wasted: 'In future all machines crossing the line have been ordered to carry at least four bombs for promiscuous bombing to break up the morale of the enemy troops.'

It is easy to forget that all these operations were being undertaken by tiny numbers of men in formations of three or four machines over vast land areas. Only occasionally do the implications of this, in human terms, peep through the laconic reports. Thus, during the move to Beketovka, three machines safely made the trip but a fourth had to land in open country *en route* and be recovered for repair. The dangers and the difficulties involved in simple tasks like this, in a theatre with few landmarks and non-existent means of communication, are all too easily overlooked. When aircraft had to land behind enemy lines, these risks increased exponentially. This is why no account of 47 Squadron in South Russia is complete without the story of Captain Walter Anderson and Lieutenant John Mitchell.

During an attack on river barges and cavalry concentrations at Chernyi Yar on 30 July, two DH9s were hit by machine-gun fire from the ground. The first was flown by Anderson and, when its fuel tank was punctured and began to leak, his observer, Mitchell, climbed down onto the wing to plug the holes in the tank with his fingers. Just as they set course for Beketovka, they noticed that the second aircraft, flown by Captain William Elliot, was coming down in hostile territory with its engine stopped. Bolshevik cavalry galloped towards it, but were held at bay by gunfire from the observer, Lieutenant H.S. Laidlaw. Regardless of their own predicament, Anderson and Mitchell immediately turned back, landed beside their comrades, picked up both of them, and – with Mitchell still on the lower wing – struggled into the air as the cavalry closed in. The rescuers were awarded immediate DSOs, Collishaw noting later that 'had the incident occurred on the Western Front, instead of in such an obscure backwater as South Russia, I am sure it would have resulted in a pair of VCs'. What made their courage even more outstanding was their knowledge of the fate awaiting them if caught. On the Western Front, though facing death daily, airmen knew that they would be treated quite well as prisoners. In South Russia, the Bolsheviks made it clear that any RAF prisoners they took would either be crucified or disembowelled and hacked to pieces. It is in this context that the dangers involved in low-flying operations must be seen.

The intensity of the Squadron's operations can be gauged from the fact that, on 5 August, three machines dropped sixty-seven bombs and fired 2,300 rounds during sixteen hours in the air. The following day, 114 bombs were dropped on river shipping and on troops, and 5,500 rounds were fired – again by three machines which between them spent twenty-four hours in the air. Despite this level of activity there were no aerial combats, though Mitchell was hit in the foot by ground-fire. He was luckier than his replacement as Anderson's observer, Captain John McLennan MC. Wounded by a machine gun on 28 August, during a successful attack on an enemy balloon, he bled to death in the cockpit.

Kink joined 47 Squadron on 11 July 1919 – one of eight airmen, including Collishaw, who arrived that day. His name began to appear in the Squadron's operational records in the first week of September. From then on, it was barely out of them. Three other pilots constituted B Flight – the fighter element of 47 Squadron – under his leadership: Captain Rowan Heywood ('Bill') Daly, an RNAS veteran with a DSC; Captain William ('Tommy') Burns Thomson who, like Walter Anderson, had transferred from the Russian Volunteer Army; and Lieutenant Marion Aten, who arrived from England on 19 August. As a first step, Kink visited the base at Beketovka, in a bomber, returning to Ekaterinodar in time for the arrival of the Sopwith Camels. He collected eight of them from Novorossiysk on 15 September, by which time the special trains for A and B Flights were nearing completion. B Flight train left for Beketovka on the evening of 24 September, and the first three Camels, erected and tested, flew to the forward aerodrome three days later. Kink, Burns Thomson and Aten were the pilots, to be followed by Daly twenty-four hours later. Now, at last, the DH9 bombing and photo-reconnaissance missions could be escorted by fighters and, on 30 September, this paid off. The DH9s of C Flight carried out four raids and a reconnaissance: 'The photographic Flight was escorted by [a] Camel, flown by Captain Kinkead. Two enemy Nieuports dived on the DH9s and the Camel attacked, shooting one down into the river. The other machine left.'

Both B and C Flights were now at Beketovka and were regularly in action together. October began with a raid by Kink on shipping in the Volga. He reported little anti-aircraft fire and returned to the task forty-eight hours later, dropping twelve bombs during more than five hours in the air. Collishaw was similarly engaged, destroying a steamboat and a large gunboat amid general mayhem at Chernyi Yar, during an attack in the early hours of 3 October. The scene would shift from day to day, with raids being carried out on almost a shuttle basis. Kink and Burns Thomson attacked an artillery piece in action at 'Zokhovaev' (possibly Zhihovoye) which was surrounded by some twenty-six limbers:

> The gun was put out of action and about twenty limbers destroyed by four 20lb bombs dropped by Captain Kinkead, the remainder destroyed by Captain Burns Thomson's 20lb bombs. Both pilots then descended to within 10 feet of the ground and with gunfire completely destroyed all horses and men – completely destroying the camp. Each fired 700 rounds SAA. Captain Kinkead also reports a direct hit by Captain Anderson with a 112lb bomb.

On 6 October two DH9As, with Camels in support, scored direct hits on an armoured train. That night, Anderson and Mitchell in a DH9, escorted by Kink and Burns Thomson in Camels, attacked Bolshevik shipping at Dubovka, scoring direct hits on a large barge. The next day, the two Camel pilots engaged two enemy Nieuports – driving them down and probably destroying them. Kink's Combat Report has survived: he was flying Camel F1955 and spent an hour and twenty minutes in the air. Thirty rounds were fired during the engagement. According to Burns Thomson: 'Neither of the machines put up a fight at all.' The report was endorsed, not by Collishaw, but by Captain Leonard Slatter who had taken temporary command of the Squadron when, early in October, the Canadian succumbed to infection: 'One of the curses of the campaign was typhus,' wrote Collishaw, 'and it respected neither rank nor nationality. Somehow, despite all the sanitary precautions that we took, I was bitten by one of the lice that carry the disgusting disease and . . . I began to run a high fever.' He was not to resume command until the end of November, by which time the fortunes of the White Armies had seriously deteriorated. Slatter was thus drawn more closely into contact with Kink as a by-product of Collishaw's illness. By such chances can a man's fate be determined.

* * *

Other changes were also afoot. Since the beginning of October, the paperwork of the unit had been changed from 'No. 47 Squadron' – first to 'A Squadron' and, after a fortnight, 'A Detachment, RAF Training Mission, South Russia'. On 20 October 1919, 47 Squadron officially ceased to exist as part of the Royal Air Force. This may have resulted from pressure at Westminster, as has some-times been asserted, but the Parliamentary record does not indicate systematic concealment. Questioned in the Commons on 16 July, Churchill had robustly defended the Intervention:

> As the House is aware, we have Military Missions in certain parts of Russia, and it may be necessary, in pursuance of the policy of the Allied and Associated Powers, to add to or strengthen these Missions. *Any further personnel despatched will, however, consist of individuals rather than units* [author's emphasis], and they will be recruited entirely on a voluntary basis . . . The men who have been sent to Russia, in the great majority of cases, are men who volunteered specially for Russia, in addition to those who volunteered for the Regular Army.

Asked for what purpose British soldiers were there, he retorted:

> They volunteered to go to Russia in order to carry out the policy of the five Great Powers in Paris in supporting Admiral Kolchak and General Denikin.

On 18 August, a Written Answer disclosed that 135 British servicemen had been killed and 310 wounded; 154 were missing, presumed killed, or prisoners of war. Ten days after 47 Squadron was formally disbanded, no attempt was being made to conceal the facts. Thus, on 30 October, Churchill disclosed that 'the members of the Royal Air Force with General Denikin in South Russia' totalled eighty-two officers and 273 men. Again, on 25 November, he disclosed that the cost of the British Military Mission there was £44,000 per month – dwarfing the totals for those in Siberia (£13,000), Poland (£1,000) and the

Baltic States (£3,800). Even as late as 1 December, the Government continued to publish statistics showing that no fewer than '277 aeroplanes have been sent to the forces serving with General Denikin', and that '101 Royal Air Force officers and 300 airmen' were serving with his armies – totals higher than those revealed in late October. As the Intervention drew to its close at the end of the year, Churchill remained defiant. Challenged on 16 December to say whether 'the British Military Mission in South Russia, or any part of it, is or has been engaged in military operations against the Soviet Russian forces', the Secretary of State responded:

A few individual officers in the Royal Air Force and Tank Corps have voluntarily taken part in the fighting against the Bolsheviks. Otherwise the duties of the Mission are confined to advice and supervision in the distribution and use of British materials.

Question: Are we responsible for the payment of these officers?

Answer: Certainly.

Question: Those who are making these attacks?

Answer: Yes.

Question: Will the Rt Hon Gentleman give instructions for these men not to be so employed in the future, in view of the statement made by the Prime Minister? . . .

Answer: I will not restrict in any way the praiseworthy and gallant activities of those officers.

Question: Are these officers employing our tanks in warfare?

Answer: I said that a certain number of these officers . . . have trained the Russian personnel of the tanks we sent to South Russia, and they have gone into action with those tanks. They have carried their instruction to that extent.

Question: Is the Rt Hon Gentleman aware that this conduct is a violation of the statement made, by the Prime Minister, that we as a country were not intervening in Russian affairs?

Answer: It is no violation. On the contrary, the Prime Minister has repeatedly affirmed our intention to continue these Missions for a certain period to afford such assistance to the forces of General Denikin as it is in their power to give, and which our resources enable us to give, and there is not the slightest intention to limit them in any way . . .

*   *   *

Given that Collishaw's Squadron consisted mainly of genuine volunteers, the manoeuvrings of politicians at home made practically no difference to front-line campaigning. Throughout October, its operations grew in intensity – but so did the enemy's response. Kink and Burns Thomson came under heavy anti-aircraft fire after dropping eight 20lb bombs on troops near Dubovka on 8 October and, after successfully targeting a bridge the following day, were back attacking an armoured train and ground forces on 10 October, 'causing

1. Kink in the Royal Naval Air Service.

2. Samuel and Helen Kinkead.

4. Thompson Calder Kinkead, Kink's elder brother.

3. Helen in old age.

5. A Squadron, 2 Wing RNAS, Thasos, July 1916 – including Blandy (*back row, second left*), Bremner (*back row, fourth left*) and Kink (*front row, centre*).

6. Second Lieutenant W.B. Jones – the dauntless observer – with Flight Lieutenant C.E. Brisley.

7. Kink on Thasos, in typically relaxed pose.

. In his Bristol Scout, with stripped Lewis gun and unprotected airscrew.

. The end of Gerrard's Aegean tour.

WING COM. GERARDS
CRASH ON BE2C.

10. Kink with his Nieuport two-seater, 1916.

11. Flight Sub-Lieutenant James Bolas.

12. Donald Bremner (*right*) on Thasos.

13. Arthur Jacob and 2 Wing's 'packing-case' hut

14. Flying instructor (*back row, third right*), Cranwell, May 1917.

15. Soon to be parted, Toss (*left*) with Kink at Cranwell.

16. At Auxi-le-Château on the Western Front.

17. 'Dallas's Circus' – 1 (Naval) Squadron with its Sopwith Triplanes, Bailleul, 28 October 1917. Next to Kink (*at far left*) are Forman, Wallace and Spence. Next to Rosevear (*to right of propeller*) are Minifie, Dallas, Ridley and de Wilde.

18. Kink and James Forman, with whom he shared two early victories.

19. Cyril Ridley.

20. Kink, the Camel ace, at Téteghem.

21. Stanley Rosevear, who did not survive.

22. Two who did – Kink and de Wilde in Paris on their way home, August 1918.

ROSEVEAR. KILLED. AUXI.

23. In the control cabin of a North Sea-class airship.

24. At Leuchars with Rowan Daly (*front right*) and Leonard Slatter.

25. With a Bristol Monoplane at Leuchars, near the tempting 'target' of the Forth Bridge.

[the] enemy to retreat in disorder and inflicting many casualties with machine-gun fire'. Matters were coming to a head, with Kink and Burns Thomson each completing six successive raids in less than six hours on 11 October.

The recommendation for Kink's DSO in the field referred not only to his actions on 12 October, but to the fact that he had

> initiated here and led a system of ground strafing that has completely demoralised the Bolshevik land forces in the Tsaritsyn area ... He has carried out similar attacks on enemy troops, batteries, camps, and transport with such daring and skill as to make the deeds of his unit famous in the whole of Russia.

His method involved waiting until the target could be seen through the Aldis sight, releasing the four 20lb bombs while still diving and then opening up with machine guns. Unusually, we have a summary of the 12 October engagement in Kink's own words because, on 7 November, he and Burns Thomson received an order to 'render forthwith in your own handwriting [a] report in triplicate regarding the action for which you were recently awarded British decorations ... Very Urgent'. He complied in these terms:

B Flight KOTLUBAN

DSO

Name: Kinkead, S.M., DSC Bar DFC Bar

Rank: Captain/Flight Lieutenant

Subject: For gallant action in leading the Camel attack on Dumenko's cavalry in the region of Kotluban on 12/10/19 after the latter had enveloped the left wing of the Caucasian Army. This action saved Tsaritsyn and caused aeroplanes to drive off the field 4,000 determined cavalry with such heavy loss that they have since been withdrawn from the fighting line.

S.M. Kinkead

Captain

11.11.19

According to Collishaw's memoirs, 'the Whites claimed to have counted 1,600 Red casualties as a result of the onslaught by the four Camels'. The semi-official history published in 1923 describes B Flight as having operated against ground forces with great success, often in co-operation with Wrangel's cavalry corps under General Ulagai:

> Flight Lieutenant Kinkead and his companions would descend and bomb and machine-gun the enemy, causing great disorder, amounting sometimes to panic. Then General Ulagai would attack with his cavalry, to complete the confusion. The best work of this kind was done in October, during the great Bolshevik counter-attack against Tsaritsyn. Dumenko, the Bolshevik cavalry leader, had broken through the junction of the

Caucasian and Don Armies on the River Don, some 40 miles west of Tsaritsyn, and he was approaching that town from the south-west with no troops to oppose him. The country over which he was advancing is bare steppe-land that would hardly offer cover to a rabbit. Flight Lieutenant Kinkead with Captain Burns Thomson and Lieutenants Daly and Aten located Dumenko's cavalry division and swooped down on to them, firing continuously with their machine guns and dropping their bombs. So determined and so successful was the attack that Dumenko's cavalry were scattered over the plains in all directions and control of them was lost. Tsaritsyn was saved from the Bolshevik cavalry and Dumenko's division was not seen on the front for some time after this.

Boris Dumenko, commander of a Red cavalry division, had been promoted to lead the Joint Cavalry Corps in September 1919. The previous March, he had been lionised by Trotsky – the head of the Bolshevik armed forces – who hailed him as a hero and awarded him the Order of the Red Banner. In April, Lenin himself had sent his personal 'greetings to the hero of the 10th Army, Comrade Dumenko, and his valiant cavalry, who have covered themselves with glory in liberating Velikokniazheskaya from the fetters of the counter-revolution'; and even on 25 October Trotsky was still describing him in favourable terms, though he was now being outshone by his former deputy, Semyon Budenny. By then, of course, the tide had turned – and it was not in Trotsky's nature to mention the hammering inflicted on Dumenko less than two weeks earlier. The fact that the Corps had been cut to ribbons would have detracted from the great victory over the Whites in which the Red Army commander was exulting. However, within a few months, Dumenko was framed for supposedly shooting a commissar and summarily executed. Whether his disastrous encounter with B Flight played any part in his downfall so soon after the event, will probably never be known.

★ ★ ★

Throughout October the Squadron was operating at full stretch, with Kink and his comrades in continuous action for at least eleven consecutive days. The tempo – and the dangers they faced – clearly emerge from these extracts from the unit's War Diary:

Beketovka: 14th ... Captain Kinkead and Lieutenant Aten escorted DH9A on raid and dropped four 20lb bombs each. Captains Daly and Burns Thomson raided shipping in the Volga, Captain Daly obtaining one direct hit on a barge. Eight 20lbs dropped.

Beketovka: 15th ... Captains Kinkead and Daly escorted DH9As and dropped eight 20lb bombs. No objects observed for ground strafing.

Beketovka: 16th ... Captains Kinkead, Daly and Lieutenant Aten raided cavalry and dropped twelve 20lb bombs. No satisfactory results.

Kotluban: 17th ... Captains Kinkead, Daly and Burns Thomson, working from the advance aerodrome at Kotluban, raided cavalry and targets in enemy's rear. A battery [was] bombed and machine-gunned and put out of action – many casualties. Troops and transport were also attacked from a low altitude by machine guns.

Beketovka: 18th ... Captains Kinkead, Daly and Burns Thomson raided troops at Peskovatka – ten 20lb bombs dropped – casualties. Captain Kinkead attacked enemy Nieuport which went down in a spin.

Beketovka: 19th ... Captains Kinkead, Daly and Burns Thomson obtained effective results on column of transport in enemy's rear; two 20lb bombs were dropped – all direct hits, completely annihilating the column.

Beketovka: 20th ... Captains Kinkead, Daly and Burns Thomson carried out a successful raid north of Dubovka, twelve 20lbs dropped.

Beketovka: 21st ... In the region of Olinoye, three Camels, pilots Captains Kinkead, Daly and Burns Thomson, with twelve 20lb bombs obtained eight direct hits on column of transport – ten wagons.

Beketovka: 22nd ... Raiding the bridge at three [*sic*] with four 20lb bombs, Captain Kinkead obtained three direct hits; however, the bridge was not sufficiently damaged to prevent traffic crossing.

Beketovka: 23rd ... Captains Kinkead, Daly and Burns Thomson raided machine-gun emplacements with twelve 20lb bombs with good effect. Captain Grigson with General Maund as passenger made observation flight of enemy lines.

Beketovka: 24th ... Captains Keymer and Breakey with observers Lts. Thompson and Chubb attempted raids. Captain Keymer and Lieutenant Thompson were accidentally killed. The other machine returned from the raid. The bridge at Vareellktubonskaya [possibly Velikokniazheskaya] was again raided by Captains Kinkead, Daly and Burns Thomson in Camels with nine 20lb bombs; two direct hits.

Holman and Maund had arrived at Beketovka on 22 October. They stayed for a week, flying as observers on several operations and presenting the officers and men of A Detachment with awards for service in the field. There were two DSOs – for Kink and for Frogley – seven DFCs, including Burns Thomson's; and thirteen Meritorious Service Medals for the NCOs and other ranks. Yet, the death on 24 October of Basil Keymer, twice a DFC winner by the age of 20, and Douglas Thompson, who had also survived many dangerous missions, is a sad and salutary reminder of the primitiveness of the machines at the Squadron's disposal. In his account of the Allied Intervention, *At War with the Bolsheviks*, Robert Jackson gives an un-sourced description of what was almost certainly this accident. He states that it occurred on 20 June and happened

when a DH9 of A Flight – one of several which took off to attack enemy troops north of Tsaritsyn – was forced to turn back to Beketovka with engine trouble. As it came in to land, the observer stood up to look over the pilot's shoulder and the bomb toggle near his seat got caught in the pocket of his flying suit. A bomb dropped away and exploded on the ground a few feet under the aircraft, blowing off its wings. The fuselage immediately plummeted to earth and the remainder of the bomb-load went off. The two officers, both Canadians [*sic*], were killed instantly.

However, the Résumé of Squadron Operations for the week ending 28 June records that, although eight bombing raids were carried out on and near Tsaritsyn, no casualties were suffered. In any case, A Flight went into action, under Slatter's command, only in October.

The Detachment really resembled a Wing rather than a Squadron, with each of the Flights operating autonomously. First into battle was the original C Flight, under Captain H.G. Davis, consisting mainly of 47 Squadron personnel who had been drafted from Salonika. Most of these men were not volunteers. Having stoically done their duty, they were allowed to leave the theatre as soon as they could be replaced by others who really wanted to be there. Thus, the new C Flight was deployed in July, under Captain Frogley, and was followed – as we have seen – by B Flight in late September, under Kink's command. In the last desperate stages of the Intervention, there would even be a semi-secret Z Flight made up of further volunteers recruited by Maund from that part of the RAF Training Mission which really had been tasked with teaching White Russians to fly.

This account of the work of 47 Squadron has focused, so far, on the exploits and successes of Kink's Flight; but it is only fair to note the courage and achievements of other parts of the unit. The semi-official history made this assessment:

The respect for British aeroplanes which B Flight had instilled into Dumenko and his men was shared by the Bolshevik fleet in the Caspian. During the Bolshevik attack against Tsaritsyn, the fleet co-operated with the land troops and actually began to shell Tsaritsyn itself. In spite of heavy anti-aircraft fire from the shore and from the fleet, A Flight under Captain Slatter and C Flight under Captain Frogley attacked the fleet again and again until it retired in disorder up the Volga. The fleet never became a serious weapon of offence or defence after that. Indeed prisoners taken some time later stated that when the fleet was ordered to attack again in December there were minor mutinies because it was 'murder to come within reach of the English aeroplanes'.

Writing to a 47 Squadron archivist in 1955, Collishaw similarly stated that:

47 Squadron in South Russia achieved historically the following Air 'Firsts': (i) Put the writing on the wall, by sinking nineteen out of twenty-three armed ships which were investing Tsaritsyn (later Stalingrad) – we used 500lb [*sic*] light-case bombs and employed the near-miss technique.

(ii) 47 Squadron 'killed' cavalry as a military weapon. We proved beyond any doubt that cavalry was out. (It was still 'in' then in the British Army.) The White Army was not defeated in the field, but it collapsed because its rear turned 'Red'. (iii) 47 Squadron was the only unit to fight a war without the inspiration of the RAF ensign. We possessed our own flag. (iv) 47 Squadron was the only unit to conduct a campaign in the total absence of whisky – but not without vodka.

The separate flag to which Collishaw referred resulted, of course, from the criticism of – and subsequent retreat from – formal RAF involvement in the Russian Civil War. As well as changing its name to A Detachment, 47 Squadron was ordered to take down the RAF ensign. Instead, it adopted a tri-colour flag showing the blue of the Royal Air Force interposed between the white of the White Russians and the red of the Bolsheviks. To this day, the flag is worn on the right sleeve of the flying suits of 47 Squadron personnel – even though, paradoxically, it denotes a time when 47 Squadron officially ceased to exist. However, the white came to be replaced by yellow, supposedly as a result of discolouration of the original flag when wrapped in an oil-cloth during the retreat and withdrawal of the Squadron from Russia.

★　★　★

The terseness of official records and the embellishment of unofficial ones have led, over the years, to speculation that Kink destroyed up to ten enemy aircraft in South Russia. This seems unlikely. On the basis of the documentary evidence, he is known to have destroyed an enemy Nieuport – the first aerial victory for the Squadron – on 30 September, and, with Burns Thomson, to have successfully engaged two more on 7 October. As the War Diary shows, his third victory sent an enemy Nieuport spinning out of control eleven days later. Although no Combat Report has survived, the records contain a telegram from Holman dated 20 October congratulating him on this victory. In fact, Churchill's biographer identifies 18 October as 'the first black day for the anti-Bolshevik forces in Southern Russia'. A popular uprising in Daghestan forced Denikin to divert 15,000 of his troops away from the battlefront at this vital moment. His lines of supply were also disrupted by the anarchist bands of Nestor Makhno, and the Bolsheviks concluded a deal with Estonia which strengthened their position in the north and enabled them to concentrate maximum effort towards the south. 'In Russia,' writes Sir Martin Gilbert, 'the anti-Bolshevik successes were now over.' On 24 October, the Bolshevik cavalry corps entered Voronezh, and an appeal to the Don Cossacks to abandon Denikin soon proved successful. In the week from 26 October, Denikin was driven back from Orel to Kursk, a distance of more than 80 miles.

While the Squadron had managed to operate almost daily in October, its opportunities were soon drastically reduced – tactically by the weather and strategically by the speed of the Red offensive. First, the weather: flying proved impossible from Beketovka on 5–6, 10 and 12–15 November. However, at the end of October, B Flight's Camels had relocated from Beketovka, near Tsaritsyn, to an advance aerodrome at Kotluban – 100 miles away – more closely to engage the enemy. Kink, Daly and Burns Thomson successfully bombed troops and transport on 4 November, Daly and Aten also carrying out a major reconnaissance mission. According to its own Record Book, B Flight was next in action on 9 November – though the Squadron's War Diary lists the same raid as occurring the following day. It was an engagement which came close to disaster, probably because of the extreme weather conditions. Three Camels were involved. Daly managed to drop only two of his four bombs, the other two remaining 'stuck on [his] rack'. Aten's were released successfully, but when he descended to strafe enemy transport, he was able to fire only 'a few rounds – machine guns not working well due to cold'. Kink had just dropped his four bombs from 2,500 feet when his control stick jammed completely. The Camel began spinning earthwards on its back as he struggled to right it. At 200 feet, with just seconds to go, he succeeded – coming under heavy machine-gun fire as he did so. Nevertheless, all four B Flight pilots were soon back in the air, raiding enemy cavalry and spying out the land in a two-hour mission on the morning of 11 November. Engine trouble forced Burns Thomson to jettison his bombs and turn back before reaching the target, but Kink and Aten 'continued the raid and reconnaissance over the Don River, north of Tarovskie [possibly Torgovaya], each disposing of four 20lb bombs successfully in about 500 cavalry, causing great panic'. On 13 November they both attempted a further raid, but had to turn back owing to thick ground fog. The following day flying also proved impossible. From 16–18 November, however, B Flight were again heavily engaged. During these three days, Burns Thomson's engine twice forced him to turn back – a symptom of the battered state of the Camel Flight by this stage – but Kink was able to press on with bombing attacks on both cavalry and infantry formations, despite coming under heavy anti-aircraft fire. On 18 November, he reported: 'Dropped four bombs on infantry north of Lozno [Loznoye] with good effect. Enemy advancing on whole front. Machine-gunned infantry on road south of Lozno causing panic.'

After another spell of bad weather, B Flight evidently decided to bow out on the Tsaritsyn Front in style. On 21 November, Kink and Daly were in action in both the morning and afternoon, together with Grigorieff in Camel F1957 on the first of these raids. The target was an armoured train which they bombed successfully from 3,000 feet, using all twelve 20lb bombs 'with good effect, Flt Lt Kinkead obtaining direct hit'. But this was little more than a defiant gesture: subsequent reconnaissance showed Bolshevik infantry continuing to advance along the entire front. Though the final operation from Kotluban, later that day, saw Kink and Daly bombing a military convoy and machine-gunning a cavalry formation, their role as an effective force in the Russian Civil War was all but over.

Following his bout of typhus and his good luck in finding shelter while recovering, Collishaw rejoined the Squadron and reassumed command at

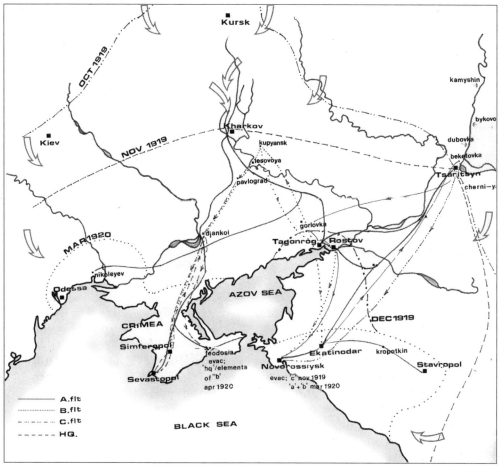

Final movements of A Detachment in South Russia, November 1919–March 1920. (*47 Squadron Archives*)

Beketovka on 27 November. Among the changes in his absence had been one consolidating the identity of the youngest of the British armed forces:

> The new RAF ranks had been officially adopted in August, although it took some time for this to filter through to us. Now, however, I found myself a Squadron Leader rather than a Major, and my Captains and Lieutenants had become Flight Lieutenants and Flying Officers.

B Flight had relocated to Beketovka on 22 November and C Flight had been re-formed – with RE8 reconnaissance/spotter biplanes – under Anderson, newly returned from hospital after being hit by ground-fire on 10 October. With Slatter arriving from Ekaterinodar, most of the Squadron personnel were briefly reunited in the last week of November. The headquarters train, consisting of twenty-two trucks, had shifted the unit's infrastructure to Beketovka

85

in preparation for the redeployment of the individual Flights. B Flight was intended for the Kharkov Front, arriving on 5 December, followed by A Flight and the headquarters train four days later. Both were operating from Peschanoye – but not for long. The War Diary states that 'Flight Lieutenant Kinkead and Flight Lieutenant Daly carried out a successful reconnaissance in the area Urazovo, when large enemy concentrations were attacked and scattered in disorder by machine-gun fire from a low altitude'. The date given is 8 December, though B Flight's own Record Book puts this mission as between 11.00am and 1.00pm the next day. In any event, the rapid retreat of the Volunteer Army caused numerous evacuations from short-lived bases.

By now, C Flight was out of contact, still fighting on the Tsaritsyn Front. A Flight – with General Holman gallantly but unwisely spending much of his time in the air – was constantly charting the Bolshevik advance and warning the White forces whenever possible. The Camels had been pushed beyond endurance. Though retreating with the headquarters to Kremennaya on 10 December, within twenty-four hours B Flight was *en route* to Taganrog to try to refit its machines. When A Flight and the headquarters train attempted to follow suit, the way was found to be blocked. Collishaw and the others eventually withdrew to the Crimea, where they continued to fly and fight until the end of March 1920. The monthly summary for the period to 31 January records the efforts of A Flight, on arriving in the Crimea, to obtain and renovate a couple of bombers belonging to the White Russian forces. It notes in passing that 'B Flight had to retreat hurriedly from Taganrog, and had been out of communication'. To understand what had happened to Kink and his men, we must turn away from the official records and examine instead the reminiscences of the only member of his Flight who lived to write in detail about their desperate situation.

Chapter Four

Russia – The Aten Chronicles

In September 1961, the American publishing firm Julian Messner produced the only full-length memoir by a member of B Flight in Russia. Marion Aten DFC had died the previous May, but had been working in partnership with a professional writer, Arthur Orrmont, on the manuscript of a book he wanted to call *Cossacks of the Air*. The volume which appeared, *Last Train Over Rostov Bridge*, was dedicated jointly to Air Vice-Marshal Raymond Collishaw and the late Captain S.M. Kinkead, and attracted attention in the United States, Canada and the United Kingdom where it was published by Cassell the following spring. In his foreword, the distinguished American journalist Quentin Reynolds described the Russian Civil War as 'probably the worst-reported conflict of modern times' and endorsed the book for its attempt to present that conflict in human terms.

The same observation was made by David Footman, an expert on revolutionary Russia and a former British Intelligence officer, in a perceptive and balanced review which commended *Last Train* for giving 'something that academic historians are so often unable to provide, the feel and the smell of actual participation in human struggle and human tragedy'. He noted that the official records of 47 Squadron were still 'rigidly withheld' – under the then fifty-year retention rule – and that Collishaw had yet to publish his own recollections. Footman regarded Aten's overall portrayal of the political, social and military scene as sound and concurred with his positive view of Wrangel and criticisms of Denikin. Yet, he divined some of the problems of compiling an account so long after the event, with a professional 'popular' author and in the absence of official documents:

There are pages of verbatim dialogue, which, after forty years, can hardly be authentic. The language too is not quite the language of the young officers of 1918 (of whom the writer of this review was one). The battles, when we come to them, are rather too tidy, the girls all rather too good-looking. The appearances of Nina (who plays the role of the heroine) come just as they should in the succeeding acts of a well-constructed drama. One feels that Mr Orrmont has perhaps been almost too efficient, that it would be good to have some slabs of Aten's unprocessed tape recordings. And yet, as one reads on, conviction comes. The language may not be quite right, but it is very nearly so. And Flight B is completely authentic. Young pilots were free from the drab exhaustion of trench routine ... Sorties were a sport – highly skilled and highly dangerous – but still a sport; and life was a round of drink, girls, parties, and absorption in the techniques of air combat. And such, for a time, life remained for these young pilots in their railway siding on the plain in front of Tsaritsyn ... Convincing too are their relations with the Russians whom they met. White officers, refugees, women and girls all come to life as these young men would have seen them. We are made to share their moods, the rosy hopes of the summer, the doubts, and then the crisis as, almost overnight, Flight B with its panache, its gaiety, and its comradeship was immersed in the confusion and misery of utter defeat.

In the aftermath of the book's publication, the Aten family naturally worked hard to promote it. Marion's brother, Boyce, had been killed in the Battle of the Argonne Forest in September 1918; but his sisters, Imogen and Eloise, and another brother, Ira Aten – named after their father, a famous Texas Ranger – all survived him. A lively and revealing correspondence ensued with Collishaw in West Vancouver who had not known, until too late, how often he had visited that part of California where Aten was living in retirement. To Imogen's delight, her approach to the Air Vice-Marshal elicited three detailed letters in September and October 1961. As will be seen, these illuminated and to a considerable extent validated the main themes of the story which her brother had told. Nor was this the first time that Aten had collaborated with a popular author to publicise his experiences: five long articles, entitled 'Flying Madmen', had been published in successive issues of the US weekly magazine *Liberty* between 31 August and 28 September 1935, just over fifteen years after the events they described.

Though significantly 'novelised', both the articles and the book give insights into the personalities comprising the Sopwith Camel Flight of 47 Squadron. Thus, 'Kinkead commanded us: dark, short, magnetic, with the shrewd down-drooping eyes of a really careful pilot who could appear a daredevil. He had thirty-nine [*sic*] confirmed victories on the Western Front.' Of the other pilots whom Aten identifies as belonging to B Flight, its War Diary constantly refers to Kinkead, Burns Thomson, Daly and Aten, but never to the Canadian Edgar ('Eddie') Fulford who features most prominently in the articles, the book and even some semi-autobiographical poetry which Aten subsequently wrote. Fulford, who flew RE8s with Z Flight and was Mentioned in Despatches at the end of the Intervention, was a close personal friend of Aten – which probably explains his determination to make him central to the narrative. Nevertheless, one should not discount Aten's portrayal of individual personalities: 'there was Captain [*sic*] Grigorieff, otherwise Russky, our liaison officer ... he believed in landing by the altimeter'. As for Kink, he 'meant to put his command on the map right from the start, and he did it ... Almost his first time up, Kink shot down a Nieuport into the Volga.'

What Aten's narratives lack in precision is, therefore, redeemed by colour and by atmosphere. Here is his vivid description of a typical air-to-ground attack, comprising an early form of dive-bombing followed by the seamless aerial strafing which soon became B Flight's trademark in the Russian Civil War:

> Kink's guns spurt dust ahead of me. His ship swerves up and passes a few yards to the right. I don't see him; I can't take my eyes from the ground. 500 feet. There is the ravine; the crowding masses of cavalry are white with upturned faces. I press the triggers and ease the joystick slowly back so my bullets will sweep that doomed line of men ... my plane shoots upward and I'm out of the dive. Up, straight up. Kink is above me, doing a cartwheel turn into line behind the last of our ships as it passes him in its dive. As fast as that – as fast as thought!
>
> At the top of my zoom I cartwheel into line behind Kink. Thus we've formed an endless chain of attack. As fast as one has fired his short burst, he zooms and cartwheels back into line for another. Rifles are popping at us vainly ... It is not fighting, it is not murder; it is systematic slaughter ... The river of cavalry has burst out of the ravine, fleeing in all directions, spreading over the steppe ... A red Very light falls from Kink's ship – the signal to regain formation ... we head for home and breakfast. One hour and fifty-five minutes ...

What Kink and his Flight were doing was to apply, in the context of a cavalry-dominated war, the technique of ground strafing which played so large a part in halting the Germans during their March 1918 offensive. According to Denis Winter's study of Great War fighter pilots, 'the aim was to fly in at about 1,500 feet so as to be below anti-aircraft fire and above effective machine-gun range; then to operate in a series of dives and zooms with short, rapid climbing turns, fitting the gun-firing in between'. Despite the difficulty of hitting a fast-moving fighter from the ground, some of the greatest 'aces' perished in this way – Mannock, certainly; von Richthofen, probably:

> It was therefore with good reason that most ground strafers flew with flattened steel helmets on their seats ... The German solution to the particular problem of low-level target shooting was to create specially trained battle Squadrons equipped with machines whose engines and petrol tanks had been armoured. The British never did this.

There was also the ever-present danger of simple pilot error which could be fatal at such low altitudes. In *Last Train*, Aten recounts one occasion where sheer carelessness nearly killed him during a ground attack:

> My guns were raking the convoy and doing a nice bit of damage, but when I tried to pull out of the dive I couldn't; my metal map case had fallen off its hooks and jammed the stick. I had about eight seconds to think of where I would crash the plane ... The stick came free when I kicked at it a last, desperate time, and I zoomed up and over the lorries ... I was

homeward bound. Back at the field Charlie counted thirteen bullet holes in my fuselage. Kink came over, scowling. 'Dammit, Bunny, I told you to have those map hooks fixed and you didn't.' My mouth dropped open foolishly; though his X-ray eyes had seen through my plane to other operating deficiencies in the past, Kink's talent for diagnosis never failed to amaze me. He always knew what had gone wrong, sometimes before you did. This time his omniscience annoyed me, and I was still a little peeved at the way he had spoken to Tommy this morning, so I said: 'It wasn't the map case. It was the stick itself that jammed.' Kink looked at me steadily and said, 'You know, Bunny, if you weren't my friend, I'd say you were a liar.' Then he walked away. 'Call me a liar, Charlie,' I said to my mechanic. Charlie sighed. 'I know, sir, ain't it a caution? Sometimes I wonder if that man ain't God.'

Aten's 1935 narrative is replete with poignant contrasts. None of the B Flight pilots doubted the brutality shown by both sides in the Civil War; but none of them surrendered to the temptation of moral relativism. After the Whites captured Tsaritsyn, Aten and his comrades toured what was left of the city: 'I looked into one house and saw what a hand grenade had left of a father, mother and daughter. That was enough. In a ravine behind the city, 12,000 citizens had been piled in unburied heaps and left to the sunshine. As Bill Daly said, the Reds were wholesalers.'

Yet, such horrors could not dampen the spirits of young men living on the edge. Inspired by the example of some Cossacks at one of the wilder parties, Kink 'decided to take a crack at the dagger dance himself, and collected some knives around the table'. The Cossack General clapped a cap over Kink's ears and 'out he went full tilt. At his first whirl, he began to spill knives. One of them went through a Cossack boot and foot, which ended the dance. Everyone, even the wounded Kuban, thought it a huge joke.' Against this picture of confidence that Christmas would be celebrated in Moscow, Aten depicts the reality – with the dead General lying in the snow and remnants of the former party-goers staggering back, away from the Russian capital, surrounded by 'a tide of death and suffering so vast that the brain could scarce comprehend it'.

* * *

Kink is portrayed as taking the lead not only militarily, but also politically. Aten writes in scathing terms about the decision to transform 47 Squadron from a combat unit into part of the RAF Training Mission. This, he rightly notes, took place at the high point of White success against the Bolsheviks, when, for example, those manning the river fleet – shattered by the bombers of C Flight – chose to mutiny rather than return to face more aerial attacks against shipping on the Volga.

'To hell with instruction school,' said Kink. 'We came to Russia to fight, didn't we? Let somebody else do the teaching.' We agreed. Collishaw went back with word that Squadron 47 was here to fight and intended to

90

fight. Very well, replied the brass hats; Squadron 47 of the RAF was getting out, and getting out right now. If we wanted to stay and fight, with General Holman and anyone else who cared to stay, it could only be as a unit of the Russian Army. And did we thumb our noses! ... Let them take away the name. Let them disband the Squadron so far as the War Office [*sic*] was concerned; that was no skin off our noses. But we were going to Moscow, not to London.

Yet, as we have seen, there was no real attempt to conceal the scale of the RAF presence in South Russia. At most, this was a cosmetic effort to ensure that those fighting the Bolsheviks were formally attached to the White Armies, rather than participating as members of separate RAF units. Collishaw, who had recruited so many of the volunteers, was pragmatic about such details. As his later writings show, he had few illusions about the Whites but never let that blind him to the depravity of the Bolsheviks:

> There was divided support at home for the job that the British and other Allied forces in Russia were doing to aid the counter-revolutionary movement, with many voices being raised in aid of what they claimed was a struggle of the oppressed working classes against the grasping landlords and the parasitic aristocracy. No doubt these people at home, who were thus able to portray the whole affair in such simple tones of black and white, mustered some fragments of truth in their arguments. Nevertheless, I should dearly have loved to have taken a group of them on a tour of inspection of a town just evacuated by the Reds. They would doubtless have found it difficult to have rationalised away the many mutilated bodies of old men and women and young girls as an essential part of the struggle against the oppressive ruling classes.

He thus gave credit to Maund – by then an Acting Brigadier-General – for protesting that it would have 'a most deplorable effect' if 47 Squadron became a non-combatant instructional unit, as it was 'worth as much as the whole White Russian Air Force put together'. Maund successfully argued that the officers and men 'had gone to Russia to fight'; they wanted no part of training duties; and they would prefer to join Wrangel's Volunteer Army if the Squadron were disbanded.

This firm stance by the head of the RAF Mission contrasts with a shocking allegation, in Aten's narrative, which is difficult to assess. Both his 1935 articles and his 1961 book are absolutely specific that Maund betrayed Kink and everyone else on the B Flight train as they desperately sought sanctuary on the far side of the River Don. Crawling towards Rostov from Taganrog during the final retreat – a journey of 37 miles – the train was overtaken by the last one from headquarters. It was carrying Maund as well as his staff, and Aten makes no attempt in the *Liberty* articles to disguise his personal hostility:

> We had met up with him at Kotluban and, behind his back, had dubbed him Impromptu, because he was only a temporary Acting General. He

was agreeably foppish and a tall and airy talker about his own experiences and achievements. He now rose a trifle in our estimation for thus bringing up the rear. Later, we were to learn that the Russian staff had simply decamped with everything in sight. The British staff knew nothing about it, but Wrangel, returning suddenly from the front to Taganrog, gave Impromptu a train and so saved all concerned.

Next night we were stalled behind a jam of trains near a lonely station, about 5 miles from Rostov. And there, on the other track, was Impromptu's train, blocking the line; the engine had gone dead. All engines, of course, were heavily guarded. To get another meant a battle. Impromptu and his crowd were just out of luck. Sooner or later a refugee mob would get up the nerve to roll their cars off the track ... We suddenly found Impromptu among us. He had come alone and unannounced ... 'Our engine's dead, Kink,' he announced. 'Novocherkassk has fallen, by the way.' This drew a grunt from us. Novocherkassk was the capital of the Don Cossacks, 20 miles north of Rostov. It meant that Rostov was doomed – with 5 miles of packed trains between us and that bridge. 'I'll drop part of my train, sir,' said Kink, 'and pick up part of yours.' 'No,' said Impromptu. 'You push along when you get a chance. I'll not leave till I see you safely away. I'll have an engine down from Rostov soon.' Good old Impromptu! We had wronged him sadly. When he took his leave we said as much – to each other ... We were opening a fresh jug of rum when Impromptu's train clanked and started off.

'What the hell!' Scotty [Burns Thomson] jumped to the window. 'Under way, all right! Where'd he get his engine?' 'Probably came from Rostov while we were talking,' said Kink, then turned at a sturdy rap. 'Come in!' The corporal of the guard stepped inside. 'The General's took our engine, sir.' 'What?' 'Put 'is own guard on in our place, sir, and said as it was all right. I 'ad to tyke 'is orders, sir.' 'Was it the General himself or one of his officers?' 'Hisself, sir, and two 'eadquarters sentries with 'im.'

We looked at one another – hard. Good old Impromptu! He was running true to form after all. 'He – he'll send back an engine for us.' 'Like hell!' flared Scotty. 'The elegant gentleman took our liquor, soft-soaped us, then sneaked our engine and left us to die. Would he send back anything?' Scotty was right and we knew it. We were done for; and the mutter of gunfire across the night made the fact clear beyond mistake.

When Aten published these words in 1935, he must have been confident that he would face no legal action from Maund who was still serving in the RAF, and who continued to do so until his death as an Air Vice-Marshal seven years later. Evidently there were no repercussions and the charge was repeated in both the American and the British editions of *Last Train Over Rostov Bridge*. But there was an intriguing difference between the two. Whereas the 1962 British edition identified Maund by name throughout, the American edition the previous year changed his name to 'Mudd'. This would have been little defence against a libel action, since the position he held within the British Military Mission was unique and the 1935 magazine articles had named him correctly. Probably neither the American authors nor their publisher knew for certain that Maund was no longer alive, and the change of name was simply a routine precaution advised by an in-house libel lawyer. In any event, this manoeuvre led Raymond Collishaw to remark, in his final letter to Imogen Aten, that:

The General Mudd, mentioned in Marion's book, was in reality Acting Brigadier-General Maund of the Royal Air Force. *Maund did a dastardly thing in stealing Kinkead's locomotive* [author's emphasis]. Maund was the RAF representative with General Holman's Mission, whose business was exclusively concerned with the provision and supply of British military equipment being provided to General Denikin's Army.

It seems highly improbable that Collishaw, as Commanding Officer of 47 Squadron/A Detachment, would not have known if this episode occurred. Yet, the mystery remains: how could a senior officer have continued in his career if he had acted so treacherously towards his own fighting men? Although Maund's Service Record has not yet been made public – because he remained in the RAF long after the Great War – I understand that no mention of the alleged train incident exists within it. Aten's articles also claim that Maund's status suffered after he left the theatre. Having re-formed at Ekaterinodar:

We raised hell generally, and so did everyone else. One bright gleam came our way. Impromptu, no longer a General, had been sent home with his tail between his legs. We outdid ourselves celebrating his debunking. That stolen engine was something that nobody in B Flight would ever forgive or forget.

Naturally, Maund's own report on the evacuation of Taganrog tells a radically different story. Compiled at the Advanced HQ, Ekaterinodar, on 25 January 1920, it states:

Our railway journey was a long and uncomfortable one. The distance from Taganrog to Rostov is only 40 miles, yet it took five days to complete! On the way, B Flight was passed, their train having been broken in half by a coupling breaking, and the locomotive connecting rod bending. Just outside Rostov, where two different railway systems converge, a complete railway block occurred; engines ran out of fuel and water. We filled our own engine four times from streams, by forming a queue of RAF personnel and our Russian Labour Corps, and thus saved the train with Mission Headquarters personnel and BMM [British Military Mission] rear party ... On arrival at Rostov on the 6th [January], the train personnel, Mission Headquarters, proceeded direct to Novorossiysk, whilst I stayed behind to try and get through B Flight and A Detachment store train, which were finally held in the block at Khapri. By degrees,

93

however, they were brought closer, and were eventually reported at the Ekaterinovskoe Station, Rostov. To get them as far as that needed the additional pressure of General Brough, Railway Adviser, BMM ... Unfortunately, the hoped-for stand by the Volunteer Army, on the line outside Rostov and Novocherkassk, did not materialise ... another repetition of the Taganrog evacuation began, and all semblance of order was lost. General Brough was unable to save the two RAF trains, standing just a mile and a half from safety and, on the morning of the 9th, ordered the RAF to evacuate their trains. As the Russians had abandoned trains of wounded alongside of these two trains, it was impossible to burn them; but all material that could have been of any use to the enemy was rendered unserviceable beyond repair. Five DH9As, seven Camels, four lorries, two tenders and a Crossley car were among the abandoned material, and shells were already falling in the vicinity when our men left. They managed to get on a train at Bataysk, and have now been sent to Novorossiysk to get new kit as, having to march, they could only take with them what they could carry through heavy snow.

Maund's report then refers in scathing terms to the 'disorganising hand' of Major-General Vladimir Kravtsevich, whose removal as head of the Russian Air Force he secured at the price of his own resignation. In this, he clearly had full backing from the head of the British Military Mission:

General Holman is convinced, with me, that the supply of machines to the Russians, so long as General Kravtsevich is in command, is a waste of public money and, therefore, instructed me to put in an application to be relieved of my command ... This I have done and the result has been that General Kravtsevich is being removed from his command ... General Holman has advised General Denikin to appoint General [Vyacheslav] Tkachev in his place ... He is a brave man, a fairly efficient administrator, and beloved by the Russian Aviation. Should he be appointed, the task of my successor will be an easier one in every way, as General Tkachev is a strong Anglophile and desirous of co-operating.

There can be no doubt that Maund's action in resigning was strongly supported by Holman who wrote to the War Office, also on 25 January, to tell them that:

His action in resigning, communicated by me to General Denikin, has had the effect of securing the removal of General Kravtsevich, who has been responsible for the unsatisfactory state of the Russian Aviation Service ... I wish to place on record my appreciation of the hard work which Wing Commander Maund has done here in South Russia. His devotion to duty and unremitting exertions have been worthy of the highest praise.

Thus it was that, on 12 July 1920, when the *London Gazette* listed those honoured for service in South Russia, 'Squadron Leader (Acting Wing

94

Commander) Arthur Clinton Maund DSO' was seen to have received both a CBE and a Mention in Despatches.

⋆　⋆　⋆

Collishaw's correspondence with the Aten family sets out a story of headlong retreat similar to that experienced by the officers and men of B Flight. Just as Aten refers to his train being packed with refugees because 'Kink let them occupy every untenanted inch', Collishaw describes a grindingly slow journey to the Crimea in an RAF train comprising ninety vehicles hauled by three locomotives: 'we must have had thrust upon us perhaps two thousand people and it was a terrible handicap'. On one occasion, Bolshevik sympathisers sent a runaway engine in pursuit:

> It collided with our train with a terrific impact and caused the mass of wooden cattle trucks to collapse and telescope one another. The stoves in these trucks set our train on fire from end to end. The only undamaged part of the train was the steel coaches occupied by the RAF. The result of the collision was pitiful for the refugees, hundreds were killed and injured ... With heavy hearts, we had to abandon all the Russian people in our train who had come to us for succour and so we steamed out of that hell-hole just in time.

Aten's account is similarly harrowing. Although his book is called *Last Train Over Rostov Bridge*, B Flight train itself remained stranded on the far side. It almost reached the bridge, courtesy of a tow from an armoured train, but could go no further. With the Red Army entering Rostov, Kink was ordered to abandon it and march his men across the railway bridge:

> The railroad yards were teeming with life; the trains were emptying, a rolling flood of foot refugees was engulfing everything in a frantic wave of panic. The ice was aswarm with scurrying figures. On the bluffs above us the Vickers was spraying on them like a hose ... more machine guns came into action. Then, from the rear, a shrapnel barrage began to sweep the river, bridge and south bank. There was no response until Kink had our machine guns open on the bluff and swept it with bullets while we got formed up. Ahead of us lay the armoured train, useless ... A wounded Russian officer dragged himself from somewhere, imploring us to take him away. He could only lift the upper part of his body on his hands. Kink explained that it was doubtful if we could get ourselves away, much less carry anyone. The officer became calm, and shifted his weight to one arm. Instead of speaking, he whipped out a pistol and shot himself through the head at Kink's very feet.

Both the book and the 1935 articles give an indication that even in such dire circumstances humanity was not dead. Kink was supposed to destroy all military equipment rather than allow it to fall into the hands of the Bolsheviks.

95

As his men prepared to set the wagons alight, however, Kink realised what this would mean:

> Suddenly his voice failed. He glanced at the refugees thronged there around us, [and] at a hospital train next to ours. 'As you were – the order's countermanded. That carload of bombs, dash it! Attention, Flight; form fours! Right turn. By your left, quick march.' We moved towards the bridge ... The hordes of refugees were screaming in panic. A mob followed us, pressing close as we marched between two lines of trains ... Ahead, we could see where the lines of sidings began to converge upon the double tracks that aimed for the bridgehead. We came abreast an engine, when the voice of Kink rang out from the lead. 'Flight, *halt*! Fall out, the officers.' We gathered around him. He said nothing, but pointed ... at this particular point there was on every track a gap. A gap of perhaps two freight-car lengths scattered with dead and dying refugees. Up on the bluffs a machine-gun outfit was sweeping that open space without a pause ... A smudge of smoke had drawn down the river. It was clearer now and closer. The icebreaker was smashing its way down towards the bridge; when it got there, the bridge would be blown up. Kink lit a cigarette. 'Speak up, you fellows,' he said, calmly enough. 'No time to lose. Do we take to the ice or keep going?' We said nothing.
>
> ... 'Hold on, hold on!' There was a break in Kink's voice. He was pointing towards the bluffs. They were disappearing. So was the river. A fine mist, accompanied by a thick rolling fog, was sweeping in ... 'Flight, attention!' Kink's voice rang suddenly. The machine guns on the bluffs were ceasing their chatter. Fog was rolling around us, smothering us; the bluffs were lost to sight. 'Close column. By your left. *Quick march*!' Quick march it was and no mistake ... Below us the icebreaker was a grimy shadow, belching smoke. The death and horror fell away from us and was gone ... We marched on, and the gunfire died out. No more screaming; just the refugees ploughing along in the snow. What had happened to the immense numbers cut off at Rostov was very simple: they no longer existed.

★ ★ ★

What had brought the fortunes of the Allied Intervention so rapidly to such a dismal situation? Clifford Kinvig's study, *Churchill's Crusade*, records that the events of early October 1919 seemed to the Secretary of State for War 'to provide a complete vindication of the almost ten months of incessant and passionate effort that he had devoted to the anti-Bolshevik cause'. Although the Prime Minister had disapproved, MPs were generally supportive, except for some left-wingers, including one – Lieutenant-Commander Joseph Kenworthy – who was to make a fleeting appearance at the end of the Kinkead story. By 15 October, the British had finally withdrawn from North Russia, in accordance with Lloyd George's policy, but Churchill remained optimistic that

96

the Whites would hold their own. In South Russia, Denikin had captured Orel and 'taken a quarter of a million prisoners, 700 guns, 1,700 machine guns and thirty-five armoured trains ... On 18 October, in a private letter to the CIGS, General Holman, the mission commander, declared, with quite inappropriate precision, that he hoped to see Denikin in Moscow by 15 January 1920.' Churchill, too, was exultant: 'The Bolsheviks are falling and perhaps the end is not distant. Not only their system but their regime is doomed.'

Such optimism was short-lived. The Bolshevik counter-offensive, which recaptured Orel after just one week, drove south unstoppably to the Don. Wrangel was belatedly promoted – but too late to make any difference. It was in the backwash of this rout that Kink, Collishaw and Aten found themselves swept along. By the end of December, even Churchill was conceding that a total Bolshevik victory seemed imminent; and, in January, minds began to be concentrated on how to extract the remaining British personnel safely. For the rest of his life, Collishaw believed that political blundering by Denikin had been decisive. Writing to a 47 Squadron archivist in May 1955, he recollected that:

> General Denikin's White Army had conquered from the Bolsheviks an area of South Russia some 2,000 by 1,000 miles. On all sides there was great enthusiasm for the cause of ousting the Reds and for the restoration of a conservative government. Alas! There was too much over-confidence and reactionary tendencies. The former landowners in Denikin's Army pressed him to publicly announce that the replacement regime would restore private property to its rightful owners. General Denikin's momentous pronouncement produced immediate and frightful consequences. In a week, what had been a glorious advance became a fearful collapse. The home front turned 'Red' and the campaign tottered into disaster.

Collishaw's frustration with Denikin was to be a recurrent theme. He admired the Cossacks but despised the former Tsarist Army officers whom he felt responsible for the collapse of the White Army. Writing to Imogen Aten in 1961, he again alluded to Denikin's promised restoration of Russian land to its former owners:

> One can imagine how such a policy would react upon the millions of people, who by that time had each grabbed a piece of land for himself. He was now called upon to disgorge his spoils and to revert to the serfdom and slavery of his ancestors ... Even the Cossacks in the White Army defected. The Volunteer Army were the principal sufferers in the collapse. Only a week before, they had been day-dreaming of the recovery of their properties and their riches and now, suddenly, they became the object of destruction from all sides. Civil war between the rich and the poor is far more cruel than international wars. It deliberately embraces the women and children in its destruction. Only a relative few of the poor Volunteer Army women and children escaped.

One person who did not escape a terrible fate was loyal Lieutenant Grigorieff, the Russian liaison officer with B Flight. Like Collishaw, he contracted typhus; but, whereas Collishaw was nursed and saved by a kindly Russian refugee, Russky was admitted to Rostov Hospital. According to Aten, his British comrades learned that he and all the other patients and staff were massacred when the Bolsheviks captured the city.

Over the years, questions have been raised, with justification, about the accuracy of Aten's narratives. With access to the contemporary Squadron records, it is clear that embellishments were added – probably with the encouragement of commercially-minded publishers. Yet, his former Commanding Officer did not feel that the overall record had been unduly distorted. In thanking Collishaw for all the information he had supplied, Imogen Aten wrote:

> Marion relived the Russian Campaign many, many times. He had written and rewritten the story over and over but failed to get it published until he came into contact with this writer [Orrmont] who rewrote it according to his idea of a saleable book. We feel that it would have been a stronger story had he not played up the love-interest so much and had stuck to the historical facts more closely. However, we are not experts on what appeals to the public.

The Air Vice-Marshal replied in the same generous spirit:

> Yes, I fully agree about the love-interest in Marion's book: but Mr Orrmont doubtless had in mind that movie directors almost invariably introduce spurious female characters into historical sketches, so as to induce reactions from an interplay of passion, pathos, tragedy; and I fancy that popular writers tend to follow similar lines. Manifestly, Orrmont told Marion that it was essential for him to introduce a thread of love-interest into the path of the story, and so poor Marion weaved a web of fanciful female characters into the picture ... Marion's book seems to be getting round, because several people have written and telephoned to me about it. Perhaps it was the love-interest that did it!

Collishaw also mentioned how he 'went to see some of Kinkead's family in South Africa in 1941. They had only the vaguest ideas concerning Kinkead's adventures in South Russia.' In trying to reconstruct Kink's personality, even the more imaginative parts of Aten's book can strike a chord: one section of the dialogue has Kink declaring: 'when a man joins the RAF, it should be part of the articles he signs that [he] guarantees not to fall in love. Love ruins more men than drink.' Despite the addition of aerial dogfights, when such combats were few and far between, and despite the process of 'novelisation' both in his book and his articles, Aten succeeds in conveying a genuine sense of atmosphere, while repeatedly giving insights into the nature of Kink Kinkead: dauntless yet humane; disciplined yet carefree; cynical yet wholly committed to his cause.

Chapter Five

Counter-Insurgency in Iraq

In the spring of 1920, soon after his DSO citation appeared in the *London Gazette*, Kink prepared to return to England. He left Constantinople on the *Hildonan Court* on 18 April for the two-day voyage to Port Said, where he was briefly attached to 70 Squadron. On 10 June, he finally embarked for post-deployment leave. The name of the troopship, *Czar*, may have raised a grim smile, given the theatre he had just left. His Mention in Despatches for service in South Russia was gazetted on 20 July, just as his month's leave ended. The next day he was posted to the RAF Cadet College, Cranwell, where he remained on the staff until October 1921.

With the shrinkage of the Royal Air Force at the end of the Great War, only a minority of those who wished to do so could continue their flying careers. A Written Answer in Parliament at the end of 1919 revealed that: 'The number of Air Force officers has been reduced from, approximately, 30,000 at the date of the Armistice, to about 4,000.' Kink's permanent commission had been confirmed in August 1919 – but only as a Flying Officer. Not until New Year's Day 1922 did he regain his wartime rank of Flight Lieutenant. This was just in time for his last and longest spell of Active Service: more than two years' continuous deployment in the British-mandated territory of Iraq, formerly Mesopotamia. In preparation for this, from October to November 1921, he had spent four weeks with 24 Squadron, honing his flying skills on the De Havilland 9A. His refresher course was graded: 'Assessment Superior. Suitable as Instructor.' But the RAF had another plan: the fighter ace was to be a bomber pilot.

The Confidential Reports in Kink's Service Record show the regard in which he was held, but also the problem facing any biographer. 'A very fine officer,' states one. 'An excellent officer,' says another, 'keen, plucky, hard-working and thoroughly reliable.' 'One of the best type of successful Service pilots,' but also 'Very unassuming.' No correspondence, no private diaries, no paper-trail at all. The nearest Kink came to keeping an archive was his extensive collection of snapshots, many neatly annotated. His time at Cranwell suggested potential for higher command: 'A very efficient officer. Has great personality and aptitude for command.' And at 24 Squadron: 'Sound pilot. Of the right type ... I consider that he would make a good leader.' His career in Iraq was assessed by some particularly distinguished airmen. These included Raymond Collishaw, now confirmed in the rank of Squadron Leader and briefly re-united with Kink after their shared hazards in Russia.

Collishaw, as Commanding Officer of 30 Squadron, to which Kink was posted at the end of January 1922, had this to report of the period in which their service in Iraq overlapped: 'Exceptionally efficient Flight Commander. Has personally led 68 bombing attacks and reconnaissances during 1922 with greatest determination and devotion to duty. Brilliant pilot, superior officer, most trustworthy, with ability to command.' A later report, endorsed by Air Vice-Marshal Sir John Salmond, the officer in overall command in Iraq, stressed the same virtues: 'Very efficient officer in every branch of work. An extraordinarily good leader and his work has shown that he is thoroughly reliable. Would make a very good unit commander.' Both of them recommended Kink for accelerated promotion; and it looked as if he was being prepared for a prominent role in the higher reaches of the RAF.

What might have been his destiny, had he not been diverted into the High Speed Flight? Certainly, James Robb – who commanded 30 Squadron during part of the Kurdistan campaign and eventually retired as an Air Chief Marshal – recommended Kink for RAF Staff College, expecting him to 'become [an] efficient and capable Staff officer with further experience'. Others described him as 'Promising ... with quiet habits ... and self-reliance'. He had 'made good progress in Staff duties and should do well. Most popular officer.' To the end of his life, all the reports were in the same vein:

> Shows great initiative. Has knack of getting the best out of subordinates and has done exceedingly well on detached duties ... Excellent in every respect ... great success ... has done exceptionally well ... Steady and intelligent ... An exceptional officer of the right type, possessed of initiative, pluck and determination. Should go a long way in the Service.

The final prediction, poignant in retrospect, was the view of Air Vice-Marshal Scarlett, in overall command of the Schneider Trophy team.

The consistent theme of the self-effacing, modest leader of men means that one looks in vain to Kink himself for an account of his own adventures. Worse still, unlike in the Russian campaign, where official archives survived at unit level, only occasional glimpses of Kink can be found in the records of Iraq Command. The same applies to the memoirs of other participants. The most substantial personal narrative is that of the Great War ace, Ira Jones, whose recollections were published as *An Air Fighter's Scrapbook* in 1938. Jones was a fiery Welshman who began as a Royal Flying Corps air mechanic, winning a Military Medal on the ground, followed by a Military Cross, two DFCs and a DSO in the air. Like Kink, he had volunteered to fight the Bolsheviks, though serving in North Russia on the Archangel Front. He arrived in Iraq in the autumn of 1923, more than halfway through Kink's long deployment, and recalled, in retirement, the many 'good shows' which were carried out there:

> During my period in the country the ones which stand out most vividly in my mind are concerned with the work of a junior officer, Flight Lieutenant S.M. Kinkead, DSO, DSC, DFC of No. 30 Squadron. 'Kink', as he was

popularly known to his friends, commanded a detached Flight at Kirkuk Aerodrome, which was situated on the western border of Kurdistan. His Flight's duty was to patrol the restive Sulaimaniya Valley and to carry out punitive raids against the recalcitrant Sheikh Mahmud, who had once been appointed the ruler of Kurdistan by the Baghdad Government, but who in 1923 led a revolt ... I remember once having a taste of Kink's gay fighting spirit. I was at Kirkuk on wireless duty, and Squadron Leader (now Group Captain) J.M. Robb, the popular and efficient commander of No. 30 Squadron, asked me if I would care to go as Kink's passenger on a flight to Helebja. 'Kink and I,' he said, 'are going to drop pamphlets on the villages, warning the inhabitants not to give help or pay taxes to Sheik Mahmud. Kink will be flying up the left side of the valley and I shall be on the other side.' Just before we took off Kink said to me: 'Your job is to keep an eye on Robbo, in case he has a forced landing. But see that your machine gun is working in case we forced-land.' We had passed Sul without any incident. About 6 miles farther on I noticed about twenty horsemen riding in file on our left front. I tried to tell Kink what I could see. He wouldn't listen and shouted back: 'Keep an eye on Robbo.' This I had been doing all along, but I was fascinated by these horsemen and could not resist tapping Kink on the shoulder again and pointing them out. Kink became very annoyed, at first pointing at his eyes, then pointing in the direction of Robb. I knew what he meant, so I gave up watching the horsemen who were now only a short distance in front of us. They must be friendly Kurds, thought I, and as I did so the nose of our machine plunged violently and Kink's front gun was splashing bullets all round the horsemen who were scattering helter-skelter in every direction. Kink flattened out at about 50 feet and gave me the signal to fire. We spent ten hectic minutes until all our ammunition was expended. I shall never forget a fat old Kurd, dressed in black, who remained on his pony during the engagement when all his comrades had dismounted. My bullets could be seen hitting the sand in front and behind him but he refused to panic and kept firing at us until the end. A brave man, that old Kurd. These horsemen turned out to be Sheikh Mahmud's bodyguard, and the fat gentleman on the pony was the brother of the great man. Mahmud was not among the party. I don't think I hit anyone although Kink went so low at times that I could see the whites of their eyes.

Such memories of Kink in Iraq are frustratingly few and far between, but that should not prevent us telling the story of the campaign against the dual threats of Turkish intervention and Kurdish insurrection with which he and 30 Squadron were so heavily engaged.

★　★　★

The history of 30 Squadron, from its inception in 1915, is one of continuous involvement with Mesopotamia. In this theatre, British and Indian troops confronted Turkish forces, notably during the disastrous siege of Kut-al-Amara, which fell to the Turks at the end of April 1916. Only one-third of the 12,000 men who surrendered survived the 700-mile forced march to Turkey. 30 Squadron had flown almost 140 sorties in a fortnight, making the world's first food air-drop, in a desperate attempt to sustain the besieged garrison. Only thirteen of the fifty members of the Squadron, captured when Kut fell, survived the cruel aftermath. At the end of the Great War, a much-reduced 30 Squadron continued to function, with one Flight at Mosul to the north and the other in Persia. In April 1920, the British were granted a Mandate to govern Iraq, under Article 22 of the League of Nations Covenant. How that Mandate should be discharged soon became a matter of fierce controversy. The campaign in which Kink would be involved decided not only the fate of Iraq, but also of the fledgling Royal Air Force.

The political background to the Kurdistan campaign – and, especially, its crucial role in securing the future of the RAF as a separate Service – has been admirably summarised by David Omissi in his study of *Air Power and Colonial Control* between the wars. Despite the disaster at Kut, the British eventually emerged victorious in Mesopotamia, capturing Baghdad in March 1917 and occupying Mosul just after the 1918 Armistice. If all this effort were to seem worthwhile, if secure routes to India and across the Middle East were to be established, and if the United Kingdom were to benefit from Iraq's untapped oilfields, it was obviously unacceptable simply to abandon the Mandate. Yet, the post-war Coalition was desperate to reduce the national debt, built up during the war, and military spending was an obvious target for reductions. Predictably:

> Tension between the three Service ministries was therefore heightened as each tried to defend its share of a shrinking budget at the expense of the others. As the smallest and newest Service, the Royal Air Force was especially vulnerable to Army and Navy attack. The various schemes for the cheap Air Ministry control of Iraq were advanced to ensure the survival of an independent Air Force at a time when the existence of this Service could best be defended on financial grounds.

Just as he had exerted decisive influence in initiating the Dardanelles Campaign and the Intervention in Russia, Winston Churchill determined the course of events in Iraq. As Secretary of State for War and Air, he saw both the scale of the problem and the nature of the solution. There was no way in which 25,000 British and 80,000 Indian troops could continue to be supported in the country. Even when the numbers started to come down by early 1920, the cost to the British economy was about £18m a year. Churchill invited the Royal Air Force to submit a scheme for aerial control which would enable as few as 4,000 British and 10,000 Indian troops to be deployed at a fraction of the existing cost – and so it proved, with expenditure falling from £23.36m in 1921–2 to only £7.81m the following fiscal year and less than £4m in 1926–7. The Army was furious, warning with some justification of the military risk involved.

Indeed, in the summer of 1920, a serious uprising occurred in Mesopotamia which took several months to contain, and both the Army and the RAF sought to put the best possible interpretation on their respective roles in suppressing it.

Churchill remained determined that an affordable scheme of control must be found and, at the end of 1920, events moved swiftly in his favour. The Cabinet decided that British responsibility for Palestine, Transjordan and Iraq should be vested in a new Middle Eastern Department under the Colonial Office. At the beginning of 1921, Churchill took over the new department and was installed as Colonial Secretary. One of his first moves was to gain permission to convene a conference in Cairo to review and make recommendations for the management of the British Mandates in the Middle East. It was at the Cairo Conference that the Air Staff's scheme was approved, in conjunction with a schedule of payments to be made as subsidies to key Arab leaders in the region, provided that they agreed to keep the peace:

> These subsidies were directly related to the strategy of air substitution and the emerging system of informal control. If the British garrisons in the Middle East were to be successfully reduced, the frontiers of the mandated territories had to be protected from tribal raids. It was hoped that the thousands spent to purchase the neutrality of the independent Arab states would be recouped many times over in future when millions were saved by air control.

Omissi relates how the War Office fought a rearguard action to try to keep at least seven British battalions in Mesopotamia; and he contrasts it with Lloyd George's preference to quit the country completely. For once, Churchill could be seen as the advocate of compromise – a compromise, what is more, underpinned by the prospect of essential reductions in military expenditure. In August 1921 the Cabinet approved his plan based on the Air Staff's scheme endorsed at Cairo. Much of the preparatory work had been undertaken by Air Vice-Marshal Sir Geoffrey Salmond who, like his brother John, would later be appointed Chief of Air Staff. Salmond had despatched the Squadron to Somaliland which cheaply and swiftly crushed the 'Mad Mullah' and his Dervishes early in 1920. Now it was decided that eight RAF Squadrons, just four infantry battalions (two British and two Indian), three companies of armoured cars, and a number of ancillary units, would be enough to maintain security in Iraq.

The new military strategy was designed in conjunction with a supportive political scheme. The British decided to offer the throne of Mesopotamia to the Emir Faisal whom they regarded as a credible potential monarch, combining nationalist credentials with religious tolerance and hostility to Bolshevism. He had upset French interests in Syria and been expelled from Damascus for his pains. The French were bought off, however, and Faisal – having arrived in the country only in July – was duly crowned King of Iraq in the same month that the Cabinet approved the air control plan. It was a skilful package, but one ultimately dependent on the continuing availability of military force. As Omissi concludes:

> The reduction of the garrison, the elevation of Faisal, the payment of subsidies to Arab leaders and the purchase of French acquiescence were all aspects of a single strategy of indirect rule intended to reduce the cost of imperialism in Iraq. Its ultimate success depended upon air control.

The road to that 'ultimate success' was, nevertheless, to be long and convoluted. The new King had a difficult balance to strike between the interests of his British sponsors on the one hand, and the demands of Arab nationalists on the other. This was the situation when Kink arrived at Basra on 6 March 1922 for the start of his long deployment. He had sailed from the United Kingdom in the troopship *Princess* on 31 January, arriving at Bombay on 23 February and embarking five days later in the SS *Varsova* for Basra. His period in Iraq, from March 1922 to mid-October 1924 – though not documented at an individual level – is set out in depth at an official level in a series of reports and despatches by successive RAF and overall commanders. It is to these that we must now turn.

★   ★   ★

Although the scheme for air control had been approved in August 1921, it was not due for formal implementation until 1 October 1922, when Air Vice-Marshal Sir John Salmond was due to succeed Major-General Sir Theodore Fraser as Commander of British Forces in Iraq. In the meantime, the Royal Air Force contingent was under the command of Group Captain (Acting Air Commodore) Amyas Borton, who drew up a full account of events from the beginning of February to the end of September. The RAF began this period with two Squadrons at Hinaidi, one each at Mosul and Shaibah, and three – including 30 Squadron – at Baghdad West. An eighth Squadron came into the theatre during March and April, and the early months were punctuated by occasional bombing attacks on aggressive tribesmen but, more usually, so-called 'demonstration flights' to persuade recalcitrant groups not to withhold their taxes from the Government. Work also continued in re-marking aerial routes overland and upgrading the landing sites enabling them to be flown in stages. All this changed on 18 June when Captain Sidney Bond, the Assistant Political Officer of the town of Chemchemal, and Captain Robert Makant from the local Iraq Levies were murdered at the Bazyan Pass by Kerim Fattah Beg of the Hamawand tribe:

> During the few days immediately following the murders, the gravest fears were entertained by the political authorities as to the danger of the disaffection spreading over a large area, and subsequent reports from many sources confirmed that it was due to the action of the Royal Air Force that the trouble was localised.

On 19 June six DH9As were despatched to Sulaimaniya, and on 23 June four more were sent to Kirkuk. As we have seen from Ira Jones's memoirs, this was almost certainly the detached Flight under Kink's command. There now began a process of tracking the murderers and raiding any villages which gave them support. Nine villages were attacked in six raids at the end of June, and twenty-seven more were bombed during twelve raids in July:

> The prompt retribution, which overtook any village which afforded hospitality to the enemy, had the effect within a few days of definitely convincing the many sheikhs who were wavering that the moment was not a propitious one for identifying themselves with Kerim Fattah Beg.

The fugitive headed north at the end of July; but, on 5 August, he and fifty horsemen crossed the River Zab near Koi Sanjak *en route* to Rowanduz, which they reached on 9 August. The town was duly attacked by 55 Squadron, but it was recognised that Kerim Fattah Beg had managed to elude capture. Retribution would eventually overtake him, but this episode demonstrated both the power and limitations of aerial policing. On the one hand, trouble-makers could be put to flight with minimal casualties, and tribesmen deterred from rallying to their cause. On the other, agility and guerrilla tactics made it most unlikely that they would be caught and permanently eliminated.

Borton noted, with satisfaction, that during the operations to suppress Kerim Fattah Beg, which lasted from 19 June to 9 August, thirty-three bombing raids and a demonstration flight had been carried out. Thirty-four villages had been on the receiving end of a total of 11 tons of bombs, and 10,000 rounds had been fired from the air. Yet, this was a very different type of bombardment from that practised, over a decade later, by the Luftwaffe in Spain. Kink's 30 Squadron colleague Stanley Vincent has described the technique:

> we had to drop messages on all villages to say that we would destroy any village – by bombing – that supplied KFB with shelter, or food for his followers and their horses. The luckless villagers were placed in a difficult position as KFB in turn would threaten to pillage their villages if they withheld supplies. But our method did pay off as the villagers hid their grain and KFB was kept under control. With Sheikh Mahmud's villages – and town of Sulaimaniya – and with those who would not pay their taxes to the British Administrative Officer, we had to drop warning messages from the air saying that if their head man did not come in by such and such a date ... we would destroy his village ... After the necessary time had expired, back we would go and drop messages saying we would bomb the village in thirty minutes.

The bombers would then circle the target while the villagers rushed to remove their valuables and, if possible, their livestock during the half-hour period of grace. When their mud houses were abandoned, high-explosive bombs would be used to break up the roofs so that the exposed timber could be set alight by showers of small incendiary devices. Sometimes petrol would be dropped to add to the conflagration and sometimes the villagers' livestock would be machine-gunned. Contrary to legend, although there was discussion about the possible use of gas from the air – primarily of an incapacitating rather than a lethal nature – this did not occur during the Iraq campaign.

Sir John Salmond was in no doubt of the effectiveness of the air control method compared with the cost in time, treasure and casualties of the ground control alternative. Sending out an Army column, he wrote, involved:

> the burning of entire villages, wholesale destruction and confiscation of livestock and almost inevitably also the loss of numerous lives, both of the tribesmen and of our own troops. The punishment which control by ground forces can inflict, being uncertain and slow, must be very severe; for it is the nine stitches where one, sewn in time, would have sufficed. With air control it is the reverse ... It is easy to apply. This means that in practice it will be applied; and while the disorder is in its initial stages; and that it will therefore need to be applied only on a very limited scale.

The problem facing Borton was not confined to the risk of insurrection. Turkey had been experiencing a remarkable revival under the leadership of Mustafa Kemal and was seeking to obtain the best post-war settlement possible. This included an attempt to maximise Turkish influence aggressively in Iraq – the base for its operations and propaganda in Kurdistan being the town of Rowanduz, where Turkish irregular forces led by Euz Demir and other Turkish officers were gathering their strength daily. This had led to four bombing raids on Rowanduz, extensively damaging what were believed to be the Turkish barracks in mid-July – even before Kerim Fattah Beg had headed for the town. The Turkish menace was by far the greatest threat to the maintenance of British rule in Iraq. It was not at all certain what the outcome would be of this undeclared war. The risks were demonstrated in August when a column of Sikhs and local Levies, sent to Rania to deal with Turkish re-inforcements in the area, was beaten back and forced to withdraw. This, as Borton recounted, had wider ramifications:

> The evacuation of Rania resulted in the Sulaimaniya Valley being threatened, and on 4 September it was decided by the GOC that Sulaimaniya itself should be evacuated by air ... The operation was commenced at dawn and completed by 12.30 hours. A total of sixty-seven persons were evacuated to Kirkuk, and a quantity of W/T stores, bomb components and machine guns brought away ... The objective ... was entirely achieved, i.e., that nobody should be left in Sulaimaniya who by his particular adherence to our regime would be endangered by our evacuation.

The rescue mission was carried out by twenty-nine aircraft, including sixteen DH9As from Kirkuk and eight more from Baghdad. Each bomber could carry just two people squeezed into the rear cockpit, though twenty-one of those rescued were brought out by two large Vickers Vernons. In all these operations

– offensive and defensive alike – Kink and his fellow-pilots knew that the prospect of landing a Ninak on inhospitable terrain, without at least a serious injury to everyone on board, was practically nil. The work of both mechanics and pilots in ensuring the reliability of their machines was thus of critical importance. Between 1 February and 1 October 1922, when the RAF took over responsibility for the overall campaign, over 7,200 hours were flown, yet only three officers and three other ranks lost their lives and six officers and one other rank were injured.

* * *

On assuming overall command, Salmond was in no doubt that the Turkish threat must be his top priority. This was the one factor which had not been anticipated when the Cairo Conference planned the reductions in Army strength and the transfer of responsibility for Iraq to the RAF. The setback at Rania had encouraged Turkish infiltration, with bases being established at Koi Sanjak and in nearby areas. Salmond had no illusions about Turkish strategy:

> She would certainly employ against us every means she could devise of exerting an indirect pressure ... by trade embargo, by organised political intrigue and systematic propaganda, by promises of armed support, by presents of arms and ammunition, and by the penetration of our border districts with irregular forces, and, more recently, by concentrations of troops on the frontiers.

Not only were the Turks dominant in Rowanduz – 'the natural gateway from Turkey into Kurdistan' – but the withdrawal from Rania had not gone unnoticed by potential insurgents:

> Prestige had naturally suffered severely. The wild and crafty Kurdish tribes were only too ready to exploit the advantages of their position between two masters ... and our hold over the greater part of Kurdistan in Iraq was, to say the least, more than precarious.

The British then made a serious misjudgement which would shape the course of their presence in Iraq for almost a decade – they decided to install Sheikh Mahmud as Governor of Sulaimaniya.

Mahmud certainly fitted the picture of an agile and slippery character capable of playing off one power against another. Although he caused immense long-term problems to the British, even at the time there was a grudging admiration for him. After his final surrender in 1931, Captain Holt, the officer who accepted it, declared:

> Sheikh Mahmud fought cleanly and with courage and, when the odds against him in men, armament and organisation are considered, it must be conceded that he fought extremely well ... It is said that Sheikh Mahmud has repeatedly broken his promises, that he is cruel and tyrannical, that he is selfish and ambitious ... But the defence has really a stronger case ...

107

His tyranny is the will of a tyrant, but it is mellowed by the generosity of a prince ... His ambition and his pride cannot be denied, but they are for his nation and not for himself alone ... perhaps the wisest judgement is that his greatest fault is that he was born a century too late.

Such was his persistence and resourcefulness that he was dubbed 'The Director of RAF Training' by the Service which had to mount so many operations against him in Kurdistan. Mahmud was the head of the family of Barzanji Saiyids and the great-grandson of 'a Kurdish holy man of fabulous virtue and power'. His father, Sheikh Said, had been murdered by the Turks in 1909 as part of their plan to undermine the immense influence of the family in Southern Kurdistan. This encouraged the British to try to recruit him as their representative in Sulaimaniya in 1918; but the plan was thwarted by the return of the Turks, who initially imprisoned him before deciding that it was necessary themselves to install him as Governor of the town. The British went one better, on their return, appointing him Governor of Southern Kurdistan; but then, worried by his ambitions and intrigues, belatedly sought to curb him. In May 1919, Mahmud raised an insurrection but was wounded, defeated and sentenced to ten years' imprisonment. Soon this was downgraded to exile in Kuwait – and at this point the gamble was taken to invite him back to Sulaimaniya in the hope of his helping the Government's authority to prevail.

Unlike in Faisal's case, importing such an influential figure to defuse rebellion proved to be an expensive error. Mahmud resumed his balancing act between the British and the Turks and evidently decided that Mustafa Kemal was the better bet. By November 1922, the British were alarmed to find him 'in almost open correspondence' with the Turks, and in February 1923 Salmond received reliable intelligence that the Governor, whom the British had installed, was planning to attack Kirkuk and Koi Sanjak in March. In collusion with Euz Demir's Turkish irregulars, Mahmud was plotting a general uprising in return for recognition as ruler of Kurdistan. The British had, in short, made a terrible mistake in bringing him back.

Salmond now faced serious and simultaneous threats from Turkey in the Northern or Rowanduz Sector of Southern Kurdistan; loss of prestige in the Central or Rania Sector; and a charismatic opponent of enormous influence in the Southern or Sulaimaniya Sector. How could he juggle the need to counter these parallel dangers? Since taking command, he had always felt that the solution lay in recapturing Rowanduz. This had been impracticable during the severe winter, though the use of air power against Koi Sanjak, following an ultimatum, forced the Turkish detachment established there to quit the town. Throughout the winter months, similar Turkish posts were immediately bombed on discovery – thus keeping them continually on the move and unable to consolidate a grip on people or places:

This air attack was the first definitive and effective check which the Turkish plans had received. It was carried out over difficult hill country and throughout the hard Kurdish winter, under often very adverse flying conditions. It was maintained on a frontage of more than 100 miles by a force which for the most part consisted of two Squadrons and at no period exceeded three.

Salmond was sure that Turkey aimed to recover Mosul, without which her hold on that part of Kurdistan inside Turkey might fail. As well as the irregulars already within Mosul, the Turks were thought – by late January 1923 – to have overwhelming forces just two weeks' march away. This meant that British reinforcements would arrive too late to meet a sudden attack. Logically, a defensive rather than a forward strategy seemed sensible, but Salmond regarded that as potentially disastrous. Abandoning the Mosul region to the Turks would be a huge blow to Britain's reputation:

> Withdrawing to Baghdad we should stand self-confessed as the defeated side, and without, therefore, in an Oriental country, one single friend. Our prestige would be non-existent and our position impossible ... At its present strength, therefore, the garrison of Mosul was in a thoroughly unsound position and constituted a dangerous detachment. It had ceased to be a deterrent to an attack and had become an inducement. Either it ought to be withdrawn at once or its strength so increased as to preclude the possibility of a surprise attack being made with success.

Salmond concluded that the only hope lay in reinforcing the Mosul garrison with all the strength at his disposal. This included the Iraqi Army placed under his command by the newly-installed King Faisal. The redeployment was achieved by 5 February, demonstrating to the Turks that, instead of facing British troops operating unaided in a hostile country, they would be confronting 'a British force in alliance with a national force fighting to defend its territory'. It was within days of this move that Mahmud's insurrectionary plot was discovered. Salmond regarded him as 'clever, headstrong and fanatical, but of a very unstable character'. Certainly, the Sheikh had decided to throw in his lot with the Turks at precisely the wrong time.

By early March, Salmond believed that the Turkish leadership at Angora (later Ankara) had become less bellicose. Although an external threat to Mosul could not be ruled out, he convened a conference there on 12 March at which it was decided to take the risk of removing the very forces he had sent to Mosul only a month earlier. They would be used, temporarily, to clamp down on Mahmud in the south and also to forestall the danger on the frontier with Turkey near Rowanduz – the key location he had always identified. Soon, these forces would be reduced in size, as part of the scheme for air control, so it made sense to utilise them fully while they were still available. This would also assist the British bargaining position at the Lausanne Peace Conference – soon to reassemble – in fixing the *status quo* in Iraq to best advantage while negotiating a treaty with the Turks.

Thus were created two mobile columns of ground troops – one, entitled Frontiercol, was to concentrate at Erbil before occupying Rowanduz and reinforcing the border; the other, Koicol, would head for Koi Sanjak to secure both it and Kirkuk against possible attacks by Mahmud from the south or the 'powerful and warlike' Pishder tribe in the Central Sector of South Kurdistan. Crucially, each of these mobile forces would always be in contact with the other, and with Headquarters, by wireless telegraphy and other forms of air messaging. True to the policy of seeking local legitimacy, a co-operative figurehead – Saiyid Taha – was enlisted to bring in key leaders in the north to parley rather than to rally to the insurgency. Salmond described him as 'a man of considerable religious and temporal influence' and 'a champion of Kurdish interests against Turkish pretensions' – which he had been forced to conclude that Sheikh Mahmud was not. Some 8,000 proclamations, many bearing the seal of Saiyid Taha, were dropped from the air exhorting the tribes not to interfere with the advancing ground forces. Three RAF Squadrons would be in constant touch with the columns until Koicol reached its destination, when the role of protecting it would be carried out from Kirkuk.

Despite floods and wrecked bridges, Koi Sanjak was reached on 4 April and, by the following day, Frontiercol was in place at Erbil. On 6 April a letter of protest was received from a shaken Euz Demir, describing himself as 'Commandant Rowanduz Group'. Salmond ignored it. By the end of April, Koicol was successfully established in Rania, wiping the slate clean after the failure of the August 1922 expedition; but the main prize had always been Rowanduz. After personally surveying the route from the air, Salmond dropped instructions to the Frontiercol commander not to attempt a head-on assault in one particularly mountainous area, until Koicol could outflank the enemy's principal strongpoint. An ambush was beaten off, with the help of continuous aerial bombing and strafing; concealed positions were neutralised; and the strongpoint on which Euz Demir had relied for the defence of Rowanduz was abandoned during the night. As a result, 'his tribal following melted away, disheartened by the emptiness of his assurances of successful resistance'.

Early on the morning of 20 April, despite dreadful weather conditions, Frontiercol occupied the abandoned stronghold. A bloody battle had been completely avoided by the judicious use of aerial reconnaissance and communication. From there to Rowanduz were two extremely difficult alternative routes; but intelligence and aerial observation showed that, while one was defended, the other was not. By the early afternoon of 22 April, Frontiercol had reached Rowanduz, to be joined by the advance guard of Koicol at 5.30pm. The campaign had been one of perfect air-ground co-operation. All Salmond's objectives were achieved at a cost of one British serviceman killed and seven British and seven Indian servicemen wounded from the Koicol force. Frontiercol suffered no casualties at all.

The Rowanduz operation thwarted Turkey's aim of annexing Kurdish territory in league with Sheikh Mahmud. By the end of April 1923, all Turkish

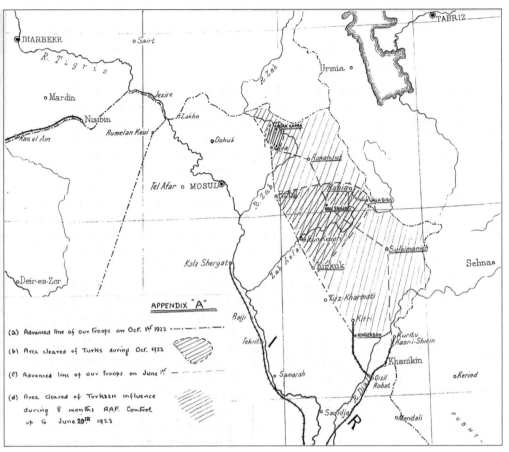

Map labels (from image):

DIARBEKR · oSairt · R. Tigris · Mardin · Nisibin · Rumelan Keui · Ras el Ain · Jezire · B.Zakho · Dohuk · Tel Afar · MOSUL · Kala Shergat · Deir-es-Zor · TABRIZ · Urmia · G. Zab · Rowanduz · Rahia · KALA DIZA · KEUPRI · Kirkuk · Sulaimaniah · Sehna · Tuz Khurmati · Kifri · KINGERBAN · Kuritu · Kasr-i-Shirin · Baiji · Tekrit · Khanikin · Samarah · Qizil Robat · Saqidja · Mendali · Kerind · PUSHT

APPENDIX "A"

(a) Advanced line of our troops on Oct. 1st 1922 ·—·—·—·—·
(b) Area cleared of Turks during Oct. 1922
(c) Advanced line of our troops on June 1st —— —— ——
(d) Area cleared of Turkssh influence during 8 months RAF. Control up to June 20th 1923

troops had retreated into Persia and Turkish propaganda had lost all its influence. Salmond detected a new spirit of co-operation among tribal leaders in the border areas. Still, Mahmud and other rebels could not be expected to give up easily, despite the neutralisation of the Turks. Having secured Koi Sanjak and Rowanduz, Koicol therefore moved on to Sulaimaniya at the end of May, in order to break up Mahmud's organisation. The British High Commissioner was ecstatic, reporting to the Colonial Office that:

> It is difficult to exaggerate the improvement of the political situation effected during the past three months, first by the move of troops to Mosul, and later by the successful operations in Kurdistan. The impression that the return of the Turks was imminent has now vanished and this has had great effect in Baghdad, Mosul and among the Euphrates tribes.

There was equal elation in the Air Ministry. Sir Hugh Trenchard, the Chief of Air Staff forwarded Salmond's first Despatch to Sir Samuel Hoare,

Churchill's successor as Secretary of State for Air, under cover of an enthusiastic commentary by his Deputy CAS:

> The report is of interest as it is the first time that the Air Staff views as to the correct use of ground troops have been carried out. Any opposition was entirely defeated by air action, with the result that these two columns were able to cover a very large part of disturbed territory with practically no casualties. The lessons learned by this should be applied to the Indian frontier ... if we can only get military commanders to avoid using ground troops as they have done in the past, and as they are doing even at the present time, I think there can be no doubt that the result will be that a far smaller number of troops will be required, and that the casualties will be enormously reduced.
>
> This is also the first occasion on which air has played such an important part in the transport of necessaries for the troops and the evacuation of [the] sick. The only alternative would have been enormous convoys of mechanical and horse transport, with the necessary escorts, which have always provided a bait for the enemy in the past and have been responsible for most of our regrettable incidents ... The great use made of aircraft and W/T as a means of rapid intercommunications was undoubtedly one of the factors which led to success.

In expressing his own appreciation of 'the success with which Sir John Salmond has overcome great difficulties, and proved in a most distinguished manner the capacity of Air Forces, when properly directed', the Secretary of State would have quietly reflected that the risk of the RAF being dismantled and reabsorbed by the Royal Navy and the Army had now dramatically receded.

With the threat of invasion eliminated, and the Lausanne negotiations proceeding slowly but steadily, it became possible to reduce ground forces in Iraq to meet the targets set at Cairo. This was virtually achieved by February 1924. A pattern had also begun to emerge of what could be expected from Mahmud in the future. Salmond hoped that he might, in his present frame of mind, 'be ready now to behave himself and to renounce his former unhappily conceived association with Turkish schemes'. In the course of time he might come to realise 'that his best interests lay in affiliating himself with Iraq'. After Koicol had departed from Sulaimaniya, it came as no surprise to learn that Mahmud had reappeared there. A message was sent to him clearly explaining that, if he confined his activities to an explicitly defined area, he would be left alone, but that action would immediately be taken if he were found to be interfering in any of the surrounding districts which had now been detached from the Sulaimaniya Division.

Once again, this optimism was not fulfilled. Soon Salmond was laconically noting that whenever this man 'of inordinate vanities and ambitions ... lapsed into evil causes ... air action has promptly restored the situation'. In August, and again in December 1923, Mahmud was discovered to be meddling in the surrounding districts, and he spurned an invitation from the High Commissioner to come to Baghdad for talks 'under guarantee of safe conduct'. The British were convinced that he was merely playing for time until he could collect enough money from dues on the autumn tobacco crop to enable him to raise and maintain an armed following. Thus, on Christmas Day 1923, 'an air attack was made upon his quarters, pamphlets being at the same time dropped, explaining the reasons which had made this attack necessary'. Total war, this was not: it was almost a minuet or a chess game between seasoned professional performers. Fortunately, despite the absence of detailed individual Squadron records, this is one of Kink's innumerable operations in Kurdistan for which we do have an account.

★   ★   ★

Taffy Jones shared the sporting sense of admiration for the Sheikh and, fifteen years after the event, vividly recalled the Christmas Day raid:

> Mahmud was known to be occupying a house in the town of Sulaimaniya, so a surprise attack was carried out in an endeavour to destroy him. Kink had by experience found out that it was no use approaching Sul (brief name by which Sulaimaniya was known) up the valley from Kirkuk, as Mahmud's scouts on the top of the hills gave him a warning by the use of fire smoke. Sir John Salmond therefore decided to start the raid from Mosul which was to the north-west of Sul, the approach being over very mountainous country and from a direction which the Sheikh would least expect.

Four machines participated in the actual bombing, while Salmond watched from the observer's seat of a fifth DH9A. Usually such raids dropped 112lb bombs from a height of 2,000 feet. This one was different: each aircraft carried a 500lb bomb with a fifteen-second delay fuse. They were to be dropped from just 500 feet or less. The pilots were Kink, another 30 Squadron Flight Commander, Eric Routh, and their comrades 'Monkey' Sherlock and 'Foxy' French. Jones's narrative continues:

> Mahmud's home was a large square house in the middle of the town. Down went 'Monkey' first to 500 feet, he missed by several yards; then Routh 'had a go' and also missed; 'Foxy' was near; then Kink went down to about 200 feet and let go his cargo, fifteen seconds later Mahmud's house was hidden from view for several seconds but when the smoke and dust had cleared away a large crater was seen in the yard, and the house was only badly shaken. Each pilot wondered how the Sheikh had fared in such a blasting. It became known later that he had been warned and was enjoying 'the show' from a point of vantage a mile away!

The five Ninaks made for home, via the Sulaimaniya Valley, apparently in safety. Suddenly Routh's machine began to descend and was seen to land about a mile from the town. Immediately Kink and Salmond's own pilot,

Arthur Jones-Williams, descended too. In a re-enactment of Walter Anderson's achievement in Russia, they gathered up the stranded airmen:

> There was no time to waste. Arab horsemen, yelling madly, were seen galloping towards them in the distance. 'John Willy' with Routh sitting on Sir John Salmond's lap, and Kink with Routh's mechanic in his back seat, were off the ground to the accompaniment of much cracking of musketry. A grand show, typical of the spirit of the RAF.

The same thing happened again, in even more dangerous circumstances, soon afterwards. According to Taffy Jones, Kink led a Flight of four on a bombing raid to punish a sheikh who had killed a Political Officer. Presumably, this was Kerim Fattah Beg. In the course of the bombing, a lucky shot from the ground hit one of the aircraft:

> Suddenly, Darley Whelan's machine was seen to glide to earth and land in the valley. Whelan was in a bigger predicament than Eric Routh had been, for the ground was rough and to rescue him was a hazardous operation. But no situation of danger was too hazardous for the doughty South African. Down went Kinkead without hesitation and landed nearby; 'Monkey' Sherlock followed suit, and before the angry Kurds had sized up the situation Whelan was in the air again in Kink's machine, and his mechanic in Sherlock's. Danger, however, was not yet over. As the valley was narrow and the 9As overloaded, it required the greatest skill to keep the machines aloft as well as manoeuvre them so as to avoid crashing into the hillside. Then there were the Kurds, who had been hiding in the hills, firing madly at them. It took ten minutes of clever manoeuvring before they were able to get clear of danger. When the machines had landed safely at Kirkuk and admiring pilots congratulated Kink, he looked right through them and said: 'Let's have a drink.' No wonder that everyone who served with him worshipped the ground that he trod.

Stanley Vincent, who like Collishaw became an Air Vice-Marshal, has another anecdote from the advance on Sulaimaniya, though he places this in 1924 rather than the previous year. The town was actually occupied on 16 May 1923 – three weeks after Euz Demir and his Turkish troops were forced to cross into Persia, where they were disarmed and sent home, and a few days before it was learned that Mahmud and his main allies had also fled to Persia.

After describing how 30 Squadron had escorted Koicol troops safely through hills and passes near to the town, he relates how 'Kinkead and I, as the two Flight Commanders, thought we would do the final sortie to witness them arrive, and were in position over the town some forty-five minutes beforehand'. Both aircraft were badly affected by a local wind phenomenon which made it necessary for them to come down on the small landing ground adjacent to the town:

> We thought we would rather face angry humans than an angry sky. We kept our engines running for a time in case we had to make a run for it, but

had to shut down fairly soon to stop boiling. Our passengers stayed by their Lewis guns in their revolving Scarff mountings and Kink and I, automatics in holsters, signed for the gathering townsfolk to sit down in a circle about 30–40 yards away. The notabilities of the town then appeared and virtually handed over the town to us with formalities restricted to the friendly exchanges of cigarettes. The Army shortly arrived and found, to their disgust, that we had stolen their thunder.

If Sir John Salmond knew of this escapade, he wisely decided to leave it out of his comprehensive Despatch – in which he rightly showered praise on Colonel Commandants Dobbin and Vincent, the leaders of the Army columns. Salmond naturally felt that his tenure in overall command had greatly reduced the external threat to Iraq, while containing potential insurrection and proving the value of the independent RAF:

> Air action ... does not involve detachments or lines of communication. There is little chance to the tribesmen of loot or of making any reply to its attack, and no chance of inflicting serious loss. It can interfere severely with the processes of agriculture, ploughing, the digging out of water channels, and the harvesting of crops. It can deny tribesmen access to their villages often even by night. It can destroy their reed hutments and stores of grain or fuel or knock their mud houses about. It can force them to flee altogether from their districts ... and [is able] to deny the tribesman his normal life, and his means of livelihood indefinitely. Except, however, where intensive action is taken, the casualties which it inflicts are extremely few ... Air control achieves its result not by its severity but by its certainty and swiftness and its deterrent effect.

However, Army critics would undoubtedly have emphasised the good fortune that sufficient troops were still in Iraq when the external Turkish threat came to a head. By the time Salmond handed over command to Air Vice-Marshal John Higgins in April 1924, British and Indian forces had been cut to the four-battalion basis envisaged at the Cairo Conference. Higgins was also in executive command of the local Iraq Levies, but was well aware that such forces were intended to deal only with internal security. As he later noted,

> they were not designed to meet external aggression by the Turks or any other power. True, the energetic action taken by my predecessor in April 1923 had dealt a severe blow to Turkish designs and had driven back their forward posts to the administrative boundary. But, as I was subsequently to learn, Turkish ambitions had been checked – not defeated.

A more immediate problem was Mahmud, re-established in Sulaimaniya and levying harsh taxes on small villages in the district as well as tribes travelling through the area. On 4 May, a minor dispute between some Christian Assyrian troops and a Muslim shopkeeper escalated in Kirkuk, causing serious conflict between Levy soldiers and the local community. There were several

115

fatalities on both sides before the riots were suppressed, and this gave the Sheikh his next opportunity. He declared a *jihad* or Holy War against the British and the Assyrians, and was once again thought to be in close contact with the Turks. Higgins concentrated the whole of 30 Squadron at Kirkuk and messages were scattered over Sulaimaniya calling on Mahmud to surrender himself by 26 May. The deadline passed and, as threatened, the town was bombed heavily for two days:

> A total of 28 tons of bombs, the equivalent in explosive to 15,000 18-pounder shells, were dropped upon the town; the Bazaar was gutted by fire, and the Custom House and Tobacco Khan destroyed; the inhabitants, forewarned by proclamation, had abandoned the town and therefore suffered no casualties.

Mahmud sat out the bombardment in caves nearby, but when he returned on 1 June, he was greeted with marked hostility by the inhabitants of the town. As his followers melted away, he moved his family and his assets across the Persian border. On 19 July, Sulaimaniya was reoccupied, without opposition, by two regiments of Iraqi cavalry and 100 police supported by armoured cars and aircraft.

Meanwhile, the Turks were preparing their final throw of the dice in respect of Mosul. The League of Nations was due to determine the border between Turkey and Iraq before the end of the year. On 11 September, small parties of Turkish troops were reported to have crossed into Kurdistan. Two days later an urgent warning was received that they would try to seize the border town of Zakho. What followed was a textbook example of intelligence, communications and air power in action:

> Nine Bristol Fighters arrived at Zakho on the morning of 14 September ... At 08.05 300 cavalry were observed crossing the River Borana ... The formation leader reported the facts by W/T and added that he was withholding action. I received the message in Baghdad, 300 miles away, at 08.12. I ordered immediate offensive measures. At 08.21 the aircraft came into action: by 08.30 the Turks were in full retreat.

They did not, however, vacate Iraqi territory for several more weeks. After a number of significant further clashes, a Turkish withdrawal was eventually agreed and took place, in stages, between 12 October and 20 November 1924. On 30 October, the Provisional Boundary – later known as the Brussels Line – was approved by the League of Nations. Higgins noted with satisfaction that 'It was substantially identical to the original Administrative Boundary'. The Turkish gambit had failed.

It was at this point that Kink's role in the campaign came to an end. Taffy Jones noted angrily that Kink 'did not receive any decorations or promotion for his magnificent ... work' – though, at least Marion Aten was given a Mention in Despatches 'for gallant and distinguished services in the field' in the 1923 Kurdistan campaign. On his Service Record, Salmond wrote of his 'Great keenness for flying and devotion to duty', adding that Aten had 'Lots of determination and can always be relied upon to see a job through'. Kink had been in theatre for two years and seven months. His accumulated leave entitlement was 166 days. More than five months' relaxation beckoned, and he left Iraq for the United Kingdom on 18 October, as the crisis with the Turks came to an end. Yet, the Mahmud saga was far from over. The Sheikh's next appearance was in April 1925 but he was driven back to Persia in June. The cycle was repeated twelve months later, but this time two RAF airmen were captured and taken to Persia. When their health began to deteriorate, Mahmud agreed to repatriate them; but, despite giving an undertaking to the Iraqi Government in 1927 that he would not re-enter the country, he soon re-appeared and did not finally surrender for another four years. According to the history of 30 Squadron, when the Sheikh gave himself up on 13 May 1931, he approached an RAF officer and remarked 'You are the people who have broken my spirit.' The 'Director of Training' had finally retired – in a wave of guarded affection from compatriots and adversaries alike.

The career of Kerim Fattah Beg came to an equally appropriate end, on 29 June 1926, when he was killed in a fight with villagers near Chemchemal – the very town where he had murdered the Political and Levy Officers four years earlier. Higgins remarked that 'the villagers were emboldened to resist this famous robber' because of the success in patrolling the district by Iraq's 1st Levy Cavalry Regiment. It is probable that Kink learned of the demise of the nastier of his two main opponents, for his next posting brought him back to the Middle East – where his organisational rather than his combat skills were about to be put to the test.

Chapter Six

Imperial Links –
The Cape Flight

Kink's next posting came through on 28 March 1925, four days before the expiry of his long leave in the United Kingdom. It was to Cairo for Staff duties at Headquarters, RAF Middle East. Although he did not know it, the seeds of his next great challenge had just been sown by Sir Samuel Hoare. Speaking in a debate on the Estimates on 12 March, the Secretary of State for Air was in propitiatory mood:

> One or two Hon. Members have alluded with regret to the fact that we have been very unfortunate, as a country, in regard to winning any of the international air races in recent times. I am very sorry that that is so; but, at the same time, it should be remembered that, if you are going to set yourself to win one of those international competitions, it does mean the expenditure of a very large sum of money.

The American Government had invested heavily in the team of US Navy flyers who had carried off the Schneider Trophy – the foremost prize in competitive aviation – at Cowes in October 1923. Currently, there were few Air Ministry resources to spare for such contests; but Hoare hoped that, 'as the finances of the country become less stringent, we shall be able to do more in the future'. He also announced support for two long-distance flights within the Empire: one from Cairo to Lake Chad, the other from Cairo to Cape Town and back:

> That is only a beginning, and year after year it is hoped we may make these long-distance flights and show the flag in the air over a great part of the British Empire.

Hoare kept his word. Within days, Government backing was confirmed for the development of new racing seaplanes – notably R.J. Mitchell's Supermarine-Napier S4 – in the hope of matching the Americans. It was not to be: despite setting a new world speed record for seaplanes of 226.75mph in September 1925, the S4 crashed at Baltimore a month later in pre-contest trials for the Schneider Trophy race. On 26 October, the Americans triumphed again, beating the remaining British and Italian entrants by margins of 33mph and 64mph respectively.

The Press was not happy. Five days after the contest, the Aeronautical Correspondent of *The Times* set out what he described as the 'Lesson of the

Schneider Cup Race' in the light of the 'handsome victory' of the United States:

> The Americans have now the accumulated experience of four years or more of high speed flying, and their winning Curtiss racers were the result of endless wind tunnel experiments, and other experimental work. If speed is of value in aircraft work, as undoubtedly it is, then Great Britain has considerable leeway to make up ... It may be said that the funds available do not permit of an intensive effort being made, but it is as well to remember that the motor trade is convinced that it pays to secure records in the big international motor races and trials. America, it is to be noted, is selling aero engines in Europe ... The Services have so far played little part in any consistent effort to impress the world with the qualities of our aircraft, and if it were possible to combine some of the operational training work with the showing of the air flag, nothing but good would result. The first big effort of this description that is to be made will not be before next spring, when a Service flight is to take place from Cairo to the Cape.

It was true that the promised RAF expedition from Egypt to Nigeria was now under way – three DH9As under the command of Squadron Leader 'Mary' Coningham, a close friend of Kink's, having left Cairo for Kano on 27 October; but these were older, wartime aircraft and were fitted with engines of American origin. *The Times* felt that this detracted from the flight's 'value to us for a propaganda purpose'. At least the Air Ministry had assured the Society of British Aircraft Constructors that the Cape Flight would be undertaken with entirely British equipment. Perhaps this indicated greater Government will to promote British aviation, but more needed to be done:

> America has definitely established speed supremacy by concentration upon securing that quality. Great Britain must make some other attribute of aircraft its strong lead, and one of the first means of enhancing the prestige of the industry in this country is to secure other records, or else carry out flights which have a practical value, easily demonstrable to the world generally.

Over the next three years, the RAF was to set standards in both long-distance and high speed flying: Kink's role was to be pivotal in both.

* * *

The prospect of an air route from Cairo to Cape Town dated from the years immediately after the Great War. Indeed a chain of landing grounds had been surveyed by the RAF in 1919, and a flight undertaken by two highly-decorated South Africans, Pierre van Ryneveld and Quintin Brand, the following year. *The Times* had offered £10,000 for the first pilot to fly from London to Cape Town, and the South African Government had paid for a Vickers Vimy bomber – repainted and renamed *Silver Queen* – to make the attempt.

The prize eluded them because they wrote off two aircraft before reaching their goal; but both were knighted for their pioneering zeal and perseverance. In trying to emulate their journey, the Government had two main aims. Militarily, they wanted to develop a system of mobile Empire defence, enabling threats to be met and outposts reinforced with the minimum of delay. Commercially, they sought to blaze a trail by laying the foundations of a future network of Imperial air routes. Although *The Times* had been unimpressed by the Cairo to Kano flight using standard Service machines, to the Secretary of State this seemed encouraging. As he told the Commons in February 1926, it showed how 'to bring Nigeria and Egypt within a week by air, whereas by motor car it would have taken a month, and by primitive native transport more than six months'. Coningham's three DH9As had flown 6,268 miles, in eighty flying hours, over very difficult territory without mishap. In colonial terms, it had been an outstanding success:

> The amount of interest that was taken in it, over this route between Egypt and Nigeria, is almost incredible. Hundreds of thousands of natives gathered to see the arrival of the machines, and Emirs in considerable numbers were taken up for joy-rides ... The pilots were generally addressed as 'bird-masters'.

If the much harder task of flying from Cairo to the Cape and back were similarly to be managed without incident, meticulous preparation would be essential.

As in Iraq, Kink's contribution was to be central but poorly documented. What has survived is his report at the end of the Cape Flight, and a covering letter for the AOC, RAF Middle East, to submit to the Air Ministry. This time, Kink was operating outside his element. The fighter ace and precision bomber pilot was now part of a nineteen-strong team, but only eight of these men were flying. The remainder were responsible for ensuring that, every time the aircraft landed, the local airstrips were fully prepared and provisioned to receive them. At the head of the Cape Flight was Wing Commander C.W.H. Pulford AFC, who had served on the seaplane carrier HMS *Ark Royal*, survived two crashes, and helped pioneer the technique of using airborne torpedoes against shipping. Looking back on the Cape Flight, he modestly observed:

> The ground organisation was so thorough that all we had to do was to get in at one place and out at another, and that was all there was in it. The strenuous period, and the one which gave most work and anxiety was the preparation for the flight. There was so much that had to be provided for and every detail had to be gone into; but once all preparations were complete, the actual flight was easy.

It was not so easy for the men on the ground. Kink was in charge of the Northern Section of the route – from Egypt to the Southern Sudan border. The AOC's letter acknowledged what he had endured and achieved:

120

I consider that the way in which the search for, and preparation of landing grounds was made, reflects great credit upon Flight Lieutenant Kinkead. Much of the country in which he was working is situated in the sleeping sickness area, and is infested with Tsetse fly. All land travelling had to be done on foot. Flight Lieutenant Kinkead trekked over 500 miles along rough tracks, and despite many difficulties always succeeded in arriving at his destination in good time to complete the work required.

Addressing the Royal United Service Institution in December 1926, with Sir Samuel Hoare in the chair, Pulford paid his own tribute. He explained that the Northern Section stretched from Cairo to Nimule on the Sudan–Uganda border. In between were the landing grounds at Assiut, Aswan, Wadi Halfa, Atbara, Khartoum, Kosti, Malakal and Mongalla:

> As far as Khartoum, supply was a fairly simple matter, since the landing grounds between Cairo and Khartoum were in general use and were well served by the railway. South of Khartoum, however, matters were not quite so simple. All transport had to be done by river steamer, which took longer, and as river steamers do not go beyond Rejaf, to get to Nimule meant a long march as well. Supervision of all landing grounds in the Southern Sudan was done by Flight Lieutenant Kinkead DSO, DSC, DFC. This officer left Cairo at the end of December 1925, though the Flight did not arrive in his section till 8 March 1926.

He was to sweat it out for more than four months.

Kink's party was formed in Cairo on 17 December. Its tasks were to establish the ground organisation needed throughout Southern Sudan, maintaining each airstrip until the return journey had used it, and winding it up when the expedition ended. To assist him, when setting out three days before Christmas 1925, he could call on the services of a sergeant and one other airman. They spent over a month travelling to Nimule: via Wadi Halfa and Khartoum, then more than 1,100 miles up the White Nile to Rejaf, and finally by car and on foot with native 'carriers'. The Northern Section Ground Party arrived at Nimule on the last day of January, eventually returning by a similar route. Their round trip covered 5,640 miles.

Kink's report explained how stores and aerodrome equipment had been sent from Aboukir to Khartoum by rail and river steamer, and fuel despatched from Suez to Khartoum via Port Sudan on the Red Sea. From the Sudanese capital, these supplies were conveyed to the landing grounds by boat, motor vehicle and native bearer. In his view, a serious mistake had been made in selecting the most southerly of his airstrips:

> Nimule Landing Ground is situated on cotton soil about 2 miles from Nimule village and is only serviceable for about four months in a year. The surface is fairly good in the dry season, but in the wet season the ground becomes more or less a swamp and covered with grass about 5 feet high. In order to keep this aerodrome serviceable, it would be necessary to clear

the ground at least once a month, and this would involve a considerable amount of labour and expense; and it would also be necessary to send an officer from Mongalla to supervise the clearing. Nimule is a Sleeping Sickness station, only 110 miles from Mongalla, with one European, a Syrian doctor, and is of no importance from a civil or military point of view.

In the event of a second Cape Flight, Jinja in Uganda should serve as a jumping-off place or as an emergency landing ground between Mongalla in the Sudan and Kisumu in Kenya. Indeed, Nimule was used only on the outward journey, Jinja being selected when the Flight returned. Kink was determined that no-one else need sample this particular spot:

I interviewed both the Governor, Mongalla Province, and the Officer Commanding the Equatorial Battalion, and they both agreed that Nimule was of no importance ... I strongly recommend that this landing ground be excluded from the list of permanent landing grounds in the Southern Sudan.

Nor could many other locations be relied upon:

it is essential before leaving Khartoum to take care there is nothing lacking, as anything forgotten cannot be purchased in the south. Good servants, with previous experience of the country to be covered, should be engaged in Khartoum ... Feeding is a difficult problem, especially in the Dinka country, vegetables are very scarce ... Sporting rifles are essential 'for the pot' ... Travelling is done by carrier and kit should be arranged in loads not exceeding 50lb, the recognised load of a carrier. A push bicycle will save many a long trek ... White ants destroy most things and care should be taken in protecting all equipment.

Given that the Cape Flight did not re-enter the Northern Section until 19 May, Kink's Ground Party had more than three months' sojourn in its most southerly region, and plenty of opportunity to savour the conditions and, especially, the climate. This alternated between heavy rains and thunderstorms for half the year, and heat and drought for the remainder. A detailed meteoro-logical study had been undertaken when planning the expedition, and had identified the period from March to July as by far the best option. With luck, the Flight would have crossed Uganda and the British East African colonies before the heaviest rains set in, while further south the worst of the rainy season should be over. On the return journey, the worst should also have passed in Uganda, while in the Southern Sudan during June it would not yet have developed fully. These predictions proved broadly accurate for the men in the air, but were of lesser value to the men on the ground. Kink laconically reported:

During January and February the grass is burnt and the heat is intense especially on the banks of the Nile, and these months are as a rule the hottest. This year the first rains fell towards the end of February and heavy

122

rains were frequent further south at Nimule during February and March. During the early months the rains usually approach from the East ... and later on they seem to approach from all directions, at times the same storm passing over twice. Rejaf, south of Mongalla, is known as a centre of earthquakes and slight tremors are felt every year. The maximum temperature experienced by the Ground Party was 42.8° [109°F] on 13 April 1926 and the minimum was 19.42°C [67°F] on 7 May 1926.

He felt it inadvisable for NCOs and aircraftmen to journey south of Khartoum unless 'fully equipped for the conditions prevailing in the South Sudan', and noted that NCOs of the Sudan Defence Force received the same allowances as officers when travelling in these regions, while being 'encouraged to put up a good show and to impress the natives in the interests of prestige'. The environment posed serious risks to health. Practically the whole course of the Nile was mosquito-infested, and strict precautions were vital to ward off malaria, water-borne diseases and sleeping sickness. Medicine chests should always be carried and generously employed: 'the natives look upon the white man as a "medicine man", and any little help is greatly appreciated and does no end of good'. Another challenge encountered was the problem of communicating between different landing grounds and aerodromes in Kenya, Uganda and the Sudan:

a great deal of anxiety was caused through not being able to get in direct touch with Kisumu [Kenya] from Mongalla [Sudan] during the homeward journey of the Flight ... The average time taken for a priority signal between Mongalla and Kisumu was ten hours, which is not much use considering that on three occasions Mongalla Aerodrome was unserviceable after only five hours' rain. One telegram sent from Kisumu to Mongalla via Nimule on 6 April was received on 17 June.

Within the Sudan, however, the telegraph system was satisfactory and the Government ran a bi-monthly steamer service from Khartoum to Rejaf, far to the south, calling at all destinations *en route*. Kink was pleased to utilise this service which took, on average, fifteen days upstream and ten days downstream. Naturally, the worst parts of his journey were overland whenever roads became unserviceable during the rains, or none existed at all. In such situations, all travelling had to be done with the aid of native carriers who could be hired via District Commissioners at a couple of days' notice:

Carriers are loaded up to 50lb, do an average of 20 miles a day, and should be changed every third day. Their rates of pay vary according to the Tribe ... and a sufficient quantity of small change should be carried for this purpose.

Kink and his companions covered 566 miles in this fashion.

In the context of a military report, Kink did not allow himself much descriptive licence. An exception was his journey on the White Nile, after leaving

Khartoum by steamer. For the first 150 miles, to Kosti, the river was 'immensely broad and ... practically no scenery exists'. After Kosti, the country was thickly wooded with the riverbanks covered in tropical vegetation as far south as Malakal. After bending westwards, the river reached the Sudd, where the landscape consisted of open prairie dotted with trees and large anthills:

> The Sudd is a large area of matted and rotting vegetation, about 400 miles in length and covered with papyrus ... up to a height of 20 feet. It is estimated that the Sudd covers an area of 40,000 square miles, a dreary and lifeless desolation.

Eventually the terrain changed character: it was 'undulating, thickly wooded and with many well-defined mountain ridges'. Through such forests and such landscape Kink and his team soldiered on, preparing all the landing grounds for the incoming aircraft.

★ ★ ★

To reconstruct the story of the Cape Flight, we can draw on two principal sources – the account given by Pulford to the Royal United Service Institution and the full Air Ministry report, eventually published in April 1927. These set out its five specific aims: to visit the Dominion of South Africa and the various British colonies *en route*; to gain experience in long-distance flying in formation, in accordance with a scheduled timetable, and so 'to test the regularity with which reinforcements can be despatched by air'; to gain experience in flying through changing climates and conditions, and over new country; to co-operate with local forces stationed near the route followed; and, finally, to visit the South African Air Force – now commanded by Sir Pierre van Ryneveld. There was no intention to break any records. According to the official report, the expedition was 'purely a Service flight carried out in the ordinary course of Royal Air Force training'. Yet, the intensive planning, the scale of the enterprise, and the final choice of pilots and machines belied this modest claim.

In the first place, quite detailed plans had been initially drawn up for ordinary Ninak bombers to undertake the flight. These had been used successfully for the Egypt to Nigeria project. Yet, this time, twenty-four different landing grounds were involved, several of which were at high altitudes. Experiments were conducted 'to find out the estimated length of run before take-off, in various densities and winds, of a DH9A', loaded as it would be for a flight. As the results were 'rather disquieting', in mid-October 1925 the decision had been made to use instead the Fairey IIID, fitted with Napier Lion Series V engines:

> This type had recently done very well in Singapore. They had a quicker take-off than the 9A, a fair turn of speed, came to rest after landing very quickly, and had an exceedingly strong undercarriage. The Lion V engine ... had proved most reliable.

Secondly, it had originally been intended to select the aircrews from a single Squadron; but, given the narrow window of opportunity identified by the meteorologists, it was necessary to obtain pilots with appropriate experience of this machine:

> The Fairey IIID is an aeroplane designed for naval co-operation, but to obtain pilots from the Fleet Air Arm was quite impossible. Luckily, there were three pilots who had become surplus to requirements and these were posted to the Flight.

The Cape Flight came into existence at Northolt Aerodrome, west of London, on 6 November 1925 – though some personnel were still joining as late as 1 December. There were three pilots in addition to Pulford: Flight Lieutenant P.H. Mackworth DFC, Flight Lieutenant E.J. Linton Hope AFC and Flying Officer W.L. Payne. In charge of navigation was Flight Lieutenant L.E.M. Gillman, with Flying Officer A.A. Jones and Sergeants Hartley and Gardiner maintaining the aircraft and their engines. Making up the Ground Parties were Kink, his sergeant fitter and AC1 rigger, already based in Cairo, as well as two more Flight Lieutenants and half-a-dozen 'other ranks', responsible for the Central and Southern Sections of the route.

Similar care was taken with the choice of machines. Northolt Aerodrome had been selected for its proximity to the Fairey Aviation Company works, where the aircraft to be used were still being built. While these modified versions were under construction, others were made available for practice and experiments. Soon it was found that the cruising speed would be 80–83mph and the rate of petrol consumption 20.5 gallons per hour. The round trip was divided into thirty-nine stages involving more than forty flights – the longest of which was some 350 miles. Simple mathematics showed the normal petrol tank on a Fairey IIID to be inadequate, so an extra tank was incorporated in place of the middle seat of the aircraft. Wireless was dispensed with, to save weight and because it was unlikely to be of help, and extra-thick treaded tyres were fitted in an attempt to reduce the risk of punctures.

Pulford insisted that the machines must not be overloaded, especially given the altitude of so many landing grounds. In his RUSI lecture, he spelt out the problem:

> After taking into account the various alterations and additions made to the machine, we found that we had 350lb to play with; 350lb may seem a lot, but when we came to fit things in it seemed very little. Weight mounted up in an incredible way, and we had literally to consider the utility of every-thing purely and simply from how much it weighed. There was certain equipment, such as maps, tools, spare wires, wheel chocks . . . emergency rations, medical outfit, rifles and ammunition, which all machines had to carry, but the heavier items had to be split up amongst the four machines . . . Two machines carried a spare propeller and two a spare wheel, whilst the machines which did not carry spare magnetos carried a tail skid or

jack. Our aim was to get all machines to weigh exactly the same if possible, thus ensuring the same strain being thrown on all four engines.

He decided to limit the overall weight to 5,050lb, the ordinary Service load. Ballast weights in the nose of the aircraft were dispensed with, but compensated for by equipment stowed as far forward as possible. Even the 'screw pickets', to peg down the aircraft on the ground, were specially manufactured in duralumin to save weight. Each aeroplane carried a .303 rifle and fifty rounds of ammunition, as well as twelve days' emergency rations for the crew of two if they had to make a forced landing. Although the question of rations was carefully considered, it was obvious that the weight of those normally issued would be prohibitive. In June 1924, George Mallory and Andrew Irvine had perished attempting to climb the world's highest mountain; but Pulford felt compelled to follow the precedent of their Everest expedition:

we decided that our rations should be similar to theirs. It may be that a ration which was good for individuals working in an altitude of over 20,000 feet in extreme cold would not have been at all suitable for men in a hot climate; however, we didn't worry our heads very much about that, and as we had no forced landings, I am unable to give an opinion on their suitability.

The amount of kit for each individual was limited to 32lb, including the weight of a hammock, a groundsheet and a sleeping bag, plus a change of uniform and two or three changes of underclothing. Even normal maps could not be taken, for reasons of weight and space. For the first time, the pilots and Flight navigator found themselves using maps with a scale of 32 miles to the inch, rather than the customary 4 miles to the inch.

Before we started, none of us had ever flown on such a small scale, but when we came to use them we found the maps very accurate and easy to fly by. The total weight of maps carried by each machine came to 9lb. Each stage had its own map pasted on a piece of mill board, on the back of which was pasted a large-scale map of the vicinity of the landing ground at which the Flight was to land.

During the first week of December, the new aeroplanes were completed and tested. They were then despatched by road to the packing depot at Ascot, which constructed extra-large cases so that the middle sections could be sent with their undercarriages in place, in order to save time at Aboukir where they would have to be reassembled:

The intention had been to send four aeroplanes and most of the stores by a ship sailing on 14 December; however, owing to the abnormal size of the aeroplane cases, the ship could only take one.

The remainder left for Alexandria on 28 December where they were off-loaded on 25 January and, 'except for carrying away most of the overhead electric light cables and thus fusing all the lights in a street in Alexandria', were transported by road to Aboukir without incident. The first aeroplane was tested on 29 January, the remainder at daily intervals. There was still a good deal of work to be done on the aeroplanes before they could be considered ready for the flight, and a variety of minor adaptations were carried out, as well as engine tests and weight checks. Fully loaded, the four aircraft were found to weigh between 5,098lb and 5,121lb. This illustrates the high degree of accuracy with which the loads had been calculated and distributed – especially as some different items were being carried in each. The engines were run for approximately six hours, care being taken to ensure that there was parity between them all. Instruments were calibrated and the crew exercised to a peak of fitness:

> We used to run a mile or two every evening after we had finished work. The result of our training was that we started the flight in as fit a condition as any of us had ever been, and though, as events proved, we had no hardships to endure, I think our training repaid us, for none of us fell sick during the flight and nobody felt any undue fatigue at any time.

On 25 February, the Flight moved to Heliopolis and made ready to set off at 7.00am on Monday, 1 March – instead of 8 March, as originally planned. Reports from the Sudan had warned that heavy rains would make the landing ground at Mongalla unusable by the last week in May. It was therefore decided to begin the expedition a week earlier and to return to Cairo by 28 May instead of 14 June. In fact, the schedule was compressed by a further twenty-four hours, once it appeared that a return trip from Egypt to the United Kingdom would be added to the plan. It would take Pulford's aeroplane 140 hours 55 minutes' actual flying time to travel to the Cape and back – 68 hours 21 minutes on the outward flight and 72 hours 34 minutes on the return. Apart from replacing one magneto, two propellers and all the oil tanks – which showed a tendency to split – no significant repairs were needed. After the first two or three days, a routine had been established and little thought was given to the prospect of forced landings. The four aircraft flew in a V formation, 500 yards apart. If one was forced to land, the plan was for a second one to descend and assist if possible, while the remaining two circled overhead. If this could not be done, all three remaining machines would head for the nearest landing ground to seek help. Fortunately, the situation never arose. Pulford attributed this reliability to the aircraft not being overloaded, which meant that they could cruise with the engines throttled down: 'A Napier Lion running at these revolutions runs like a clock and will seldom give trouble.' The other key factor was careful inspection and detection of any faults caused by vibration after every segment of the flight. On arrival at each landing ground, the pilots would refuel their own aircraft while the technical officer and the fitter checked the engines and the rigger inspected the wires.

The Flight always taxied in after landing with the RAF ensigns flying. They were not flown in flight as they wore out quickly. This procedure was

127

always strictly adhered to for the benefit of the native population and also to show others that they were a Service Flight. As soon as the engines were stopped the personal gear was taken out ... covers were put on and air intake plugs were put in. The aeroplanes were then lashed down to four screw pickets (one to each wingtip, one to the airscrew and one to the tail), and the controls secured for the night. Routine aeroplane and engine inspection and refuelling were then carried out. The time taken varied, but three hours' work was generally necessary before everything was done.

For take-off about forty-five minutes would be required, the Commanding Officer always being last to leave. They would assume cruising formation immediately, unless there was a Governor present to be honoured with a fly-past and dipped-wing salute.

Communications were a problem, Pulford later explained, especially in parts of Southern Sudan, Tanganyika, Uganda and Northern Rhodesia:

telegraphic messages had in certain places to go a very long way round before they reached their destination ... On the homeward flight a wire was sent to Abercorn from Pretoria fourteen days before we were due to land there, but we found on arrival that the message had arrived only five minutes before we did. The wires were down and the message had had to be brought over 100 miles by a runner ... In Egypt and Northern Sudan, and from N'dola southwards, however, the communications are very good ... On the outward trip we had, on the whole, extremely good weather. We struck a sandstorm at Khartoum which made the visibility very low ... [This] persisted until 100 miles south of Nimule, a distance of about 1,100 miles. The rainy season had started in Kenya by the time we arrived and was ceasing in Tanganyika when we passed through on the way south. We experienced a good deal of rain when on the ground, but in the air we managed to dodge any rainstorms that we saw. These storms are very sharply defined and can nearly always be avoided. The visibility in the Central and Southern sections of the flight was extreme. The fact that we were able to see the spray of the Victoria Falls when over 70 miles away from them illustrates how wonderfully clear the air was on this part of the route.

The weather on the return flight was good until the rainy season was again encountered near Lake Victoria:

We ran first into clouds which stretched from the ground to about 16,000 feet, and after we had cleared them, into a series of heavy rainstorms. The Flight split up and each machine found its own way to Kisumu ... we narrowly missed hitting the tops of trees and the sides of hills ... our petrol was running short ... [and] the emergency petrol specially carried for such an occasion in tins in the rear seat could not be pumped into the tanks as the pump had jammed. However, we landed all right.

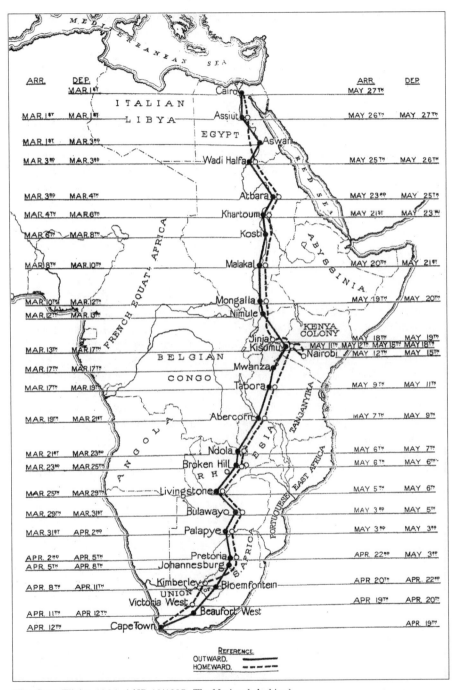

The Cape Flight, 1926. (*AIR 10/1297, The National Archives*)

129

Sandstorms could spring up very quickly and generally appeared to occur at sunset.

Africa, to the average person, is generally associated with heat, and since none of us had ever been out there we expected to find it extremely hot. We imagined that the Equator would be the hottest part of all, but we were pleasantly surprised. Egypt and the Sudan lived up to expectations, for it was 105 degrees in the shade at Khartoum on 5 March and 115 degrees when we landed there again in May. Mongalla and Malakal were also very hot and sticky ... Though it was warm from an English standpoint at the remainder of the places we landed at, it was never uncomfortable. It was quite cold at Cape Town. Landing in the Sudan was an experience which to me never lost its novelty. At 6,000 feet it was cool, at 2,000 feet one began to feel warm, whilst on landing the blast of hot air on one's face felt as if a furnace door had been left open ... We used to fly in khaki slacks or jodhpurs and woollen bush shirts. These we found were neither too hot on the ground nor too cool in the air.

In his address to the RUSI, Pulford included a useful descriptive passage:

In Egypt the main impression received was that of a sluggish river flowing between a narrow strip of vegetation which grew narrower as we flew south. On both sides of the river the desert stretched as far as the eye could reach. After Luxor this strip of vegetation practically ceased altogether. The Northern Sudan appeared from the air to be a wilderness of sand with numerous black and rocky hills dotted about. 200 miles south of Khartoum the desert gave way to scrub, and from there southwards the vegetation increased. The country then alternated between sparse bush, thick bush and flat open plains ... The country rose ... until the Central African Plateau was reached at Kisumu ... Except for the mountainous district between Beaufort West and Cape Town, when forced landing would have been difficult, the country we flew over in the Union of South Africa was, from a flying point of view, one of the best in the world. We could, if necessary, have landed practically anywhere.

The Flight always sought to take off before the sun was well up, in order to obtain the assistance of greater air density. Navigation was 'practically entirely by compass ... Our greatest error in position on any flight was 12 miles in a distance of 350' – but even this was because of course alterations to avoid rainstorms barring the way. The navigation officer, Flight Lieutenant Gillman, was given credit for his accuracy as were the maps for theirs. Compasses were routinely recalibrated at various points en route. Height was adjusted to keep radiator temperatures at 70°C and oil temperatures below 60°C. This involved flying at 6,000–7,000 feet over Upper Egypt and the Sudan, but elsewhere at an average height of 3,000–4,000 feet except where mountains – such as those on the way to Cape Town and Nairobi – required altitudes as great as 11,000 feet.

Efforts were made to reduce the discomfort of long-distance flying in open cockpits. Except in cold air over Cape Town, where Sidcot suits had to be worn, the woollen bush shirts and khaki slacks or jodhpurs proved to be adequate: 'The majority of the Flight wore tropical flying helmets ... and found them excellent', as were anti-glare goggles for use on the ground. To guard against deafness, each member of the Flight was issued with a pair of ear-defenders 'such as are used for gunfire'. Ear-plugs of cotton wool offered negligible protection. Conditions were at their worst in Kink's Northern Section, as was quickly discovered on arrival at Khartoum:

The blast of hot air on landing felt as if an oven door had been left open. It was learnt afterwards that it was 105 degrees in the shade ... Viewed from above, the difference in colour between the Blue and White Nile is most marked. From the air the difficulties of defence that General Gordon must have been faced with during the siege of Khartoum spring to the eye at once. The Flight remained at Khartoum from 4 to 6 March ... The Commanding Officer called on the Governor of Khartoum and the OC British Troops. He regarded the landing at any place as being somewhat similar to the visit of a Squadron of ships to a port ... [and] wherever necessary, he always reported his arrival officially to the local authorities.

On the second night a sandstorm struck at sunset and was 'very unpleasant'. This did not prevent the aircraft getting away the following morning, but the resultant poor visibility – often under a mile – forced them to navigate by following the river to Kosti. The whole village turned out to see them land and, as the visibility had grown worse rather than better, it was decided to stay the night: 'During the stay at Kosti the officers slept at various bungalows, the sergeants slinging their hammocks by the aeroplanes.' These distinctions were maintained throughout the expedition, although usually the NCOs were offered a roof over their heads. It took two attempts to reach Malakal, the headquarters of the White Nile Province on the eastern bank of the river. There, the official report made the first of several admiring comments about the native population. Referring to the local Shilluk tribe, it stated: 'They are a fine tall race, their average height being over 6 feet ... Whilst at Malakal the Shilluks, armed with spears and shields, gave a war dance in honour of the Flight; about 200 of them took part.' A version of the report sent to newspapers in the Dominions added that the Shilluks 'are born actors and their sense of rhythm wonderful'. Later, at Nimule, the flyers were approached by the Chief of the village who came up and saluted:

though no-one could understand what he said, it was easy to discern what he meant. Apparently he remembered the visit to Nimule of a twin-engine aeroplane, for he gave in pantomime a very good description of her landing and taking off. This aeroplane must have been the *Silver Queen.*

Another positive experience occurred in Tanganyika, where flights were given to the Governor and to the Commanding Officer of the 2nd Battalion of the King's African Rifles.

> Before leaving Heliopolis the War Office had asked if the Cape Flight could bring back some information as to the degree of visibility of troops from the air in East Africa. Whether they did so or not was left entirely to the discretion of the Commanding Officer.

Pulford arranged to do this with the 2nd Battalion KAR on 18 March:

> It can be stated ... that once troops get into bush or elephant grass it is practically impossible to detect them unless flying low. The sun glinting on accoutrements might give them away, but this could be got over by dulling everything which shines.

He took up both the Governor and the OC 2nd Battalion – the latter confessing that he could see nothing once the troops moved away from the roads. During this flight, the soldier's borrowed goggles blew off and fell in thick bush, which meant that one of the aircrew would have to manage without a pair. However, Pulford reported:

> Early next morning, about two minutes before taking off, a native was seen running fast across the ground towards us. On reaching us he handed me the goggles quite undamaged and then walked away. Where or how he had found them I never discovered, but the incident bears witness to the honesty of the average native.

He also noted that the 2nd Battalion KAR, who accommodated the Flight at their mess

> are recruited largely from amongst the Angoni and Yao tribes in Nyasaland. They are an extremely fine and fearless-looking lot of men. They wear a black fez, blue jersey, shorts and blue puttees without boots. Practically every man wears at least two medals.

Only after leaving the Northern Section had conditions suddenly improved. From Malakal to Mongalla, a distance of 350 miles, visibility remained poor: 'All were heartily tired of the constant murkiness, as they could see very little of the country, and sitting for nearly four hours with nothing to do beyond steering a compass course became very monotonous.' Another 124 miles brought them to Nimule, a village of some thirty native huts on the eastern bank of the Nile. Here Kink was waiting to meet them, with a large crowd of natives, when they landed ten minutes before noon. Also present was Squadron Leader Coningham who was on his way back to Cairo after attending a conference of Governors at Nairobi. The official report throws further light on this unhealthy location – where the Flight had an unscheduled overnight stay to avoid 'a race against daylight' on the way to Kisumu:

132

There is a small rest-house in the village which contains two rooms. The Flight put up there for the night. The officers slept in their hammocks for the first time, and they proved very comfortable. All hammocks were provided with mosquito-netting which covered the hammock like a bag. The occupant, after getting into his hammock, could make it mosquito-proof by pulling taut the draw-string of the mouth of the bag. They found that to get into a hammock when it was pitch dark with the hammock swaying violently, and then to pull the draw-string tight before the mosquitoes could get in, was a task which required considerable agility and unlimited patience.

One can see why they were happy to be on their way – a feeling compounded when, after ninety minutes in the air,

> they appeared to break through the pall in which they had been enveloped ever since leaving Khartoum. The contrast in visibility was extraordinary, for inside ten minutes a visibility of about 1 mile increased to one of about 50 miles . . . It is an interesting fact that the visibility was so bad for so great a distance (over 1,200 miles).

Such conditions were most unusual and no explanation of the cause was ever forthcoming. Their passage to Kenya was uneventful and the landing ground at Kisumu – 'perfect and one of the best in Africa' – hosted a large, welcoming crowd including Flight Lieutenant Emmett MC DFC, the head of the Ground Party in the Central Section:

> It was at Kisumu that the personnel first experienced that overwhelming hospitality which they were to meet for the rest of the flight. Everybody was bent on entertaining them as much as possible . . . Whilst at Kisumu the Air Ministry was cabled for permission to prepare Jinja landing ground for use on the return flight, as Nimule would probably be unserviceable owing to rain. The submission was approved.

The pattern of hospitality was consistent. In N'dola, Northern Rhodesia, a 'large dance' was held in their honour and they were given a guided tour of the Bwana Mkuba Copper Mine. At the next stop, Broken Hill: 'two dances were given in honour of the Flight'. When the Flight reached Pretoria, on the way out and on the way back, their programme was 'filled with entertainments. Lunches, dances, dinners and visits to places of interest were arranged, and all were given an extraordinary time.'

In terms of goodwill, the expedition was a triumph:

> Large crowds used to meet us whenever we landed, and everybody we met seemed very pleased to see a Service Flight on its way through Africa. We received boundless hospitality wherever we landed. The dinners and dances to which we were invited were legion; in fact I may say that we found it very much more tiring on the ground than in the air.

133

As for the indigenous peoples:

The native population in Kenya, Tanganyika and Northern Rhodesia regarded us with amazement not unmixed with awe. They gave us all kinds of names ... [some] declared the gods were coming ... What appeared to impress the natives most was the speed at which we covered distances, which to them represented weeks and even months of travel.

Sometimes they were over-enthusiastic: at Palapwe Road, a small trading station in Bechuanaland, the young Regent of the Protectorate – 'who spoke excellent English' – requested the Flight to pass over the capital, Serowe, a large native town of 20,000 inhabitants some 30 miles away:

This was done the next day (1 April) ... The Flight did not stop long over Serowe, for the noise of the engines had stampeded all the cattle and donkeys. They could see them charging up and down the roads at full speed. The Commanding Officer thought it best in the interest of Serowe to cut short the demonstration and return. On landing at Palapwe the natives would not believe that they had been there and back in an hour, a journey that would take them two days.

From the point of view of the airmen too, it was an unforgettable experience to see, within the space of a few short weeks, such world-famous landmarks as the Pyramids, the Aswan Dam, the source of the Nile at Jinja, the game reserves in Kenya, the Victoria Falls, the diamond mines of Pretoria and Kimberley, and Table Mountain 'with the blue Atlantic stretching far beyond it'.

Of the five tasks entrusted to the Cape Flight, the journey south had already accomplished four: a succession of Colonies had been visited, military co-operation with local Forces carried out, experience gained in long-distance flying in formation to a tight schedule, and difficult country and climates surmounted. What remained was the visit to the South African military, and they were duly met at Pretoria by General Brink, Chief of the General Staff, and Sir Pierre van Ryneveld, the head of the Air Force, whose own Cairo–Cape flight had been so much more arduous. After lunch, the first task was a detailed examination of the Fairey IIIDs, which had been out in the open for more than a month. Apart from needing a few minor adjustments, the aircraft were in perfect order, including the fabric which was found to be 'in excellent condition'.

There followed a visit to Swartkop Aerodrome, south-west of the town centre. Here the South African Air Force was based in countryside 'very much like that of the Central Flying School'. The SAAF was tiny – the headquarters staff consisting of just three officers overseeing a single Flying Squadron, Training Flight and aircraft depot. Half of the Force's fifty-two aeroplanes were stored in reserve. All of them had been donated by the British in 1919, when the RAF was decimated after the Armistice. They included DH4s,

DH9s and SE5 fighters. Of about twenty officers in the SAAF, all but one were pilots:

> Nobody below the rank of Major has a permanent commission, and as there are only two of them, the total permanent establishment of officers is only five. All the remainder serve on a short service basis. Captains can serve till they are 35 and lieutenants till they are 30 years of age. At present all pilots are either ex-RFC, RNAS or RAF, but eight cadets are under training to replace those who will shortly be going to the Reserve.

The entire Force was concentrated at Pretoria, but landing grounds had been laid down throughout South Africa, 'so that machines can reach the most distant point in a day'. The SAAF impressed everyone with their keenness and efficiency. Their formation flying was excellent and, on the return visit to Pretoria, the Flying Squadron carried out live bombing and machine-gun practice from the air. Twenty aeroplanes took part and the bombing was 'astonishing in its accuracy', the first salvos landing all around the target and the second destroying it completely.

It was at Bloemfontein that the only serious mechanical problem was discovered. Half an hour before landing, one of the aircraft – S1102 – began losing oil, and subsequent examination revealed that the tank was badly split. Though a replacement was soon fitted, the same thing happened on 12 March as the Flight climbed to 11,000 feet to cross the Drakensberg Mountains *en route* to Cape Town:

> the Commanding Officer saw 1102 climbing vigorously, and finally lost her above him at about 16,000 feet. On taking up close formation . . . there was no sign of 1102; however, the ground underneath looked good for a forced landing. As they passed Wynberg Aerodrome, 1105 signalled that 1102 had landed, so the formation went on to fly over Cape Town before landing. The view that burst upon them as they rounded Table Mountain was superb. They then returned to Wynberg and landed at 13.07 hours in the presence of a very large crowd. They were met by the Minister of Defence, the Chief of the General Staff, and the Mayors of Wynberg and Cape Town.

When the crews were reunited, it was discovered that all the oil tanks needed replacement – the reason for S1102's rapid ascent having been to gain enough time to select a landing site if the engine seized. Fortunately, the problem was solved when sturdier replacement tanks were manufactured and fitted during the RAF's week-long stay in Cape Town. During this time, Pulford and his team were guests of honour at lunches hosted by the Mayor at City Hall, the Minister of Defence at the House of Representatives and the Governor-General at his residence. Yet again, they found themselves invited to dances and dinners every night.

The return to Cairo was, for the most part, a mirror-image of the outward flight; but there were several difficult and dangerous moments. At some

80 miles south of Kisumu, they ran into a series of blinding rainstorms, and when not battling these they encountered low cloud, sometimes to ground level: 'collisions with the sides of hills and the tops of trees were narrowly averted. On arrival at Kisumu it was found that the fabric on the airscrews of 1102, 1104 and 1105 had in places begun to strip.' The next stop was the Kenyan capital:

> An enormous crowd had assembled, as these were the first aeroplanes that had ever visited Nairobi. They were welcomed officially by the Acting Governor, H.E. the Governor being away ... The Flight were received with open arms by everybody and given a very good time during the stay. All managed to get some shooting.

When the time came to depart, after three days of steady rain, columns of spray rose as each aircraft took off. When they next landed, it was found that 'a snake which had crept in and twined itself round the spokes of the leader's port wheel while at Nairobi, was still there'. The Cape Flight was now re-entering Kink's Northern Section and, true to form, the weather did its worst. At least Nimule was omitted; but, at Mongalla:

> There had been rain two days previously and the landing ground was very soft in places. 1104 was bogged taxiing in, and again when taking off the next morning. The other aeroplanes were lucky not to get bogged as well, for the tracks of 1104 were only 3 feet to the left of the track followed by the remainder. Flight Lieutenant Kinkead proved of great service here.

The round-trip from Cairo was almost at an end, but extreme conditions in the Northern Section persisted. It was 115°F in the shade at Khartoum where the Flight stayed from 23 to 25 May, before struggling from Atbara to Wadi Halfa through the murk and gloom resulting from a heavy sandstorm. On the penultimate stage, some of the trickiest problems arose. The Flight had to turn back to Aswan after twenty-five minutes, when two aircraft experienced falling oil pressure, and it also became necessary to change the propeller of a third. The official report chronicled Pulford's frustration:

> On landing the second time, there was nobody at the aerodrome and we could not open the petrol store. As there was a strong headwind, it was essential to put in the amount of petrol used up on the abortive flight. After having waited for nearly three hours for someone to arrive, I gave orders for the door to be broken down. This could not be done, and we only succeeded in breaking the lock. Finally, in desperation, I bought 32 gals of MT spirit in the Aswan bazaar, and had that put into the tanks ... Over Sohag it looked as if another sandstorm was coming on, and, although we were at 7,000 feet, it was extremely bumpy. 1105 was thrown about to such an extent that a flying wire parted. Later we found that we had passed over a small sandstorm. All the aeroplanes nearly crashed on

landing at Assiut through striking ridges which were not marked and could not be seen from the air.

At 6.05am on 27 May, the Flight left Assiut for Heliopolis. As the four aircraft approached, escorts took station on either quarter: 'They were back again, having seen more of Africa in three months than most men see in a lifetime'; but they already knew that their work was far from finished. Even before the expedition began, it was hoped that the aircraft would be capable of flying home to England after conversion to seaplanes in Egypt. At Cape Town, these orders were received and a route and provisional timetable were supplied to Pulford. This involved stops at such destinations as Crete, Athens, Corfu, Brindisi, Naples, Berre (near Marseilles) and Brest, *en route* to Lee-on-Solent. Two days after arriving at Heliopolis the Cape Flight flew to Aboukir where each aircraft was thoroughly overhauled and cleaned, and new propellers – suitably sheathed for floatplane work – were fitted.

The Fairey Aviation Company had sent out their float expert to assist in the task of changing the undercarriages, fitting tail and wing-tip floats and making other relevant adjustments. Although each aircraft was now some 200lb heavier:

> The lift exerted by the floats was such that, in spite of this extra weight, lower revolutions were required to maintain height when cruising than on the land flight.

The aircraft, with their wings folded, were taken on trolleys to the beach at Aboukir Bay for thorough testing, and practice flights showed that they were 'much easier to land as floatplanes than as landplanes'. The Flight set off at 10.15am on 9 June and finished on time at Lee-on-Solent at 1.02pm on 21 June. Over the sea the height was generally about 1,000 feet. Their course was set by compass, Pulford reporting that: 'Flight Lieutenant Gillman deserves great credit for his navigation on the flight between Brest and Lee. We were in fog from the time we left Ushant until we sighted the Needles dead ahead.'

At all stops *en route* the floatplanes were beached or brought up slipways, if possible. Otherwise, the floats had to be pumped out prior to take-off:

> The flight home was much more tiring when compared with the flight to the Cape. The actual flying was the same, but the work on the ground was more strenuous. Aircraft had to be hauled up slipways or else beached. Floats had to be pumped out continually. After a rough take-off, the engine installation had to be very carefully gone over. When lying at buoys for the night, there was the constant fear that a float might have been damaged when landing and had filled up with water.

Pulford had been given £150 for travelling expenses before leaving Aboukir. This proved more than enough. Greek, Italian and French pilots all seemed very interested in the Flight and impressed by its punctuality, the reliability of its machines and the quality of its formation flying. Each Fairey IIID spent more than forty additional hours in the air, but no significant repairs were needed apart from one change of propeller. Efficient ground organisation and help from the Greek, Italian and French authorities made it possible to keep to the timetable at every point bar one.

One hazard occurred between Brindisi and Naples. Pulford was crossing the mountains of Calabria when his aircraft plunged, without warning, from 8,000 to 6,800 feet. Another was the Channel crossing from Brest on the last day. It had to be done at 50 feet, in 'the thickest of thick fogs'.

Among the waiting spectators was a correspondent from *Flight* magazine, who described the 'dismay' when only three of the four Cape Flight aircraft hove in sight at 12.45pm on 21 June. Flying Officer Payne had become sep-arated from the others, and great was the relief when he came out of the mist and managed to land, just a few minutes later:

> The formation flying of Pulford, Mackworth and Hope was very fine as they passed over the sheds at Lee ... All alighted simultaneously in the Solent. The taxiing up in line abreast was a very pretty sight. The Wing Commander was the first to come ashore, on the back of a wading airman. Clad in a tropical tunic, which looked as if it might once have been either white or light blue, with badges of rank on the shoulder straps, khaki shorts and stockings, he was tanned to a coppery hue, and looked a picture of physical fitness. All his seven companions looked equally well. They drew up on the beach, and Air Vice-Marshals Sir Geoffrey Salmond and Sir Ivo Vesey shook hands with each officer and airman, and Sir Geoffrey, in the name of the RAF and the Air Council, thanked them all for 'the splendid success of their enterprise'.

The magazine stressed that the Flight was 'unique in many ways' and that the airmen and the Ground Parties had performed a service not only to the Royal Air Force but also to the British Empire. There had been 'no other instance on record of a formation of four aeroplanes flying over 14,000 miles, across two continents, from the Northern temperate zone to the Southern temperate zone and back without change of personnel, of aircraft or of engines'. Kink, Flight Lieutenant Emmett, and Flight Lieutenant W.E. Reason, in charge of the Southern Section, had 'shown themselves to be possessed of exceptional organising abilities'. Altogether, the Cape Flight had been 'a triumph of British organisation and achievement'.

The Secretary of State for Air took exactly the same view in a telegram to Pulford:

> I heartily congratulate you and the personnel of the Cape Flight under your command on their arrival in this country. The successful accom-plishment of this flight of 14,000 miles over land and sea without a hitch by four Service machines is a most creditable achievement and the regularity with which you have been able throughout to adhere to your

timetable is striking testimony of the high standard of training of the Royal Air Force and the reliability of the Fairey machines and Napier engines employed. There could be no more convincing demonstration of the assured future of aviation as a mobile and economical instrument of Imperial Defence and as a reliable means of speeding up communications between this country and the Dominions.

Kink's contribution had involved much background labour in conditions of maximum hardship and discomfort. He returned to Cairo, resumed his Staff duties and wrote up his report. At the end of September, he was posted home, embarking on the SS *Mooltan* from Port Said and arriving at Tilbury on 9 October 1926. After graduating from the 22nd Flying Instructors' Course at the Central Flying School on 24 March 1927 – 'Category A1· Excellent flying instructor and pilot' – Kink was sent to 5 Flying Training School. There he remained until 29 June when, after six months' manoeuvring by Leonard Slatter, he was finally recruited to the Marine Aircraft Experimental Establishment at Felixstowe. Like the pilots of the Cape Flight, he made the transition from landplanes to seaplanes. In doing so, he moved from virtual anonymity to the centre of the stage.

Chapter Seven

High Speed Flight – The Whitehall View

The Cairo to the Cape expedition was a way of asserting British prestige in the air with a minimum of controversy: not so the parallel issues of high speed flight and international air racing. Here the choices were much harder, with the final decisions emerging only after intense internal debate. Following the crash of the S4 at Baltimore, a review was carried out by Sir Geoffrey Salmond, the Air Member for Supply and Research, who was convinced of the value and the necessity of competing for the Schneider Trophy. This contest was conceived by Jacques Schneider, prior to the Great War, as an equivalent event for sea-planes to the annual James Gordon Bennett race for landplanes. Schneider, the son of the owner of a French armaments factory, trained as a mining engineer, then qualified as a balloon pilot in 1911 and broke the French altitude record, two years later, with a height of 10,081 metres. Often referred to as a Cup – which it was not – the Trophy, donated on 5 December 1912 when Schneider was just 33, was a silver and bronze sculpture on a large, dark-veined marble base. It was valued at the princely sum of £1,000 and depicted 'a nude winged figure representing speed ... kissing a Zephyr recumbent on a breaking wave'.

Although its donor died impoverished in obscurity in May 1928, his prize became the symbol of a quest for aerial supremacy between France, the USA, Italy and the United Kingdom. Its full title was *La Coupe d'Aviation Maritime Jacques Schneider* and, in order to carry it off permanently, a country had to win the race three times within five years. Initially an annual contest, it took place over the open sea for a distance of at least 150 nautical miles, with each country able to enter a maximum of three aircraft. These were stringently tested for seaworthiness just before the race. Competitors had to be sponsored by a society affiliated to the Fédération Aéronautique Internationale (FAI) – which, in the case of the United Kingdom, was the Royal Aero Club.

The first Schneider Trophy contest was held at Monaco on 16 April 1913 and consisted of twenty-eight laps totalling almost 174 miles. It was won by a Frenchman, Maurice Prévost, at an average speed of 45.75mph. Five of the other six contestants were also French, the exception being an American. A year later, the winning speed rose to 86.78mph, when Britain's Howard Pixton won in a Sopwith Schneider seaplane; but the return match had to wait until September 1919, at Bournemouth, where the only competitor to complete the course – an Italian – was ruled to have done so incorrectly. Italy was, nevertheless, chosen to host the fourth Schneider race, which took place at Venice in September 1920 and was won by the sole competitor not to withdraw – an Italian – at an average speed of 107.22mph. This rose in turn to 117.9mph, again at Venice, in August 1921; to 145.7mph at Naples in August 1922 – a British victory by Henri Biard in Mitchell's Supermarine Sea Lion II; and to 177.38mph at Cowes in September 1923. That American success took the contest to Baltimore in October 1925, where Mitchell's record-breaking S4 crashed during trials and US Army Lieutenant James Doolittle's Curtiss R3C-2 beat Hubert Broad's Gloster IIIA by 232.57mph to 199.17mph. It was this wide margin which had so upset the Aeronautical Correspondent of *The Times* when he recommended that the British should concentrate on 'some other attribute' of aerial record-breaking, given the speed supremacy established by the Americans. It also led to a degree of soul-searching within the Royal Air Force.

Geoffrey Salmond reported his findings to Sir Hugh Trenchard, Chief of Air Staff, on 27 November 1925. He was sure that the S4 could have attained an average speed of 215mph, which was 'close enough to American design in high speed aircraft that we can have confidence in producing an aircraft of sufficient speed to win the race'. Yet, this would not happen unless the RAF decided to enter a team of its own, rather than simply supporting civilian contestants:

> However good our material may be, all efforts in this direction will be wasted unless the pilots, personnel and ground organisation is of the highest efficiency. In this connection it is to be remembered that we have to compete with the United States Air Service . . . Since the pilot question is equally as important as the machine and ground personnel, I suggest that certain pilots of suitable physique and capacity should be specially selected . . . I am taking steps to order three high speed machines from the Supermarine Company, Gloucestershire Aircraft Company and Messrs Parnall, requiring a specified performance of 260mph for delivery by 1 July next year . . . In addition, I am proposing that, should any aircraft firm build a machine to beat 260mph, we will be prepared to purchase it.

Supermarine was not the only aircraft company still in the racing seaplane business. Hubert Broad's machine at Baltimore, which gained him his second place at an average speed of nearly 200mph, had been N194 – a Gloster III powered by a 700hp Napier Lion engine. Salmond decided to make two of these seaplanes available to train the specially chosen pilots for the proposed RAF team. Initially, they would also have the use of a third Gloster machine, with a curious name and a distinguished history: the Bamel. These three aircraft had a pedigree comparable to those created by Mitchell, for they sprang from the mind of a first-class designer of similar experience and calibre.

The Gloucestershire Aircraft Company had been formed in June 1917 by a merger between the Aircraft Manufacturing Company, on the outskirts of London, and H.H. Martyn & Co. of Cheltenham. By the spring of 1918, it was constructing up to forty-four aircraft per week. The period of rapid expansion came to a shuddering halt with the Armistice, but the firm did at least manage to keep going. The same could not be said for the Nieuport and General Aircraft Company at Cricklewood, whose chief designer, H.P. Folland, began working for Glosters in 1921 after its demise. A devotee of the biplane, Harry Folland was an extremely successful designer of military aircraft, including the SE5 and the SE5A 'reckoned to be the finest single-seat fighters of the 1914–18 war'. He established his reputation at Farnborough between 1912 and 1917, when he transferred to the Nieuport Company. It was Folland who designed the Gloster Mars I – conceived and built in less than a month – and nicknamed the Bamel, because it resembled a cross between a camel and a bear. As a wheeled biplane, the Bamel set up a British speed record of 196.4mph in December 1921 and also won the Aerial Derby for three years in succession. Purchased by the RAF after its 1923 victory, it was later converted to a floatplane for the High Speed Flight.

At first Salmond's plan seemed to be in danger. Trenchard was thoroughly opposed to the RAF entering either its machines or its pilots as contestants in air races. This resulted less from fear of failure than of the consequences of success. The CAS profoundly distrusted what he called 'company promoters and pageant merchants – and especially firms who want to build machines as an advertisement – [who] would then press us to enter for every single race in this country or in others'. Even worse, if the British succeeded, 'we should be pressed by the newspapers and firms to run it and bear the cost of it for subsequent years'. Money lay at the heart of his concerns:

[A]re the Treasury likely to agree to paying the expenses of three pilots, their pay and allowances, their passage across, their maintenance in America on a fairly expensive scale, and the cost of the machines and their transport across? I feel that in this [sic] two years of economy the Treasury would not agree.

Nevertheless, his mind was not completely closed. Trenchard knew that a hybrid civil-military effort would probably fail and was determined that 'if the Service are going to take a hand, they must do the whole thing, and be completely responsible in every way'. Therefore, if a decision to compete were taken, a special Flight should be formed under a Squadron Leader or Wing Commander 'with four first-class pilots, and the machines run as a purely Service show' backed up by a qualified Technical Officer attached to the Flight.

Faced with the choice between Trenchard and Salmond, the Secretary of State for Air did not hesitate. Writing to the former on 3 January 1926, Hoare conceded that it would be important to choose 'the line of least resistance' where the Treasury was concerned. It was also true that, once the precedent had been set for participation in air races, it might be difficult for the RAF to withdraw in the future. Yet, the Schneider Trophy possessed a special status:

You can judge much better than I can as to the value of a few very swift machines, and highly trained expert pilots, to the Air Force. From the

142

26. 47 Squadron, South Russia, B Flight train.   27. Marion Aten.

28. B Flight train with (*from left*) Rowan Daly, 'Russky' Grigorieff, William Burns Thomson and Marion Aten.

29. RAF officers at Ekaterinodar – including Walter Anderson (*second right, front*), John Mitchell (*second left, back*), William Burns Thomson (*third left, back*) and Kink (*third left, front*).

30. On the steppe, South Russia.

1. In his B Flight Camel, 47 Squadron – one of the best-known pictures of Kink.

2. Major-General Holman, head of the British Military Mission, South Russia, preparing to go on
reconnaissance in an RE8.

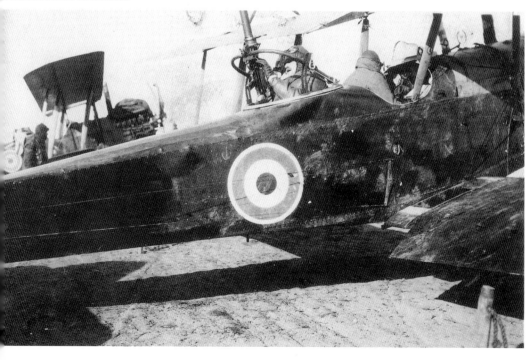

33. Kirkuk Aerodrome, where Kink commanded a detached Flight of 30 Squadron's DH9A bombers during the campaign in Kurdistan.

34. The wily and elusive Sheikh Mahmud, with firearm prominently displayed.

35. Mahmud's house (*centre right*) in Sulaimaniya, pictured in May 1924, showing the craters from 30 Squadron's punitive bombing.

6. A fine study of Kink in his DH9A over the Bazyan Pass, 6 August 1924.

7. End of an odyssey: the Cape Flight arriving at Lee-on-Solent, 21 June 1926.

38. Secretary of State for Air, Sir Samuel Hoare.

39. Reginald Mitchell at work.

40. Schneider Trophy pilot Henri Biard with Mitchell and the S4 seaplane.

. The High Speed Flight, Calshot, 9 August 1927: (*from left*) Harry Schofield, Oswald Worsley, dney Webster, Kink and Leonard Slatter.

. How the Gloster IV design kept drag to a minimum.

43. At Venice in the ungeared Gloster IVA, N222, September 1927.

44. Before the Schneider Trophy race ...

45. ... and shortly after his emergency landing

point of view of the public, I am convinced that to win the Cup would do real good to British aviation. With anything so new as flying, special efforts must be made to enlist the support of public opinion. I can scarcely imagine a better way of enlisting this support than by winning a Cup which, rightly or wrongly, is regarded as the blue ribbon of air racing.

Precisely because the contest was now so famous, a degree of politics was coming to the fore. In 1924, having gained her first Schneider victory at Cowes the previous year, America had shown great sportsmanship in agreeing to postpone the contest. Both the British and the Italians had suffered setbacks which forced them to withdraw, and the USA could have flown over the course unopposed to claim a second victory. Given the size of Doolittle's winning margin in 1925, the likelihood is that the Trophy would then have gone to the United States for a third time and the contest would have been finished forever. This, to Trenchard, seemed a desirable outcome. He noted that the Royal Aero Club had told the Americans that British participation in 1926 would be impracticable. If the Americans did not postpone the race for a second time, Trenchard mused:

is it not better that the matter should end there if possible? This would mean the end of the Schneider Cup and all the difficulties and expenses connected with it, rather than have an Air Ministry official intervene and getting the race postponed ... We definitely decided that we could not enter this year and, therefore, if the race is not postponed the Schneider Cup comes to an end, as I have said above.

In a sense the contest had become a victim of its own success. The technology of the engines and of the airframes had reached such a level of complexity that the development opportunities offered by a twelve-month gap in the racing cycle were quite inadequate. 'An interval of one year is really too small for a European nation to build a high speed racing machine, test it and transport it over to the United States in order to win the Cup,' Salmond wrote to Trenchard on 5 February. He understood this also to be the view of the Italians and the French; but, although the United Kingdom's request for postponement had been forwarded via the FAI in January, the Americans had insisted that it must go ahead in October 1926. For once, good sportsmanship had its limits – as the British themselves demonstrated in 1931 when they won the Trophy outright with a 'fly-over' by a single contestant.

Salmond still hoped that the Americans would not proceed with the competition in 1926 if they were the only entrants. He actually dissuaded two private would-be competitors from seeking to take part, and proposed an announcement

that our policy with regard to international high speed seaplane races is [that] (i) such races can only suitably be held at two years' intervals; (ii) provided this is accepted, the Air Ministry will do its utmost to assist private enterprise to compete in such races.

He reported that, at a round-table meeting with the Royal Aero Club, the Society of British Aircraft Constructors (SBAC) and would-be private competitors on 19 March, it had been unanimously agreed that no entry should be made in 1926 – a decision released to the press four days later.

The proposed construction of new high speed aircraft was set to proceed, and the SBAC requested that 'definite officers should be now selected and trained' on existing high speed machines, so as to be ready to fly the new ones as soon as they became available. Salmond raised this with Trenchard, and duly confirmed that if a contest were held in 1927: 'the Air Ministry would do their utmost to obtain authority to undertake the race themselves, provided the industry cannot find the personnel'. He also came up with a fall-back position, in case the Americans went ahead and won the Cup permanently: the Air Ministry should support an attempt to capture the World's Speed Record in the United Kingdom, if a suitable machine were available

> immediately after the result of the Schneider Cup is known ... If this is done, there can be no question but that any advantage which the Americans may try to achieve by winning the Schneider Cup under such circumstances will immediately disappear if the British record is put up.

Hoare endorsed this plan on 1 April, noting that:

> If the British [Aircraft] Industry decide, as it seems likely, that the best chance of success [in 1927] is to train RAF personnel, I understand from CAS that, provided that the arrangements remain in his hands, he is prepared to agree to the training of a certain number of selected officers. My own view is that without trained personnel of this kind we shall never do much good and I hope that this will be the arrangement adopted.

On 7 June, Salmond reported to Trenchard:

> The first of the Gloster [IIIA] machines is now in the erection stage at Felixstowe and will probably be ready ... early in June. The second machine, the Bamel, and the third machine, the Gloster IIIB, will probably be ready ... in July and September respectively. Furthermore, by September or a little later, the three new high speed machines will probably be ready ... [A] programme of propeller tests has been drawn up for the Gloster IIIA, the results of which will be required for the design of the propellers for the three new machines ... I do not consider that any undue risk would be incurred by allowing Flying Officer [Oswald] Worsley, who is one of the test pilots at MAEE, to carry out this programme on the Gloster IIIA ... the question of pilots for the subsequent flights now arises ... If only one pilot is available, the tests would be unduly drawn out, as weather and other conditions have to be chosen very carefully. It would be an economy both in time and flying if you would agree to the temporary posting of three or four pilots from Service units to carry out the work with Flying Officer Worsley. They could combine their

training with these tests and return to their units, if necessary, when both were complete until the three new machines for 1927 were ready . . . If you approve, I should like the officers to be available from the end of July.

It was to Trenchard's credit that, despite his doubts and antipathies, he was determined to make the enterprise succeed: 'the first thing to do is to choose a good Squadron Leader, who shall be responsible for all these high speed machines'. If the RAF were to participate, he added: 'I must watch that our best pilots, those used to high speed flying, are not sent overseas if we are likely to want them.' The High Speed Flight would be formed initially at the Marine Aircraft Experimental Establishment (MAEE), which had been set up on the Suffolk coast at Felixstowe on 1 April 1924 as the principal unit for testing and evaluating floatplanes and flying boats.

Before the end of June, Salmond knew that the Italians intended to compete and that the 1926 race would probably proceed. By now, the new generation of high speed machines was under development and RAF pilots would need to be trained to test them, whether or not a further race were to be held in 1927. For Trenchard, the key question was

if any such race should materialise, would we be in a position to compete? The only way is as we have already agreed . . . although I have agreed to this, I really do not think it is worth it; but I must do it.

The CAS asked for the names of two or three Squadron Leaders from whom he could select the officer to command the High Speed Flight. Salmond replied on 13 July, nominating Squadron Leader W.H. Longton DFC, AFC; Squadron Leader S.R. Watkins AFC; or Squadron Leader L.H. Slatter OBE, DSC, DFC. With regard to pilots, he noted that 'experience of seaplanes, and small weight and stature, are advantages; but they are not, I think, essential'. As for training aircraft:

The only machine we have at Felixstowe at present is the Gloster IIIA . . . we expect the Bamel to be at Felixstowe about the end of this month and the Gloster IIIB in September. The three new high speed machines should be ready towards the end of September or a little later . . .

a prediction which proved distinctly over-optimistic.

Trenchard asked the Air Member for Personnel (AMP) to consider the three suggested names. The Flight leader, he wrote, should be someone 'medically very fit . . . who could stand the high speeds necessary' and, preferably, who had served in the field in France. Their choice fell on Leonard Slatter, a 31-year-old South African who had studied as a teenager at Battersea Polytechnic and London University, before enlisting in the RNAS in 1914. Beginning as a despatch rider with the Naval Armoured Car Division, Slatter took part in the Second Battle of Ypres before becoming an observer and then a pilot. As well as securing seven aerial victories, he excelled in attacking enemy warships; and he won a bar to his DSC for bombing Ostend Seaplane Station from only 400 feet, in the face of intense anti-aircraft fire. He also held a DFC, won over the Western Front, and an OBE for his work with 47 Squadron in South Russia. More than anyone else, it was Slatter who ensured that Kink became one of the elite band of Schneider Trophy pilots.

On 23 August, before Slatter had been appointed, Wing Commander R.B. Maycock, in command of the entire MAEE, sent a full report to the Air Ministry. Two high speed seaplanes had already arrived, but no definite information about a policy for the High Speed Flight had yet been received. A suitable shed was available on the site of the original air station:

> A few repairs to the roof and additions to the lighting would . . . be necessary, after authority to proceed is forthcoming . . . It appears particularly desirable to keep the work and aircraft of this Flight as secret as possible. This is a particular reason for moving the Flight to the Old Station, away from observation of people on the Harbour Pier, and from out of the present shed where visitors are continually shown round and contractors' men are at work.

The Commanding Officer of the Flight should be selected and sent as soon as possible. Specialised high speed work needed the undivided attention of a responsible individual. The pilots chosen for the Flight would have to prove themselves in terms of skill and temperament during their probationary period. The unit would need at least one fitter and two riggers for each machine and one sergeant fitter and one sergeant rigger as well.

> At least one high speed motor-boat (25 knots, if possible) will be required as a stand-by for rescue work, and getting to aircraft that have forced-landed in the shortest possible time, to effect salvage . . . a speed course . . . will be necessary, also a course approximating to the Schneider Cup course in the number of turns and distances apart of the turning points.

As the towns of Dovercourt and Felixstowe lay to the east and west of the MAEE, it was necessary sometimes to fly over them before the pilots had time to turn. This had generated several complaints from residents, regarding noise and potential danger. Maycock assured the Air Ministry that: 'No noises or danger to the public which can possibly be avoided will be permitted, and the pilots have been given written instructions on this point.' Finally, special tanks were installed and facilities prepared for the storage and handling of petrol and benzol at the Old Station, so that such highly inflammable fuel could be kept secure and safely transferred to the aircraft.

Although scheduled for 24 October 1926, the ninth Schneider Trophy contest was postponed, at the request of Italy, until 11 November. It was held at Hampton Roads over a triangular course close to the Naval Operating Base. The three American servicemen flew Curtiss biplanes which had successfully participated the previous year. One crashed during the navigability test and had to be replaced by a much less powerful reserve machine. All three Italians flew Macchi M39 monoplanes with 800hp Fiat engines. Major Mario de Bernardi won easily at 246.496mph. US Lieutenant Frank Schilt came second with an average speed of 231.363mph. Lieutenant Adriano Bacula was third at 218mph, while Lieutenant William Tomlinson in the reserve plane could manage only 136.953mph. Captain Arturo Ferrarin had to retire with a broken oil pipe at the end of his third lap, while Lieutenant George Cuddihy went out on his seventh with petrol pump failure. Against the odds, Italy had prevented America from permanently claiming the Trophy: the Royal Air Force now had to fulfil its pledge of an all-out effort to enter and win.

There was no shortage of setbacks – including on the political front. By 22 November, Geoffrey Salmond was reporting to Trenchard and Hoare that the new machines were now expected in February or March 1927: 'Their completion has been delayed owing to the coal strike and other matters.' Trenchard, however, suspected that it would 'probably be more like June before we see them – certainly before we get all three'. On 2 December, Trenchard wrote tetchily to Salmond that matters were lagging in terms of pilots being attached to the Flight as full-time personnel. It was two months since Slatter had been appointed, and he himself had not flown any of the Gloster machines, this being done solely by test pilots from MAEE. Within a week, however, it was confirmed that Flight Lieutenant John Chick and Flying Officer Rex Stocken were in place at Felixstowe, in addition to Slatter and Worsley. Slatter and Chick had 'got as far as taxiing on the Bamel'; Stocken had flown the Bamel and was ready to fly the Gloster IIIs, and Worsley had flown all three machines.

The Fédération Aéronautique Internationale had agreed in October to the Royal Aero Club's proposal to hold the contests every two years in future. This should have scheduled the next race for 1928. Yet, after Italian pressure, by the end of 1926 a date late in 1927 seemed more probable. Such constantly changing predictions exasperated the Chief of Air Staff, who wrote a long minute to Salmond on 26 January 1927:

I saw in the paper this morning that the Schneider Cup is now going to be run this year. Every bit of information that has come to me about the Schneider Cup from the Royal Aero Club during the last two years has been incorrect. It is inconceivable to me that the Royal Aero Club should have ... voted for the Schneider Cup to be run this year, when only a few months ago they agreed to run it every two years ... I thought we had members who were in closest touch with the Royal Aero Club. Anyhow, the damage has been done ... On 1 October 1926, nearly four months ago, Squadron Leader Slatter took up this job. Three months afterwards, he had still not flown any of the machines. I see now ... that it was proposed to order four machines for the Schneider Cup this year in addition to the three that have been so delayed in coming forward ... and it is now learnt that these three machines will not be handed over to the High Speed Flight until about April. Under these circumstances, I consider that the High Speed Flight should be handed over [from the MAEE] to the

Service Department at once, and that they should be made to go on practising with the two others – the Bamel and the Gloster IIIA, with a couple of Flycatchers which I would propose to give them, so as to keep them in constant practice ... One of the chief reasons for the failure two years ago, I was informed, was the bad arrangements in organisation, practice and pilots chosen ... I need hardly say that I do not want the responsibility, but, as I said I would take it in the past, I consider that – if I have got to take it – I must ask that it be handed over to me in sufficient time to get it going.

Within forty-eight hours, Salmond and Trenchard had agreed that the Flight should be transferred from the Director of Technical Development to the CAS at the end of May; that it would consist of Slatter, the three pilots already at Felixstowe, 'and a fourth one to be selected by AMP'. Salmond was confident that a gap of three months between this handover and the race itself would be ample for all necessary preparations. On 22 February, he reported to Trenchard that the race would be held in September and that each of the three brand-new machines should be ready in good time – a Gloster IV by mid-March, the Short-Bristol Crusader by the end of that month, and a Supermarine-Napier S5 during the first week in April. Two more Glosters and two more S5s were also being ordered, and should be available in August.

Trenchard wrote, somewhat grudgingly, to Hoare the following day asking him to consider various points 'if you still decide that we must enter':

The time will be very short, but I am prepared to take it over on these conditions if you wish me to do so, though I would point out that, owing to the fact that the new machines will not be ready till August, and to the further fact that it has only just been decided that the Schneider Cup shall be run this year, the time is all too short to make it a success from a Service or an organisational point of view; but I can and will still do my best. Secondly, Treasury sanction would have to be obtained, and we should have to appeal for them to be allowed to have travelling allowances and extra allowances which I am afraid would be heavy, as the officers and men must be properly looked after if they go as a Service unit to Italy, and we ought to send probably at least a Wing Commander, if not a Group Captain, in charge of the whole party.

Such were the implications of the RAF entering the contest as a unit and bearing all the resultant expenses. Alternatively, the machines, pilots and ground crew could be lent to the Royal Aero Club and/or the manufacturers, who would then have to pay the extra expenses involved in sending them all to Italy. Trenchard concluded with the remark:

I have not repeated in this minute all the old arguments on the subject, nor what I consider the great mistake of rushing this contest into this year because our manufacturers consider they will score a point by pushing forward the date unexpectedly.

Hoare was quite insistent that the whole undertaking must be borne by the Royal Air Force and that all necessary steps taken to secure Treasury compliance – on the precedent of what the Americans and, if applicable, the Italians and the French had already been doing. Detailed information was duly received, from the US Assistant Naval Attaché for Aviation in London and the British Air Attaché in Rome, about the arrangements made by America and Italy when sending teams abroad to compete for the Trophy. A bid to the Treasury was despatched on 29 March explaining why nothing less than a fully organised RAF expedition could be expected to succeed:

> The expense involved (seeing that the aircraft are already the property of the Air Ministry) would consist of the cost of transporting the machines, including a spare one, to Italy and back; of their running expenses, and of the travelling and adequate subsistence allowances of the personnel concerned, which would be twenty to twenty-five in number for a period of about three weeks. It is estimated that the total expenditure on these services will not exceed £2,500. The Air Council are far from contemplating that Service representation in the Schneider Cup race should be an annual event and their view is, in fact, that it will be impossible for sufficient suitable entries to continue to be obtained for a yearly contest; but they consider that, for this one occasion at least, an adequate British entry is highly desirable and that it cannot be secured otherwise than on the lines they have indicated, which they trust that Their Lordships will approve.

The Treasury responded with a number of alternative suggestions, but the Air Ministry view was now settled:

> It is the considered opinion of the Air Council that the building and flying of high speed aircraft is productive of most valuable results, both to research and technical development; that non-competitive flying trials can never supply the same stimulus either to the designers or pilots as does actual competition in an international race; that to secure these results it is essential that the aircraft should be tested at an Air Ministry Experimental Establishment, and subsequently flown in the race, by Royal Air Force personnel as a Service exercise under Service organisation and discipline; and that, whether the Schneider Cup be won by this country or not, the results of an entry on these lines will be well worth the expenditure involved – for which purpose funds are available on Air Votes.

To sweeten the pill, the letter concluded by referring to the prospect of reducing the cost of participation by making use of the aircraft carrier HMS *Eagle* which, by coincidence, would be cruising in the Adriatic in September. On 13 May, the Treasury agreed additional expenditure of up to £2,500 for the RAF to enter the September 1927 race, noting the assurance that the Air Council were 'far from contemplating' annual participation in the future. Their

Lordships also trusted that 'no steps will be taken (such as the purchase of special racing machines) which could be interpreted as committing the Council to undertaking responsibility for an entry in any future year' without prior Treasury sanction.

The contest itself was just over four months away and a vast amount of work remained to be done. The Chief of Air Staff was anxious that instructions should be drafted at once for the Air Officer Commanding Coastal Area to take over control of the Flight and to be briefed by Salmond on how it had been organised thus far: 'This is very urgent,' Trenchard had written on 11 May

> as time is all too short for AOC, Coastal Area, to see that the Flight will be all right for the Schneider Cup race in September. I hope I can be told in a week's time that AOC, Coastal Area, has had all this information.

He had also stressed the importance of a Technical Officer being attached to the Flight. Salmond was consulted and agreed that 'the best officer to carry out these duties is Mr L.P. Coombes who is a Scientific Officer and is at present at Felixstowe; he has up to date been carrying out work on the High Speed Flight', and should be available if needed to accompany the team.

The stage was now set for serious plans to be laid. On 14 May, the Air Ministry wrote to the AOC Coastal Area, Air Vice-Marshal Francis Scarlett directing him to assume full responsibility for the organisation and training of the High Speed Flight, currently at Felixstowe. Everything should be done to give it the best chance of success at Venice, and a report was requested on the present state of the Flight together with any recommendations which needed to be made. Attached was a memorandum giving details of the aircraft currently available and yet to be received. By this time, two of the three new types had arrived to join the Bamel, the IIIA and the IIIB. The Gloster IV had been completed during April and had carried out taxiing trials, but had yet to undertake airborne trials including test flying and airscrew testing. The Crusader, built by Short Brothers, was also still undergoing contractors' trials. The first of the Supermarine S5s was almost complete, while construction of the Gloster IVA was proceeding rapidly. The second S5 was well under way, but production of the Gloster IVB and the third S5 had only just begun. The Crusader was fitted with a Bristol Mercury engine; two of the Glosters and one of the S5s with the Napier Lion VIIA ungeared engine; and one Gloster and two S5s with the Napier Lion VIIB geared engine. High Speed Flight pilots could also practise on a Flycatcher seaplane at Felixstowe, capable of about 130mph, and on two land machines at Martlesham – a Heron and a Gamecock – capable of speeds of about 150mph.

Formal responsibility for the High Speed Flight passed from Sir Geoffrey Salmond to Air Vice-Marshal Scarlett on 20 May. With just four months to go, Scarlett did not intend to waste time. He interviewed both Maycock and Slatter at Coastal Area Headquarters in London on the day he took over, then visited Felixstowe early the following week. On 26 January, Slatter had unsuccessfully asked for Kink and Richard Atcherley – another officer he admired – to be allowed to join the team. On 11 February, he had tried again:

Further to my letter ... dated 26 January 1927, it is requested that the following officers named therein should be attached to this Unit for training on High Speed Aircraft: Flight Lieutenant S.M. Kinkead DSO DSC DFC and Flying Officer Atcherley. It is understood that certain difficulties exist with reference to attaching these officers. I would like to point out, however, that I consider it essential that I should have officers whom I personally know and whose flying ability I am acquainted with. In view of the short time available for training, it is considered a good deal of time will be saved in training pilots if I have had previous personal experience with them.

The Air Ministry response of 17 February was to tell him bluntly that 'it has not been found possible to post to your establishment the officers for whom you apply. Flying Officers H.M. Schofield and S.N. Webster have, however, been posted for training on high speed aircraft in their stead'. Now that Scarlett was in charge, Slatter tried for a third time, using the AOC-in-C's report to the Air Ministry in May as his vehicle:

At present one Squadron Leader and four other officers are attached ... and are considered satisfactory pilots. I am of the opinion that Squadron Leader Slatter can run this Flight satisfactorily ... It is thought, however, that one other officer should be earmarked ... either Flying Officer R.L.R. Atcherley or Flight Lieutenant S.M. Kinkead ... The former is the most suitable. If it is agreed to earmark either of these officers, it is recommended that he be sent now to Calshot ... to obtain preliminary seaplane instruction and then to Felixstowe to fly one of the High Speed Flight aircraft to ensure that he satisfies the requirements of the Officer Commanding Flight ... At present four NCOs and twenty airmen are attached to the Flight.

Scarlett was confident that all the pilots could fly the existing high speed machines 'with certainty and precision'. They were well experienced in taking off and landing the Gloster IIIA, and had used it to begin practising high speed cornering – though this had to be kept within limits as that machine had been 'declared unsafe for quick turning at high speed ... The aircraft are comparatively easy to fly in the air, but the art of flying high speed machines successfully lies in taking off [from] the water and landing again' – the former being the harder task. Once the Gloster IV had completed its acceptance tests, the team would be able greatly to intensify practice flights over a triangular course.

By early June it had been decided that six officers, eight riggers, eight fitters, two NCOs, a storekeeper and three airmen with motor-boat experience would constitute the party travelling to Venice. Over 500 tonnes of equipment would need to be shipped – including aircraft in their cases which could not be sent overland by rail because the giant crates were too large to pass through the railway tunnels into Italy. This meant that, in order to arrive on the desired date of 1 September, the aircraft would have to leave England early in August. During June, Slatter drew up a series of weekly reports listing the amount of flying undertaken by each pilot and the state of preparedness of each machine. Matters were not helped by periods of low visibility and unsuitable sea conditions, but Flight Lieutenant Sidney Webster and Flying Officer Harry Schofield managed to try out the Gloster IIIs at Felixstowe. Meanwhile, Flight Lieutenant Worsley was detached to RAF Calshot, the seaplane base on the Solent, where he successfully flew the first of the Supermarine-Napier S5s. This left Flight Lieutenant Chick – but not for long. Slatter reported his being 'posted away' from the Flight on 22 June. As will presently be seen, this may have been the result of bad luck or of an injustice; but, in any event, a vacancy now existed enabling Kink to join the team – just as his friend and comrade from battles past, Leonard Slatter, had intended all along.

At a meeting in the Air Ministry on 29 June, chaired by the Director of Organisation and Staff Duties (DOSD), Scarlett, Major J.S. Buchanan (one of the Air Ministry's representatives on the Schneider Cup Committee of the Royal Aero Club) and other officials agreed that the High Speed Flight should be moved from Felixstowe to Calshot, but the slower machines should not. Scarlett had previously found 'propellers designed in England and sent out to the Mediterranean to be under-pitched'. It was therefore agreed that several spare propellers of varying pitch should be sent with the team to Venice:

> The AOC, Coastal Area, stated that he was anxious to have more information of what the Italians were doing and it was agreed that this matter should be taken up by DOSD with Air Intelligence, and that the AOC, Coastal Area, should be kept fully informed of all information obtained.

Travel arrangements were also determined. The Flight would be sent in two detachments, the first probably consisting of the Crusader, one Gloster IV and one or two of the three S5s. These would leave England on 17 August, by steamship, arriving at Malta about ten days later. An Admiralty collier would then take them to Venice, arriving on 2 or 3 September. At Malta a Fairey Flycatcher would be added for use for practice flying around the course. The second contingent, consisting of the remaining one or two S5s and the Gloster IVB, would leave England, by steamship, for Malta, ten days after the first, and would then trans-ship onto the aircraft carrier HMS *Eagle* which would arrive at Venice on 8 September. Some non-flying personnel, including the two spare pilots, would travel out with these shipments, but those taking part in the race, as well as the remainder of the Flight's personnel, would travel overland to Venice in time to meet the earlier shipment at the beginning of September. It was hoped to use the aircraft carrier to transport the whole Flight back to Malta after the contest.

In parallel with these preparations, thought was being given within the Air Ministry on what to reveal to the press. On 7 May, a brief article in the *Morning Post* by the distinguished aviation correspondent C.G. Grey caused some anxiety. It described one of the new machines – the Short-Bristol Crusader – and went into detail about its radial engine. Each cylinder was covered with a separate cowl or 'helmet' in order to reduce head resistance, and the engine was

> one of the greatest feats in aeronautical engineering. Its compactness is astonishing, more than 700 horse-power being compressed into about the space taken by a woman's hat-box.

After some discussion, officials decided that all three of the new racers should be taken off the Secret List and placed on a 'Part Publication List', with the manufacturers given discretion as to how much technical information to reveal. The Ministry stressed, nevertheless, that 'the engines incorporated in these high speed aircraft are to remain secret'.

From time to time, the RAF had received press enquiries about the forthcoming contest, but had generally respected the advice of C.P. Robertson, head of the Ministry's Press Section, to wait until nearer its date. In late July, it was agreed that the press should be invited to visit Calshot to see the Supermarine and Gloster aircraft a week before they set out from Southampton: 'this is about the latest date that we can arrange and the manufacturers concerned have agreed that this will allow sufficient time for packing'. On 5 August, Robertson sent Scarlett an extensive collection of draft notes for release to the press as background information. The viewing of the new S5 and Gloster IV was confirmed for 11.30am on Tuesday, 9 August. The Short-Bristol Crusader could similarly be inspected at Felixstowe two days later. It was stressed that journalists should not, for the time being, publish 'actual or approximate speeds of the aircraft ... nor should the horse-power or revolutions of the engines be given'. There need be no reporting restrictions apart from the technical details of the engines.

Thus it was that the country learned for the first time about the men and machines of the High Speed Flight, and the task they would face in Venice. Seven circuits would be flown, each of 50km – just under 27 nautical miles – making a total of almost 190 nautical miles around a triangular course. It would be covered in an anti-clockwise direction, involving twenty turns in all:

> The first leg is 11.4km (7.1 land miles) and the first turning point (an obtuse angle) is at Porto di Malamocco. The second leg is 13.86km (8.6 land miles) with a turning point (a sharp acute angle) opposite Chioggia. The last and long leg, 24.74km (15.5 land miles), runs to the starting-point, where the turning is also exceedingly sharp.

Brief biographical summaries were given of each of the pilots, and the scale of the effort being made was indicated by the fact that twenty-seven RAF mechanics, and a few more from the aircraft firms, would be needed in Venice

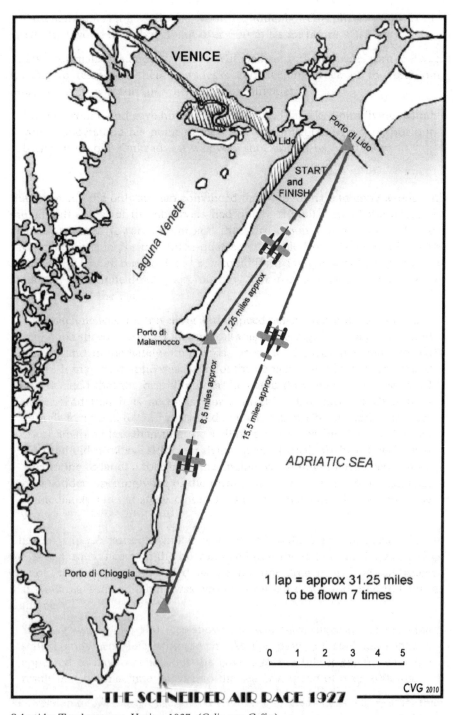

Schneider Trophy course, Venice, 1927. (*Colin van Geffen*)

154

to support the team. Among the senior civilian personnel who would also be going were the Chairman and Managing Director of the Supermarine Aviation Works, Commander James Bird; the firm's Chief Engineer, R.J. Mitchell; the Managing Director of the Gloster Aircraft Company; the Managing Director of D. Napier & Son; and Oswald Short of Short Brothers. The real interest, however, lay in the seven racing seaplanes – three S5s, three Gloster IVs and one Short-Bristol Crusader:

The SUPERMARINE-NAPIER S5 is a low-wing monoplane twin-float type seaplane, and is a development of the Supermarine-Napier S4 which won the world speed record for seaplanes in 1925, and still holds the British speed record for both land and sea planes ... The S5 has a number of very novel features ... All the fuel is carried in the starboard float. The effect of this is partially to balance the engine torque and make the machine more pleasant to fly. The fuel is carried to the engine by means of an engine-driven pump. The fuel tank is constructed as a section of the float. The wing surface radiators are an entirely new development ... They cool the engine without adding any resistance whatsoever to the machine, having a perfectly flat outer surface. The fuselage is constructed entirely in metal, the skin taking practically all the stresses. The engine mounting consists of a cantilevered extension to the fuselage ... The floats are constructed of duralumin ... The wing is built of wood and is covered with special laminated wood underneath the ... radiators, thus eliminating the resistance which would occur if the corrugations of the radiators were exposed. The oil is cooled by passing it along both sides of the fuselage in contact with the skin through specially constructed oil coolers, the corrugations of which can be seen by looking at the sides of the fuselage. The metal propellers have been designed and manufactured by the Fairey Aviation Company Limited, Hayes. The fuselage is probably smaller in cross-sectional area than any fuselage previously designed, and the pilots have had to be specially fitted to the machines. The area of the maximum section is only just over half that of the S4. Fresh air ducts are fitted to clear the cockpit of exhaust fumes and hot air during flight.

The GLOSTER-NAPIER IV ... is the latest of a long series of Gloster racing aircraft ... The designer is Mr H.P. Folland ... The fuselage is of laminated spruce monocoque construction ... removable petrol tanks are carried in the fuselage ... Wing radiators ... are situated on the top and bottom planes. The wings are of multi-spar type, entirely covered with laminated spruce, waterproof glue being used for all woodwork ... The inter-plane struts are built up of duralumin forgings to reduce frontal area. The floats are ... in duralumin, special care having been taken to obtain a good streamline shape ...

The SHORT-BRISTOL CRUSADER built by Short Bros Ltd of Rochester and engined by Bristol Aeroplane Company ... is probably the lightest loaded machine per horse-power in existence. The weight of the whole structure with the engine fitted is less than was considered a reasonable weight for the engines alone in the earlier days of aircraft development ... The fuselage ... is constructed in the main of double plank mahogany, but the forward part consists of steel tubing to take the engine mounting. For a seaplane of this class the machine is particularly easy to fly and no modification has been necessary at any stage since the first flight ... [It] has proved to have an excellent degree of stability and manoeuvrability ...

The NAPIER LION RACING ENGINE ... is designed and built by D. Napier and Son, Acton W3, London ... a development of the famous Napier Lion in use in commercial and military aircraft all over the world. It has twelve cylinders, fan shape, in three blocks of four cylinders each ... one outstanding improvement is a substantial reduction in the frontal area ... everything has been done to reduce head resistance ... The amazing power which this tiny engine develops must also remain a mystery for the present, but when it is possible to give figures of performance, it can be promised that the power output obtained from an engine of such compact size will be remarkable. Another advance which has been made in this engine is that it has been fitted with a special reduction gear. This enables a slower-running airscrew to be used, which gives a higher efficiency ... and this alone marks a unique development in British aero engine design ... The Napier Lion is a water-cooled engine. It is a significant fact ... that since the war all the winners of the Schneider Cup have been [fitted with water-] cooled power units.

The BRISTOL 'MERCURY' AIR-COOLED STATIC RADIAL ENGINE ... is built by the Bristol Aeroplane Company Limited, Filton, Bristol. The designer is Mr A.H.R. Fedden, who has been responsible for the ... 'Jupiter' Air-cooled Radial Engines ... not only largely used in Royal Air Force single-seater fighters ... but ... for service on the Cairo-Karachi commercial air-route ... The power developed is enormous ... It is without doubt the highest-powered air-cooled engine in the world ...

Until this point, everything had been shrouded in secrecy. Soon the names of the S5 and Gloster IV pilots, Webster, Worsley and Kinkead, would feature in thousands of articles in hundreds of newspapers all over the world. A newsreel of their 9 August photo-call still exists. It shows them posing, with Schofield and Slatter, in front of one of Mitchell's machines. Smiling, relaxed and slightly self-conscious, they seem a carefree and good-humoured team; but the task ahead of them was formidable. 'Good luck to the Flying Bullets' pilots!' reads the narrative of the silent movie clip. Every one of them would need it.

Chapter Eight

High Speed Flight – The Pilot's View

Of the members of the High Speed Flight who went to Venice in 1927, only Harry Schofield has left a full account. The Technical Officer, Lawrence Coombes, gave lectures on the Schneider Trophy contests, years after his move to Australia in 1938 to establish an aeronautical research laboratory; but the text of his presentation suffers from errors of detail, no doubt caused by the passage of time. He also entertained a jaundiced view of Slatter, describing him in an interview as 'not the most popular of COs' and in his lecture notes as 'not a good Commanding Officer'. This meant, he claims, that the spirit prevailing in the team was far from happy:

> Early on, Rex Stocken was dismissed. He had flown the Gloster III in rather a nasty wind and after landing taxied up to the motor-boat to be taken in tow. On stopping his engine the crosswind and the chop, combined with the small reserve buoyancy of the floats, caused the machine to heel over sideways and backwards till it capsized. Stocken got clear but Slatter ruled it was bad seamanship and threw him out.

According to Coombes, a similar fate befell Chick who had been chosen to test the first Gloster IV at Felixstowe:

> It was an extremely blind machine and, as it had very little water clearance for the propeller, the early stages of the take-off occurred in a cloud of spray; it was not until the machine was travelling at 40 to 50mph that the pilot could see in which direction he was heading. Chick spent a great deal of time in taxiing trials and it was rumoured that he had no intention of actually flying. However, one evening he actually did take the aeroplane off and, after a short flight, landed again safely. There was much jubilation in the Gloster camp, but Chick's triumph was short-lived. Very soon after, Chick arrived late one morning for flying and was immediately put under arrest by Slatter and thrown out of the team. Kinkead thereupon took over the Gloster IV and performed nobly, both in test flying and during the race.

Whether Slatter deliberately tried to create vacancies for the pilots he wanted on his team, or whether he was simply a strict disciplinarian who did not believe in giving second chances, it is now impossible to determine. Certainly, he set great store by those whom he knew of old and trusted. One such was Schofield, who submitted his name 'with hundreds of others' and soon forgot all about it. Much to his surprise, he was chosen and 'very late one very wet night in February 1927, after a filthy drive', he arrived at Felixstowe from London. There he met Worsley for the first time and duly reported to Slatter: 'We had been together at Leuchars two years before, which was all to the good.'

Chick and Webster had already been attached to the unit, while Stocken was preparing to leave. Schofield was impressed by his first sight of the training seaplanes:

the Glosters IIIA and IIIB, perched up near the roof of the hangar on their massive launching trolleys, looked simply gigantic. Glistening and beautiful and strangely placid in appearance, the first impression was one of awe; it was impossible not to be thrilled in contemplation of such masterpieces of ingenuity, capable of such magnificent power and effort, yet in the changing lights and shadows of their resting place, so subdued, so calm and so quiet.

His first task was to gain experience and knowledge about water conditions – in particular, the phenomenon of the long swell of the waves, which was regarded as the 'worst enemy' of the high speed pilots. This was because

the run required for a racing seaplane in taking-off is so long, and the speed before she can leave the water so high, that the crests of the swell which are far apart and usually impossible to anticipate, tend to throw the machine into the air before she is properly 'airborne', and she leaves the water completely out of control, and flops back again in a most unpleasant manner.

The instinctive reaction of most pilots would be to keep the throttle open and try to force a way through the difficult water; but the effect of this would be worse each time the crest of another wave was reached at a higher take-off speed than before. Eventually, a serious crash would be inevitable, unless the pilot had the self-discipline to close the throttle and wait for the adverse conditions to subside. One of the hardest tasks was to unstick the machine from the surface until it rose onto the 'steps' on the underside of the floats. There was also the problem of engine torque, which tended to force one wing towards the surface of the sea.

Once on the steps, however, the controls become more or less normal, and it was only necessary to remember instructions and not try to pull her off too soon – just to wait patiently until plenty of speed was apparent, or else the dreaded porpoising would result ... At the commencement of a take-off, the floats ride well down in the water, and as the machine starts to become 'airborne', and the floats to hydroplane, they rise, and the machine is then said to be 'on the steps'.

Schofield also found that great patience was necessary in trying to land the streamlined high speed machines which were 'extremely difficult to glide at anything under 150 miles an hour'. An age would seem to pass while he held his seaplane roughly 2 feet above the surface until the speed decreased sufficiently to touch down. Even taxiing on the water was difficult and risky unless the wind was very low, and there was always a prospect of total loss:

> The slightest error is sufficient to capsize a racing machine – just a little wind forcing the tails of the floats into a small sea, or the weight of the pilot disposed too far back as he leaves or enters the cockpit are sufficient to turn the craft right over backwards.

It was also hazardous to start up a racing seaplane 'whilst drifting on the end of a rope from a motor-boat', with the profusion of starter leads which had to be pulled aboard or cast off prior to take-off. Schofield felt that hardly a minute of the programme at Venice was not fraught with the risk of seeing the floatplanes go to the bottom.

After landing, the pilot would be in the hands of the motor-boat crew. These fast seaplane tenders would gently take the aircraft in tow until it could be manoeuvred over a submerged cradle or trolley which would enable it to be drawn up the slipway. Finally the pilot could clamber out and be carried, piggy-back fashion, to the shore by a mechanic kitted out in waders and life-jacket. Only then would he discover, in trying to deal with endless questions posed by the watchers, that he was virtually deaf and would remain so for an hour or more:

> nobody seemed to quite realise or believe that we often could not hear a thing, and later, when we adopted the policy of ignoring everybody and just vanishing after coming ashore, many must have thought us an ill-mannered bunch of toughs.

Gradually the pilots became superlatively fit, spending the many hours when flying was impossible exercising, playing golf or tennis, or swimming. This could breed frustration and occasional tensions but, on the whole, 'the more troubles we had, the firmer did we become cemented together in the common cause'. The pilots knew that their work 'carried with it an increase of speed of a proportion unheard of before or since'. They were operating at the margins of physical endurance and they soon came to terms with the danger of blacking-out when making high speed turns. Schofield described the process vividly, explaining that, if the weight of a pilot is known as one 'G', and a turn has been done at five 'G', it means that the weight of the pilot has been magnified fivefold and that a force of five times his normal weight has been concentrated upon the cockpit seat:

> At five or six 'G', there is every prospect of the sight failing through centrifugal force drawing the blood from the back of the eyes, and a most unpleasant feeling it is ... As the joystick is pulled back and the turn

tightened, black spots suddenly appear before the eyes and develop into a curtain; the whole body feels uncomfortable, and well it might, because all the various organs are being projected towards the seat at many times their normal weight ... Of course, the force can be applied in a reciprocal manner, for instance, if after a steep fast climb the joystick be put sharply forward, the most appalling sensation is felt. The machine changes direction and the body wishes to go straight on at perhaps 300 or more miles an hour, and when after an appreciable time I recovered from my first experience of this nature, I found it hard to believe that my shoulder straps had really been strong enough to hold me into the cockpit.

Experience showed that five 'G' was the tolerable level at which fast turns could be made in a race at speeds approaching 300mph; but the pilots' main concern – which almost became an obsession – was not to lose their 'edge' through insufficient flying practice. Thus, if the weather grounded the high speed trainers, they were allowed to fly simpler types from Martlesham Heath, just 9 miles from Felixstowe:

we took full advantage of the arrangements, dashing over and roaring all over the sky at every opportunity, and soon feeling again that we could cope with anything.

Early in April 1927, Schofield graduated from the Bamel to the Gloster IIIA and began practising at speeds of up to 225mph. He soon became accustomed to the terrific sensation of speed at low levels, watching tiny objects on land and water growing rapidly into large ones, then flashing away behind; but the problems of landing were harder than ever:

The difficulty in losing speed was incredible. If I took my eyes off the dash for a few seconds and kept the nose in what appeared to be a reasonable position, she soon felt as though she would fall out of my hands, yet a glance at the dash showed an air speed of 130 miles an hour. The approach seemed endless, she just would not lose speed or come out of the air, and it seemed like hours later when we found ourselves whistling just over the surface wishing to goodness she would stop and settle.

The hazards involved in alighting at such speeds were soon illustrated when the Crusader – the first of the three new types destined for Venice – arrived at Felixstowe together with the famous long-distance flyer Bert Hinkler. He was asked to take her up for the first time and, after a successful trial, nearly crashed on landing. Schofield was in the high speed motor-boat, which was so essential to recover seaplanes quickly before they could capsize and to recover pilots if anything did go wrong. As Hinkler came in to land, they saw a disaster in the making:

He was pretty near the water and did not quite level up before his left float touched the surface. It was only the merest stroke, but the effect on the machine was terrific. She did the vilest twitch towards us and leapt into the air again. Whether we were shaken more than Bert I do not know. I only know that there did not seem to be the slightest chance of avoiding the devil of destruction that so suddenly came straight for us, and was less than 100 yards away; also in the flash one sometimes gets under trying circumstances, we saw that the undercarriage wires were hanging in festoons and the struts were bent. I am not quite clear how it all sorted itself out. Bert must have been very cunning with the rudder, because just as we were ready to take a header over the opposite side, she sat down with a funny little waggle which just put everything right, and to our amazement, although she did rather emulate a half-set jelly, stayed in a more or less normal position.

Schofield's memoirs hint at a side to his character which some might dismiss as superstitious, but others would see as spiritual. He had what he described as a 'curious, indefinable feeling' of foreboding about the Crusader, and his wife, for no explicable reason, exclaimed on viewing the machine: 'I do wish you were not going to fly that.' Later, another member of their family would have a premonition which sadly proved all too accurate. Successive flights in the Crusader did little to generate confidence. The engine had a disturbing tendency to cut out and on one occasion the supercharger died, 'then shot in again with a bang that . . . all but gathered me into the rear end of the fuselage'. Visibility from the cockpit was largely obstructed, and the task of landing was fraught with difficulty.

As for the other new machines, a visit to Woolston showed that the Supermarine-Napier S5s would be ready, if at all, only just in time for the September contest; but the first of the Gloster IVs made a great impression on arrival at Felixstowe:

I do not remember anybody looking at her without some sort of expression of amazed admiration, and what a really beautiful picture she made when she stood assembled there for the first time. The colour scheme – sea-blue fuselage and gold wings and tail – gave her the appearance of some weird and beautiful tropical fish, and we never tired of looking at her and touching her intriguingly streamlined shapes and gadgets.

The pilot chosen for the Gloster IV at this stage was John Chick, a Great War ace credited with sixteen victories in Bristol two-seaters, and a skilled aerobatic flyer. His experience with the Gloster was to be as traumatic as Schofield's with the Crusader. The view was terrible – it being impossible to see anything at all over the upper wing, or anything below it except at the tips. So much water was thrown up while taxiing that Chick could see virtually nothing through his goggles, and hours were spent on preliminary trials with Schofield 'watching him career in blind frenzy in all directions, sometimes just leaving the surface, but never staying off for more than a few seconds'. Chick's personal courage

161

was beyond question, but he was perturbed at the prospect of having to put the biplane onto the water at 90–100mph without being able to see what he was doing. He was right to be worried. After successfully achieving 246mph, with power to spare, on his first flight, he was horrified to hear a loud twang as a bracing wire snapped:

> He looked at the floats, and saw that they were swaying from side to side; the wings were literally flapping ... there was Johnnie, all alone and with the whole outfit wobbling and banging about; but it had stuck together, and though he still did not believe that it would for more than a few seconds, it did, to the end, and was a most inspiring example of aircraft design.

Chick felt his way down to the surface of the water, judging his height as best he could from the side view which was all he had. He was sure that the float assembly would disintegrate rather than take the strain but, after a 'violent convulsive shudder' on touching down, he brought the machine to a halt. This was, in Schofield's view, a most terrifying experience and many people thought it the reason for Chick's departure from the team shortly afterwards. Schofield, however, cryptically recorded that 'it had little or nothing to do with it' – which suggests that Lawrence Coombes may well have been right in attributing Chick's removal to some minor breach of discipline. On the other hand, Coombes's account of the maiden flight of the Gloster IV makes no mention at all of the disaster which nearly overtook Chick and which was authentically described in detail in Schofield's book published only five years after the event.

Whatever the real reason, Slatter at last could have his way and, at this relatively late stage, Kink arrived at Felixstowe to take over from Chick. Schofield had not met him before and was 'strangely struck from the first by his quiet, slow, and steady mannerisms and speech'. They were introduced by the Station Adjutant one evening, in the dusk outside the mess. Writing only four years after the crash which claimed 'one of the whitest and finest men that ever breathed', Schofield was convinced that Kink somehow already knew the 'dreadful fate' that awaited him:

> My wife and I grew very fond of him, but for some unknown reason, our small daughter seemed to fall under a strange spell in his presence. He wanted, and tried, to make friends with her. He would sit sometimes and hold her hand, and talk softly to her, smiling all the while; but, after a while, as though influenced by some depressing shadow somehow connected with him, she would break down and sob pitilessly.

Schofield was adamant that this was not something he became aware of retrospectively, but a definite impression felt at the time. Even at the 'risk of appearing ridiculous', he believed that 'some indefinable suggestion spread from Kink, and found a sympathetic chord' in his child. In any event, he summed up his attitude to Kink in words barely distinguishable from those later chosen by Taffy Jones in his own memoirs. Schofield wrote:

I can say, with utmost confidence, that there is not a soul in this world who can think of a bad word to say about him. Such was his reputation. As brave as a lion, to which his glittering array of hard-won decorations bore testimony, a man anybody was proud to call a friend, and whom one instinctively tried to emulate in every possible way.

★ ★ ★

A measure of Kink's demeanour, and the admiration it inspired, can be gained from Schofield's account of his first flight in a high speed seaplane. This was the Bamel, which had already caused alarm in Schofield's hands,

when a smell of burning and a growing straggle of smoke from somewhere in front caused me to drop her into the harbour like the proverbial red-hot poker ... Inside the hangar again, we found that the fireproof bulkhead just behind the engine had been damaged.

No cause could be established and, after the burnt woodwork was repaired, Kink took off in the machine:

He had been in the air only a few minutes, and we had lost sight of him, when he suddenly reappeared heading for the centre of the harbour leaving a dense trail of smoke behind him. It was a meteoric descent and only a pilot of Kink's calibre could have pulled it off as he did. As he passed us, he was hidden in a dense cloud of smoke, and he made a priceless 'landing' towards the mouth of the Orwell, and almost before he had stopped moving, we saw him fairly leap from the cockpit to the floats, and start to wrestle with the cowling. He still had his usual calm smile when he came ashore, and seemed to think it a matter unworthy of discussion or worry of any sort, but his bloodshot eyes, and smoke-begrimed face, hands and clothing told their own tale and the more proud we felt that we were in the same show with him.

In the middle of July the High Speed Flight moved from Felixstowe to RAF Calshot at the entrance to Southampton Water. Costal defences and Calshot have been synonymous since the time of Henry VIII, when the risk of invasion led to five sites in the area being selected for fortification: East and West Cowes, Hurst Castle, Netley Castle and Calshot. Much of the stone used to build Calshot Castle between 1539 and 1540 is thought to have come from monasteries nearby which the King had dissolved. The fortification was restored and neglected, in turn, as fears of invasion grew and receded. Shortly before the Great War, the Admiralty planned a chain of air bases for naval aircraft working with the Fleet and, in April 1913, a seaplane station was constructed on Calshot Spit, adjacent to the Castle. It consisted of three hangars, accommodating twelve seaplanes; but, even from its earliest days, it was involved in research and experimentation. During the war, the air station was part of a network – including Portland and Bembridge – known as the Portsmouth Group: in 1917 alone, the Group's seaplanes spent over 3,500 hours in the air on convoy protection and anti-submarine patrols, and 270 pupils were trained as seaplane pilots. The Armistice led to a role teaching naval co-operation and aerial navigation, but Calshot remained inextricably linked with the development and use of flying boats and seaplanes.

Worsley had been there for some time, testing the first S5 which, Schofield recalled, now stood 'in sole and solitary occupation of the huge hangar'. She seemed incredibly slender, compared with the Gloster IV, but just as beautiful in her silver and sea-blue livery. Worsley's trials had been shrouded in secrecy, but the rest of the team now learned that N220 had already touched 280mph. From then on, they could be confident of possible victory in Venice. Before Schofield could try out the newest machine, he, Slatter and Kink returned to Felixstowe to unveil the Crusader to the press. As the sea-state ruled out high speed flying, they spent most of their time explaining to reporters why a racing seaplane could not be flown in such conditions, while ordinary ones 'were operating with nonchalant ease'.

Back at Calshot, Schofield's chance to fly the S5 was not long in coming:

> Little thrills ran all over me. I don't think that I feared anything, but . . . it was difficult to realise that in a very few minutes one would be cramped in a tiny cockpit behind vast power, crashing through the atmosphere in the fulfilment of another step in the advancement of science and the prestige of our country and Service.

While the S5s had been under construction, several of the pilots were shown how to gain access to the tiny cockpits by squeezing in sideways and down as far as possible, then turning to face the front and wedging their shoulders underneath the top fairing of the slender fuselage. There were 'many sighs of relief from watching design staff when the last man had been "tried-in", for it had to be a near thing' and there was a real risk that the dimensions would simply be inadequate. Although the cockpit had a hinged canopy, the pilot's helmeted and goggled head was still in the open. Soon Schofield was storming through the air at 280mph:

> I put my head slightly to the left, forgetting for a moment, and drew it back with a start as a searing wave of flame reminded me. To the right, the same procedure made my head vibrate in a fight to keep it from being dashed backwards . . . I was flying in shorts and a tennis shirt, and had little or no clearance from the sides of the cockpit, but had been told that they got hot due to the oil coolers on the outside . . . I unwittingly touched the side of the cockpit with my elbow, and the shock which the burn . . . gave me, nearly made me jump out of the machine.

Although the controls and responsiveness of the aircraft and its engine were a pure delight, danger lay in the stalling speed – which meant that the S5 could not stay in the air below some 95mph. All the problems of torque on take-off were accentuated in those seaplanes fitted with engines geared to ensure lower propeller revolutions and greater efficiency. Schofield wondered how a geared S5 ever got airborne at all:

> Directly I opened the throttle, the port wing almost buried itself in the water, and the whole outfit started to swing to the left. The maximum use of opposite control seemed to produce no effect, and to add to the apparently hopeless state of affairs, a dense cloud of spray hid practically the whole of the outside world from view. Suddenly she would get up on her steps, and instant relief was given. She was controllable in every direction, and free from spray altogether. We never got used to the first stage however, never felt quite certain about it until she came into her own.

The second S5 duly arrived and was found to be more streamlined than the first. The hundreds of tiny rivets all over its metal skin were flush with the surface, instead of protruding like tiny knobs. It had been realised that a machine could be retarded not only by the pressure of air against even such small protrusions, but also by the eddies and the suction caused behind poorly streamlined objects. Significant horsepower would be wasted, and measurable speed lost, in overcoming the extra drag.

As well as the buffeting of the pilot's head in the open cockpit, it also became clear that there was a danger of being gassed. Schofield and the others 'had been warned that the fumes from our special brand of petrol were acutely poisonous', and that there had been ventilation trouble with the S5s. He experienced such problems in the Gloster IV as well, 'but a nip of oxygen and a glass of milk kept ready for the occasion soon put things right again, although I felt the effects of the poisoning, as we all did occasionally at that time, for two days afterwards'.

The pace was now quickening at Calshot with every possible variable being tried out and tested. Different types of propeller were fitted and different types of speed turn attempted, in order to achieve decisive effect. Indeed, it became obvious that the race could be lost almost from the outset by the slightest mistake in the method of turning. Yet, as always, the team were at the mercy of the weather. Schofield describes one of Kink's earliest flights in an S5 as having been on a day similar to that on which he died:

> Sullen and steely grey everywhere, a feeling that outside the vague sort of cocoon that encased the immediate landscape, the powerful sun was trying to break through, but was only succeeding in making the inner existence humid and depressing. Sky and sea blended together so ethereally that it was impossible to tell where one finished and the other started ... Yet Kink insisted that he knew exactly what he was doing, and put up his usual faultless show. For the greater part of the time he cannot have known in what direction he was flying ... Who could ever hope to

master such visibility in which one lost all sense of direction and height, especially when the height from the water was usually only some 150 feet.

From such a height, at 300mph, it would take about one-third of a second to hit the water. These were the conditions, Schofield noted sadly, and this was the location where Kink 'suddenly turned down and vanished forever' only a few months later.

At the end of August, after a few days in London buying tropical kit and other clothing, Kink, Webster and Schofield met at Victoria Station for the boat-train to the Continent. Slatter and Worsley were already in Venice preparing for the arrival of the machines and their minders, safely ensconced in the aircraft carrier *Eagle*. Thirty hours later, they found themselves stranded on the Italian mainland, for want of a boat to take them across the few hundred yards separating them from the Lido and the Excelsior Hotel. When they finally arrived, they were warned not to fall into the trap of booking any extras which would all be greatly overpriced for the Excelsior's 'revoltingly wealthy and acquiescent' clientèle. At least the reception from their Italian competitors was warm and unfeigned, though none of them knew any English – except de Bernardi, 'who, as a result of his visit to America, spoke pidgin Italian-English with a marked American accent'. Gradually, the sheer horror of their financial exposure dawned on the members of the British team. Not only had they paid for the tropical uniforms themselves, but a misunderstood offer from the Italians had led the Air Ministry to reduce their special allowances 'to a mere few shillings'. Increasingly desperate efforts to keep track of expenses bills, which they feared were being run up unwittingly, were baulked by the hotel management who 'regretted that it had not been possible, owing to overwork, to get them ready'. Finally, the best efforts of the doughty airmen succeeded, and their worst fears were confirmed:

> I have never seen such brazen robbery and downright swindling practised anywhere. Tea, supposed to be included, had been cleverly wangled to make everything but the bare tea an extra; small cakes were almost the price of their weight in silver ... Small glasses of light beer which we had thought we were pretty safe on, had cost us six shillings and sixpence each, dozens of them. Liras for going on the beach, more for going into the sea, liras for service; washing, in the cases of most of our garments, had been far more each time than we paid for the articles ... Nothing would induce me to stay in that den of thieves again, for all the overrated pleasures of the Lido ... Of course, the object of prolonging the production of our bills was to carry on the good work for as long as possible and, had we not been forewarned, there is no knowing to what extent we might have become involved.

In contrast to the obscene wealth of the Lido, the team nearly came to grief when recognised in a less salubrious part of the city by 'a seething mass of very young ruffians', who quickly grew into a crowd threatening to pen them in.

Only by throwing handfuls of small coins as far as possible in the opposite direction was an escape route opened up:

It was a rather dangerous thing to do, we were told afterwards, for under similar circumstances on other occasions, numbers of the young lunatics, crazed by the unusual sight of money, had fought so furiously that large numbers of them had finished up in hospital with very serious injuries. But what were we to do?

Schofield's brief role in the Kinkead story was rapidly approaching its close. He was scheduled to make a trial flight in the Crusader – or 'Curious Ada', as she had come to be known without much affection. Whereas the Italians had developed the superior technique of transporting their machines over the water on lighters, the British still proceeded by motor-boat and tow-rope, causing constant fear of capsizing. On 11 September, the Crusader was taken to the Lagoon in this manner and Schofield strapped himself in. It had already been decided not to use her in the front line, as her top speed clearly did not match those of the S5s and the Glosters. She had been assembled, inspected and duly accredited by the appropriate civilian and Service personnel. In his memoirs, Schofield was understandably defensive about his own omission of pre-flight checks:

I must admit that I did not go to the extent of checking up every point. Perhaps I should have done, but who would have done under such circumstances? Anyway, far from trying to find excuses for what happened ... even had I spent some time in the process, I doubt whether I should have hit upon the cause of the trouble to come.

That is, at best, debatable: for, when the machine had been reassembled, the aileron wires had been crossed. By connecting them to the wrong flaps, a rigger had ensured that any attempt to correct a roll in the aircraft would have exactly the opposite effect. Schofield took off in the direction of the Lido, holding the machine close to the surface in order to check that some mischief was not about to happen immediately. Suddenly, a bump forced the starboard wing upwards to an angle of 60 degrees. At about 150mph he made the correction; but, instead of flattening out, the Crusader immediately rotated past the vertical, the port wingtip struck the surface and with a tremendous crash the aircraft took him to the bottom of the Lagoon. By some miracle, the cockpit broke apart and a fierce surge of water shot him to the surface, stripped of all his clothing:

I was told, when I came round many hours later, that not only had I been swimming at a terrific rate when the Italian speedboat caught me, but that I had put up a fearful scrap when they tried to get me aboard ... Our own motor-boat returning later saw two wee black shapes bobbing up and down on the swell, and picked up my shoes which were being supported by a bubble of air in each toe.

167

On recovering consciousness in hospital, he found he had no broken bones but not one spot of white skin anywhere on his body – which was 'all the most beautiful blacks, blues and reds'. Though thankful to be alive, he naturally had no idea of the cause of the crash, which emerged only when the wreckage was recovered a few days later. Some impulse had prompted him to change his normal glass goggles for Triplex safety ones. This undoubtedly saved his eyesight. A kindly visit from General Balbo, the Italian Air Minister, and his retinue was some consolation; but the knowledge that, prior to the accident, he had been selected to fly the fastest of the British machines, was a bitter pill to swallow.

Chapter Nine

Victory at Venice

In December 1927, nine of Kink's fellow airmen – including Taffy Jones, James Robb and 'Mary' Coningham – presented him with a gilt-edged volume of newspaper and magazine reports, which they had commissioned from Durrant's of Holborn Viaduct, the leading press cuttings agency. It is typical of Kink's career that the largest collection of material about his adventure in Venice was created not by him, but at the behest of others. The album begins in the week prior to the Schneider race, originally scheduled for Sunday 25 September, and concludes a month later with reports of Kink's impending selection to mount an attack on the World Speed Record. Dozens of different publications combine to paint a vivid picture of what happened to the team in Italy.

First reports indicated that as many as 200,000 spectators were anticipated. Among them would be diplomats, dignitaries and, possibly, dictators. On Wednesday 21 September, Sir Philip Sassoon MP arrived after a 6½-hour flight. The Under-Secretary of State for Air said he was optimistic that the British team would succeed; and everyone was keen to stress the goodwill and sportsmanship of the competitors. Yet, there were political undertones. The correspondent for the *Liverpool Post* was told that day that the race would be watched 'by Signor Mussolini, who is taking a great interest in the effort to retain the Trophy' – and this was a factor in Sir Samuel Hoare's decision to stay away. Thirty years later, he recalled:

> I myself did not go to Venice. I was doubtful as to whether we could win, and I did not want to be present when Mussolini and his Fascists were sure to turn an Italian victory into a triumph of dictatorships over democracies. Besides, I had received a royal command to be the Minister in Attendance on the King at Balmoral at the very time when the race was due to be flown. I accordingly refused Mussolini's invitation, and waited anxiously in London to hear the result. I actually received the news of our victory when I was already on the night train for Scotland.

It quickly became clear that, far from being the favourites, the Italians were the underdogs. This probably accounts for the eventual non-appearance of *Il Duce* at the Lido. The same report which suggested his likely presence also demonstrated the potential of the RAF team:

> The Supermarine-Napier S5 is probably the speediest of the British machines, and the Italians themselves are inclined to the opinion that it

will be the fastest craft taking part in the race. At the same time, I am assured by the pilots that the Gloster-Napier IV machine, which will start the race and will be flown by Flight Lieutenant S.M. Kinkead, has not yet shown its fullest speed. This is really the 'dark horse' of the race. I am assured authoritatively – and there can be no harm now in stating it – that the Gloster has touched a speed of 296mph and could probably be 'pushed out' a little more … Britain's chances may be written down as excellent … The Italians have given all the help possible to the British team. They have shown themselves thoroughly good sportsmen, but I rather fancy that they are anxious about the result. There are a host of Italian experts here, and one of them quite frankly expressed to me today the view that the Supermarine-Napier S5 was generally regarded as the most likely winner.

Trials had been under way for the past few days and the airmanship shown by the RAF pilots had attained 'a remarkable degree of perfection'. When Kink took one of the Glosters out over the actual course for more than half an hour, the press were enthralled. 'That was a marvellous performance, and there is no danger of any breakdown in the human factor,' commented one journalist. Another suggested that Kink's average speed had been 294mph, and exulted: 'If this can be repeated on Sunday, there should be no doubt about a British triumph. It was a remarkable tribute no less to the skill of the pilot than to the stability of the engine.' It was true that the preliminary seaworthiness tests, in which the aircraft had to remain afloat, untended for six hours, might eliminate one or two machines. However, it seemed that 'the only way in which Britain can fail to secure the Trophy is by the whole trio of competing machines being forced down during the race and failing to finish the course'.

This impression was reinforced by the obvious problems of the host team. The *Daily Mail* correspondent, Paul Bewsher, explained that the Italians were having

difficulty in obtaining satisfactory revolutions from their engines. While being tested this morning, an Italian engine burst into flames. Watched by the English team, on the opposite side of the canal, the Italians frantically pumped the contents of the extinguisher on it and subdued the fire. The engine was working again a little later.

Bewsher, a former RNAS observer with a DSC to his credit, was a gifted poet and writer with a vivid turn of phrase. He fully understood the risks and pressures which the airmen would face:

Never have air pilots been called upon to undergo such an ordeal as will be the case on Sunday. It is possible that the machines may reach a speed of 300mph, and that the pilots will travel faster than any human being has ever done before. This morning I was awed by the sight of machines out for a trial spin. A seaplane flashed down the long beach of the Lido like a shell and with the same rapidly rising and rapidly dying wail. One moment the machine was a scarcely seen dot on the far left; the next moment it was disappearing out of sight on the right.

For all the talk of good sportsmanship and goodwill, Slatter did not want to take any chances. Lawrence Coombes was one of two Technical Officers attached to the team, the other being Flying Officer Tom Moon. In keeping with his acerbic style, Coombes's account tells that, by the time of his arrival, 'Moon was already in a state of revolt'. In order to prevent any sabotage of the aircraft, 'Slatter had ordered him to sleep down at the air station with the machines, and he had been eaten alive by mosquitoes. He flatly refused to spend another night there, when there was a wonderful hotel to sleep in.' And who could blame any young officer for thinking this way, in such a location, with 'languid beauties ... lolling in gaily-hued diaphanous silk pyjamas on the most exotic beach of the world' – as the *Weekly Dispatch* described it? Indeed, for the airmen, much more was on offer than just the Trophy. Under the heading 'Lido Women in a Fever', Keith Ayling of the *Sunday Chronicle* revealed that:

A charming bride awaits [the] winner of the Blue Riband of the air, the Schneider Cup race – if he wants her. That is the offer of her mother, a wealthy American woman who is staying on the Lido. She announced her intention this afternoon of offering her daughter's hand to whatever hero of the air pulls off the great race. Not one of the aviators to whom I have spoken, however, is exactly enthusiastic over the idea ... Large crowds, including British, German, American and Italian visitors, have gathered to see the contest ... Among them are thousands of women who seem to have lost their heads in the general excitement. Crowds of them waited this afternoon for a glimpse of the airmen. Each one is a hero, and lockets and favours containing their photographs are being worn by hundreds of women. Never has there been such a carnival in Venice. Crowded trains arrive, one after the other, and the Grand Canal is a seething mass of boats. This afternoon I saw three gondolas laden with flowers that American women had sent as their tributes to the airmen.

Fortunately, the RAF fliers were resistant to such temptation – at least, before the race. According to Bewsher:

The British pilots are keeping in the most careful training for the terrific nerve and body strain of this high speed flying. Their very carefully ordered life is in striking contrast to that of the cosmopolitan men and women, clad in gaudy silk pyjamas, who fill the huge fashionable hotel at which the pilots are living. This morning I saw members of the British team, looking in superb physical condition, chatting on the beach. Naturally, the airmen are the heroes of the holidaymakers, but they lead Spartan lives, despite all attempts at lionising.

As well as the attention of the ladies, individual pilots were a natural focus for the press. The *Manchester Guardian* claimed that the 'Italian team ... consider

Ferrarin the first string', but that the British would not reveal any preferences of their own. The *Belfast Evening Telegraph* thought that 'Flight Lieutenant S.M. Kinkead and Captain Ferrarin are generally considered to be the two best airmen in the rival teams'. The Aeronautical Correspondent of *The Times* drew attention to what he called 'a most interesting race within a race, so far as the British seaplanes are concerned'. This was because, to the surprise of the British team, 'both the monoplane and the biplane appeared to have practically the same top speeds, whereas purely theoretical assumptions would indicate that the monoplane with its single wing should be the faster'. One report referred to annoyance within the British team at 'the exaggerated reports of speeds published in some English papers', adding that, 'nevertheless, our pilots are all quietly confident'.

As the race drew closer, emphasis was laid on the sheer physical strain for both men and machines. In the seven years since 1920, Schneider race speeds had risen from 107mph to something close to 300mph. 'Can the human heart endure the ordeal of such terrific speeds as 5 miles a minute?' was the question posed in one article. Its author recalled the belief of Victorian doctors, when considering the railways, that anyone travelling at 60mph would die. Modern-day fears could not be dismissed so easily:

> It is not a question of the technical efficiency of the machine but of centrifugal force. It was found that at speeds above 250mph centrifugal force, when turning, drew the blood from the pilot's head to his feet, with the obvious chance of disaster. Both the British and Italian pilots have met the same problem, and it has been part of their training to overcome it.

Naturally, the risk would be greatest when repeatedly tackling acute turns at high speed. Taking a wide circle around a marker pylon was the safest method of cornering, but involved too great a loss of time. There remained the alternatives of 'placing the wings in a vertical position and mounting higher at the same time', or inclining the machine 'three-quarters towards the marking pole without rising higher' and gaining time by turning much closer to the pylon. Either of the latter 'acrobatic' methods carried with it the danger of blacking out.

Unlike the British with their three different prototypes – reduced to two after the Crusader crashed – the Italians put all their faith in a single type of seaplane. This was the Macchi M52 monoplane, which derived its designation from a touch of superstition on the part of Major de Bernardi. When he won the Trophy in America, his machine had been a Macchi M39. To this he added the number 13, as that had been both the date of the race and the total of competitors taking part. For Venice, five Macchi M52s had been prepared – one for training, three for the race and one as a reserve. They had been built from the wood of the 'Californian silver spruce fir, which combines lightness and strength'; but were nowhere near as slender in body, or as compact in engine design, as the Supermarines. One account suggested that, of twelve engines manufactured by the Italians, no fewer than six had been destroyed in tests intended to boost their maximum speed.

Commenting on 'The Fastest Race in the World' for the *Morning Post*, was Major Oliver Stewart MC, a former Sopwith Pup ace who later received an Air Force Cross for his post-war experimental work. He contrasted the new generation of seaplanes, which were capable of 270–300mph, with racing cars, locomotives and motor-boats – and concluded that the seaplanes could 'make rings round the next fastest vehicle on earth'. These aircraft travelled at more than one-third of the speed of sound. The sight of one of them passing over-head made a tremendous impression:

> It first appears in the sky as a black dot which grows in size at a fantastic pace. The engine sings the note of a far distant bell. Suddenly the ground beneath the spectator's feet trembles, the bell note disappears, and the air is rent by the *fortissimo* crash of a thousand horse-power. There is a streaming glimpse of a blue fuselage and the seaplane is a diminishing dot, pelting for the horizon ... This physical assault upon Time and Space is one of the newest expressions of applied science. The machines are indeed vehicles of exploration. Their pilots are adventurers in unknown places, facing unsolved problems.

Fewer than a dozen men had ever travelled at such extreme speeds, and questions were sometimes asked why it was important to do so. Stewart listed his answers in short order. First, as the Schneider race was the greatest test of aeronautical design and engineering skill, the winning country would gain in prestige and in commercial opportunities. Secondly, progress would be made in techniques of research and development: 'Some of the greatest technical advances in both Service and civil aviation may be traced directly to the Schneider Trophy races.' Yet, to Stewart, as an aviator, such practical justifications were not really necessary. Like the mountaineer faced with an un-conquered peak, the aeronaut viewed the search for speed as an end in itself:

> The pursuit of absolute speed affords an intrinsic satisfaction. It is, as it has been said, a form of exploration in unknown places. Few will rest content until a voyage of discovery has been attempted.

Before any records could be challenged or competitors vanquished, the Schneider Trophy aircraft had to pass a 'Navigability and Watertightness Test', laid down in the rules of the race. The two parts of this elimination process were designed to prove the seaworthiness of the aircraft. Each machine had to complete a course of from 5 to 10 nautical miles on and over the water:

> For this test the competitor must taxi over the starting line, then rise and continue the course, during which he must taxi the machine over two distances of half a nautical mile at a minimum speed of 12 knots ... The remainder of the course will be covered in flight. The competitor must,

however, alight again before completing the course and taxi over the finishing line.

Each contestant was entitled to a second chance, if something went wrong; but, after crossing the finishing line, the machine must be moored immediately to a buoy, where it had to stay afloat unattended for six hours:

> Any machine leaving its mooring during this period will be disqualified. No repairs will be allowed during the ... tests. Except for changing the airscrew, which is allowed, the machine must not undergo any modi-fication between the above tests and the speed contest. It will be stamped to ensure this.

Shortly after 9.00am on Friday 23 September, the British machines left the airport at St Andrea, towed in procession by motor-boats to the starting-point in the Triporte Canal, north of the Lido. Under a cloudy sky with a light breeze blowing, each seaplane had to undertake two ascents, two descents and various taxiing manoeuvres, while Sir Philip Sassoon, Signor Balbo and a large assembly looked on. Kink was the first away in his Gloster IVB, N223, fitted with a geared Napier Lion engine. This meant that two of the three British aircraft finally selected were powered in this way and only Worsley's S5 was not:

> This decision to use two geared and one ungeared-engined machine was partly due to the satisfactory trials with the geared engines. These have given more confidence and there is, therefore, good reason for taking advantage of their slightly superior speed. The Gloster when taxiing at slow speed covered herself with spray, and in fact came along in a cloud of her own making, but directly the pilot opened out and her speed increased she rose cleanly. She took off in good style, and Kinkead did most of the flying part of the test, holding the machine on a cant, which makes very striking flying ... The Italians not being ready, Flight Lieutenant Webster came next, in the Supermarine-Napier, with geared engine ... He, too, got away all right, and was followed by No. 6, Flight Lieutenant Worsley, in the Supermarine-Napier with the ungeared engine. Before 12 o'clock the three British machines were at their moorings.

Oliver Stewart described all three British pilots as making 'faultless take-offs and landings', but regarded Webster as the most impressive in the air. The choice of the correspondent of the *Daily Chronicle* fell on Kink who, he said, 'created a great impression by his handling of the Gloster-Napier'. All the pilots, in reality, were at the top of their form – not least the Italians:

> Bernardi took off on a climbing turn which made one's hair stand on end. The little blood-red Macchi-Fiat ran along the water a short way, rose, and at once climbed steeply and banked to well over the vertical, describ-ing a huge arch against the sky and plunging down with the velocity of a bomb. There were shrieks of delight from the Italian spectators ... For

174

almost the first time in the history of the Schneider Cup the nearer the race approaches the more difficult it is to spot the winner. Usually one type of machine shows an appreciable superiority of design. This year there is no such difference and there are no accurate figures showing the speeds.

Stewart identified one potential weakness on the Italian side, arising from the extent to which the Fiat engines had been pushed to the very limit in order to give what he called 'a frightening power output, more than one horsepower being extracted from every pound weight'. This had caused trouble the night before, with team mechanics still hard at work at 4.00am and the noise of the engines rising and falling as last-minute adjustments were made. By contrast, the Napiers, 'although they also have been squeezed to give the ultimate drop of power, have given very little trouble'.

Even when the aircraft operated perfectly, taking them up was an exercise in discomfort. The *Daily Telegraph* noted that all the British pilots suffered from exhaust fumes blowing into the open cockpits, particularly when the machines were turning: 'They feel indisposition soon after landing, but it soon wears off. Invariably they are as black as sweeps when they have finished a flight.' According to Ralph Barker's narrative, Kink suffered two distinct setbacks during his practice flights. On one occasion

> when Kinkead was about to alight in the Gloster IVB, his spinner came adrift and struck the propeller, causing damage to the propeller shaft. Even worse was the news that fumes in the cockpit, a fault that it was thought had been corrected at Calshot in both the S5 and the Gloster by ventilation from air ducts in the wings, had affected Kinkead so badly that he was confined to his room all next day. The excuse given out was that he was suffering from malaria.

Paul Bewsher remarked that Kink 'had his face, arms and body black with exhaust smoke from the engine. It is said that, if he had looked over the side of his machine during its flight, the side of his face would have been burned' – an added complication given that the forward view of the biplane was so obstructed. Bewsher contrasted the conditions of the pilots with those of the spectators:

> With British naval officers in white ducks, Fascisti in black shirts, Royal Air Force mechanics in khaki drill, and a few Englishwomen in light summer frocks, the gathering was a picturesque one. The crowd on the pier cheered each British pilot when towed in his machine to the mooring buoy after the landing tests.

By the time he wrote those words, however, the weather had deteriorated, a thunderstorm was raging and doubts were growing about the possibility of holding the race at all on 25 September. If it were held successfully, the *Manchester Guardian* noted, nothing would ever be the same for the victor.

Unlike de Bernardi and Ferrarin, the names of Kinkead, Webster, Worsley and Guazzetti were practically unknown to the world:

> yet on Sunday, perhaps, one of these names will become as famous as a Derby winner. Eleven years ago Ferrarin won fame by his Rome-to-Tokyo flight, and last year, de Bernardi won the Schneider Cup in America. The British pilots are still hardly known, but already they begin to arouse interest. Kinkead, a South African, short and stocky, Webster red-haired and jolly, Worsley taller and good-looking.

The teams had apparently become the best of friends and it was said that, when they tried to 'pump' each other for information, someone would always give the game away by bursting out laughing. It seemed a bad omen for the Italians that mechanics were fiddling with the engines right up to the last minute and that Ferrarin in particular almost missed the deadline for the elimination tests. Writing on the Saturday, the *Observer*'s correspondent referred to the pilots as 'heroic pioneers of war aviation', and predicted that: 'Their small aircraft will develop as war scouts.' This was, in effect, 'a contest between two Ministries, the only Air Ministries in the world', in order to be the fastest. Yet, there could be no doubt of the genuine warmth extended to the RAF team:

> Captain Ferrarin, who is such a wonderful pilot, told me today that he thought our machines were perfectly splendid, and there was no mistaking his sincerity and enthusiasm. Captain Ferrarin and the three de Bernardi brothers, who are airmen, told me they have very friendly feelings for England and her airmen. Other Italians remarked on the fine display of the 'deck-landers' in alighting on the deck of the aircraft carrier *Eagle*. Much comment has also been made on the fact that our men have been enjoying themselves, playing tennis and so forth, quite free of the care of their machines, while the Italians criticised themselves severely for working up to the last possible moments on their own.

At a higher level, elements of one-upmanship were just discernible – the *Sunday Express* referring, for example, to the Squadron of eight Italian warships moored in the harbour along with HMS *Eagle*, and the 10,000 people who had gathered in the Piazza di San Marco on the Friday night 'to listen to a magnificent orchestral and vocal concert which was held to raise funds to present the Italian Government with a seaplane from the citizens of Venice'. One potential problem was resolved on the Saturday, when Sidney Webster successfully retook the navigability test. He had been given no warning of any infringement when attempting it the first time, and had been told to proceed to the mooring-out; but his initial disqualification at 4.00pm on the Friday did not upset his equanimity or his concentration. Now he was safely poised for the main event.

It was still intended to stage the race on 25 September, despite the thunderstorm on the Friday afternoon, when the six moored seaplanes had been battered by giant hailstones – causing fear of possible damage to the radiators in the wings. The *Sunday Times* explained that the beach in front of the Excelsior Hotel would be cleared on the day of the race, so that the authorities could charge spectators £1 for a seat and 'hundreds of Lido loungers in bathing costumes [could] watch the men gamble their lives'. A fresh breeze had sprung up after dark on the Friday, when the last of the seaplanes completed its mooring test and was towed to the sheds 'over a dangerous swell'. The paper believed that Kink would be likely to win: 'The daring pilot created a record for speedy turning and straight flying [and] cornered the course with remarkably little loss of speed.' However, it had learned of the risk he faced of being 'rendered unconscious by the engine gases'. He was due to be the first competitor and de Bernardi the second. Nowhere in the reports is there a mention of Mussolini appearing at Venice; but General Balbo, the Under-Secretary for Air, gave a lunch on the Saturday to all the competitors, at which the toast was 'May the best team win!'

It was well known that the winning speed of the nine Schneider races to date had risen from 45.7mph to 246.49mph. Now the goal of 5 miles a minute was drawing closer. A speed of 300 miles per hour 'would take one from Charing Cross to the far end of Hampstead Heath in one minute; from London to Paris in fifty-eight minutes; to New York in ten hours; and around the world in 3½ days' – these were illustrations supplied by the *Weekly Dispatch*. Its report summed up the personalities of the RAF team whose combined ages totalled just eighty-six years:

> The favourite is Flight Lieutenant S.N. Webster, who has the fastest machine (a Supermarine-Napier S5) and is the most dashing. Boyish-looking, with reddish hair, he is always full of high spirits and is utterly fearless … Flight Lieutenant S.M. Kinkead, who pilots the first machine to start, is a quiet, thoughtful man, regarded as the brains of the team. As calm judgement whilst travelling at 300 miles an hour is the most important factor, his chances of victory are also considered to be excellent. Flight Lieutenant O.E. Worsley, the third British pilot, is regarded as the most temperamental and is considered by some as the 'dark horse' of the team.

The newspaper explained that although some pilots used special harnesses to try to avert blackouts when cornering, both competing teams had trained specially to tighten their turns, by stages, over a period of months to remove the symptoms and the danger of unconsciousness:

> All the same … the ordeal of today's race will be tremendous, terrifying. The screaming roar of engine and propeller, the strain of the rush through the air, the anxiety to make each of the many turns with the least possible falling off in speed – this will make this year's race such a supreme test of man as well as machine that none but a superb, trained-to-the-hour athlete, one who has magnificent physique as well as outstanding aerial skill, could possibly hope to survive it.

The popular Sunday papers were working themselves up into a frenzy. As well as revealing the 'bride-on-offer', the *Sunday Chronicle* stressed that there had never been an air race 'fraught with such perils'. A slip or a miscalculation would mean almost certain death, and the British pilots would be flying in shorts and sweaters 'as anything like flapping clothes or protruding buttons might mean disaster'. Webster was said to be the 'star' but Kink was 'also much fancied':

He is the most-decorated man in the British team, and declared this afternoon that he would 'do or die' in his attempt to bring home the trophy. Once fitted into his machine he must get off the water quickly or he stands in danger of being suffocated by the exhaust fumes from his engine. A human incident occurred this afternoon when a Canadian who fought with Kinkead over the German lines arrived to see the race. He has travelled over 4,000 miles to be with his former comrade.

The correspondent for the *Sunday Herald* was preoccupied with insect and other metaphors:

Flight Lieutenant S.M. Kinkead is expected to win ... He has achieved the fastest speed yet, and he has accomplished some brilliant banking round the twenty sharp turns that make the triangular course so difficult. The Italian pilots say they experience faintness when making these acute turns, but our men have conquered this sensation ... The Italian machines look like red gnats, and the British seaplanes resemble blue-gold flying fish as they glint over the water, almost too fast for the eye to follow ... Lieutenants Kinkead, Worsley and Webster told me today they were very fit and well and would make a good show, adding that they must not underestimate the Italians ... It is impossible to obtain details of the machines, which are closely guarded by armed squads ... The price of a Lido stand has been trebled and there is a great boat ramp. It is impossible to buy, hire or borrow anything that will float ... Prices charged by the boatmen would make a Thames waterman's mouth water. There are plenty of mosquitoes here which sting – like the hotels, where you pay even for the hire of air. It is said that this week will explode the high-price bubble. The gondola business was never so flourishing in the Grand Canal – the equivalent of our Oxford Circus.

Yet, much of this enterprise was in vain. When Bewsher filed his despatch for the *Daily Mail* on the Sunday evening, it was not to report the result of the contest. The next day's headline read: 'GALE STOPS GREAT AIR RACE – AMAZING SCENES IN VENICE – 250,000 VISITORS – HOPE FOR TODAY'. A quarter of a million people, many at a fever-pitch of excitement, had had to be let down. Bitter was the sense of disappointment when the decision to postpone, taken only at 11.00am on the Sunday, was announced. More than 100,000 spectators had already gathered in anticipation of the event scheduled for 2.30pm. Soon the steamboats were returning to Venice packed

178

with dejected travellers, some seriously out of pocket and unable to stay for a further twenty-four hours. Bewsher described what had happened and why the delay was unavoidable:

For more than twenty-four hours special excursion trains had been arriving from all parts of Italy, especially from the densely populated cities of the north. The Government had cut railway fares by half for the occasion, and patriotic Italians came in droves in the hope of seeing their champions win the world's most important air race. The gaily beflagged, narrow streets and the canal bridges were so packed as to be almost impassable. Throughout yesterday, until the early hours of this morning, a special service of steamboats took sightseers to the Lido, where hundreds slept on the beach and in open spaces. Many others slept in the open in Venice . . . [And when the] steamboat service was resumed at 4 o'clock this morning . . . tens of thousands of men and women, carrying flasks of wine and parcels of food, crossed the sparkling lagoon, among warships, to the long island of the Lido, which provides a superb grandstand for the race.

However, on the Saturday night, a strong wind sprang up. By Sunday morning the sea, which had been calm for days, was very rough. Sassoon told Bewsher:

It is very disappointing not only for the crowds but also for the pilots, who are keyed up to racing pitch. I understand that not for ten years has there been such a strong wind at this time of year. It is a pity the weather should have chosen this day.

The seaplanes could have taken off safely from the sheltered waters of the Lagoon behind the Lido; but, if one were forced down at sea during the race, it would probably capsize and drown the pilot, even if he managed to alight without disaster.

By noon on Monday, however, the sea-state had been transformed. Despite heavy cloud, there was just 'a bare semblance of wind' and the surface became perfectly calm. For some the change came too late, and the crowd was much diminished although still very substantial. A report in the *Star* drew attention to further hazards:

Apart from the great danger of engine breakdown . . . the possibility of colliding at the turns cannot be entirely ruled out. From their low cockpits the pilots can see but little around them. In some cases the seaplanes are almost 'blind'. At the dangerous turns . . . there will be no more than seconds separating the competitors. Though there is an interval of five minutes between the despatch of each plane from the starting-point, so that the first away will have nearly completed the 217 miles before the last starts, it is inevitable that there will be bunching at some of the turns as the great thrilling contest proceeds. That is why Lido spectators will be gazing this afternoon on a flight which may mean death to any unfortunate who makes the least slip.

On the afternoon of Monday 26 September, all the speculation and anticipation came up against reality. Oliver Stewart's account in the *Morning Post* set
the scene:

A high layer of grey cloud hid the sun when the time approached for the
start of the race. The 15-mile strip of sand of the most expensive and most
exclusive resort in Europe was black with people. The Crown Prince
entered the special royal box on the roof of the Excelsior Hotel at 2 o'clock.
Two minutes before 2.30 the hubbub of conversation died down and
all eyes were turned to the north. Then the loudspeakers announced that
the first machine, Kinkead in the Gloster, had taken off. A black dot could
be distinguished moving over the distant sky. It climbed to 4,000 feet and
the crowd held their breaths as it swooped for the starting line. 20 feet
above the sea and 30 feet in front of the spectators it hurtled past and the
air seemed filled with the thunder of its engine. Straining eyes caught a
glimpse of the helmeted head of Kinkead crouching at the controls.

In the *Daily Mail*, Paul Bewsher's description was equally vivid:

From beginning to end the race was full of thrills. Just after half-past two,
when it was due to start, a wave of excitement passed over the crowds
packing the beach when a tiny black speck was seen in the grey, overcast
sky far away. It grew rapidly larger; its drone rose to a wail, its wail to a
roar, and then, with an ear-piercing scream, the bronze and blue Gloster-
Napier biplane, piloted by Flight Lieutenant Kinkead, flashed like a
meteor only 30 feet above the sea. For a brief moment, while one's heart
was forced to one's mouth by the sight of the awful speed, one's eyes were
able to hold a clear image of the seaplane. Then, with its scream dying to
a wail, it was a fast-shrinking dot in the sky. A few minutes later amid
the frantic cheers of thousands of Italians, the blood-red torpedo of the
Macchi-Fiat monoplane, piloted by Major de Bernardi, howled by in
pursuit some 60 feet above the land immediately behind the beach. Four
tense minutes passed. Then far out over the smooth waters of the Adriatic,
just above the tiny orange sails of a fishing fleet and the stately grey British
warships, I saw a little black shape moving rapidly towards the left. It was
Flight Lieutenant Kinkead who, having made a right about-turn round the
distant pylon 10 miles away to my right, was heading back to the pylon
4 miles on my left. As he approached this pylon great excitement was
caused by speculations as to how he would go round it. It was seen that he
circled it in a wide sweep. Major de Bernardi, who followed a few minutes
later, rose up into the sky and shaved it close with a dizzy, vertical bank.

When Webster's turn came to cross the starting line, it seemed to Stewart to
introduce 'an altogether new conception of movement'. The S5 appeared to
stride over the face of the sky 'as if entirely detached from the ordinary forces
governing the movements of earthly objects'. He reported the cheers of the
Italians dying away, to be succeeded by 'silent astonishment'. Guazzetti,

Worsley and Ferrarin followed in steady succession, and it was clear that every machine was being driven to its limit. 'As the machines tore by,' Stewart wrote,

> it was impossible not to think of the men who piloted them with such skill and daring. Trapped in their tiny cockpits, with the terrific heat of the engine being driven back onto them by the rush of air like a blast from a furnace, they flew superbly.

Kink's first lap was quickly displayed on the official timekeepers' board – 6 minutes, 59 seconds. De Bernardi's was given as 7 minutes exactly, and a close contest seemed likely. It was not to be. Engine trouble forced down the Italian after his first circuit, just as it did to Ferrarin whose Macchi emitted a puff of smoke and a tongue of flame when crossing the starting line. A few minutes into the race, only Guazzetti and the British remained in contention – with the Italian's speed appreciably slower than theirs. It seemed as if the geared machines were both on course for victory. Kink was flying as low as possible, to maximise his sideways view and firmly keep his bearings. His second lap, once into his stride, was 6 minutes, 43 seconds, while his third was stated to be 6 minutes, 26 seconds, constituting more than 289mph if confirmed. At one point, he overhauled an S5 – which had started later – and passed it near the Porto di Lido turn. Bewsher thought it was the N220:

> Flight Lieutenant Kinkead, who was clinging to the tail of Flight Lieutenant's Webster's machine round one lap, passed him right opposite the grandstand. With fearless daring, Flight Lieutenant Kinkead thrust his machine down to only a few feet from the water and shot ahead right underneath his comrade.

However, *Flight* magazine correctly identified the other machine as Worsley's N219 and captured the moment in an iconic photograph. The two were flying close together at the turning point:

> After they had straightened out, a terrific race ensued … and it came somewhat as a surprise to see the Gloster-Napier biplane actually pass the monoplane opposite the Excelsior.

The *Aeroplane* was similarly impressed with Kink's phenomenally tight cornering, which sharply contrasted with the extravagant climbing turns on which the Italian team relied:

> At the end of [Worsley's] first lap, Flight Lieutenant Kinkead was about 100 yards behind him. Flight Lieutenant Kinkead put on a steeper bank and practically did a half-circle concentric with Flight Lieutenant Worsley's, coming out on a line for the hotel about 100 yards in front of him and 50 feet or so below him. It was quite the prettiest sight of the whole race, and it showed how beautifully both pilots were cornering. After that, both Flight Lieutenant Webster and Flight Lieutenant Worsley took their corners a good deal closer, with a steeper bank.

Major C.C. Turner, writing for the *Daily Telegraph* was enthralled to have witnessed 'the most remarkable aeroplane race ever seen':

> The spectacle of the race far exceeded all anticipations ... The Gloster biplane, in its coat of copper and blue, was a thing of sheer loveliness. In a rare gleam of sun it looked like a tropical hummingbird. Its speed was unmistakable, and the roar of its engine, clean and sonorous, sang of strength.

He also believed that Kink had achieved a third-lap speed of 289.76 miles per hour, over 50 kilometres. Although it seemed that 'a small correction may have to be made', he thought there was 'no doubt that Kinkead flew faster than any other pilot in the race, and therefore in the world'. In fact, the Gloster IVB had become the fastest biplane seaplane which ever flew, but it had not beaten Mitchell's creation. The timing for Kink's third lap had been faulty and, in a late-night press *communiqué*, it was revised from 6 minutes, 26 seconds, to 6 minutes, 45 seconds – reducing his speed to 277.18mph, in comparison with Webster's fastest lap of 284.2mph.

The cause of the error was obvious to Coombes – observing for the Air Ministry – who could see the whole of the course from the roof of the hotel:

> The official timing hut was situated on the beach in front of the Excelsior Hotel. The observers had a difficult task as their field of vision was restricted ... and warning of approach was inadequate.

Despite the correction of this mistake, which appeared in the press two days after the race, most subsequent accounts have suggested that Kink's speed 'fell away' after his third lap. What actually happened showed much greater consistency. By flying so low after his first circuit at 6 minutes, 59 seconds, Kink shaved more than 16 seconds from his initial timing and then completed three more laps within a margin of difference of just 3.39 seconds. The fourth lap took 6 minutes, 46 seconds and only on the fifth did his speed falter – as something went critically wrong with the aircraft. Soon after completing that circuit in 6 minutes, 55.35 seconds, Kink rapidly turned away and landed safely in the Triporte Canal. The cause of his exit was the Gloster IV's spinner – the streamlined cone fitting over the hub of his propeller. This had come adrift during his practice flight on 21 September, striking the airscrew itself and causing damage to the propeller shaft. Only by working flat-out had the RAF mechanics made the necessary repairs in time for the navigability test. Now the same fault had apparently recurred, setting up a vibration which led Kink instantly to abandon the contest. According to an account in the *Aeroplane*:

> the spinner on the airscrew boss of the Gloster had cracked just where the blade of the screw passes through it, and ... a strip of the cracked metal had wrapped itself round the blade of the screw and so had thrown the whole thing out of balance – such is the effect of even a tiny piece of metal at those colossal speeds. Anyhow, it was enough to set up a vibration

which shook the whole machine and did, one believes, actually jolt loose the carburettor intake pipe in spite of the locknuts and all forms of assurance. An RAF officer who had been at St Andrea when the engines were being run up just before the race told one afterwards that he had spotted at the time that the spinner was a trifle out of truth, but that as he was there entirely unofficially he had not liked to comment on the fact. It was rather a pity he did not.

The historian of the Gloster Aircraft Company, Derek James, gives a slightly different emphasis:

When N223 was back in its hangar the propeller was removed and, despite the popular theory that it was a 'thrown spinner' which caused the retirement, it was discovered that the Lion's splined propeller shaft had a crack going three-quarters of the way round it. Thus, Kinkead's decision to retire from the contest almost certainly saved the aircraft and his life from an untimely end. This race marked the last appearance of a biplane in the Schneider Trophy series, but Glosters had the satisfaction of knowing that N223's third lap of 277.1mph had set an all-time record for biplane types.

It had been an extremely narrow escape, but also a fine result for an aircraft with such limited visibility. (Despite this handicap, James also notes that the ungeared Gloster IV – N222 – 'is known to have been looped and rolled by Kinkead, the first high speed aircraft of this type to be used for aerobatics', though no other reports of this seem to exist.)

Only Guazzetti remained to challenge Webster and Worsley, albeit that his best time was slower than Britain's worst. He was just coming to the end of his sixth lap when, to everyone's surprise, he shot out of sight behind the hotel and did not reappear. 'The spectators waited for the crash,' Bewsher reported, 'but later it was learned that he had landed safely in the Lagoon.' Webster and Worsley then passed the finishing post, in that order, 'still travelling almost at the same speed as at the start'.

Webster was under maximum pressure, until the last moment. Almost disqualified at the outset, he was determined not to lose on a technicality. The British had tried to guard against pilots miscounting the number of circuits flown. They had a simple device consisting of a piece of board with holes in it covered by paper. Punching one out at the end of each lap should provide a foolproof method of keeping score. David Mondey's history of the race explains why the winner flew an extra lap:

Webster had duly punched out his seven holes, but a glance at his watch showed an elapsed time of only forty-six minutes out of an anticipated fifty-plus. Had he slipped up with his 'counter'? He could not be sure that he had not punched a hole at the beginning and end of one lap. On the ground, both Scarlett and Slatter were afraid that Webster would run out of fuel on this eighth lap, with the attendant dangers of an unpowered landing. It was with considerable relief that his approach was heard some minutes later, the Lion giving a roar of victory as it swooped over the finishing line.

★ ★ ★

The British victory was not only a triumph for the country, the Royal Air Force and its pilots, it was a massive vindication of the design genius of R.J. Mitchell who – in less than a decade of life left to him – went on to create the Supermarine S6A and S6B from which in turn sprang the Spitfire. It is barely conceivable that the fighter planes upon which Britain's survival depended in 1940 would have been developed when they were, but for the impetus of the Schneider Trophy contests. The ungeared Napier Lion engine had given Worsley an average speed of 273.01mph over the 217-mile course. Webster's record-breaking win, with the geared Napier Lion engine, had averaged 281.66mph. This meant that, on a seven-lap course involving twenty difficult turns, the S5 had still beaten the fastest time ever achieved in the air – by a land aeroplane over a straight course of just 3 kilometres. The *Daily Telegraph* remarked that, where seaplanes were concerned, this was true of Kink and Worsley too:

> Although ... the corrected timing deprives Flight Lieutenant Kinkead of the honour with Flight Lieutenant Webster, of beating the aeroplane record – land as well as sea – which is 278½ miles per hour for a land machine, his speed of 277.18mph is a seaplane record, the previous figure being 258.3mph for this class. Flight Lieutenant Worsley's 273.07mph also exceeds that record by nearly 15mph.

Newspapers were also quick to translate such figures into everyday examples. At 280mph, they pointed out, one could travel from London to Brighton in eleven minutes, to Cardiff in thirty, to Penzance in fifty-five and to New York in 12½ hours. By comparison, one noted, the day after the race: 'The world's longest non-stop train run was made yesterday by the LM&S train *Royal Scot*, which covered the 300 miles from Carlisle to London in 5 hours 45 minutes.'

Everyone had come through the contest safely, though at various times danger had loomed. Not only had Kink's sensitivity and skill saved him from disaster, but all three of the Italians were at risk when their engines failed at very high speed. Even the winner faced problems, as the *Telegraph*'s correspondent recounted, while the act of alighting safely, but inaccessibly, could also be hazardous:

> Soon after Webster started, a slight breakage occurred in the cowling of his engine, and this undoubtedly reduced his speed slightly, and it is further of interest to note that he was not at all times flying with throttle fully open. His speed was very even, and his wonderful piloting has impressed everybody here. But the flying of all the members of the British team was

184

exceptionally good. They came over the line again and again at the same height and place.

Bernardi had a forced landing out on the course, and he was for two hours rocking about on the swell in heavy rain. Eventually he was rescued by a British destroyer and, as he was suffering from chill and exhaustion, he was removed to hospital. No ill results are expected. Elaborate precautions had been taken by the Italians for rescue work, and many fast craft were on the course. Arrangements had been made even for doctors to swim from the first-aid boats to a wrecked seaplane. Bernardi's experience shows how great are the difficulties of locating seaplanes when down on the water.

According to the *Daily Express*, all the Italian pilots declared that they retired because of trouble with engines or oil pumps. The British pilots were described as looking more like minstrels than members of the RAF, so smoke-filled had the cockpits been. Under the headline 'Matchless Skill and Daring', the *Daily News* called the event 'the most thrilling race in the history of flying':

> Expert prediction that failure of machine, engine, or pilot would be followed by a dreadful crash and death was fortunately not realised. The course, with its two extremely acute turns in each of the seven laps, imposed a fearful test on the stamina and skill of the racers, but man again rose superior to the conditions imposed on him. Nothing finer has been seen than the matchless daring of all the fliers at these acute turns ... Webster was helped from his plane by cheering mechanics. His face was black with oil and exhaust fumes, his sweater and shorts streamed with oil, and the exhaust gases which swept into the cockpit as he throttled down his engine to land had slightly affected him. One of the first things he asked for was a cigarette. In company with the other members of the British team he had been placed in strict training months before, and he had sometimes complained since he arrived on the Lido that it was fifteen weeks since he had had a smoke or a drink.

As soon as news of the result came through, Sir Samuel Hoare cabled his congratulations to Scarlett:

> Delighted to learn successful issue of today's contest with our Italian friends, whose skill and sportsmanship have been so abundantly shown in previous races. Please convey Flight Lieutenant Webster and all concerned my heartiest congratulations on magnificent victory of Supermarine and Napier Lion engine, which is one more proof of unsurpassed excellence of British personnel and material.

The day after the race, *The Times* ran a leading article headed 'The British Triumph' on precisely the lines to which the Secretary of State had subscribed when urging official participation in the contest:

> The race for the cup, as everyone knows, has for some time past ceased to be a race for any competitor not representing the whole resources of his

country in manhood and engineering; it is a contest in which nation is pitted against nation, the best of its men and the best of its machines being chosen for it after exhaustive trials.

Webster had exceeded the previous year's winning speed by about 35mph – 'an immense leap forward and one that is unprecedented for any single year in the history of the race'. Victory had been secured at a time when some believed that the country was not living up to its earlier reputation in the air:

> It has now been shown that there is nothing that Great Britain cannot do if she gives her mind to it . . . Apart, however, from the international prestige of the victory, on which the eyes of the whole world have been fixed, the country has gained enormously in technical knowledge and experience by preparing for the competition; and there is every justification for continuing a policy of consistent and co-ordinated research and for participation in some of the more spectacular feats from which hitherto British airmen have held aloof.

Congratulations flowed in from near and far. In France there were 'expressions of the highest admiration', despite Webster having exceeded in a seaplane the world speed record held by a Frenchman in a landplane. The *Petit Journal* said that the result proved that human beings could travel at speeds previously regarded as probably fatal. It also showed what could be done by indomitable will, energy and perseverance. Following setbacks in the Schneider Trophy contest, the British had quietly set about creating the fastest seaplanes in the world, and they had done so in a patient and painstaking way which made ultimate victory certain. 'What an example for us,' the journal declared, 'a seaplane has beaten our airspeed record, established in 1924, which we had not thought it necessary to try to improve.'

In the United States, there was generous praise at the highest level for the British victory. Edward Warner, the Assistant Secretary of Naval Aeronautics, gave credit to the effort made in engine design. Quite recently, British aviators had looked to America as an engine supplier, but it now appeared that their own designers, when properly supported financially, could compete with the world. At home, there was sympathy for Kink's near miss at glory. Under the heading 'A Fine Effort – British Flier's Bad Luck at Venice', the *Daily News* declared that he 'flew a magnificent course in his Gloster-Napier biplane till he was forced down by the breaking adrift of the spinner over the propeller boss'. It also paid tribute to his 'distinguished war record', listing his five principal gallantry awards. More whimsically, 'The Londoner' commiserated with him in the *Evening News*. In a piece entitled 'Speed and Change', just before news came through of the reduction in Kink's third-lap time, the columnist wrote as one of the 'creatures that crawl slowly on the face of the earth':

> As for my London journeys, I doubt if starting from this house where I sit writing I might be in Hampstead before the swift Webster, leaving at the same time, would have come down at Paris. Yet they say that even

Webster's speed was passed, over one lap of the course, by Kinkead who, flying straight, must have flown at more than 300 miles an hour. Alas, that the spinner of Kinkead's plane should have broken loose. I have no idea of what a spinner may be; they who tell me that it is a cone-shaped piece of metal placed over the propeller boss to give streamline form to the nose of the fuselage do not help the understanding of a man who winds up his clock timidly, being ignorant of all mechanical things. But yet I can grieve that this spinner should have broken loose, forcing the valiant Kinkead to come down at the end of his sixth lap. Honour to Webster who flew on until the end! Honour also to Kinkead who might not go on flying for that evil spinner's misdoings. May the angels, who must ever have sympathy for other fliers, have a care of those two stout-hearted ones in all their bold flights, for indeed such men live perilously.

Chapter Ten

Reactions to the Race

The defeated Italians hid their disappointment well, entertaining the British team at a luncheon sponsored by the Royal Italian Aero Club. This was a prelude to greater celebrations at home, where the aviators were due to arrive on the Saturday after the race. An Air Council luncheon at the Savoy Hotel in honour of the team had already been announced for 4 October. Originally the intention was for the team to return by boat and train but, as Schofield related in his memoirs, a sense of drama led to their being flown in from Le Bourget by Imperial Airways. As the *Manchester Guardian* noted on 29 September:

> A week ago the Italians could not always spell the name Webster, and once it was actually written on a scoring-board at Venice as 'Vegster'. Today the name is familiar in all mouths ... The cheerful, phlegmatic young officer who has sent the air reputation of Great Britain soaring to the zenith, and his no less worthy companions, Worsley, Kinkead, and in fact all the team, must not be allowed to steal into London without a fuss.

However, as the newspaper's Venice correspondent related, some people were mightily relieved that the contest was over:

> The genial head barman of my hotel broke down at last and wept from sheer fatigue. He said he had had no sleep the night before, just time to shave and change his shirt and then on duty again. He would remember 'Coppa Schneider' all his life. I assured him that the British would take the Trophy away, and at that he cheered up and began to smile again.

The Italian press was gracious but determined, as a revealing article in *Tribuna* made clear. Britain had made 'formidable preparations' both in improving the Napier Lion engines and designing the Supermarines. Italy had been unable in one year to prepare and build a new engine capable of outperforming those 'whose construction and trial was begun twenty months ago'. The British victory meant that preparations should be started immediately for the next contest: 'To the victorious Lieutenant Webster we offer the salute of the Italian people; to the Italian pilots and engineers a word of encouragement for next time.'

Indeed, before the team departed, Webster told *Tribuna* that he expected his timings to be improved upon in England before the next Schneider race. The paper also reported that members of the Italian team would, within a month, attempt to beat Webster's winning speed. The question of which records had actually been broken was clarified in the *Daily Telegraph* on 1 October:

Although in the course of the Schneider race Flight Lieutenant Webster actually broke not only the seaplane but also the land aeroplane record in absolute speed, he was not timed over short distances. The only official record he broke was that of speed over 100 kilometres, which he did at 283.6 miles per hour. At the present moment the 3-kilometre record is officially held by the French aviator Bonnet (278.4 miles per hour). Flight Lieutenant Webster flew 350 kilometres (217 miles) at more than 281 miles per hour, but until he has flown an officially observed 3-kilometre 'straight' Bonnet's record will stand.

The newspaper understood that the S5, and possibly also the Gloster IV, would be flown in an attempt on the world speed record over a 3-kilometre course, soon after the team's return. It seemed certain that 290 miles per hour or more would be reached, if only because of a much lighter fuel load which would need to be carried for a few short runs. Before any of this could be considered, the members of the High Speed Flight had to survive the journey home and the attendant newspaper publicity. The *Aeroplane*, which regarded itself as a cut above the rest of the press, was scathing about the Imperial Airways flight:

The weather was of the very worst and others who travelled in the same machine suggested that some members of the team were afflicted with the human malady of air-sickness. Just why the team should have been compelled to come from Paris by air is not very clear. One imagines that it must have been an Air Ministry order in response to the popular news-paper clamour for the public arrival of the heroes of the day. It was an entirely unnecessary piece of cruelty. The only thing that an experienced pilot hates more than being piloted by somebody else, is being shut up in a closed cabin. It is several degrees worse than being driven by somebody else in a closed car after one had been accustomed to driving open speed cars.

At Croydon Airport on the Saturday after the race, only a couple of thousand of the hardiest souls gathered in the wind and rain which greeted the returning victors. The Argosy landed to loud cheers at 2.15pm, having been escorted, in arrow formation, by eight Gloster Grebe fighters on the approach to the airfield. Waiting to meet it were Sir Philip Sassoon, Air Marshal Sir John Salmond and representatives of the Air League, the Royal Aero Club and the Society of British Aircraft Constructors, among others. There was an 'embarrassing pause' while the cameramen went to work and then the team, lashed by the torrential rain, climbed into an open car for a brief 'triumphal tour' along the front of the public enclosure, with policemen riding on the running-boards. They drew up at the Imperial Airways building where, before taking questions from the press, Scarlett declared to cheers that 'we went out to Venice as a team, we worked there as a team, and we bring back the Trophy as a team'. He paid tribute not only to the military and civilian members of the team, but to their Italian opponents who had proved themselves to be 'true sportsmen in the very best sense of the word'. Asked about discomfort suffered by the pilots, he conceded that: 'They felt a certain amount of effect from exhaust gases, but a glass of milk and a little oxygen put them all right.' The greatest danger the pilots had to encounter was the possibility of collision because of the imperfect view from their machines. He considered that we might anticipate within the near future a speed of 300mph.

As for the pilots at the centre of attention, the *Aeroplane* commented approvingly:

One is fairly sure that the members of the team strongly objected to the publicity that they received. And certainly their terse replies to newspaper people craving interviews must have been enough to prove, even to the intelligence of Fleet Street, that officers of the Royal Air Force have no desire to be put in the same class as movie stars. Nothing could have been more proper than the reticence of all members of the team. One hopes that now Fleet Street will believe that other officers of the Royal Air Force who have avoided publicity have acted according to their own wishes and have not been muzzled by the Air Ministry.

An editorial in the *Daily Telegraph* noted that, although the public welcome arranged for the returning team had been 'robbed of much of its exuberance by Saturday's pitiless rain', many thousands of radio listeners 'were thrilled by the broadcast description of the actual arrival'. The BBC had enabled indirect participation in the reception of the team whose success constituted 'a national triumph'. In an article in the *Army Quarterly*, Oliver Stewart predicted that the good effects of the decision to enter the race would be seen 'in a year or two ... [in] improvements in the standard fighting plane'. First, however, the airmen, the officials and the politicians were entitled to savour their success.

*   *   *

The Air Council luncheon duly convened at the Savoy with Sir Samuel Hoare – so recently at Balmoral – announcing from the chair that the King had awarded Flight Lieutenant Webster a bar to his Air Force Cross. Webster modestly replied that it had not been his individual victory: 'I happened to have been the pilot who was given the fastest machine in the race, and I did no more than anyone else would have done.' Scarlett described Webster, Worsley and Kinkead as having proved themselves great pilots, with Kink putting up 'a most extraordinary show'. For the first time it was publicly disclosed that if the Gloster had continued flying for a few seconds longer, a terrible crash might have resulted: 'Kinkead remained in the race until, as we discovered after-wards, another few revolutions of his engine would have been the end.' In reporting this, the *Morning Post* remarked that Kink 'had been flying lower and cornering faster than any other pilot in the race'. (The *Post* would reiterate this in a tribute to Kink, four months later: 'So evenly did he make the turns, and so exactly did he maintain his height of a few feet from the water, that it appeared as if his machine were running on rails.') Before proposing the toast to the team, Hoare frankly admitted: 'In recent years we have not made a habit of winning international competitions of any kind. I do not disguise from you my delight now that victory has again smiled upon us.' He praised the team's spirit from start to finish, and also the sportsmanship and hospitality of the Italians. Yet, considering the reasons set out in his memoirs for not going to Venice, his description of the Fascist leader – as reported in *Flight* magazine – seems distinctly overdone:

> Signor Mussolini, the statesman who with an eagle eye long ago saw the future of the air, and ... General Balbo, his brilliant lieutenant, who had set other ministers an example difficult to follow for he had added to the laurels of the politician the wings of the pilot.

No doubt it was in keeping with the diplomacy of the times.

On the same day as the luncheon, the High Speed Flight went with Scarlett, Sassoon and Hoare to 10 Downing Street, where they were received by the Prime Minister. The level of adulation surpassed all expectations. Webster had been met at Croydon by his MP and the Mayor of his native Walsall. Returning to his home town on 6 October, he was greeted at the boundary by his widowed mother and friends, before making a triumphal progress to the Town Hall along a route lined by 15,000 schoolchildren waving flags. The band of the 5th Battalion, the South Staffordshire Regiment, struck up 'See, the Conquering Hero Comes' and the Mayor presented him with an Illuminated Address and an oak plaque 'bearing in silver the figure of Victory flanked by models of the Schneider Cup machine'. Once again, Webster stressed that it had been a team effort, and he singled out the mechanics who had worked around the clock for three days before the race. He had, he said, flown over a hundred different types of aircraft – but the S5 was the best.

Before another week elapsed, two more set-piece events were staged in London and in Felixstowe. The first was a banquet given by the Royal Aero Club, the Royal Aeronautical Society, the Air League of the British Empire, and the Society of British Aircraft Constructors. This, too, was at the Savoy and both the Chief of Air Staff and the First Sea Lord were present. Brigadier-General Lord Thomson, a former and future Secretary of State for Air in the first two Labour governments, was in the chair. He showered praise upon the Air Ministry, the Secretary of State, Trenchard and Air Vice-Marshal Sir John Higgins who had succeeded Geoffrey Salmond as Air Member for Supply and Research, as well as upon all the designers and experts. The Royal Navy had given great practical assistance, both in transporting the machines and providing moral support by its presence at Venice. According to a long report in the *Aeroplane* magazine, Trenchard remained typically uncompromising when supporting the toast:

> Speaking as far as he could on behalf of all ranks of the Royal Air Force and without wanting to detract from those whom they have all come to honour, the Schneider Trophy team was only typical of the young officer of the RAF. He assured his audience that the RAF had many others who could as worthily have upheld the honour of the Country ... To Air Vice-Marshal Scarlett and the team, on behalf of the RAF, he could only say 'We congratulate you for what we all expected of you, you are a credit to the RAF.'

Webster, in responding, described Slatter as having been given a most difficult job and having surmounted innumerable obstacles, without overlooking the smallest detail. For example, the pilots had found a note inside their cockpits just before the race 'which had conveyed to them just the appropriate message'. The Chairman of the Royal Aeronautical Society, Colonel the Master of Sempill, announced the award of the Society's Silver Medal to the technicians of the Supermarine Company, the Napier Company and the Fairey Company for their share in the victory. Reginald Mitchell and Captain G.S. Wilkinson, Chief Designer at Napiers, received well-deserved ovations. The First Sea Lord stressed the value of seaplanes to the Royal Navy and the Counsellor of the Italian Embassy assured everyone present that his country 'had been very happy to have the team amongst them and would be even happier to welcome them back again as soon as possible'. In equally good-natured competitive banter, Hoare teased his Labour rival about the fact that the losing machines had been painted red; Thomson promptly responded that, when the day of reckoning came for the Conservative Party, a Labour government would at least be able to say 'For all you have done for the Air Force, may some of your sins be forgiven you'! On that bipartisan note, the dancing began and continued into the early morning.

Finally it was Felixstowe's turn. The date was Thursday 13 October, giving the team all of twenty-four hours to recover from the revelry at the Savoy, return to East Anglia, and assemble at 11.30am for a victory march from Felixstowe Air Station to the Town Hall. The *East Anglian Daily Times* declared that Felixstowe and Martlesham had followed the fortunes of the High Speed Flight more closely than any other community in the Empire. This had been from the moment when it first emerged that the 'task of asserting air supremacy' was being entrusted to officers and men 'who in their daring duties have all had association with this part of the Suffolk coast'. The whole town turned out for the event as the airmen 'wheeled out of their station to the skirl of the bagpipes'. Soon the marchers were among friends:

> Every hive of scholastic activity must have been deserted, for at intervals the youth of school life, in charge of its tutors, was met and heard. Flags were flown, and as the town was approached ... the inhabitants thickened

in number until on arrival at the Town Hall there was a dense throng. The drum and fife band played the RAF officers and men to the front of the platform.

Schofield, still under medical supervision, together with the Commanding Officer of RAF Martlesham and the Chairman and Members of the Urban District Council formed the reception committee. Cheers rang out when the Chairman of the Council thanked Wing Commander Maycock for giving the community an 'opportunity of showing the respect and appreciation in which they held him, the officers, NCOs and men of the RAF Station'. That evening, almost 250 people sat down to a banquet at the Felix Hotel. Responding to the Council Chairman's tribute, Scarlett made special mention – not for the first time – of the NCOs and men who had tended the racing seaplanes. He appealed to businessmen to be sure to offer employment to the 'other ranks', if and when they left the Royal Air Force. As for the actual fliers:

> He could assure them that he had never had a more difficult task than that which he was required to perform when choosing out of the five selected pilots the three who were to fly in the race. Flight Lieutenant Kinkead was given an extremely difficult machine to fly, and he was not going to say that if things had gone otherwise he would not have been second. Flight Lieutenant Webster, as he had always told him, was chosen because he was so good-looking (laughter). Flight Lieutenant Worsley flew a direct-drive machine, and it showed that it had the necessary speed and got round the course as anticipated. That was the known history of the race. The unknown history was that the pilots were flying machines from which vision was practically nil. It was a very fine feat on their part, and he gave them every credit for what they had done.

Scarlett praised the sportsmanship of the Italians and referred to the regret-table news, discovered only on the eve of the contest, that Jacques Schneider was now living 'in great poverty' in a small cottage on the coast of France:

> It was very hard to realise what he must feel at seeing that the competition which he had started had now become an international affair. In con-clusion, he paid a tribute to Felixstowe itself, saying that thanks were due to its residents, because they had raised so few objections to and com-plaints against the flying which went on at all hours of the day and night in their midst.

This gave Webster – the Martlesham test pilot – his cue, pointing out that 'a little while ago he used to be the most hated man in Felixstowe at 5 o'clock in the morning'. He singled out the 'tireless and unending' contribution of Flying Officer Moon, who had done all the 'dogsbody' work and could still raise a smile. Finally, Sir John Higgins paid tribute to the people of Felixstowe for their support, not only for the team but for the RAF as a whole. Higgins was the most senior Air Ministry representative present at the Felixstowe banquet and ball – and it is to the deliberations of the Ministry that we must now return, in order to understand how Kink Kinkead found himself on a Solent shore on a freezing afternoon, in March 1928, with the eyes of the world upon him.

★ ★ ★

Despite general euphoria at the outcome of the race, it was only natural that an occasional dissenting voice would be heard. On 28 September, just two days after the victory and while Parliament was in recess, the Scottish Labour MP William Wright sent a handwritten note to Hoare quoting the *Star* newspaper of the day before. This had stated that the 'all-in cost to Britain of this year's race will be about £100,000', and Wright wanted to know if this figure was correct. Air Ministry officials felt that it might be wise to reveal the contract price of the six aircraft sent to Venice, in addition to the £2,500 of extra expenditure sanctioned by the Treasury to cover the costs of travel and of accommodation in Italy. They feared that unfriendly questioning in Parliament might actually force the disclosure of a total figure which would be 'considerably larger' than just the cost of designing and building the aircraft. In fact, the total purchase price of three S5s, two Gloster IVs, one Crusader, five Lion VII engines and one 'Mercury' engine amounted to some £83,000. The grand total for 1927, however, was an estimated £125,120 – twice that for 1926 (£62,620) and four times that for 1925 (£32,180). Hoare was unconvinced and overruled his officials on 8 October:

> I certainly think it would be a great mistake to give here and now figures for the total cost of the six Schneider Cup machines. This would merely be to provide an unfriendly critic with a figure which he could ... use as a stick to belabour the Air Ministry. As at present advised, I do not propose to give any figure at all beyond the £2,500.

A letter was duly despatched to the MP on 13 October, citing the £2,500 figure as an estimate of the cost of the actual race arrangements, and asserting – with some economy of truth – that to supply a figure for 'preliminary expenditure on the construction of the machines and flying them for experimental and development purposes', could not be done 'without a quite unjustifiable amount of clerical labour'. The Secretary of State was on stronger ground when claiming that, even if the Schneider contest did not exist, the Air Ministry would still have to carry out experimental and development work on high speed aircraft:

> Such work is, of course, essential to aeronautical progress. Speed is only one of many desiderata and, in just the same way as we have built and flown these high speed seaplanes, we build and fly machines designed to secure an advance in other vital factors, e.g. range and carrying capacity.

Thus, he argued, 'even if it were practicable without an undue expenditure of time and labour', there would be no grounds for isolating the cost of the high speed seaplanes used for the race from the cost of all the other work in hand on different types of experimental machines.

At the same time, plans were being laid for the future: 'My mind is quite made up that if the next contest is to be held in England the Air Ministry must be responsible for seeing that there is a really efficient British entry,' Hoare minuted to the CAS; but Trenchard's attitude remained hostile to the whole enterprise, as his reply on 12 October made clear:

> I consider that we should certainly make an effort to have the race run every other year instead of yearly. The expense of running it yearly is much too great for any country to continue paying and it does not give time for sufficient progress to be made. I also consider that we should at once write to the [Royal] Aero Club to ask them to find out from the manufacturers if they will be prepared next year, if we lend them the machines, to organise and run the race themselves. To me it is of the utmost importance that this is done. First of all, we are almost committed to the Treasury to say that we should not do it as a Service Flight again. Secondly, I can say from what I have seen and heard since the race that it is definitely to the detriment of officers in the Royal Air Force to be used for this sort of competition every year, or every other year.

The Schneider Committee of the Royal Aero Club reacted with predictable dismay. They were unanimous that, unless the Air Ministry gave the same level of support as in 1927, 'the prospect of retaining the Trophy in this country would be exceedingly remote':

> The emphatic opinion was that the assistance of Service pilots and personnel was one of the determining factors in winning the Trophy this year and it is not seen how the Trophy can be defended with any hope of success unless such Service personnel are again available ... [D]uring the past five years the competition for the Trophy has assumed the character of a competition between Governments, and each time the Trophy has changed hands the victory has been due to the extensive financial and practical backing afforded by the respective Governments of the winning countries.

The Committee believed that both of the other likely contestants would receive maximum Government support and that 'any relaxation of the national effort in the forthcoming contest would gravely imperil British prestige in the air'. A pattern was unfolding in precisely the way that Trenchard had predicted. 'It is known that the Treasury only gave their consent this year to the cost falling on public funds on the understanding that this was not to form a precedent,' wrote the CAS, in a long minute to Hoare on 14 November:

> The race, held in England, and supported by our Government, would cost infinitely more than it cost [us] last year when the Italians were the hosts. The fact of its being held in England would probably produce ten times

the number of guests who would expect to be put up, lunched, dined and entertained.

He had learned that President Coolidge was 'definitely and firmly determined' to end US Government support to Schneider Trophy competitors: 'He thinks it is wrong.' The CAS also took the view that 'competition between Governments in a race of this kind will lend itself to innumerable complications and even diplomatic incidents'. The British should tell all the Aero Clubs involved that the race should not be held in 1928:

> If this fails, I consider that the British Government should firmly state that they will not compete in this race except once in every four years, and the Aero Club should state that they will only compete every two years, if they wish to. I regard this letter from the Aero Club as all plain bluff. Except from the commercial point of view, I am quite certain that a further race is of little value to the Royal Air Force and will not help the prestige of the RAF. I would also point out the bad results the race has on the young officers who have to carry out the duties of this nature for the Royal Air Force. With the best of officers in the world it is bound to have a deleterious effect, through no fault of theirs. It is wrong that officers of that age and seniority should be feted by all the great ones of this country for carrying out a flight in a fast machine, which is not very difficult for them. There are hundreds of others who could do it. It is the organisation, the machine and the engines that win it! There is no need so far as I can see for this race for *research purposes from a Service point of view* [Trenchard's emphasis] ... and I cannot see any great value in getting another 10 or 15 miles an hour in speed, although it has been of benefit in the past.

If the Secretary of State disagreed, the CAS advised, he should ask Sir John Higgins what the costs and advantages might be of building more machines at present

> because I feel that although AMSR in the past – and I agreed with him – has said that high speed trials are absolutely necessary for the development of machines, I feel that they are not absolutely necessary annually, although I think that one every now and then would be of the greatest value.

Hoare therefore decided to take a strong line with the Royal Aero Club, convening a special meeting at the House of Commons on 21 November with Higgins in attendance. The Secretary of State suggested that, if a public subscription were started by the Lord Mayor of London, he personally would give it every support. It was agreed to write to all the Aero Clubs affiliated to the FAI proposing that the race should be held every two years, thus allowing adequate time to design and build new aircraft. The Government had not yet decided whether full RAF participation would be resumed if the race were put off to 1929, and the Royal Aero Club remained worried that the country 'may have to abandon defending the Schneider Cup'. Fortunately, help arrived from an unexpected quarter – General Balbo, who visited London for discussions with Hoare in the middle of December. As the latter's Private Secretary recorded:

Events in connection with the holding of a contest for the Schneider Trophy in 1928 have moved rapidly during the past forty-eight hours ... The Secretary of State saw General Balbo on Wednesday and again yesterday, and elicited from him that the Italians were definitely averse from [sic] a contest in 1928 (General Balbo tried at first to hedge a little with a view to putting responsibility on our shoulders but was ultimately quite frank on the point) and also were prepared to subscribe entirely to our proposal that as soon as possible the contest should formally be put on a bi-annual instead of an annual basis.

Balbo wished to make this public immediately but Hoare asked him to wait for twenty-four hours, to allow time to tell the Royal Aero Club what had been agreed. The Club, in turn, approved the announcement and drafted a message to be forwarded to its counterparts in America, France, Italy and Germany – 'in whose hands the actual machinery for the contest rests' – via the British Air Attachés in each country.

By 23 December, the Air Ministry had received confirmation from both the National Aeronautical Association, USA, and the Deutscher Luftrat, Berlin, agreeing to the change. Now that the pressure of an annual commitment had been removed, the development of successor aircraft could proceed. Hoare's Private Secretary advised Trenchard and Higgins at the end of January 1928 that:

The Secretary of State has written privately to the Chancellor of the Exchequer following on a recent conversation which he had with him at Chartwell to say that he proposes to incorporate in our programmes for 1928 and 1929 the necessary measures for developing further types of machine, improving existing engines and also for producing a new engine if possible. He has added that this will not increase the total figures of expenditure already agreed by him with the Chancellor. The Chancellor and other Members of the Cabinet, with whom the Secretary of State has discussed the question, have all pressed the view that the Air Ministry should spare no endeavour to secure another victory in 1929 and that, in particular, we should undertake responsibility for developing the necessary machines and engines.

Trenchard was now content to proceed. He expected the next contest to be held in the late summer or autumn of 1929 and, on 5 March 1928 approved the establishment of a new High Speed Flight to take over the new machines and engines in twelve months' time.

★   ★   ★

197

Kink's place in the scheme of things had already been finalised. In late 1927, Slatter and two representatives of the Royal Aero Club accepted an invitation to visit Lancashire to consider whether Blackpool, Southport, Fleetwood or Morecambe Bay might be suitable for the race. Only the last of these was thought to have the necessary facilities, and the Schneider Cup Committee decided to explore this. On 30 December, *The Times* reported that the prospect of the race being flown in the Liverpool area had 'received some encourage-ment', the previous day, 'when Captain Wilson, of the Royal Aero Club Schneider Cup Committee, and Flight Lieutenant S.M. Kinkead, one of the competitors in the race at Venice last September, visited the city to inspect the proposed course'. By then, however, the likelihood of the RAF using its own facilities had substantially increased, and nothing further came of the initiative. Also in December, Kink, Slatter and a civilian representative of the Marine Aircraft Experimental Establishment met Air Commodore John Chamier, Director of Technical Development at the Air Ministry, to discuss in detail the practicability of future high speed work at Felixstowe. Chamier reported to Higgins that:

> The recent very high speed aircraft require a 2–3 mile run for a get-off. This can only be had at Felixstowe with the wind blowing from the sea, and under these conditions it is usual to have a swell sufficient to upset these frail craft. The point was discussed exhaustively and was fully established. If high speed work is to go on with any steadiness, Felixstowe is really impracticable. From the point of view of sheltered water to three points of the compass, Calshot is better: it really seems to be the only place ... [B]efore the next race we must, I think, face having the Flight at Calshot for six months. The Gloster view has been much improved and the work of converting the IVB to a V is to start at once. There remains the question of the IVA. Slatter and Kinkead are quite serious on the point that the IVA is unsafe, particularly because a pilot may yaw without knowing it and get into trouble. They are so sure in their opinion of this matter that I do not think we are justified in asking them to take the risk of flying her just for development work. At a cost of perhaps £2,000, we could improve the view ... but keep the original floats, tail surfaces, etc. In that condition she should be ... of use for practice, which she is not now, after all the money spent on her.

Chamier asked permission to make that alteration, and on 12 January 1928 he submitted to Higgins his proposals for future high speed experimental work:

> The High Speed Flight to form at Felixstowe forthwith from the existing personnel under Flight Lieutenant Kinkead and as part of the existing organisation there ... The duty of the Flight will be the training of pilots at Felixstowe in high speed flying ... and also experimental high speed work on Supermarine 5s and [the] Gloster V when ready. Since Felixstowe is unsuitable for very high speed work, the latter duties will have to be carried

out at Calshot. For this purpose a minimum detachment of one officer assisted by a good WO or NCO and one fitter and one rigger per machine, and a crew for a high speed motor-boat will have to be stationed at Calshot.

Technical assistance would be provided by Supermarine and, when necessary, by the Air Ministry:

normally when work is in progress Flight Lieutenant Kinkead will himself be at Calshot and the work at Felixstowe will be carried on by his deputy. Flight Lieutenant Kinkead, being in charge of the high speed work as a whole, will be able to raise the strength of his detachment at Calshot by temporary transfer of officers or men from Felixstowe when the magnitude of the work and the settled weather conditions demand. On occasions of special work . . . the services of a Research Officer from Felixstowe should be available for the assistance of the Flight. On special occasions OC Felixstowe will further assist the Flight by the loan of personnel to work camera-guns etc. over the speed course.

Orders confirming these arrangements were issued to the Commanding Officer, MAEE, on 13 February by the Director of Technical Development and the Director of Scientific Research. Kink would deal with the Supermarine Company and with the Air Ministry directly on technical matters, and would be free to raise the strength of his detachment by temporary transfers subject to the approval of OC Felixstowe. A copy of this letter to MAEE was sent to Air Vice-Marshal Scarlett, as AOC Coastal Area, on 20 February – the same day that MAEE told the Air Ministry what was happening to the third and last Supermarine-Napier S5, the N221: 'the geared engine is being installed in this aircraft, which will be ready for transport to Calshot on the 22nd instant by RAF lorries, which are due to arrive at Calshot on the afternoon of Friday, the 24th'.

This news was passed to Coastal Area Headquarters on 23 February with a request to inform OC Calshot; but Scarlett was unhappy not to have been involved sooner with changes affecting stations under his command. Higgins was apologetic, but noted on 24 February, after writing privately to Scarlett, that

the AOC Coastal Area does not quite realise that this so-called 'High Speed Flight' is not at all the same unit which he was administering direct last year, but is merely a convenient term for referring to a portion of the establishment at Felixstowe which is dealing with high speed research.

However, the argument rumbled on, generating correspondence including a statement by the Air Ministry on 1 March that: 'It is not intended to re-form a High Speed Flight as such, but merely to detail certain selected personnel and aircraft of the existing establishment of the MAEE for the further development of this specialised form of flying.'

Regardless of ruffled feathers, N221 was going to Calshot for a very special exercise in high speed 'research' – if all went well, she would make her pilot the fastest man in the world.

Chapter Eleven

Disaster in the Solent

Less than a month after the triumph at Venice, reports appeared in the British press that Italy was in no mood to concede mastery in the air. At first it was thought that de Bernardi had set a new world speed record of 301mph, over a 3-kilometre course at Venice, in the second half of October. This would have meant that, according to FAI rules, a challenger needed to achieve 306mph in order to beat it by the required minimum of 5mph. In fact, de Bernardi's official result – achieved on 4 November – raised the bar to just 296.94mph, leaving the prize of reaching 5 miles a minute still to be claimed.

Kink's name was already being mentioned: the final newspaper cutting in the scrapbook presented by his friends came from the *Birmingham Gazette* of 25 October. Entitled '306 MILES AN HOUR – AIM OF BRITISH AIR RECORD ATTEMPT', it suggested that he might be the pilot in a British attack on the world's speed record to take place at Calshot 'almost immediately, if the weather is favourable'. A more detailed account in the *Daily Telegraph* claimed that: 'In British aeronautical circles satisfaction was expressed on receipt of the news ... that the Italians have not submitted tamely to their defeat in the Schneider Trophy contest.' Given that Major de Bernardi's fastest lap in the race had been only 263.1mph, compared with Webster's 284.1mph and Kink's 277.1mph, it might seem remarkable that

> in the few weeks since the race one of the Italian machines should have been improved sufficiently to attain a speed, on the straight, of 301mph [*sic*]; but it must be borne in mind that in flying the short course less petrol has to be carried, and there is no cornering or turning points, whilst the adverse effect of wind is ruled out.

This was because speed record attempts had to be flown in both directions along the timed 3-kilometre course. It thus seemed reasonable to assume that, on the basis of the British performance at Venice, an S5 should be able to set a new record of between 305 and 310mph.

Despite speculation about a bid for the record in mid-November, it was only in late January that a definite announcement was made. An S5 and its Napier Lion engine were being overhauled and upgraded for an attempt in March. By now it had been confirmed that de Bernardi had achieved a speed of just under 297mph, so the target for the S5 would be a minimum of 302mph.

The Operations Record Book of RAF Calshot states that a detachment of the High Speed Flight arrived from Felixstowe on 24 February 1928, but the next public sighting of the project was not until Tuesday 6 March. That morning, a press and newsreel photo-call was staged in front of the main hangar – just as had been done the previous August before the team left for Venice. From then onwards, in stark contrast to the first dozen years of his military career, Kink found himself at the centre of concentrated media attention which charted every aspect of the final phase of his life. He neither sought personal publicity, nor did he let it irritate him. Probably, the media frenzy surrounding the Venice competition had warned him what to expect. The most comprehensive coverage was to be found in the Southampton-based *Southern Daily Echo* which, being an evening paper, was always first with the news; but so great was the interest in high speed flying that most major journals had correspondents at Calshot – some of whom provided syndicated reports overseas. What happened over the next few days would make headlines around the world.

The S5 selected for the record attempt was the brand-new N221. Though completed in time for the 1927 race, it had been transported to Venice as a spare machine but had never taken to the air. The first news despatch from Calshot set the scene for what was to follow: 'Attack on the World's Flying Record – Everything Ready for the Test – Weather Conditions Deciding Factor.' Having been assembled and rigged by Monday 5 March, N221 – it was hoped – would make a trial flight immediately after the photo-call the following day. This was ruled out as 'an almost entire absence of wind' resulted in poor visibility caused by a persistent haze over the water. Instead, the journalists were treated to a demonstration of the power of the Lion engine. Its roar was described as deafening and everyone present felt the vibration of the concrete base on which the seaplane stood. N221 was declared to be absolutely 'fit'. It would need to be for the task ahead: the 3-kilometre course would have to be flown no fewer than four times – twice in each direction, with the average calculated to determine the official speed. Measurement would be no easy task. The attempt on the record, including the turns at each end of the timed runs, would probably take little more than fifteen minutes as the seaplane covered a mile every twelve seconds, during the measured section of the course.

Commander Harold Perrin, Secretary of the Royal Aero Club, was in charge of validating the arrangements, and it was soon determined that the timed section would run from the jetty of the AGWI Oil Company at Fawley to the small pier at the extreme end of Calshot Spit. Measuring-posts were set in concrete at both locations together with additional posts 500 metres beyond each end of the timed section. Perrin explained that the aircraft had to be in level flight no higher than 50 metres above the surface of the water for the entire 3-kilometre stretch, and also for the 500 metres flown prior to entering it: 'The effect is to ensure that no fictitious speed is gained by diving down on the speed course.' Although the time-keepers appointed by the Royal Aero Club would be in sole charge of determining the official speed reached, the

Air Ministry had sent its own scientific representative to experiment with a camera-gun designed to photograph the aeroplane as it passed each measuring-post, while simultaneously photographing a moving strip of paper showing the seconds and fractions of a second which elapsed during the flight. This scientist was Lawrence Coombes, whose own Service record was considerable. Like Kink, a former Sopwith Camel pilot in the RNAS and RAF, Coombes had been involved in fifteen victories on the Western Front, had won the DFC, and had worked as a specialist at both Farnborough and Felixstowe, before travelling to Venice with the 1927 Schneider team.

Before any attempt on the record could be made in earnest, FAI rules stipulated that the aircraft must make two separate landings. This was why a trial flight in front of reporters and photographers had been planned for 6 March. As it was, the press and the newsreels had to be content with posed shots of N221 being wheeled out, inspected by Kink and his team, started up by the Napier engineer, and then used as a backdrop for the uniformed pilot. The resultant portrait is probably the best-known of Kink – standing alone, rather diffidently, in front of his tiny craft with its huge floats and exposed mighty engine. Over his right shoulder flutters an RAF flag, and in the background are the square shapes of period automobiles looking incongruous against the streamlined fuselage of the S5. Kink's pose suggests a degree of reluctance at the media attention. This would have been entirely in keeping with what is known of his character. Despite everyone's increasing frustration at the extraordinary weather, the day-by-day reports confirm that he never allowed exasperation to undermine his even temper. Nevertheless, it does seem likely that external events may have influenced his judgement, while the knowledge of what Mitchell had created in the S5 must have fuelled his determination to prove its potential.

Gradually it dawned on the assembled media that their ingenuity would be taxed to maintain interest in the story. The early headlines – 'World's Air Speed Record . . . The Man and The Machine' (7 March) – gave way to more gloomy ones. 'Waiting at Calshot – Keeping Watch on the Weather' (8 March); 'Flight Further Postponed – Waiting for the Right Conditions' (9 March); and then, when N221 finally took to the water, 'Flight Lieutenant Kinkead Baulked Again' (10 March). Time after time the pattern was repeated. Kink would drive to the hangar from his quarters in the Upper Camp, very early in the morning, in the hope of carrying out the preliminary flights. Day after day the reports told a similar story:

[6 March] The weather conditions will be the deciding factor. For instance, this morning . . . a haze hung over the water causing poor visibility . . . the misty weather caused a postponement until tomorrow . . . [7 March] The weather prevented the Supermarine-Napier S5 . . . from taking [to] the air this morning . . . at daybreak it was raining, and visibility was too bad for high speed flying . . . The weather became worse this afternoon, and flying was out of the question, so the attempt was definitely postponed until tomorrow ... [8 March] It was much clearer and brighter at dawn this morning than for several days past, but there was a disconcerting wind which, while it offered no difficulties to ordinary flying, made high speed flying dangerous, if not impossible ... [9 March] There was considerable improvement in the prospects of high speed flying at Calshot this morning. When Flight Lieutenant S.M. Kinkead ... arrived on the station at 7.00am the visibility was good and the wind, although inclined to be a little gusty, was more favourable than yesterday. Flight Lieutenant Kinkead, the picture of imperturbability, paced the concrete with brisk steps, weighing up the prospects ... although flying was not possible at the moment, the chances of improvement were such, with a little luck, he might be able to go up later ... The airman signified his intention of returning to the station after breakfast ... The Air Ministry expert said the sea was likely to get smoother, but whether the wind would rise or fall he was unable to say. Everybody adjourned for breakfast in an optimistic frame of mind. Their hopes, however, were doomed to disappointment. The wind increased to a force of about 20 miles an hour, and when Flight Lieutenant Kinkead came to the station after breakfast he was compelled to further postpone the flight.

★   ★   ★

While Kink, his team, the Royal Aero Club and Air Ministry officials, and the encamped media were wrestling with the technicalities and safety-margins of a record attempt at Calshot, the Government was groping – with limited resources in a bleak economic climate – towards a future for military aviation. On the evening of 8 March, in an edition which Kink may well have seen, the front-page lead story in the *Southern Daily Echo* set out the plans of the Secretary of State for Air, Sir Samuel Hoare:

> More money is wanted for the Air Force. The new Air Estimates issued today show a total of £16,250,000 net and £19,135,100 gross. The corresponding figures for 1927 were £15,550,000 net and £19,986,400 gross. While the gross estimates show a reduction of £851,300, there is an increase of £700,000 in the net amount.

The Secretary of State's accompanying memorandum said that the present strength of the Royal Air Force was approximately equivalent to sixty-nine Squadrons, including eight on a non-regular basis. By the end of 1928, this should rise to seventy-three Squadrons, while the addition of two new Flights to the Fleet Air Arm should bring its total to twenty-five – equivalent to twelve-and-a-half Squadrons:

> The process of rearmament with new aircraft and aero engines will be continued. The control of aircraft at low speeds by means of slots in the wing structure is being actively developed ... A parachute is now supplied for every aircraft in the Service which is capable of carrying it, that is over

203

75 per cent of all machines. This percentage will rise to 86 per cent in 1928 ... [Despite] considerable difficulties ... which have ... prolonged the period of construction [of the new airships R100 and R101] ... these are being satisfactorily surmounted, and the completion of both airships and their flying trials in this country are provided for in these estimates.

The Royal Air Force was, in reality, suffering from the perennial problem of Armed Services in peacetime. No obvious enemy was on the horizon, though democracy was under strain in different ways in various parts of Europe; the country had weathered a General Strike but the economic outlook was grim; and the technical dilemmas of choosing between lighter- and heavier-than-air craft had yet to be resolved in favour of the latter. To some, the entire high speed project seemed an expensive blind alley. After all, the racing seaplanes, as they had evolved in the context of the Schneider competitions, had little to offer commercial aviation. As they were operating at the extremes of physical performance, it was equally unclear what benefit they could bring to military aviation. Certainly, the creator of the S5 had no illusions about the risks involved. In his definitive study of Reginald Mitchell's design career, *Schneider Trophy to Spitfire*, Dr John Shelton quotes a speech given by Mitchell to a Rotary meeting in Southampton soon after the 1927 contest:

> The designing of such a machine involved considerable anxiety because everything had been sacrificed to speed. The floats were only just large enough to support the machine, and the wings had been cut down to a size considered just sufficient to ensure a safe landing. The engine had only five hours' duration; after that time it had to be removed and changed. In fact everything had been so cut down it was dangerous to fly. Racing machines of this sort are not safe to fly, and many times I have been thankful that it was only a single-seater. The machine itself has been a source of anxiety to me right from the start, and I am pleased to know that at this moment it is safely shut up in a box.

By the second week of March 1928, however, as Mitchell well knew, N221 was out of its box. The *Echo* correspondent described it vividly:

> The beautiful stream-line Supermarine-Napier S5 seaplane remained in its grey-painted shed waiting, like a steel greyhound straining at the leash, for a test which it is hoped will regain for Great Britain the world's speed record and the honour of possessing the first seaplane officially to exceed a speed of 5 miles a minute.

* * *

And so it went on, hour after hour, while the pressmen stood around, the officials whiled away the time, and those most intimately involved in the project continued to weigh up the odds. At last, after four postponements – from Tuesday 6 March, onwards – it looked as if Kink's run of bad luck might be over. The *Echo* correspondent saw him at the crack of dawn on the Saturday:

'I am going to have a shot at it.' With this crisp sentence Flight Lieutenant S.M. Kinkead, the RAF pilot, intimated to me at 6.25 this morning his intention of taking up the Supermarine-Napier S5 seaplane ... The imperturbable pilot arrived on the air station at twenty to six this morning before anyone but the guards were astir. He waited for the crew to man a pinnace, and in this he repeated his trip down Southampton Water which he made yesterday morning in order to observe the state of the wind and tide out in the waterway over which his course is planned. The wind was rather fresher than he hoped for – it was blowing at a force of about 10 miles per hour – but the water was comparatively smooth, while the visibility too was as clear as it had been for several mornings past. Flight Lieutenant Kinkead ascended the steps of the jetty with a look of determination on his tanned and rugged face, and made the remark quoted above to me in reply to my inquiry.

Ordering the RAF engineers to prepare N221, Kink set off in his two-seater car for his quarters. The great hangar doors slid open and the tiny blue and silver racing plane – 'the embodiment of speed and mechanical beauty' – was rolled out for fuelling. Just before 7.00am Kink reappeared, but it was obvious to all that no time could be lost: 'Every minute the wind seemed to be getting up more and delay in getting into the air might mean further postponement.' As the engine was started and gradually speeded up, Kink emerged from the administrative offices to watch N221 vibrating into life. With a cheerful smile he went to change into his flying kit: a brightly patterned Fair Isle sweater, Service trousers, flying helmet, goggles and gloves to protect his hands until he was ready for take-off. A contemporary newsreel shows him clambering into the cockpit before discarding the gloves and wedging himself in. At one point the wind catches the partial canopy cover, slamming it down on his forearm before he is ready, but no harm appears to be done. What followed was to be yet another anti-climax:

The smiling pilot turned up his thumbs as the S5 was slowly run down the slipway by a rope to which a line of airmen held on. The craft took [to] the water, and immediately she was afloat the wheels were drawn from beneath her floats. The blue paintwork and silver wings glinted in the brilliant sunshine and made a superb picture. It was bright but bitterly cold, and no-one envied the airman in his confined and uncomfortable cockpit. The machine taxied across the fairway towards Lee-on-Solent, and was completely enveloped in spray thrown up by its passage through the water. In the centre of the channel the machine turned with its nose pointing towards Southampton. Suddenly the hum of its engine ceased. The cloud of spray dispersed, and the machine could be seen rocking gently on the water. What had happened?

Before anyone could begin to speculate, a serious situation developed as the wash of a cruise-liner bound for Southampton, combined with that of a tug-boat in close attendance, nearly capsized N221. One of the two RAF launches which had sped to the scene managed to break the force of the disturbed water, and although the seaplane rocked violently, it did not overturn. N221 was towed forlornly back to the slipway. Kink extracted himself from the cockpit and was carried the short distance to shore by one of the launch party clad in heavy waterproof gear. He knew what was wrong: the plugs had sooted-up. Otherwise the engine was perfect; and, when the sea was less choppy and the plugs had been replaced, he would try again. It was not to be. Soon the wind was blowing so strongly that all prospect of another attempt once again had to be shelved.

A sharper edge was beginning to show in part of the media. In its title, a cinema newsreel posed the ironic question: '300 Miles An Hour? – Bad Luck Mars First Attempt of Flight Lieutenant Kinkead & RAF Wonder Plane to Beat World Record.' Yet, Kink was undeterred – and on Sunday 11 March, while some of the doubters were still in their beds, he was at last able to seize his chance.

'Thrilling Flying at Calshot' was the ecstatic headline in the early edition of the *Echo* the following day, with *The Times* more sedately proclaiming: 'Flying Speed Record – Successful Trials'. Kink had achieved outstanding results on the first of his two preliminary flights. The *Echo* correspondent, his most conscientious and committed supporter in the press, drew heavily on a stock of superlatives: 'One of the most inspiring and thrilling spectacles imaginable was witnessed from Calshot Air Station by a few privileged people shortly after 7 o'clock yesterday morning,' he declared. Having seen N221 in action, he was certain that its potentialities were

> truly staggering ... it was apparent that the machine is capable of an amazing velocity. If there was one thing which impressed itself on the minds of observers besides the speed of the seaplane, it was the superb manner in which the pilot handled her. Flight Lieutenant Kinkead is admittedly in the front rank of the world's air pilots, and his magnificent control of high speed aircraft is almost superhuman.
>
> Five days of fruitless waiting – mainly for an improvement in the weather – by a small army of journalists and photographers were well rewarded when the graceful streamlined craft carried out a 17-minutes' flight, which for sheer thrill nothing could surpass. The tiny monoplane, with its mighty engine, screamed over the water at a height of barely 100 feet, to disappear in the distance in a flash, leaving onlookers breathless with amazement.
>
> Quick-actioned cameramen, waiting with cameras levelled to attempt a lightning 'shot', swung round as quickly as is humanly possible, hoping to snapshot the 'flying bullet' as it sped past, only to find that it had passed out of their line of vision before they could accomplish their purpose.

The fastest biplane seaplane flight in history: Kink's geared Gloster IVB, N223, overtaking orsley's ungeared Supermarine-Napier S5, N219, Venice, 26 September 1927.

47. The welcome home: Kink, Webster and Worsley greeted by Sir Philip Sassoon (*second left*), Under-Secretary of State for Air, and Air Marshal Sir John Salmond (*right*), Chief of Air Staff.

48. The lap of honour, Croydon Airport, 1 October 1927.

FELIXSTOWE HONOURS the SCHNEIDER CUP TEAM.

On Felixstowe Town Hall steps, (*from left*) Slatter, Webster, Kink, Worsley, Schofield, Moon and ing Commander R.B. Maycock, CO of the Marine Aircraft Experimental Establishment, receive the uncil Chairman's praise.

Webster, Kink, Slatter, Schofield and Worsley with the Schneider Trophy.

51. World speed record press event, with N221, Calshot, 6 March 1928.

52. Carried ashore after t successful flight, five day later.

53. The last flight, 12 March: N221 emerging from the hangar, with snow still on the ground.

4. N221 is made ready, as Kink looks on.

5. The final launching.

56. 'Good luck …'

57. On the steps.

8. The engine salvaged.

9. Fawley Church, 16 March 1928.

60. Kink's grave at Fawley.

61. Cranwell's Kinkead Trophy, still awarded annually.

62. Members of the Kinkead-Weekes family visit the Kinkead Room in the original hangar at Calshot Activities Centre: (*from left*) Paul (great-nephew), Mark (nephew) and Roddy (great-nephew).

Cinematograph men with stand instruments [*sic*] found themselves hope-lessly beaten by the racing 'plane as it bore a rocket-like course through space. The only result that could be hoped for was a blur if the machine passed their lens at the crucial moment.

As the monoplane hurtled through the ice-cold air the noise of its powerful engine lagged a mile behind. It was a strange and remarkable circumstance: it was as if sound was pursuing a creature of the air which it endeavoured in vain to outstrip. During its flight the S5 was 'put through its paces' very thoroughly by the daring pilot, who, to all appearances, was as happy and carefree in the narrow limits of his cockpit, with the wind whistling in his helmet-covered ears, and swirling against the face of his goggles, as any schoolboy in his play-hour.

Up and down the waterway at varying heights flashed the tiny speed 'plane, buzzing like an angry mosquito at its greatest height, and giving vent to a peculiarly penetrating scream when at a lower level, which rose and fell in a few moments, and died away as the distance increased. Flight Lieutenant Kinkead took the turns ... in a steep banking climb, which sometimes meant that the monoplane was practically vertical. Over the Isle of Wight roared the little seaplane at the southernmost point, and the sound of her engine disturbed the slumbers of many Southamptonians as she turned at the most northerly point.

Kink had lost no time in getting clear of the water, and apparently experienced no difficulty in doing so. As soon as he was seaborne he had headed into the wind, in the direction of Hamble, taking less than 500 yards before the floats left the surface. Everyone was impressed – not least the correspondent of *The Times* who described how satisfied Kink clearly was with the controls of the S5, as he turned at 1,000 feet, and flew in a wide circle over the New Forest, back over the Solent, and again over the length of Southampton Water:

After another circle, Flight Lieutenant Kinkead turned at the top end of the speed course, came down to within 50 feet of the water and flashed past almost level with the top of the castle in a straight flight which never veered from the horizontal. Coming back, Flight Lieutenant Kinkead turned on an almost vertical left bank high up over the station, swung out to sea, and then, turning again, came in on a long flat glide to be water-borne once more. This process was watched with interest, but not anxiety. It was a pleasure to watch the perfect way in which the pilot, who had never before flown this particular type of high speed aircraft, brought the monoplane onto the water at probably 100 miles an hour, or just over. He chose an angle of glide which almost imperceptibly brought the floats nearer and nearer the water until the monoplane was just skimming the surface – a grey insect over a grey sea. Then a tiny feather of white foam broke behind the floats and rapidly grew bigger. The machine seemed about to settle, but lifted just once in a long hop and then, touching again, threw up a spurt of spray, and gently floated on the water.

207

According to the *Echo*, the landing was 'a masterpiece of skill and neat calculation', with other RAF pilots present describing it as one of the finest they had witnessed. At a speed of almost 100mph, N221 had descended until just touching the waves before rising a foot or two then gliding smoothly to a standstill. It was bitterly cold and Kink gladly recovered his overcoat which, like his gloves, he carefully wore up to the time of entering the cockpit. The whole flight, covering an estimated 60 miles, had lasted just over a quarter of an hour.

The record seemed tantalisingly close; but, by the time accounts of Sunday's success appeared in the Monday newspapers, the intense cold had already caused yet another postponement. Kink had arrived at the hangar even earlier than usual, on what was to be the last day of his life. It was soon after 6.00am – and N221 was quickly rolled out of its hangar, with the engine running at low throttle. Only ten minutes later, a leak in the oil cooler – caused by the extreme temperature – was discovered. The cooler was immediately detached and sent by speedboat across Southampton Water to the Supermarine Works at Woolston. By midday it had been repaired and returned, in the hope that a flight might be possible in the afternoon. The auguries were not good. So extraordinary was the weather that the *Echo* ran a special story about the 'striking contrast' between the previous two Sundays:

> True to tradition, March, after coming in like a lamb, has developed lion-like attributes, and everyone shivered in the cold easterly wind over the week-end. Overcoats discarded last Sunday were donned again yesterday, and those people who could remain by their firesides did so. There was a difference of 21 degrees in the maximum day temperatures of yesterday and the previous Sunday ... With eight hours' sunshine, temperature on Sunday, March 4th, rose to 58 degrees, which was approximately the peak of the warm spell. Yesterday, the thermometer rose to only 37 degrees. There was nearly as great a difference in the night temperatures. On the night of Saturday–Sunday (March 3rd and 4th) the thermometer did not drop below 40 degrees. Last night it fell to 21, or 11 degrees of frost.

For the remainder of 12 March, the weather forecast predicted 'moderate north-east winds; mainly fair, but snow showers probable; very cold' – and so it transpired. As the *Daily Express* correspondent noted later, Kink had already spent an hour supervising his team in bitterly cold weather, when he saw him on the slipway at daybreak that last morning. The delay caused by the oil leak seemed to be decisive, as 'the prospects of good weather receded while the repair was being effected'. In the afternoon, the chance of a flight appeared to be

> quite hopeless for the rest of the day, for a snowstorm succeeded the heavy white frost. 'I ought to have a fair view of 10 miles before I start,' he said to me. 'This machine travels so fast that you need the best visibility, and I certainly must be able to see the horizon.' In that snowstorm there was no

horizon. Then came a magical change. The snow disappeared and the sun returned ... The blue and silver monoplane was brought out of its shed to the head of the slipway, and an army of mechanics promptly prepared it for flight. The powerful 875hp engine was started up, and an engineer ran it for some moments before leaving his seat.

Lieutenant Kinkead was ready to take his place. He had stripped off his tunic, for the cockpit is so small that he had to reduce the amount of his clothing in order to fit tightly into it ... [A] number of photographers asked him to pose. 'Not now,' he replied. 'Wait till I come back.' Then he climbed the little steel ladder to the cockpit, turning round just before he entered it in order to smile to his friends. Immediately afterwards the machine was taken down to the water, and the watchers followed its course as it taxied away from the shore.

*　　*　　*

As Kink and his team waited tensely but patiently for the snowstorm to dissipate at Calshot, they and their enterprise – and the Service of which they formed a part – were under serious scrutiny at Westminster. It was a Supply Day in Parliament and the debate on the Air Estimates, which had been published the week before, was getting under way. The opening speech consisted of a major statement by Sir Samuel Hoare. The Secretary of State for Air was keen to justify the very existence of the Royal Air Force as a separate Service; to defend investment in civil and military aviation at a time of economic stringency; and to articulate the need for national defences, in contradiction of those who promoted pacifism and disarmament as the answer to international strife.

He began with Government plans to develop commercial aviation 'between London and the various capitals of the Empire', and turned to the RAF only in the second half of his presentation. The Air Force had been created just ten years previously, with no permanent organisation of any kind. The lack of barracks, and of all the other paraphernalia of a long-established Service, meant that heavy and exceptional expenditure had been unavoidable at first. Yet, in the Middle East, the RAF had shown how economical air power could be. Within a year of taking over responsibility from the Army in 1922 for the garrisoning of Iraq and Transjordan, the RAF had reduced the cost from £27,000,000 to £13,000,000. Five years after that, it was now running at only £2,000,000. Hoare then came to the last of his key issues:

the question is whether or not the organisation of the Air Force has justified its existence in providing powerful machines and engines and in keeping abreast with aeronautical developments all over the world ... I believe I am justified in claiming that over these 10 years we have made not unsatisfactory progress. Let me give an illustration or two to point the claim I am making. There is the well-known illustration of the Schneider Cup machine ... and the fact that in the first contest held after the War the speed at which the race was won was 107 miles an hour, whereas this year

209

it was 280. An attempt to pass the 300 miles per hour mark is being made this afternoon at Calshot, and I hope, if all goes well, a world's record may be established.

With a closing tribute to 'the sound judgement and the resolute purpose' of Sir Hugh Trenchard at the head of the RAF for most of its first ten years, the Secretary of State yielded the floor for opponents of the Government – and of the Royal Air Force – to make their contributions.

This was the ninth year of national subservience to the now-notorious Ten-Year Rule which did so much to cripple British defence preparedness prior to the rise of Japanese and German militarism. The theory was that defence expenditure should be reduced and restricted as long as the Government could foresee no specific threat of a major war occurring in the decade ahead. Even Churchill, as Chancellor, was in favour of it; and such was the temper of the times that it came as no surprise when, responding to Hoare, Hugh Dalton for the Labour Party demanded to know

> for what purpose has the Right Hon. Gentleman doubled, as he told us, the size of the military Air Force since 1922; for what purpose does this military Air Force exist? Why is there this continued increase in the number of Squadrons and this continued increase in the one weapon in the whole range of modern weapons which is mainly useful for offensive purposes? He told us nothing this afternoon as to whether we have yet made any discovery of a defensive aerial weapon?

Dalton challenged Hoare to say whether he anticipated 'a long period of peace' following a statement to that effect by the First Lord of the Admiralty, William Bridgeman. The Secretary of State for Air, under the cosh of the Ten-Year Rule, had to agree. Dalton's riposte encapsulated an attitude – which had several years yet to run – of malign influence on Britain's capacity to defend herself:

> If he [Hoare] contemplates a prolonged period of peace, why does he ask the taxpayer to pay for four new Squadrons, and why does he claim that he has had to slow down the rate of development which he would otherwise have regarded as desirable? ... We on this side of the House view with grave concern the continued growth of offensive forces in the air. We view it with grave concern not only in this country but in other countries which, likewise, are increasing their Air Forces. We regret that the Right Hon. Gentleman this afternoon, while he indulged in many interesting, stimulating and encouraging talks, did not hold out any hope of disarmament this year, and he is not, apparently, seeking to reduce in the years that lie before us the burden which is resting on the taxpayers of this country for the purpose of building up military forces in a period when, according to his own admission, he fears no war and anticipates no enemy.

The Opposition was as good as its word, throwing full weight behind an amendment regretting the Government's failure to advocate 'bolder proposals for aerial disarmament' at a Preparatory Commission for the Disarmament Conference at Geneva, and recommending 'a programme containing the abolition of military and naval air forces and the establishment of the international control of civil aviation'. Despite the support of former Prime Minister Ramsay MacDonald, this move failed by 215 votes to 116. There then followed consideration of the Air Estimates in Committee; and this gave Joseph Kenworthy MP the chance to make his second long speech of the day, when he moved an amendment for a token reduction of 100 men in order – as he put it – 'to call attention to a number of scandalous doings of the Air Minister'. Kenworthy, a former naval officer and the heir to a peerage, had originally sat as a Liberal on the radical left of his party. One of the most ardent opponents of the Allied Intervention in Russia, he was a prolific contributor from the Back Benches both before and after switching to the Labour Party in the mid-1920s. He criticised the fact that most RAF aerodromes were in the south rather than 'well north of the central line of England [where] the main air bases should be', and deplored the fact that schoolchildren in London and the Home Counties were being encouraged by the Government to attend (free of charge) the dress rehearsals for the Hendon Air Display:

> if you are deliberately to go out of your way to organise school treats, you will lay yourself open to the suspicion that you are trying to inure the young mind to fighting in the air, and that it is part of a deliberate propaganda in which all the Fighting Services are engaged, to counteract the pacifist tendency that has resulted from the War.

After a variety of similar complaints, Kenworthy concluded:

> The Right Hon. Gentleman [Sir Samuel Hoare] talks peace, but he acts war. He increases armaments, engages in this subtle and despicable propaganda for schoolchildren; he is always ready to lend his airmen and airplanes for the making of war films at any time – the Air Force has become a film super – and it is all part of a deliberate attempt to counteract any peace propaganda that has been possible during the past few years. It is deliberately done by the Party opposite and the heads of the Fighting Services; and the heads of the Air Service are not at all behind. It is most unsatisfactory, most disappointing, and altogether wrong. It is not conducive to the peace of the world, and, therefore, I propose to reduce the Vote by 100 men.

It was now after 11.00pm, and before the defeat of Kenworthy's amendment by 187 votes to 75 – despite support for it from such Opposition luminaries as MacDonald, Dalton, Philip Snowden and A.V. Alexander – the Secretary of State for Air gave his response. Hoare's opening statement, as the press later reported, plunged the House into gloom:

> While I was speaking this afternoon a very terrible tragedy took place in the Air Force. I was describing to the House the efforts we were making to

win the World's record speed [*sic*] and I was telling the House that the experiments were actually taking place in the Solent. Little did I know that at that very moment the gallant officer who had been selected to make the attempt had lost his life, that his machine had crashed from the air, and that he had fallen with it into the sea. Let us turn aside, before I deal with the questions which have been raised in this Debate, to offer our sympathy to his family, and pay a tribute of respect to one of the finest officers in the Force – a young man with an unrivalled record who might in the ordinary course have reached the highest post in his great profession. I am afraid the way of progress is strewn with sacrifices of this kind, none the less regrettable, and particularly when they happen in the dramatic manner in which this tragedy took place this afternoon.

★   ★   ★

It had not been until 5.10pm that Kink became airborne. All the commentators at Calshot agreed that his efforts to take off had been fraught with difficulty. The *Echo* reported that he had spent 'about ten minutes in the operation'. According to the correspondent of the *Daily Sketch*:

> it seemed as if something was not right, for he stopped short, turned round again, and then set off in the same direction. The machine rose out of the water momentarily and then floated again. It was obvious to expert spectators that it was not behaving properly, but after a third attempt it rose sharply in the air and went round in wide circles. So fast it seemed to travel that it was out of sight before the sound of the engine reached the ear.

The account given by *The Times* was among the most graphic. Its correspondent explained that whereas Kink's take-off had been assisted by the wind the previous day, by 5.00pm on Monday there was a flat calm:

> After being launched he opened up the engine, disappeared as usual in flying spray, and then came out rocking dangerously fore and aft on the floats, instead of becoming airborne. The pilot of course realised the well-known danger of porpoising, shut off, and let the machine quiet down before turning round and going much further out into the deeper water. Once more he opened up, gathered speed, checked the machine as it seemed about to rock again, and then kept going at full speed until, to everyone's relief, he rose clear into the air ... It is open to question, however, whether the violence of these preliminary struggles to maintain control may not have caused the heavy surges of water, which swept over the tail unit, to strain it in some way not immediately apparent.

This was the second mandatory flight, and another landing was required before Kink could finally tackle the record. He sped off towards Southampton, then turned in a wide sweep southwards, over Calshot Air Station towards the Isle of Wight. After circling again, he alighted gently and with 'scarcely a moment's hesitation' took off for a second time, heading north once more towards

Southampton. A further turn to the left brought him over the 3-kilometre course at an oblique angle as he headed due south towards Cowes. All was set for the first timed run.

In view of what has passed into legend about the cause of the disaster, it is important to set out the eyewitness accounts in as much detail as possible. Naturally, some journalists tended to colour their accounts of the minutes before the crash in the light of their knowledge of the impending disaster. The *Southern Daily Echo* rushed out an extra edition on the Monday evening which simultaneously contained the rapturous report of Sunday's success on the back page, and an early account of the disaster on the front. Expanding on the latter in its Tuesday edition, the *Echo* described how Kink – 'one of the most modest and retiring of men' – was doubtful up to the very last minute whether to go up or not:

> One or two people advised him not to do so, and until nearly half-past four it looked as if he would probably take their advice. A lightning decision, made when brilliant sunshine was fast removing signs of the snowstorm, acted like a spur to mechanics and officials . . . Kinkead watched the proceedings with a critical eye. He seemed to be even more reserved than usual, and his quietness may have been due to the fact that he was steeling himself for the vital test [which], as he must have realised, would either cost him his life or bring him glory. Flight Lieutenant Kinkead was not permitted to forget the deadly possibilities of his flight. Immediately it was known that he intended to fly, the Station ambulance was driven up to beside the jetty, as it had been on each occasion that a similar decision was arrived at during the week. Kinkead looked at the vehicle fixedly for about fifteen seconds, and a grim smile played round the corners of his mouth as though he was amused by some secret thought . . . As he climbed into the narrow cockpit of the machine, the pilot looked as perfectly fit and quietly determined as any man could. He smiled somewhat wistfully as the 'plane was run down the slipway, and responded with a hearty 'Thank you', when some of those about him wished him 'Good luck'.

The *Daily Express* poignantly drew attention to the fact that, during all the delays, 'the most patient man was Flight Lieutenant Kinkead'. Kink was described as possessing a charming personality and no fear at all:

> One of his last remarks before his death was an answer to someone who this afternoon hazarded the opinion that to fly such a machine was extremely dangerous. 'I do not think it any more dangerous than crossing the road,' he replied. 'The risk in each case can be just as fatal.'

Another *Express* commentator claimed that Kink

> seemed to have some foreboding that all was not well. He was even quieter than usual those last few days – not nervous, but serious, as a man on whom a great responsibility has been placed.

Nevertheless, there was a high degree of consistency in the various accounts of what was seen to occur after N221 reappeared, far in the distance, hurtling north at tremendous speed for the start-line at Calshot. According to *The Times*:

> The tiny monoplane, just before entering the first timed run of 3 kilometres (nearly 2 miles), dived straight into the Solent from a height of between 100 feet and 50 feet, and now lies in at least 36 feet of water near the Calshot Lightship ... so swift was the disaster and so far away was the place from the observers on shore that it is impossible tonight to say accurately what happened. From my observation post on the flat roof of the Castle in the Seaplane Station the machine seemed but a speck in the misty sky of a late afternoon ... It was seen as a dot in the mist, its position identified more by the sound of the engine than anything else – and then came a sudden upward sweep of white spray from the grey sea. It was just as if a naval shell had crashed into the water, throwing up a column 10 or 20 feet high. I caught a momentary glimpse of a black object – the wing tip, it seemed – *diving vertically into the water* [author's emphasis] on the edge of the sudden uprush of sea – then the white column fell back, the sea became placid once more, and for a fleeting second two black dots were left, quickly to disappear in turn under the surface. The whole disaster had happened and ended in a second, and it was impossible for a moment to believe that a very skilful pilot and gallant gentleman was not still in his machine and in the air. For the time-lag of sound is such that the roar of the engine was still coming to our ears while our eyes were forcing upon reluctant consciousness that all was over. We watched the Coastal Motor Boats racing to the spot, but without hope, for no man could have survived such a terrific impact with the water, while *the manner in which the machine had dived rather than flown into the sea* [author's emphasis] ruled out any faint hope of rescue which otherwise might have been entertained.

After highlighting Sir Samuel Hoare's remarkable tribute in the Commons, the *Morning Post* was equally adamant about the nature of the fatal dive:

VERTICAL NOSE-DIVE FROM 100 FEET ...
Flight Lieutenant S.M. Kinkead, one of the most brilliant high speed pilots in the Royal Air Force, was killed at 5.25 this evening by crashing into the Solent just before attempting to break the world's flying speed record ... The aeroplane was flying at an altitude of 100 feet between the Calshot Air Station and the Isle of Wight when the disaster occurred, and the spectators at the air station, who included the French, Italian and Japanese Air Attachés, were horrified to see the machine suddenly collapse. One of the officials expressed the opinion that the machine had developed 'rudder flutter' ... Flight Lieutenant Kinkead had made his second test flight and was apparently about to begin his attack on the record. He had circled the aerodrome once when, just as he appeared to be

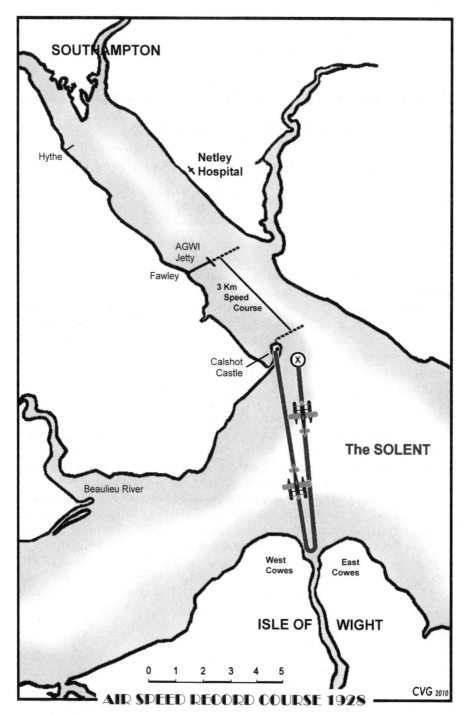

SOUTHAMPTON

Hythe

Netley
× Hospital

AGWI
Jetty

Fawley

3 Km
Speed
Course

Calshot
Castle

Ⓧ

The SOLENT

Beaulieu River

West
Cowes

East
Cowes

ISLE OF   WIGHT

0   1   2   3   4   5

CVG 2010

AIR SPEED RECORD COURSE 1928

Kink's last flight, 12 March 1928. (*Colin van Geffen*)

entering the marked course, his machine shot like a shell from a gun into the water ... It was difficult to realise what exactly happened, but *it sounded as though he had opened his engine all out. The next second the machine dived absolutely vertically into the water* [author's emphasis]. An agonised cry rang out from the onlookers, 'My God, he is down!' For a few fleeting seconds everybody seemed paralysed, and then someone rushed to summon the motor launches. Motor launches and Coastal Motor Boats from Portsmouth raced across the water, and were joined by tugs in a frantic search for any trace of the pilot or his machine. But the waters had closed over him, leaving nothing but a few splinters of wood floating on the surface.

A graphic description of the disaster was given to the *Daily Sketch* by the meteorological officer of the air station, who was on the roof of Calshot Castle:

'Standing on the tower,' he said, 'it seemed he was making clear for us, and coming at an enormous pace. As he approached he dropped lower and lower in the air, and about a mile off he was down to about 100 feet from the water. A few moments later, with about 1,200 feet between the S5 and the Castle, *the machine suddenly side-slipped – not an ordinary side-slip, but a slip at about the same speed as his forward flight* [author's emphasis]. He was over the Deep Channel then, the route of the big steamers, and when he struck the surface there was a shower of water exactly as if a torpedo or shell had exploded.'

The *Daily Express* correspondent was also

standing on the top of the old circular tower that dominates the air station, and we were looking out for a glimpse of the machine when suddenly someone cried out, 'There he is!' It could be seen in the distance – a black speck. Kinkead was coming straight towards me, but it was extremely difficult to distinguish the surface of the water in the distance from the mist that hung over it. We knew that he would be overhead in another few seconds, but, to the amazement of everyone, *the machine plunged without warning into the water* [author's emphasis]. In the cries of horror that went up the Japanese attaché could be heard calling out loudly, 'Crash! Crash!' as he dashed away towards an ambulance. The cause of the crash is inexplicable and the immediate theory was that a bracing wire might have snapped. *The machine dived nose first into the sea* [author's emphasis], and as the tail disappeared a great column of water was thrown up.

Onlookers were stunned by the tragedy, with the *Echo* describing how:

At one moment the little blue and silver seaplane, the Supermarine-Napier S5, was hurtling across the sky like a winged projectile, at the next it was *diving almost vertically* [author's emphasis] and at a stupendous speed into the sea, to be swallowed up without a trace ... The disaster was so bewilderingly sudden and complete that the onlookers were momentarily unable to speak or to act – but only to gaze with horror-stricken eyes at the watery grave of the gallant pilot and his graceful craft.

The reporter observed that, just before the almost vertical dive, Kink had 'opened out the engine, and the craft shot ahead like a thing possessed'. The sound of the roaring engine reached the shore after the plane had disappeared – giving the eerie impression that N221 was still under way beneath the surface of the sea. Among the appalled onlookers were Reginald Mitchell himself and Captain Henri Biard, the Supermarine test pilot who had won the Schneider Trophy for Britain at Naples in 1922, but had crashed into Chesapeake Bay while preparing for the 1925 contest at Baltimore. Biard had been flying Mitchell's earlier – S4 – monoplane and had no doubt that it had failed structurally, despite an Air Ministry verdict blaming him for stalling it. Writing about his own brush with disaster, he later explained that:

> As the wind caught the wings with colossal pressure on the turn, the flutter, which I had noticed so faintly before that it only seemed fancy, began with a vengeance. I worked feverishly at my controls – got the machine almost round – tried to relieve that awful pressure that was making the wings flutter almost like a moth's wings – felt the air tearing at them like a living, malicious thing, superhumanly bent on smashing and twisting and wrenching this mechanical intruder ... and then with an effort which tore at every muscle in my body, I got her righted again and on an even keel, only to find that we had lost flying speed and it was too late ...

Mitchell and Biard were 'almost too overcome to speak'. They knew that Kink had no chance of repeating Biard's miraculous escape, but had he suffered a similar mechanical catastrophe? Biard was certain that the airframe had failed once more, and he never wavered from that view. Almost thirty years after Kink was killed he recorded an interview for a radio programme on 'The Spitfire's Ancestors'. He attributed his own survival to the fact that:

> I had this huge engine in front of me. I knew – or at least I thought – if I make the engine go first into the sea and make the hole in which I will follow – well, it's better than if I go first. And that saved me, obviously. The engine made a huge hole, and we had it shown shortly afterwards on the S5 ... Kinkead – wonderful bloke – he did the same thing – exactly the same thing; but he didn't go in straight. His head was knocked off and we never found it. I know why he was killed, oh, so frightfully well ... He started to take off; shut the engine off; he did it again three times. But – instead of bringing the whole thing back and saying: 'Look, see if it's all right' – he'd been so bothered that he didn't do it. And then he took off and the thing flew beautifully ... You were allowed to go to 1,200 feet in those days. He went over Cowes and he turned and came back towards us. I was standing with Mitchell there. You had to do the speed at only 100 feet. He came down like a – oh, at great speed – and the moment he

217

flattened out . . . it gave up the ghost. It suddenly went 'phew' – only from 100 feet, you know, but doing over 300 miles an hour.

Two journalists standing beside Mitchell and Biard were torn between rushing to telephone their newsdesks and keeping track of the unfolding disaster. Biard was furious with the main offender:

I turned round and gave him such a kick. Oh, I knocked him flying. Mind you, I understand his point of view – it was business in a way; but our friend, poor old Kinkead – it was very shocking to us, you know.

★   ★   ★

Biard was not the only airman convinced that something had gone wrong with the aircraft. Most of the observers had only a frontal view of the oncoming plane as it raced towards them and the start-line at Calshot; but a Coastal Motor Boat was in position three-quarters of a mile from the point of impact. As the *Daily Express* reported, its crew could form a judgement 'not from a view hidden by a machine directly approaching, but from a broadside view'. One of its officers told the paper:

The machine was not travelling at the speed believed, but it was going at a very good speed. I noticed that the tail was fluttering. It was a pronounced flutter, and immediately afterwards, or so it seemed, the pilot slowed down. It may be that he was aware of the danger that had developed, and had decided that the best thing that he could do would be to descend. I understand that it is necessary for a machine like this, which is built entirely for speed, to land at a speed of no less than 120 [*sic*] miles an hour, for at anything less than that the stalling point is reached. It may be that Kinkead did not have sufficient flying speed. I certainly heard, as he was attempting to land, a roar from the engine which might have been caused by a sudden opening wide of the throttle in order to permit of a landing. Immediately after that he closed it, and the machine plunged into the water.

The *Daily Sketch* carried a similar account and so did *The Times*. According to the *Sketch*, the officers on the boat noticed that the tail of N221 was shaking. One of them said that it 'rippled' as the machine drew near. They all believed that Kink realised something was wrong, throttled down and tried to land the seaplane:

When it was about 100 feet above the sea, they suggest, the machine stalled and went left wing down. At the point of stalling, Kinkead appeared to have opened out the engine to the fullest extent, with the result that the machine dived into the sea at a speed of over 200mph.

The version in *The Times* described the officers on the boat as pilots rather than naval personnel, as reported elsewhere, and agreed that they were probably in the best position to have seen the last, fatal seconds. One was said to be 'positive that he saw abnormal movement of the tail unit and fin, suggesting that a sudden weakness had developed'. He was equally sure that Kink was throttling down on a glide, having discovered that something was wrong with the fore-and-aft control. It was while 'making a cool and calculated effort to regain the water before any absolute failure occurred' that Kink met with disaster:

> Flight Lieutenant Kinkead did not fly into the water, but ... after gliding down from a considerable height to about 100 feet or less, *the machine took control, suddenly altered its attitude, and dived vertically into the water* [author's emphasis].

The main dissenting voice was that of Harold Perrin who told the *Daily Express* that, just as the timekeepers were getting ready to measure Kink's velocity,

> he opened out as if he was going full throttle to get the utmost possible speed for flashing across the line. Immediately afterwards, to our astonishment, his machine plunged straight into the water. I cannot say how it happened, but it might easily be that he was not aware how close the water was to him owing to the mist that prevailed.

Perrin was much less tentative than this in an interview with the *Daily Sketch*:

> 'It seems to me,' he stated, 'that as Kinkead came down to do the 3 kilometres at top speed, he must have misjudged his distance owing to the mist that was gathering on the surface of the water. I estimate that he was travelling at full throttle. He seemed to go into the sea in a fast glide.'

This last statement clearly contradicted all the other reports which categorically described a vertical or near-vertical plunge into the sea at the end of Kink's gradual descent. Commander Perrin's third version – in *The Times* – was hard to reconcile with his other two. Here he was cited as confirming that the engine gave a sudden roar, as if opened up just before the crash. He regarded this as indicating 'that something had happened to cause the engine to race, and that momentarily the pilot's control was upset'. Brief mention was also made of the possibility that, turning out of the mist into the sun, Kink was momentarily dazzled, lost his view of the ill-defined horizon, and 'flew into the sea before he realised how close he was to the water' – but this theory was said to have few supporters and was, indeed, even harder to square with the vertical plunge which so many described.

On one point, at least, all commentators agreed. Kink's engaging personality, coupled with the violence of his death in the passage of an instant, left everyone at Calshot saddened, shaken and shocked. There could be no guarantee that the cause of the tragedy would ever be known, even after the recovery of N221, and there could be no certainty what Kink's loss would mean for Mitchell's high speed aircraft. First, the S4; now, an S5. Was there really a future for such volatile machines? Or had the accident been caused by the pilot himself?

Chapter 12

An End and an Aftermath

The letter addressed to Mrs Kinkead, out in Johannesburg, did not need to tell her what had happened to her second son. The whole world knew that. Instead, it enclosed messages of sympathy and condolence received by the Air Council in London. The Italians were especially solicitous, their Air Attaché asking for full details of Kink's funeral, in order to send a wreath, and forwarding translations of two cables just received:

> Kindly express English friends my deepest sorrow for the death of my great competitor Kinkead – Major de Bernardi.

> Grieved by accident occurred loyal generous partner Kinkead I beg to send the expression of my deepest regret to all the glorious family of English aviators – Arturo Ferrarin.

Admiral Denti, Italy's senior naval officer at Venice, also quickly contacted the British Consul:

> In the name of all the officers and personnel under my command please accept our sincerest sympathy for the death of Flight Lieutenant Kinkead whom we learned to know, appreciate and love for his brilliant qualities during his stay at Venice for the Schneider Trophy.

In Rome, the British Ambassador received General Balbo's *Chef de Cabinet* sent 'in full uniform' as a gesture of respect, and reported that Italy's own attempt to break the world speed record, 'which was to have been made at Venice two days ago', had been postponed for three days in tribute to Kink:

> The Italian press is full of solicitous expressions of sympathy, the deceased officer being generally characterised as one of the most daring and determined pilots whom Great Britain has possessed.

Messages from the United States National Advisory Committee for Aeronautics and the Society of British Aircraft Constructors were also enclosed, and it seemed that Kink's death had struck a chord throughout society. Samuel Hoare's tribute in the Commons has already been recorded, but he in turn was contacted by Buckingham Palace:

> I am grieved to learn of the loss sustained by the Royal Air Force in the tragic death of Flight Lieutenant Kinkead, who had such a distinguished

career in the Service. Please convey to the relatives of the gallant airman an expression of my sincere sympathy – George R.I.

People who knew Kink personally as their comrade in arms were deeply affected. Air Marshal Sir John Salmond, now in command of the Air Defence of Great Britain, was reported to have been 'silent for some moments' when the news of Kink's death was telephoned to him by the *Daily Express* on the evening of the disaster:

> It is very sad. It was not in the least expected. Kinkead was one of the finest pilots there has been or probably ever will be in the Air Force. I knew him well in Iraq, and I feel his death as a personal loss. Everyone had a tremendous regard and affection for him. He was a wonderful pilot and an admirable officer.

In the *Aeroplane*, C.G. Grey regretted that an attempt had not been made to break the record immediately after the victory at Venice. If that opportunity had been seized, he noted sadly, 'we might have had the record six months ago, and Kinkead might have been alive today' – but then, again, as so often happened, 'he might have been killed in a simple accident at home':

> To his friends, and even acquaintances, Kinkead was always known simply as 'Kink' – a singularly inapposite, if obvious, nickname, for never has there been a man who made more of a habit of thinking straight, talking straight, and living straight. If Kink had any enemies one has never met any of them. All who knew him admired him equally as a pilot, as a fighting man, and as an individual. Kink had that curiously quiet manner and voice which seems to be the characteristic of all South Africans. It consorted oddly with his war record. And yet it was part and parcel of his kindliness to others, his dislike of advertising himself, and that fine sportsmanship which enabled him to take his bad luck and his perilous descent in the Schneider Trophy Contest at Venice as all in the day's work.

Grey felt there to be poetic justice in the fact that Kink, 'the most modest and self-effacing of men', had been made the subject of a leading article in *The Times* – 'an honour which is reserved for the great ones of the Earth'. The newspaper had indeed paid a remarkable tribute to a young man it described as 'this brilliant ornament of the Service':

> All who have any sympathy with youth and skill and daring will feel a pang of sorrow at the sudden death of Flight Lieutenant Kinkead in the waters of the Solent ... The impact with the water must have brought death as instant as the death in battle Flight Lieutenant Kinkead had so often braved in the War. He has indeed died in action, for this attempt to break the speed record was no mere sporting adventure, but a serious experiment in the improvement of air navigation and air transport made in the interests of the Empire and with official permission and encouragement.

221

Precious lives, like that of this distinguished officer, are the price we have to pay for increase of knowledge in the science and the art of the air ... We talk of our mastery over [the forces of Nature], but it is always a limited mastery ... We are still very far from anything approaching mastery of the air, but we have learned enough ... to understand how invaluable air transport may become ... in peace and in defence. Therefore we make these sacrifices, as we make the sacrifices of war, sadly, but with pride in those who in the flower of youth and early manhood face death for the common good. Flight Lieutenant Kinkead was a South African, and South Africa is one of the remote parts of the Empire overseas which rapid communication promises more specially to benefit. He has died in the service of the land of his birth as in that of the Empire for which he fought with such prowess in the War ... It seems certain that for one reason or another, the pilot had a struggle to raise the seaplane off the water and that she rocked on her floats to a degree which appeared dangerous to onlookers on shore. Among the suggestions made is that she may have been injured in the process without the knowledge of the pilot. But really we know nothing material as yet, except the fact that a tried and gallant gentleman has gone to his death in the daring performance of a dangerous duty.

★　★　★

Not one but two investigations were quickly established. Oddly, they over-lapped, with the RAF Court of Inquiry held in private on 14 and 15 March and the Coroner's Inquest beginning in public on the second of these dates. Kink did not remain entombed for long. By noon on the day after he died, the diving ship *Excellent* arrived from Portsmouth, anchoring near the spot where the seaplane had struck the surface. It was one of the deepest parts of the Solent, in the centre of the dredged channel some 200 yards from the Castle Point Buoy. Before diving could begin, N221 had to be found and this involved scouring a wide area with chains. The task was carried out by two crews in rowing boats while ocean liners and tramp steamers sailed past, dipping their flags in gestures of respect. A 'Special Correspondent' of the *Echo* watched it all from a tug. Earlier, at Calshot, he had witnessed an 'infinitely sad' scene:

It was the sort of weather Kinkead had been waiting and watching for all the week. There was scarcely a breath of wind and the early sun made a pathway like burnished brass across the rippling waters of the Solent. It was like a golden mantle across the very spot where Kinkead vanished in last evening's setting sun. There was hardly a soul about the aerodrome. When I walked by the empty hangar where the Supermarine-Napier S5 had been housed, I noticed a man in rough overalls gazing pensively at the spot where the machine last started from. He was silent and meditative. He walked slowly away murmuring 'Poor old Kink'. He was one of the

222

mechanics who had worked on the seaplane, day after day, preparing her for the great flight, and had come to love both pilot and machine.

It took four hours of dragging and diving to locate and recover the wreckage. The engine had broken away and was brought to the surface first, then taken onboard a trawler. Once the fuselage and tail of N221 had been secured, the seaplane was slowly towed down the Solent to Calshot. On 14 March, *The Times* published a graphic picture of the shattered fuselage being winched ashore. Perhaps bearing in mind the impression which such images would make, the RAF had revealed new information about Kink's successful test flight the day before he was killed:

> Kinkead had preserved complete reticence as to the exact speed at which he travelled in his trial flight on Sunday morning, and no-one had realised that he had reached, on his air speed indicator, a rate of no less than 330 miles an hour ... Kinkead was so enthusiastic after his trial flight that he said he believed he could attain probably 350 miles an hour. It should be realised that this type of monoplane had never before been flown, probably, at more than 300 miles an hour, and ... no-one could be certain that stresses, which were within the capacity of aircraft engine and propeller at 300 miles an hour, might not rise to an unexpected magnitude when the speed was increased to 350 miles an hour. This therefore may supply a clue to the accident. Further evidence today suggests that Flight Lieutenant Kinkead had not throttled down his engine ... and there seems good reason to believe that he set his mind on scoring an outstanding success ... Kinkead had been urged to content himself with beating the existing record by the requisite 5 miles an hour, or at least to keep within a speed of 310 miles, but he, as a pilot, took a risk which designers and aircraft instructors would have rightly hesitated to permit in existing machines.

It seems unlikely that the proceedings of the RAF Court of Inquiry will ever come to light. On Kink's Service Record, the final entry gives the number of a file, which has apparently not survived, and a two-sentence summary of the findings:

> 831629/28: C. of I. held at Calshot on 14.3.28. Flying accident (Pilot) Supermarine S5 N221 at Southampton Water on 12.3.28. Accident due to stalling of the machine, the cause of which the Court is unable to determine.

Air Commodore J.C. ('Paddy') Quinnell told his stepson, Solent historian Maldwin Drummond, that he had been a member of the RAF Inquiry team:

> Paddy said [that] Kinkead, while attempting to land on Southampton Water, struck the surface hard and was killed. The Inquiry decided Kinkead had not been able to estimate the distance between his plane and the water as it was a particularly calm day and the sea was like a mirror.

One of the recommendations of the Inquiry was that a launch should be employed to ruffle the water on days of flat calm, so the pilot could better estimate the distance above the sea.

The Schneider Trophy story has inspired countless authors over successive generations. Many give Kink an honourable mention, stressing how his death grieved Reginald Mitchell – who developed the Spitfire, despite failing health, on the basis of his record-breaking seaplanes. Cancer finally claimed him at the age of 44 in June 1937. Most of these writers claim that Kink failed to pull out of a dive at the start of his high speed run. This is undoubtedly wrong, given what many eyewitnesses said at the time. It is also incompatible with what the Coroner's Inquest determined, though that in itself is open to challenge.

At 3.15 on Thursday 15 March, the Southampton County Coroner, Percy Ingleby, opened the inquest in the Library next to the Sergeants' Mess in Eaglehurst Camp at Calshot. He had previously fulfilled 'the melancholy duty' of viewing Kink's remains in the mortuary nearby. One of the witnesses he would hear that day was Flying Officer Fred Miller, who described being on board the RAF boat *Adastral* when the wreckage was brought to the surface, seeing Kink's body 'in the cockpit', and extricating it from the seaplane. This grim task was actually carried out by Charlie Etherington, a 27-year-old crewman on one of the RAF launches which dashed to the scene, together with his NCO. He was interviewed in 1980 by the popular historian Alexander McKee who had appealed in the columns of the *Echo* for witnesses of the crash. Kink's body was dreadfully mutilated:

> Head was off. Body up tail. Sergeant Temple and I had to cut tail open to get the body out. Body cut as if by fine wire. Fuselage crushed in. Half his head gone, vertical cut more or less ... I was a bearer at the funeral and I didn't like being a bearer, knowing what was in there. Thought about it all the time and remembering how he was when we got him out.

These terrible injuries resulted from the angle at which N221 hit the water. McKee's account cites a letter from Mr E.W. Gardener:

> He was the very man who had dealt with the wreckage when it had been returned to the Woolston works of Supermarine. 'The wing on impact with the surface of the water snapped off and caused the bulkhead to be pushed along the fuselage, breaking the $1'' \times \frac{1}{4}''$ steel flying wire which was bolted to the top of the bulkhead.'

Kink's life had ended in a fraction of a second. The question was, why? Mr Ingleby did his best to find out, but the odds were against him. Few witnesses gave evidence and, of those who did, even fewer had evidence worth giving. Flight Lieutenant Wilson, the Adjutant of the air station, set the scene, but had no knowledge of Kink's speed, of the fuel used, or of any ill-effects he had previously suffered from fumes. By contrast, Flight Lieutenant Peter Cundle Wood confirmed that, after the successful Sunday morning flight, Kink had told him that 'he had been very sick', but had now recovered. Edward Ransome, from the Air Ministry's Aeronautical Experimental Department, had been attached to Kink's team and inspected the seaplane before it set off from the slipway: 'It was then in a perfectly airworthy condition. If it had not been so, I should not have allowed it to fly.' Nor was there anything wrong with the engine. Reginald Garrett Smith, the service engineer from Napiers, said it was in perfect condition; but he was reluctant to answer questions about its special fuel:

> *Answer*: I do not know whether I am at liberty to answer. I do not know whether I shall be giving away official secrets or not.
> *Question*: Did the spirit contain ethyl of lead?
> *Answer*: Yes: it was not the same as the commercial spirit, ethyl.
> *Question*: Can you tell me whether the spirit is in general use here?
> *Answer*: It is absolutely special fuel for engines of this type of machine, and to the best of my knowledge not used in others.
> *Question*: Have you ever known anyone who has been overcome when using this spirit?
> *Answer*: I have known people to be affected by the fumes. The deceased was the only man I have known who had been made sick by the fumes.
> *Question*: Have you known anyone to be overcome?
> *Answer*: I have heard at third or fourth hand of people being overcome, but I have no personal knowledge of people being overcome by ethyl spirit.
> *Question*: Is it possible that the deceased was overcome by the fumes of the spirit he was using?
> *Answer*: I consider it was a possibility.

Although the Coroner focused sharply on this issue, Smith's testimony was more significant for his eye-witness account of the crash. This corresponded in every particular with the majority of the press reports immediately after the accident. N221 took off from the water, made a wide circle to the left, and disappeared in the direction of Cowes:

> The machine was out of my view ... and hearing for about three minutes. I was standing on the eastern slipway when the noise of the engine again became audible. The machine soon appeared in sight, travelling towards me from Cowes at about 250 feet above the water, and going very fast. It was impossible to tell the pace. The machine appeared to be intentionally descending, and, after a few seconds, nosedived very suddenly into the sea from about 50 feet up. I saw nothing more of it. This happened about a half to three-quarters of a mile away.

There was, in fact, no question of Kink having flown directly into the sea. It is only natural for a biographer to wish to absolve his subject from blame in circumstances like this. Nevertheless, it is a curious fact that the explanation most frequently given now was largely discounted at the time. Pilot error was ascribed, as we shall see, but it had nothing to do with misjudging a high speed dive. Perrin's varying descriptions have already been listed, and his interpretation did receive some backing, retrospectively, from Lawrence Coombes, who had accompanied the Schneider team to Venice in 1927:

Later that year [sic] an attempt was made on the world speed record. Kinkead was chosen to fly the S5 which had been specially tuned for the attempt. I was sent down to Calshot with an assistant and camera-guns to prepare for the event. Unfortunately, the weather in late October [sic] in England is not good for high speed flying. The Solent has extremely nasty tides and currents and, even when the weather was clear, water conditions are often bad. The place was swarming with pressmen who showed visible impatience with Kinkead for not making the attempt under what they considered to be reasonable conditions. After a period of rough weather, a flat calm ensued. The visibility, however, was poor, barely a mile, which was insufficient for the 300mph machine. One pressman remarked in Kinkead's hearing: 'One day it's too rough, the next day it's too calm. The whole thing's hopeless.'

Kinkead decided to make the attempt that afternoon, obviously against his better judgement. I was manning one of the camera-guns when Kinkead approached the first timing point. The rules for the speed record allow a dive from 1,000 feet to 300 feet, and this is always taken advantage of in order to increase the mean speed over the course. Kinkead came down in a shallow dive but, to our horror, instead of flattening out at 300 feet, he continued the dive and hit the water, sending up an enormous cloud of spray. Naturally, he was killed instantly. It was quite obvious that, in the glassy calm water and poor visibility, he was unable to judge his height.

The RAF Court of Inquiry, by contrast, is known to have found that the seaplane stalled – that is, lost flying speed and thus fell into the sea. This is at least compatible with what the overwhelming majority of eye-witnesses reported – that N221, having steadily been descending, suddenly turned sharply downwards and nosedived to her doom. There is, of course, an alternative explanation, namely, that something went wrong with the aircraft itself. For the moment, the Inquest's attention lay elsewhere. The Coroner knew that Kink was vastly experienced. He was also aware of his susceptibility to fumes in the cockpit. A qualified witness – Smith – considered it possible that Kink could have been overcome by fuel or exhaust fumes. It was decided to adjourn the Inquest until the results of laboratory tests on tissues were known.

*   *   *

Kink's funeral was held at Fawley on 16 March, the day after the Inquest adjourned. It was, Charlie Etherington recalled, one of the largest the village had ever seen. The first part of the service took place in the RAF Chapel at the air station. Then the procession assembled. Representatives of the Air Ministry and all three Armed Services were escorted by all the officers, NCOs and men from the base, together with a marching band, firing party and buglers. At Fawley Church, the cortège was met by the local vicar, Reverend Frank Harvey, and the last rites performed by Reverend James Black, Presbyterian Chaplain of the RAF Depot, Uxbridge:

> At the rear of the procession, the ex-Servicemen of Fawley fell in and followed to the churchyard, one of them carrying a beautiful wreath. A crowd numbering several hundred attended to pay a tribute to the gallant officer.

Among the mourners were Sidney Webster, Leonard Slatter and Raymond Collishaw. Three lorries were laden with 'magnificent flowers' including 'a representation of an aeroplane, entirely in daffodils'. A muffled peal was rung, three volleys fired and the Last Post sounded as Samuel Kinkead passed from the sight of men.

★　★　★

The loss of N221 was not the only high-profile tragedy in the news. The day Kink died, Lady Carbery – the adventurous young wife of a former Irish peer – was killed at Nairobi Aerodrome while instructing a novice. On 13 March, Captain Walter Hinchliffe – an experienced civil aviator and Western Front veteran – set out with the Hon Elsie Mackay, daughter of Lord Inchcape, attempting to cross the Atlantic for the first time from East to West. They disappeared without trace. Meanwhile, Sir Samuel Hoare was being questioned in the Commons 'about the circumstances in which Flight Lieutenant Kinkead lost his life ... whether the speed trial was approved by the Air Ministry, [and] whether such trials served any useful purpose'. He responded robustly that they did and developed this theme, on 23 March, in an address to the Birmingham Conservative Club 'on the recent air tragedies and the question raised by high speed and Trans-Atlantic flights'. Further east-west Atlantic flights would, he said, be 'most unwise ... until we have machines of greater endurance at our disposal'; but speed record attempts, though dangerous, were in a different category:

> year by year, we have made a steady advance in the conquest of the air ... but now as always the way of human progress has its tragic side. We are marching along the road to victory but, as we move forward, many a brilliant and gallant officer loses his life in the advance. Who shall assess the tragedy for families and friends, and for the country, when one of these splendid young men falls by the way? A week ago one such life was lost in that sudden plunge of Flight Lieutenant Kinkead's seaplane into the Solent. In the twinkling of an eye, a young and brilliant life was blotted out from human sight and ended in a second beneath the waves of the sea.

Such losses naturally led people to ask if the pursuit of speed could justify the sacrifice; but this was to miss the point:

> if it was only the breaking of a world's record that we were attempting to achieve, I should agree with those who ask this question. I would say, no world's record is worth such a sacrifice. I would say, the few miles more do not justify the loss of a single life. But let us remember that there is more at stake than an increase of speed, and that, just as many of the improvements in the motor car engine are directly due to motor racing, so a definite advance in aeroplane design and in engine improvement results from high speed flying. Let us then, whilst showing our deepest sympathy with Flight Lieutenant Kinkead's family, refuse to abandon an effort that is necessary for the progress of aviation and make certain that the sacrifices of the pioneers shall not have been made in vain.

Hoare's was very much the prevailing view. A fine editorial in the *Hampshire Advertiser and Southampton Times*, the *Echo*'s weekly counterpart, on 17 March all but predicted the Battle of Britain – in which the S5's successor, the Supermarine Spitfire would play a decisive part:

> The tragic fate of Flight Lieutenant Kinkead, one of Britain's most intrepid airmen, ... is a melancholy reminder of the price that must be paid for air power. This terrible tragedy was the result of no mere 'stunt' ... In the past, on land and water and under the water, our gallant men have never hesitated to risk their lives in order that the nation's safety may be assured. The future lies in the air. No country, least of all an island like our own, can afford to run the risk of being unprepared against attack from the skies. Speed is essential. To gain it, Flight Lieutenant Kinkead lost his life. Others have done so; others will do the same. It is the sacrifice that Progress demands, and it will always be nobly paid. Yet, there are circumstances about this disaster that make it particularly pathetic. Young Mr Kinkead had a brilliant flying record in the war. He was one of the team which won the Schneider Trophy for Great Britain at Venice last year. Now he has died at the moment when ardent hopes were being entertained of a new British triumph. For his country he lived and for his country he died. No simpler epitaph could be written.

★   ★   ★

When the inquest resumed on 26 March, the Coroner was forced to abandon his theory that Kink had been poisoned. The report by Wing Commander H.E. Whittingham, head of the RAF Pathological Laboratory at Halton, was decisive. It stated that Kink's blood showed 'no spectroscopic, or chemical, evidence of the presence of carbon monoxide'. No lead, or lead compound, was found in either the lung tissues or the blood samples:

> Smears of lung tissues were examined for the possible detection of crystals of lead, tetraethyl hydroxide, but with negative results. Portions of lung

tissues were submitted to distillation tests, but no odour of petrol, benzol or ethyl was noted. Nothing abnormal was observed.

Having drawn a blank on the question of fumes, the Coroner inquired if the velocity at which N221 had been travelling could have made it uncontrollable. Once again he put his questions to the Station Adjutant; once again Flight Lieutenant Wilson pleaded lack of sufficient expertise:

Question: Would the increase in the speed tend to so compress the air in front as to deflect the course of the machine?
Answer: I have not sufficient technical experience to answer a question of that sort. Only a technical expert could hope to answer that.
Question: I am only asking because it has occurred to me that it is possible that as the flight is suddenly varied by something like 70 degrees the course of the 'plane might be deviated by the compressed air in front. It may be quite impossible to theorise, but I just wanted to know about it.
Answer: I am afraid, as I said just now, only a really technical expert could hope to cope with questions like that.
Question: Is it possible that the deviation up or down or sideways was caused by the resistance of the air? I am trying to find out if there is a possible explanation of *the sudden dive of the seaplane* [author's emphasis]? If you don't think there is anything in it, I am prepared to accept your answer.
Answer: I would not like to attempt to answer it. It is difficult to come to any conclusion.

These exchanges show, yet again, that Kink did not fly into the sea. A planned descent had become a 'sudden dive', as the press reported at the time. Two possibilities remained – mechanical failure or pilot error. The inquest duly adjourned until 20 April, when the evidence of Major James Cooper, Inspector of Accidents, was heard. He was adamant that nothing whatever had gone wrong with the seaplane. No part of the aircraft, its engine or its controls had broken or failed to function normally:

Question: Did you form any opinion as to the cause of the accident?
Answer: I did.
Question: What was that?
Answer: I came to the opinion, as a result of my investigations, that the aircraft stalled at a height of something like 50 feet to 80 feet, when the pilot attempted to land.
Question: Stalling is losing flying speed?
Answer: Yes, losing sufficient speed to maintain flight ...
Question: Have you any idea why the machine should lose flying speed?
Answer: I formed the further opinion that the pilot misjudged his height above the water when attempting to land, and this led to the machine stalling.
Question: Can you tell me why you came to that conclusion?

229

> *Answer*: I think the pilot abandoned his attempt to fly the speed course because of the weather conditions at the time ...
>
> *Question*: I don't know whether you know, but it is said that the water in the Solent is very deceptive owing to local conditions.
>
> *Answer*: I believe it is.
>
> *Question*: There have been many accidents owing to misjudged heights while flying?
>
> *Answer*: We have investigated quite a number of accidents owing to errors of judgement of the height above the water ...
>
> *Question*: So far as you know, there was no reason why he should abandon his flight?
>
> *Answer*: In my opinion he abandoned it because of the weather conditions ...

Major Cooper added that under certain weather conditions, such as mistiness, little wind and a calm sea, it was hard to judge one's height over water. 'There was also the question of horizon as well.' Cooper had reached his conclusion. It had determined the outcome of the RAF Inquiry. Now it would settle the inquest as well. The Inspector would not even concede the facts established by other witnesses:

> *Question*: There is no doubt that deceased suffered from the effects of the fumes after the flight on the Sunday?
>
> *Answer*: That is a matter of opinion. It may have been the cold and taking breakfast on a cold and empty stomach.

Despite his best efforts, the Coroner succeeded only once in drawing out an admission; but that, too, was promptly dismissed:

> *Question*: Did you have any evidence that the rudder, or tail, of the machine was seen to be fluttering before the crash?
>
> *Answer*: Yes.

Asked what this indicated, Cooper said that it had been seen when the machine was turning and was probably just 'the reflection of the sunlight' from the rudder. 'I do not think that the tail was actually oscillating,' he added. If there had been such violent movement, evidence would have been seen in the wreckage. At this point, the Coroner gave up. He understood there was to be another speed record attempt, and he thought it would be 'lamentable' if there were another fatal accident. 'I think everything has been done that can be done,' replied the Inspector, and certainly there was little else for the Coroner to do. His verdict of misadventure stated that death was due to haemorrhage and shock from extensive injuries caused by violent contact with part of the seaplane when diving into the sea 'owing to lack of speed while attempting to alight'.

Not everyone found this believable. As well as Charlie Etherington, Alexander McKee interviewed other witnesses of the crash. One was T.L. 'Monty'

Banks, a corporal engineer on the fastest of the RAF rescue craft – a Coastal Motor Boat – who saw N221 diving and 'was sure he saw the tail flutter just before the machine hit the water'. According to McKee, Banks did not like the way in which the suggestion of flutter was brushed aside:

the witnesses interviewed had been on the sea wall at Calshot, much further away than the crew of the CMB. Yet their skipper had not been called to give evidence . . . A major mystery is Major Cooper's belief that the S5 stalled onto the water when landing, as everyone else described a descending high speed run to the measured 3-kilometre mark. The witnesses in the boat, being to one side, had the best view, but even those who were watching Kinkead coming at them almost head-on were in no doubt that he was travelling extremely fast . . . The landing speed of the S5 was about 120–130mph, the stalling speed 90mph. At the stall, of course, the machine would simply cease to fly and then drop into the water.

At Venice, Kink had narrowly escaped disaster with an emergency landing when he detected a mechanical fault. Until Major Cooper's evidence, no-one at the inquest had suggested he was trying to land. To have decreased his speed to the 90mph at which he would have stalled, Kink would have had to glide down with a decreasing velocity hard to confuse with an attempt on the world speed record. Thus, at one end of the scale, history relates that he went to his death in a full-speed dive from which he failed to pull out. At the other, the Inquiry and the inquest have him trying to land, but stalling and falling, because he reduced his speed after misjudging his height. These accounts are incompatible with each other and with the facts. Yet, there is another explanation: the possibility that history repeated itself. Was the last-second surge in engine power a vain attempt to regain flying speed when detecting the start of a stall – or was it instead to counter the effects of an oscillating rudder? Wing Commander A.H. Orlebar, a subsequent Commanding Officer of the High Speed Flight, wrote in 1933:

I do not know just what happened . . . From a photograph of the machine taxiing out one can see it was certainly very misty and the water was very glassy. People say Kinkead was not too fit at the time, and the combination of difficulties may have led him to make a mistake. However, there are many different opinions, and many spectators believe that something went wrong with the machine.

As has been seen, Henri Biard was one onlooker certain that the aircraft had failed. His own crash, in the S4 at Baltimore, had also been blamed on the pilot, rather than on wing flutter; but modifications were nevertheless made to brace the wings of the successor S5. Orlebar's own subsequent experience gives an indication of what may really have happened to Kink on that last, fatal flight. According to Ralph Barker's narrative:

aileron flutter had been experienced on the S5s when the controls became slack and, when the High Speed Flight began practice in 1931, rudder vibration on one of the S6s nearly led to disaster ... Climbing at full throttle, Orlebar noticed a nasty vibration, but when he eased back the throttle it stopped. After a minute or so he opened up again, and he was doing about 350mph at 300 feet, turning to keep over the Solent, when the vibration suddenly returned, in far more violent form. The rudder bar forced his feet alternately backwards and forwards, the stick moved fore and aft in his hand, and he realised he was encountering tail flutter. He slammed back the throttle but the vibration continued ... The whole plane and its outlines were blurred. Orlebar was down to about 50 feet and preparing for a crash when the flutter ceased abruptly and he alighted straight ahead. All the control wires had been stretched and the fuselage was badly buckled in front of the tail ... Mitchell at once set to work to establish the cause and find a cure. His remedy was to fit mass-balancing weights to the rudder (and the ailerons, as a precaution) and to stiffen the fuselage.

N221 was mangled by the crash and, inevitably, subjected to further stresses and strains during the recovery process. It seems surprising, to put it mildly, that the Inspector could say with such confidence that no evidence could be seen in the wreckage of the failure of any component. Dr David Kirkpatrick is a present-day expert on aerodynamics who has reviewed the contents of this chapter. He states that:

> The aerodynamic forces on an aircraft in flight are generally proportional to the square of its airspeed. If Kinkead had substantially exceeded the target airspeed of the S5 – as suggested retrospectively by the RAF – on either of his trial flights or in the record attempt, some component could have been overstrained to the point of catastrophic failure. The effects of the crash and subsequent salvage could have made it difficult to detect any conclusive evidence.

★ ★ ★

When the Secretary of State for Air paid tribute to Kink on 12 March, he described the young officer as one who might have reached 'the highest post in his great profession'. The fate of Kink's contemporaries shows this to have been more than idle rhetoric. Many reached very senior rank. Of the members of the High Speed Flight, Slatter at Coastal Command formed a winning partnership with Admiral Sir Max Horton during the Battle of the Atlantic. Knighted in 1942, he succeeded Sholto Douglas as AOC-in-C Coastal Command in 1945, became an Air Marshal in 1947 and retired from the RAF in 1949. Sidney Webster stepped down as an Air Vice-Marshal the following year – the final rank also achieved by Orlebar who, just eighteen months after Kink's death, raised the world speed record to 357.7mph in a Supermarine S6. This was N247, the seaplane in which he had almost come to grief as a result of

232

rudder flutter and which claimed the life of Lieutenant Gerry Brinton – the only naval pilot to join the High Speed Flight – in August 1931. The Schneider Trophy was eventually won outright on 13 September that year by Flight Lieutenant John Boothman, whose fellow team member, Flight Lieutenant George Stainforth, set up a world record speed of 407.5mph in an S6B on 29 September, demonstrating the tremendous rate of progress since Kink's attack on the 300mph barrier in 1928. Boothman, like Slatter, was knighted, having served as an Assistant Chief of Air Staff and also as AOC-in-C Coastal Command. Stainforth, by contrast, was killed in action in the Middle East in September 1942. He was 43 when he died, having chosen to continue flying much longer than he needed. Worsley died in a car crash in 1930; but Chick reached the rank of Air Commodore, despite his contretemps with Slatter in 1927.

Among Kink's wartime contemporaries, the same mixture of high achievement and lives cut short prevailed. Richard Bell Davies became an Admiral and Gilbert Smylie, whom he rescued, an Air Commodore. Gerrard and Samson also reached the latter rank. Both retired in 1929 but, while Gerrard lived on until 1963, Samson died in 1931 at the age of only 47. Having taken command of 40 Squadron RAF in April 1918, Stanley Dallas was shot down on 27 May. He had thirty-two victories to his credit and was 26 when he died. Cyril Ridley, still in the RAF, was killed when two aircraft collided in Germany in 1920; Max Findlay crashed fatally during the Johannesburg Air Race in 1936; but James Forman survived to serve in the Second World War. Ridley died at 25 and Findlay at 38. Collishaw and Maund became Air Vice-Marshals – an outcome which Aten would have relished in the one case and deplored in the other. Collishaw lived on until 1976, but Maund died of natural causes, on Active Service, at the end of 1942. Anderson became Chief Pilot for British Airways, but perished with two others in a night-time crash at Gatwick in September 1936. His wife of two months witnessed the accident. Walter Anderson was 46 when he died. Elliot, whom he rescued in Russia, became AOC-in-C Fighter Command, soon after the Second World War, and Chief Staff Officer to the Minister of Defence. He retired in 1954 as Air Chief Marshal Sir William Elliot. 'Robbo' also headed Fighter Command before retiring as Air Chief Marshal Sir James Robb in November 1951. 'Mary', after an outstanding career in the Western Desert, left the RAF as Air Marshal Sir Arthur Coningham in 1947; but he disappeared over the Atlantic while a passenger on a civil flight in January 1948. Three years earlier, he had been succeeded as head of the RAF in Germany by Sholto Douglas, who reached the highest rank of all – Marshal of the Royal Air Force – on 1 January 1946. The fate of the leader of the Cape Flight was especially poignant. Conway Pulford became an Air Vice-Marshal and was appointed to command the RAF in the Far East in March 1941. He chose not to abandon his headquarters in Malaya as early as he might. When he finally left, his motor-boat was strafed and forced to run aground on a malaria-infested island. By the time the

Japanese captured the survivors, two months later, Pulford had already succumbed to exhaustion and disease. He was 50 when he died and was posthumously Mentioned in Despatches.

Of the politicians who featured, more or less directly, in the Kinkead story, Joseph Kenworthy lost his Commons seat in 1931. Before he could regain it, he succeeded to the title of Lord Strabolgi, controversially awarded to his father in 1916 after being in abeyance since 1788. From 1938 to 1942, he was Opposition Chief Whip in the Lords, presumably urging greater conformity among his Labour colleagues in the Upper House than he had ever shown in the Lower one. He died suddenly in 1953 at the age of 67. Sir Samuel Hoare's name will forever be linked with that of Pierre Laval, the French Prime Minister (subsequently executed for collaboration), with whom he concocted an ill-fated plan in December 1935 to dismember Abyssinia after Mussolini's aggression against her. Whatever his failings as an appeasement-minded Foreign Secretary – and the Hoare-Laval Pact cost him that post – he had been an admirable Secretary of State for Air in the 1920s and proved to be a formidable Ambassador in Madrid in the 1940s, manoeuvring brilliantly to ensure that Spain kept out of the war. Elevated to the Peerage as Viscount Templewood, he died in May 1959.

After she lost her second boy, Helen Kinkead asked her son-in-law if he would perpetuate the family surname. Bill Weekes – who had won a Military Cross for taking a horse-drawn battery across a bridge under fire – readily agreed. Helen survived to see her three grandsons, Dennis, Bobby and Mark, achieve distinction in the South African Navy, in business and in academia respectively, before her death two days short of her 96th birthday in 1957. She outlived three of her four children, Vida having died in her fifties in 1946.

All too many of Kink's peacetime comrades died before their time. In the six months from January to June 1928, the RAF recorded sixty-eight serious accidents, excluding those at the Royal Aircraft Establishment. Kink's was one of the twenty-eight in which one or more of the occupants died. He was listed as having 2,141 flying hours to his name, in the course of his career as a 'war pilot'. According to the RAF's half-yearly report, the death toll would have been even higher but for the fact that parachutes had at last been issued in 1925. The first 'forced parachute descent' had taken place in 1926 and eight lives had been saved in this way by the end of 1927:

> During 1928, there were a further seven occasions on which parachutes were used after collisions in the air, or for some other reason ... Up to the end of 1928, fifteen forced descents by parachute had been made: eleven of these were successful, in two cases the parachutist was injured and in two cases he was killed.

All this came a little too late for Bill Daly. By 1924, he belonged to 39 Squadron, flying DH9A bombers as part of an expert display team at RAF pageants. As the Commanding Officer later testified, on 5 June Flying Officers L.G.

Lucas and R.H. Daly were practising formation flying at a height of 1,000 feet over Spittlegate Aerodrome, near Grantham:

> The former apparently pulled up his machine, and the undercarriage of Daly's machine became firmly fixed in the top plane of Lucas's machine. Both machines commenced to descend locked together. Turning into [a] half-circle, they hit the ground just as Daly, after enormous effort, had pulled his machine out of the top of Lucas's plane. Their machines had been in the air four times before during the day. The manoeuvres were being carried out under his (Squadron Leader Whittaker's) instructions. It was a pure error of judgement on the part of one of the pilots, added the witness, but it was impossible to say which. There was nothing wrong with the machines.

Flying Officer Rowan Heywood Daly DSC DFC was 26 when he died. A parachute would probably have saved his life, but nothing could have prevented the death of Burns Thomson in Egypt, where he was serving with 4 Flying Training School based at Abu Sueir in 1922. Like so many other young flyers with a disregard for regulations, he came to grief while stunting at low level. On 4 November that year, he misjudged a manoeuvre and fatally crashed into a building. He was 25 when he died and he lies in the same war cemetery as George Stainforth, at Ismailia. Of the four Camel pilots of B Flight, 47 Squadron, only Marion Aten died in his bed – in May 1961, just before his evocative but novelised memoirs were published. An Epilogue lists the fate of his principal comrades with a fair degree of accuracy, give or take a year or two. Curiously, the main exception is his particular friend, Eddie Fulford, whom he believed to have perished in a troopship off Southampton in 1942. Fulford actually survived the Second World War, having been recalled from the Reserve at its outbreak. He was one of the lucky ones. Kink, ultimately, was not. Yet, in contrast to countless others, at least his fate lay, to a great extent, in his own skilful hands.

Kink's first campaign on the Western Front was the Passchendaele offensive of 1917. His last was that of August 1918 which led to the Armistice. His courage in the air was mirrored in the hearts and actions of thousands of foot-soldiers below. Second Lieutenant Glyn Morgan wrote to his father at the start of the one, and Lieutenant Hedley Goodyear wrote to his mother at the start of the other. Both knew the odds against survival:

> You, I know, my dear Dad, will bear the shock as bravely as you have always borne the strain of my being out here; yet I should like, if possible, to help you to carry on with as stout a heart as I hope to 'jump the bags' . . . My one regret is that the opportunity has been denied me to repay you to the best of my ability for the lavish kindness and devotedness which you have always shown me . . . however, it may be that I have done so in the struggle between Life and Death, between England and Germany, Liberty and Slavery. In any case, I shall have done my duty in my little way . . .
> Your affectionate son and brother, Glyn

With hope for mankind and with visions of a new world, a blow will be struck tomorrow which will definitely mark the turn of the tide. It will be one of a grand series of victories ... A great triumph is certain and I shall take part in it. I shall strike a blow for freedom along with thousands of others who count personal safety as nothing when freedom is at stake ... I have no regrets and no fear of tomorrow. I should not choose to change places with anyone in the world just now, except General Foch ...

God bless you all. Hedley

Glyn Morgan, who joined the Army straight from school, was killed on 1 August 1917. He was recommended for a posthumous VC and was 21 when he died. Canadian schoolmaster Hedley Goodyear MC was killed on 22 August 1918. He was 32 when he died.

In reviving the memory of Samuel Kinkead, we bring back from obscurity the campaigns in which he fought, the values which he held and the goals which he sought. We shed light on the sacrifice of others, equally courageous but cloaked in anonymity. The epitaph for one heroic airman can most fittingly be drawn from the words of another. 'When Kinkead, still a Flight Lieutenant, went deep into the Solent in his Supermarine S5,' wrote Taffy Jones in 1938,

the Royal Air Force lost, without doubt, its finest junior officer. He was remarkably brave, a brilliant pilot, ideal leader, and straight as a die in all his dealings with his juniors and seniors. He was modest in the extreme and such was his tremendous personality that everyone who came in close contact with him looked upon him as someone apart from his fellow-officers. Each thought that his friendship was theirs alone: something so precious that others could not possibly have it. I think it is quite un-necessary to say any more than this about the award of decorations and promotion: Kinkead did not receive any decorations or promotion for his magnificent peace-time work. He was junior to officers who were un-worthy of cleaning his shoes. Many brave airmen had gone before Kinkead, and I feel sure that Valhalla was well lit up on the night of 12 March 1928.

Appendix I

Kink's Combat Victories

The listing below is the best available collation of a variety of reports, largely based on the work of Frank Olynyk and Christopher Shores, with a few additions, subtractions and amendments. It should be remembered, however, that the reconnaissance, bombing and ground-attack roles carried out by many fighter pilots were often more dangerous, and more militarily significant, than individual air-to-air combats.

(01) 28.08.16	Not specified	DD	NE of Zinelli	Bristol Scout	RNAS Operations Report
(02) 17.10.17 1145	DFW two-seater	OOC	Comines	Triplane	CR No. 76
(03) 18.10.17 1030	DFW two-seater	OOC	E of Poelcapelle	Triplane	CR No. 78 (shared)
(04) 24.10.17 1330	Two-seater	DES	Comines/Wervicq	Triplane	CR No. 84
(05) 29.10.17 1715	Scout/Fighter	OOC	Gheluvelt	Triplane	CR No. 87
(06) 12.11.17 1545	New-type Scout	DES	Dixmude	Triplane	CR No. 91 & DRO (shared)
(07) 15.11.17 1300	Albatros Scout	DES	Beerst	Camel	CR No. 95 & DRO
(08) 15.11.17 1315	Albatros Scout	OOC	N of Dixmude	Camel	CR No. 95 & DRO
(09) 04.12.17 1600	DFW two-seater	OOC	SE of Dixmude	Camel	CR No. 98 & DRO
(10) 06.12.17 0645	Two-seater	OOC	Forêt d'Houthulst	Camel	CR No. 103 & DRO
(11) 06.12.17 1100	Albatros Scout	OOC	N of Passchendaele	Camel	CR No. 104 & DRO
(12) 10.03.18 1455–1555	Two-seater	OOC	Menin	Camel	DRO & SRB (1)
(13) 16.03.18 1625	Albatros Scout	OOC	Roulers	Camel	CR No. 119 & DRO
(14) 21.03.18 1550	Albatros Scout	OOC	Nieuport	Camel	CR No. 121 & DRO & SRB (1)
(15) 22.03.18 1215–1435	Albatros Scout	OOC	Slype area	Camel	DRO & DSC Bar Citation
(16) 06.04.18 1315	Triplane	OOC	Bouchoir	Camel	CR No. 128
(17) 02.05.18 1010	Albatros two-seater	OOC	N of Albert	Camel	CR No. 144 (shared)

No.	Date/Time	Aircraft type	Result	Location	Aircraft	Reference
(18)	10.05.18 1950	Albatros Scout	OOC	NE of Villers-Bretonneux	Camel	CR No. 160
(19)	15.05.18 1745	Albatros Scout	OOC	E of Albert	Camel	CR No. 163
(20)	16.05.18 0645	Albatros Scout	DES	Bapaume/Mory	Camel	CR No. 164 (shared)
(21)	17.05.18 1800	Triplane	DD	NE of Albert	Camel	CR No. 173
(22)	23.05.18 0845	Albatros Scout	OOC	Arras/Cambrai/Aubigny	Camel	CR No. 181 (shared)
(23)	30.05.18 1055	Pfalz Scout	OOC	SE of Albert	Camel	CR No. 188
(24)	30.05.18 1955	Albatros Scout	OOC	Achiet-le-Grand	Camel	CR No. 191
(25)	19.07.18 1222	Kite Balloon	DES	E of Albert	Camel	CR No. 235 (shared)
(26)	29.07.18 1120	Fokker biplane	OOC	Bailleul/Armentières	Camel	CR No. 236
(27)	30.07.18 1015	Fokker biplane	OOC	S of Armentières	Camel	CR No. 237
(28)	01.08.18 2030	Fokker biplane	OOC	SE of Dickebusch Pond	Camel	SRB (1)
(29)	08.08.18 1105	Two-seater	DD	Foucaucourt/La Flaque	Camel	CR No. 240
(30)	10.08.18 0900	Fokker biplane	OOC	Foucaucourt	Camel	CR No. 246
(31)	10.08.18 1615	Fokker biplane	DES	SE of Rosières	Camel	CR No. 247
(32)	13.08.18 1105	Fokker biplane	OOC	Lihons	Camel	CR No. 252
(33)	13.08.18 1110	Fokker biplane	DES	Rosières	Camel	CR No. 252
(34)	30.09.19	Nieuport	DES	Chernyi Yar	Camel	MS/WD
(35)	07.10.19	Nieuport single-seater	DD	Dubovka	Camel	MS/WD (CR)
(36)	18.10.19	Nieuport	OOC	Peskovatka	Camel	MS/WD

Other Possible Victories . . .

Above the Trenches

A victory attributed to Kink, in a Bristol Scout on 11 August 1916, is not borne out by the Operations Report (AIR 1/2314/223/12): it states that a new-type Fokker which he attacked 'nose-dived about 2,000 feet and made off in the direction of Xanthi. The apparent immunity from damage, although attacked at close quarters, raises the presumption that the vital parts are arm[our]ed.' This machine was clearly not driven down, so the combat was indecisive. Another victory, listed for 17 September 1917, was actually the one correctly listed for 17 October: the Combat Report was wrongly dated. There is no trace in the records of 201 Squadron Record Book of a Kink victory on 11 August 1918.

FAA Museum: Gerrard Papers, 1997/207/0022: 'Early Days of Flying' by Air Commodore E.L. Gerrard (1947)

(37) The victory attributed to Kink by E.L. Gerrard over Hans-Joachim Buddecke, if factual, might be that of 28 August (see pp. 14–15 and (01) above), when an EA was driven down and forced to land. However, Gerrard states that Kink was making 'his first flight over the lines' in a Nieuport. This would not have been the case in late August 1916 if referring to his first flight over the lines *per se*; but it might have been the case if referring to his first flight over the lines *in a Nieuport* rather than a Bristol Scout. On the other hand, the Operations Report for 28 August states that Kink was flying a Bristol Scout, not a Nieuport, during this encounter. Therefore, this might have been an extra victory which was inadequately recorded, given that Combat Reports from No. 2 Wing in the Dardanelles have not survived and that a brief history of the Squadron (see below) states that he had three victories in the Dardanelles, not just one.

National Archives

(38) Although the surviving records support only a single victory by Kink in the Aegean, a short 'History of No. 201 Squadron RAF, late No. 1 Squadron RNAS', apparently prepared in 1919, lists Kink as one of four 'Well-known War Pilots who have served with this Squadron' and states: 'Captain S.M. Kinkead DSC DFC has seen service at Dardanelles with the RNAS and whilst there destroyed three enemy aircraft. Joined this Squadron on 20 September 1917 and remained with it until posted to Home Establishment on 26 August 1918, during which time he destroyed twenty-five EA and carried out much useful work during low flying operations' (AIR 1/176/15/201/1). If the Buddecke encounter is counted as one of the extra two Aegean victories, a net increase of one should be made in Kink's total.

SRB (1)

(39) 01.10.17, 1010–1105: '2 Scouts attacked by Flight Lieutenant Kinkead; one dived vertically for 1,000 feet and was then lost sight of.'

(40) 21.10.17 1145: 'A Scout engaged by Flight Lieutenant Kinkead near Lille spun down for some distance, then nosedived out of sight.'

Ronald Sykes DFC

(41) Two victories attributed to Kink by Ronald Sykes on 11 and 12 August 1918, if factual, were probably based respectively on the events of 12 and 13 August (see pp. 65–8). Sykes alone was credited with the former one (which could, in theory, be added to Kink's total as a 'shared' victory), while the latter would be that referred to under (33) above. Together with the Gerrard story, this could raise his maximum total to forty-one in all three theatres where he served as a fighter pilot. Excluding the four 'driven down', the 'extra' two in the Dardanelles/Aegean theatre and Sykes variations, but allowing the two listed in the Squadron Record Book on 1 and 21 October 1917, the total would come down to thirty-four. Thus, by a slightly different route, one comes to almost the same attribution (thirty-five/forty victories) as is estimated in Chapter Two of *Above the Trenches* (p.40).

Abbreviations

DES   Destroyed; OOC: Shot down out of control; DD: Driven down damaged.

DRO   AIR 1/40/15/9/9 – 1 (Naval) Squadron Daily Reports of Operations, September 1917–March 1918.

SRB (1)   AIR 1/1502/204/40/11 – 1 (Naval)/201 Squadron Record Book, 1 September 1917–30 June 1918.

SRB (2)   AIR 1/1502/204/40/12 – 201 Squadron Record Book, 1 July 1918–26 January 1919.

MS/WD   AIR 1/1959/204/260/28 – 47 Squadron/A Detachment Monthly Summaries and War Diary, June–November 1919.

Sources

AIR 1/39/15/9/5: 12.11.17; 15.11.17; 04.12.17; 06.12.17; 10.03.18.

AIR 1/40/15/9/9: 01.10.17; 17.10.17; 18.10.17; 21.10.17; 24.10.17; 29.10.17; 12.11.17; 15.11.17; 04.12.17; 06.12.17; 10.03.18; 16.03.18; 21.03.18; 22.03.18.

AIR 1/176/15/210/2: 04.12.17; 06.12.17.

AIR 1/1216/204/5/2634 (1 Naval Sqdn): 17.10.17; 18.10.17; 24.10.17; 29.10.17.

AIR 1/1216/204/5/2634 (1 Sqdn RFC, Part 2 – misfiled Combat Reports): 15.11.17; 04.12.17; 06.12.17.

AIR 1/1227/204/5/2634 (201 Sqdn): 06.04.18; 19.07.18; 29.07.18; 10.08.18; 13.08.18.

AIR 1/1502/204/40/11: 01.10.17; 17.10.17; 18.10.17; 21.10.17; 24.10.17; 29.10.17; 10.03.18; 21.03.18; 02.05.18; 10.05.18; 15.05.18; 16.05.18; 17.05.18; 23.05.18; 30.05.18.

AIR 1/1502/204/40/12: 19.07.18; 29.07.18; 30.07.18; 01.08.18; 08.08.18.

AIR 1/1828/204/202/18: 17.10.17; 18.10.17; 24.10.17; 29.10.17.

AIR 1/1829/204/202/21: 29.07.18; 30.07.18.

AIR 1/1959/204/260/28: 30.09.19; 07.10.19; 18.10.19.

AIR 1/2218/209/40/1: 08.08.18; 10.08.18; 13.08.18.

AIR 1/2242/209/42/17: 06.04.18.

AIR 1/2242/209/42/18: 02.05.18; 10.05.18; 15.05.18; 16.05.18; 17.05.18; 23.05.18; 30.05.18.

AIR 1/2243/209/42/20: 19.07.18.

AIR 1/2314/223/12: 28.08.16; 17.10.17; 18.10.17; 24.10.17; 29.10.17; 04.12.17; 06.12.17; 10.03.18; 16.03.18; 21.03.18.

Personnel of No. 2 Wing, RNAS (as at 22 March 1916)

Information based on Gerrard Papers, Fleet Air Arm Museum, Yeovilton – 1997/207/0072.

Wing Commander	E.L. Gerrard
Executive	Sq Cr R. Smyth-Pigott
W/T & Signals	Lt P.L.R. Fraser RNVR
Medical Surgeon	A.G. Sworn
Intelligence & Mapping	2nd Lt W.B. Jones RM
Photography	Lt P. Blair RNVR
Stores	WO W.F. Floyd & WO J. Tozer Mitchell
Transport	WO A.S. Hellawell

'B' Detached Squadron – Flight Commander H. Stanley-Adams

Pilots
Flight Lieutenant A.F. Bettington
Flight Sub-Lieutenant L.A. Hervey
Flight Sub-Lieutenant C.A. Maitland-Heriot
Flight Sub-Lieutenant H.L.E. Tyndale-Biscoe
Flight Sub-Lieutenant C.H. FitzHerbert

Observers
Lieutenant Sassoon
Lieutenant W.T. Grieves
Sub-Lieutenant A. Maitland-Heriot
Sub-Lieutenant C.B. Oxley
Sub-Lieutenant W.E. Slingsby

Surgeon
K. Wolferstan RN

Aircraft
3 Nieuports
3 Henri Farmans

'A' Squadron – Flight Lieutenant K.S. Savory

Pilots
Flight Lieutenant A.F.F. Jacob
Flight Sub-Lieutenant S.M. Kinkead
Flight Sub-Lieutenant H.V. Reid
Flight Sub-Lieutenant K.V. Hooper
Flight Sub-Lieutenant F.E.P. Barrington
Flight Sub-Lieutenant F.D.H. Bremner
Flight Sub-Lieutenant G.K. Blandy

Observers
Second-Lieutenant W.B. Jones
Sub-Lieutenant R.H. Portal

Aircraft
4 Bristol Scouts
3 Moranes
15 Nieuports

'C' Squadron – Flight Lieutenant C.E. Brisley

Pilots
Flight Lieutenant G.F. Smylie
Flight Sub-Lieutenant M.A. Simpson
Flight Sub-Lieutenant R.Y. Bush
Flight Sub-Lieutenant J.H.W. Barnato
Flight Sub-Lieutenant R.S.W. Dickinson
Flight Sub-Lieutenant P.A.F. Belton
Flight Sub-Lieutenant V. Nicholson
Flight Sub-Lieutenant H.K. Thorold

Observers
Lieutenant P. Blair
Midshipman H.E. Burnaby

Aircraft
5 BE2Cs
7 Caudrons
11 Henri Farmans
5 Maurice Farmans
1 Voisin

Appendix III

Location List for 1 Squadron RNAS/ 201 Squadron RAF

Information based on AIR 1/695/21/20/201: History of 1 Squadron RNAS/201 Squadron RAF, 1914–1929, and additional data from Jeff Jefford.

17 October 1914	Gosport	1 Squadron RNAS	
28 January 1915	Dover	1 Squadron RNAS	
26 February 1915	Dunkirk (St Pol)	1 Squadron RNAS	
10 June 1916	Furnes	Redesignated as No. 1 Wing RNAS (21 June 1915)	
		Detached Flight – redesignated as 1 Squadron RNAS (6 December 1916)	
15 February 1917	Chipilly	Attached to: 14th Wing, IV Brigade RFC and redesignated: 1 (Naval) Squadron	In support of: Fourth Army
11 April 1917	La Bellevue	Attached to: 13th Wing, III Brigade RFC	In support of: Third Army
1 June 1917	Bailleul	Attached to: 11th Wing, II Brigade RFC	In support of: Second Army
2 November 1917	Middle Aerodrome	Attached to: No. 4 Wing RNAS	
10 December 1917	Dover	Attached to: No. 4 Wing RNAS	
16 February 1918	Téteghem	Attached to: No. 1 Wing RNAS	
27 March 1918	Ste-Marie-Cappel	Attached to: 11th Wing, II Brigade RFC	In support of: Second Army

28 March 1918	Fienvillers	Attached to: 13th Wing, III Brigade RFC/RAF	In support of: Third Army
		Redesignated as 201 Squadron RAF (1 April 1918)	
12 April 1918	Nœux	Attached to: 13th Wing, III Brigade RAF	In support of: Third Army
20 July 1918	Ste-Marie-Cappel	Attached to: 11th Wing, II Brigade RAF	In support of: Second Army
6 August 1918	Poulainville	Attached to: 22nd Wing, V Brigade RAF	In support of: Fourth Army
14 August 1918	Nœux	Attached to: 13th Wing, III Brigade RAF	In support of: Third Army
19 September 1918	Baizieux	Attached to: 13th Wing, III Brigade RAF	In support of: Third Army
14 October 1918	Beugnâtre	Attached to: 13th Wing, III Brigade RAF	In support of: Third Army
27 October 1918	La Targette	Attached to: 13th Wing, III Brigade RAF	In support of: Third Army
22 November 1918	Béthencourt	Attached to: 13th Wing, III Brigade RAF	In support of: Third Army
23 January 1919	Béthencourt	Reduced to cadre	
15 February 1919	Lake Down	Cadre	
2 September 1919	Eastleigh	Cadre, until disbandment on 31 December 1919	
1 January 1929	Calshot	Reformed, from No. 480 (Coastal Reconnaissance) Flight, as	
		201 (Flying Boat) Squadron RAF	

Appendix IV

Comparison of RFC, RNAS and RAF Ranks

Information based on Above the Trenches, *p. 23.*

RFC	RNAS	RAF
Field Marshal		Air Chief Marshal
General		Air Marshal
Lieutenant-General		Air Vice-Marshal
Major-General		Air Commodore
Brigadier-General		Group Captain
Lieutenant-Colonel	Wing Commander	Wing Commander
Major	Squadron Commander	Squadron Leader
Captain	Flight Commander	Flight Lieutenant
Lieutenant	Flight Lieutenant	Flying Officer/ Observer Officer
2nd Lieutenant	Flight Sub-Lieutenant	Pilot Officer

Appendix V

Comparison of RAF, Royal Navy and Army Ranks

Information based on Air Ministry Weekly Order 973/1919, 27 August 1919.

RAF	Royal Navy	Army
Marshal of the Air (From 1925: Marshal of the RAF)	Admiral of the Fleet	Field Marshal
Air Chief Marshal	Admiral	General
Air Marshal	Vice-Admiral	Lieutenant-General
Air Vice-Marshal	Rear-Admiral	Major-General
Air Commodore	Commodore (1st & 2nd Class)	Brigadier-General
Group Captain	Captain (of 3 years' seniority)	Colonel
Wing Commander	Commander (and Captain of under 3 years' seniority)	Lieutenant-Colonel
Squadron Leader	Lieutenant-Commander	Major
Flight Lieutenant	Lieutenant	Captain
Flying Officer/ Observer Officer	Sub-Lieutenant	Lieutenant
Pilot Officer	Chief Gunner etc.	2nd Lieutenant

Appendix VI

Assessment of the Loss of Supermarine-Napier S5 Seaplane N221 on 12 March 1928

Letter from Dr David Kirkpatrick FRAeS (Visiting Professor, Defence Academy of the UK) to the author, 7 April 2010.

Dear Julian,

I have read with great interest the two draft Chapters you sent me covering the fatal accident in the Solent. I like the way the text transferred from Calshot to Westminster and back; the politicians of the 1920s were, like those of today, concerned about the effects of a peace dividend.

In historical research the preferred approach to evidence is to establish 'who said it first?' and 'how did he know?'; but in the 21st Century there is often such a torrent of statements that it is hard to establish chronology and hence which statements might have been influenced by earlier ones. In this (very rapid) accident, it is clear that many of the witnesses were watching a small aircraft from a considerable distance, and from an unfavourable angle, and could not have been sure how fast the aircraft was travelling or at what angle it hit the sea.

Also, it is an intrinsic hazard of racing or record-breaking that vehicles are optimised for performance rather than for safety or reliability, and such designs are prone to disastrous breakages whenever there are relatively minor variations in the strengths of components or in the stresses imposed on them.

There are three main plausible explanations for the accident:

1. During an attempt at landing, in response to some unspecified emergency, the pilot allowed the airspeed to fall below the point at which a wing stalled, lost lift and dropped the aircraft into the sea,
2. During an attempt on the air speed record, the pilot misjudged altitude and flew straight into the sea in a shallow dive, and
3. During an attempt on the air speed record in level flight, some failure of airframe, aero-engine or pilot caused the aircraft to change abruptly its direction of flight and to dive into the sea.

Although both the RAF and the Coroner accepted explanation 1, in default of evidence for any other, it seems to me unlikely. An experienced pilot would have been very well aware of the danger of stalling, and Kinkead had twice already successfully landed the S5. It is conceivable that if he had been ill, or distracted by some imminent catastrophe, he might possibly have diverted his attention from his air speed indicator, but I really doubt it. Biard, Perrin and Smith all agreed that just before the accident the aircraft was flying at very high speed, which virtually precludes stalling. Only an unnamed officer on a Coastal Motor Boat claimed to a newspaper reporter that the pilot had slowed down, and the phrase 'or so it seemed' in his reported statement hardly sounds confident; furthermore second-hand evidence is intrinsically less reliable.

The sudden roar from the engine noted by Perrin and the unnamed officer could have been the pilot's response to a dangerously low airspeed and thus consistent with explanation 1, or it could have been the pilot seeking maximum power as he approached the timed course for the record attempt (which the *Morning Post* and the *Echo* were probably expecting to hear), or it could even have been the result of some machinery failure allowing the engine to race while depriving the aircraft of thrust. The roar does not, in my view, settle the argument either way.

I can offer no useful comment on explanation 2, having no experience of landing seaplanes on water. Coombes' experience demands respect for his choice of this explanation, but there were very many others who insisted that the S5 aircraft made a sudden change of course from virtually horizontal to a near-vertical dive, and their observations (albeit some not very trustworthy) are incompatible with a shallow dive into the sea.

Although Major Cooper's inspection of the remains did not discover that anything had gone wrong with the aircraft, it is certainly possible that some such failure did occur and that the evidence of it was destroyed by the crash and the subsequent salvage activity, dredging the bits of the aircraft from the Solent. If the retrospective RAF evidence on the S5's speed can be believed, the associated aerodynamic forces could have exceeded the design strength of some component (a bracing wire?) so that it failed abruptly and caused the aircraft to dive. Biard had the most relevant experience of all the witnesses, and his diagnosis of structural failure is convincing. Any witness or organisation may be subconsciously inclined to adopt the most congenial explanation for an accident. Thus Biard may have wished to exonerate a fellow pilot and the RAF may have wished to preserve the reputation for airworthiness of UK aircraft. With no conclusive evidence either way, I would bet on explanation 3.

Yours sincerely,

David

Awards to Flight Lieutenant S.M. Kinkead

Held at the National Museum of Military History, Johannesburg.

Distinguished Service Order
Distinguished Service Cross
Bar to Distinguished Service Cross
Distinguished Flying Cross
Bar to Distinguished Flying Cross
1914–15 Star
War Medal
Victory Medal with Mention in Despatches Emblem
General Service Medal with Kurdistan Clasp

Foreign Awards
Order of St George, 4th Class (Russia)
Order of St Vladimir, 4th Class with Swords (Russia)
Order of St Anne, 2nd Class (Russia)
Order of St Stanislaus, 2nd Class (Russia)
King Faisal War Medal (Iraq)

Sources and Further Reading

Introduction

Aerodrome, The: Aces and Aircraft of World War I (http://www.theaerodrome.com).

Barfield, Norman: *Supermarine (Archive Photographs)* (Chalford, Stroud, 1996).

British Military Powerboat Trust website (http://www.bmpt.org.uk/index.htm).

Brown, Alan: *They Flew from the Forest* (privately published, nd).

Cruddas, Colin: *In Hampshire's Skies* (Tempus, Stroud, 2001).

Hood, Mark: Loss of Whitley bomber P5044
   (http://www.bbc.co.uk/ww2peopleswar/user/05/u933805.shtml).

Jones, Ira: *The Kinkead Memorial Portrait Fund* (nd, but probably 1929). This booklet lists more than 500 contributors, from Air Marshals to junior officers and from aviation companies to private citizens, who between them donated the total of £726 15s 5d – worth about £24,000 today. The Memorial Committee, consisting of five officers including 'Mary' Coningham, James Robb and 'Taffy' Jones (its Secretary), used £600 of this sum for the two portraits by George Harcourt, £30 for the gravestone at Fawley, and just over £49 for the Kinkead Trophy at Cranwell. I am grateful to Léonie Rosenstiel, widow of Arthur Orrmont, for supplying a copy of this document which recorded Marion Aten's own contribution, together with those of Trenchard, Borton, Geoffrey and John Salmond, Higgins, Douglas, Rowley, Fulford, French, Vincent, Brand, Pulford, Orlebar, Chick and Webster, to name but a few. The Gloster Aircraft Company donated £150 – worth about £5,000 today – whilst Supermarine and Napier gave fifty guineas each.

Lewis, Julian: Maiden Speech, *Hansard*, 20 May 1997
   (http://www.julianlewis.net/speech_detail.php?id=1).

Lewis, Julian: EDM 950, initially tabled by seventy MPs on 9 March 1998
   (http://www.julianlewis.net/edm_detail.php?id=1).

Lewis, Julian: 'The Life of Fl/Lt S.M. "Kink" Kinkead (1897–1928)'
   (http://www.julianlewis.net/local_news_detail.php?id=18).

Murley, Clare & Graham Parkes: *The Parish Church of All Saints, Fawley* (Waterside Heritage, 2007).

National Register of Historic Vessels: HSL102
   (http://nationalhistoricships.org.uk/index.cfm/event/getVessel/vref/525).

Nelson, Garry: 'Sam Kinkead', *Aeroplane Monthly*, October 1993.

Press reports: *Lymington Times* (21 March 1998); *Southern Daily Echo* (11 & 16 March 1998).

RAF Cranwell: *The Journal of the Royal Air Force College*, Vol. IX, No. 1, Spring 1929.

Rance, Adrian: *Fast Boats and Flying Boats – A biography of Hubert Scott-Paine* (Ensign, Southampton, 1989).

Shipley, Edwin: *The Green Eagles of Calshot* (privately printed, 1992).

Solent Sky Museum: Supermarine S6A – N248
   (http://www.spitfireonline.co.uk/popup/exhibit12.html).

Chapter 1: An End and a Beginning

ADM 273/4/94; ADM 273/7/81; ADM 273/30/124: Samuel Marcus Kinkead RNAS.

AIR 1/649/17/122/408: Organisation of RNAS Units in Mediterranean, April 1917–August 1918.

AIR 1/649/17/122/420: Reorganisation of Air Service in Eastern Mediterranean, January–March 1916.

AIR 1/649/17/122/421: Report on Flight by S/Cdr Davies and F/S/Lt Smylie, November–December 1915.

AIR 1/661/17/122/642: Reports on Flight from Imbros to Bucharest, October–November 1916.

AIR 1/682/21/13/2226: A Short History of the Royal Naval Air Service (compiled by J.C. Nerney, AHB).

AIR 1/2301/212/7: Personal Reminiscences of Group Captain E.L. Gerrard RAF, 1914–15.

AIR 1/2301/215/5: Arming of Aircraft, 1914–18.

AIR 1/2314/223/12: RNAS Operations Reports, Nos. 1–53, November 1915–March 1918.

Ashworth, Chris: *Action Stations – 9. Military Airfields of the Central South and South-East* (Patrick Stephens, Wellingborough, 1985).

Bremner, Donald & David Lance: 'Naval Pilot in the Aegean – 1916', *Cross & Cockade* Magazine, Vol. 5, No. 4, 1974.

Bruce, J.M.: *The Sopwith Pup* (Profile, Leatherhead, 1965).

Davies, Sir Richard Bell: *Sailor in the Air* (Pen & Sword, Barnsley, 2008).

Falls, Cyril: *The First World War* (Longmans, London, 1960).

Franks, Norman, Frank Bailey & Russell Guest: *Above the Lines – A Complete Record of the Fighter Aces of the German Air Service, Naval Air Service and Flanders Marine Corps, 1914–1918* (Grub Street, London, 1993).

Gerrard, E.L.: Collected Papers (Fleet Air Arm Museum, Yeovilton), including 'Early Days of Flying' (1947).

Jones, H.A.: *The War in the Air*, Vol. II, Ch. I, 'The Dardanelles Campaign' (Oxford University Press, Oxford, 1928).

Jones, H.A.: *The War in the Air*, Vol. V, Ch. VII, 'Naval Operations in the Mediterranean and Near-Eastern Waters, 1916–March 1918' (Oxford University Press, Oxford, 1935).

Kincaid, Bill: *This I'll Defend – The Story of the Kincaids* (Thesaurus, Walton-on-Thames, 2003).

Lewis, Bruce: *A Few of the First* (Leo Cooper, London, 1997).

Longmore, Sir Arthur: *From Sea to Sky, 1910–1945* (Geoffrey Bles, London, 1946).

Press reports: *Sussex Daily News* (4 & 5 September 1917); *The Times* (5 September 1917); *Worthing Gazette* (5 September 1917); *West Sussex Gazette* (16 September 1917).

Samson, Charles Rumney: *Fights and Flights – A Memoir of the Royal Naval Air Service in World War I* (The Battery Press, Nashville, 1990 – originally published, 1930).

Thetford, Owen: *British Naval Aircraft since 1912* (Putnam, London, 1962).

WO 339/115734: Second Lieutenant T.C. Kinkead.

Chapter 2: Glory Days – The Western Front.

AIR 1/39/15/9/5: RNAS Fortnightly Communiqués, January 1917–March 1918.

AIR 1/40/15/9/9: No. 1 Squadron RNAS, Daily Reports of Operations, September 1917–March 1918.

AIR 1/176/15/210/2: No. 1 Squadron RNAS, Daily Reports of Operations, November 1917–March 1918.

AIR 1/675/21/13/803: Notes on Air Stations & Squadrons Participating in Air Pageants, 1922–3.

AIR 1/695/21/20/201: History of No. 1 Squadron RNAS/201 Squadron RAF, 1914–1929.

AIR 1/1216/204/5/2634 (1 NAVAL SQDN): Combat Reports, 1 (Naval) Squadron, April–October 1917.

AIR 1/1227/204/5/2634 (201 SQDN): Combat Reports, 201 Squadron, March–September 1918.

AIR 1/1501/204/40/3: 1 (Naval) Squadron/201 Squadron, Field Returns, 30 March 1918–8 February 1919.

AIR 1/1501/204/40/5: 201 Squadron RAF, Standing Orders for Patrols, 28 April–16 October 1918.

AIR 1/1501/204/40/6: 201 Squadron RAF, Operation Orders Issued by III Brigade RAF, 30 May–17 November 1918.

AIR 1/1502/204/40/11: 1 (Naval) Squadron/201 Squadron RAF, Squadron Record Book, 1 September 1917–30 June 1918.
AIR 1/1502/204/40/12: 201 Squadron RAF, Squadron Record Book, 1 July 1918–26 January 1919.
AIR 1/1828/204/202/18: 11 Wing RFC, Combat Reports, September–October 1917.
AIR 1/1828/204/202/19: 11 Wing RFC, Combat Reports, November 1917–January 1918.
AIR 1/1829/204/202/20: 11 Wing RFC, Combat Reports, May–June 1918.
AIR 1/1829/204/202/21: 11 Wing RFC, Combat Reports, June–July 1918.
AIR 1/1829/204/202/22: 11 Wing RFC, Combat Reports, August–September 1918.
AIR 1/2218/209/40/1: V Brigade RAF, War Diary, August 1918.
AIR 1/2241/209/42/15: III Brigade RAF War Diary, March 1918.
AIR 1/2242/209/42/16: III Brigade RAF War Diary, March 1918.
AIR 1/2242/209/42/17: III Brigade RAF War Diary, April 1918.
AIR 1/2242/209/42/18: III Brigade RAF War Diary, May 1918.
AIR 1/2243/209/42/19: III Brigade RAF War Diary, June 1918.
AIR 1/2243/209/42/20: III Brigade RAF War Diary, July 1918.
AIR 1/2243/209/42/21: III Brigade RAF War Diary, August 1918.

Bowyer, Chaz: *Sopwith Camel – King of Combat* (Glasney Press, Falmouth, 1978).
Bruce, J.M.: *Sopwith Camel* (Arms and Armour Press, London, 1989).
Douglas, Sholto: *Years of Combat* (Collins, London, 1963).
Franks, Norman: *Dog-Fight – Aerial Tactics of the Aces of World War I* (Greenhill, London, 2003).
Gray, Randal & Christopher Argyle: *Chronicle of the First World War*, Vol. II, 1917–1921 (Facts on File, Oxford, 1991).
Green, Peter & Mike Hodgson: *Cranwell – RNAS & RAF Photographs* (Midland Publishing, Leicester, 1993).
Green, William & Gordon Swanborough: *The Complete Book of Fighters* (Salamander, London, 2001).
Hellwig, Adrian: *Australian Hawk over the Western Front – A Biography of Major R.S. Dallas DSO DSC* (Grub Street, London, 2006).
Jones, H.A.: *The War in the Air*, Vol. IV, Ch. V, 'The Battles of Ypres, 1917'; Ch. VII, 'The German Offensive, 1918' (Oxford University Press, Oxford, 1934).
Jones, H.A.: *The War in the Air*, Vol. VI, Ch. I, 'The Creation of the Royal Air Force'; Ch. XI, 'Prelude to Victory'; Ch. XII, 'The Amiens Offensive'; Ch. XIII, 'The Battle of Bapaume'; Ch. XIV, 'Victory' (Oxford University Press, Oxford, 1937).
Jones, H.A.: *The War in the Air*, Appendices (Oxford University Press, Oxford, 1937).
Lucas, John: *The Silken Canopy – A History of the Parachute* (Airlife, Shrewsbury, 1997).
Sheffield, Gary: *Forgotten Victory – The First World War: Myths and Realities* (Headline, London, 2001).
Shores, Christopher, Norman Franks & Russell Guest: *Above the Trenches – A Complete Record of the Fighter Aces and Units of the British Empire Air Forces, 1915–1920* (Grub Street, London, 1990).
Shores, Christopher, Norman Franks & Russell Guest: *Above the Trenches – Supplement* (Grub Street, London, 1996).
Steel, Nigel & Peter Hart: *Tumult in the Clouds – The British Experience of the War in the Air, 1914–1918* (Hodder & Stoughton, London, 1997).
Sykes, Ronald: Interview in Sound Archive, Imperial War Museum, Ref. 301/7, Reels 4–5.
Sykes, Ronald: 'Serving with 201 Squadron RAF', *Cross & Cockade* Magazine, Vol. 2, No. 2, 1971.

Chapter 3: Russia – The Squadron Records

AIR 1/15/15/1/67: War Diary of 'Z' Flight of the late Instructional Mission, 30 November 1919–5 January 1920.
AIR 1/408/15/232/1: War Diary of 'A' Detachment, 47 Squadron, and Instructional Mission, November 1919–March 1920.
AIR 1/408/15/232/7: RAF South Russia, Report for 16–30 April 1920.

AIR 1/448/15/303/48: Résumés of Operations, Middle East and South Russia, April 1919–May 1921.

AIR 1/1957/204/260/12: Recommendations for Honours and Awards, May 1919–April 1920.

AIR 1/1959/204/260/28: War Diary of 47 Squadron, June–November 1919.

AIR 1/1963/204/260/53: Daily States of 47 Squadron, South Russia, 1919.

Brough, Ray: *White Russian Awards to British & Commonwealth Servicemen during the Allied Intervention in Russia, 1918–1920, With a Roll of Honour* (Tom Donovan, London 1991).

Collishaw, Raymond & R.V. Dodds: *Air Command – A Fighter Pilot's Story* (William Kimber, London, 1973).

Collishaw to Boulnois: 6 May 1955 (47 Squadron archives).

Gilbert, Martin: *Winston S. Churchill*, Vol. IV, 1917–1922 (Heinemann, London, 1975).

Gilbert, Martin: *Winston S. Churchill*, Companion Vol. IV, Part 2, July 1919–March 1921 (Heinemann, London, 1977).

House of Commons: *Hansard* (16 July 1919, Col. 370; 18 August 1919, Col. 1947W; 30 October 1919, Col. 902; 25 November 1919, Col. 1605; 1 December 1919, Cols 56–7W; 16 December 1919, Cols 205–7).

Jackson, Robert: *At War with the Bolsheviks – The Allied Intervention into Russia, 1917–20* (Tom Stacey, London, 1972).

Jones, H.A.: *Over the Balkans and South Russia – Being the History of No. 47 Squadron RAF* (Edward Arnold, London, 1923).

Kinvig, Clifford: *Churchill's Crusade – The British Invasion of Russia, 1918–1920* (Hambledon Continuum, London & New York, 2006).

Kondratyev, Vyacheslav & Marat Khayrulin: *Aircraft of the Russian Civil War* (Gauntlet Publications/Military History Bookshop, Folkestone, 2009). This unusual volume, translated by Tom Hillman, identifies on p.100 the two pilots who attacked 47 Squadron on 30 September 1919 as Shchekin and Korotkov. According to eyewitnesses, when Kink shot down Shchekin into the Volga, his Nieuport did not sink immediately. They saw him 'climb from the cockpit, but to swim a hundred metres to the bank, against the current, was not to be'. Korotkov was killed exactly one month later.

Lenin, V.I.: 'Telegram to the Commander of the 10th Army', 4 April 1919 (www.marxists.org).

Trotsky, Leon: *Military Writings*, Vol. 2, Order No. 80, 2 March 1919; 'A Great Victory', 25 October 1919 (www.marxists.org).

WO 33/971: Final Report of the British Military Mission, South Russia, by Major-General Sir H.C. Holman, 1920.

Chapter 4: Russia – The Aten Chronicles

AIR 1/1963/204/260/54: Report on the Evacuation of Taganrog & the Resignation of Wing Commander Maund from Command of the RAF in South Russia, January 1920.

Aten, Marion: *A Dead Red Rose – An Aviator's Adventures with Desert Angels* (Ralph Fletcher Seymour, Chicago, 1950).

Aten, Marion (as told to H. Bedford-Jones): 'Flying Madmen', Parts 1–5, *Liberty* magazine, 31 August–28 September 1935 (Liberty Publishing Corporation, New York).

Aten, Marion & Arthur Orrmont: *Last Train Over Rostov Bridge* (Messner, New York & Copp Clark, Canada, 1961; Cassell, London, 1962). A new and revised edition, edited by Michael Aten, was published in 2011 by Thin Red Line Books (Ashgrove Publishing, London).

Collishaw to Imogen Aten: 23 September, 15 & 24 October 1961 (Gary Radder Esq).

Winter, Denis: *The First of the Few – Fighter Pilots of the First World War* (Penguin, Harmondsworth, 1983).

Chapter 5: Counter-Insurgency in Iraq

AIR 5/292: Despatches from AVM Sir John Salmond, Baghdad, 22 May & 21 June 1923 (published as a Supplement to the *London Gazette*, 11 June 1924). Publication of these Despatches, covering 15 February–30 April & 28 April–19 June 1923, was delayed at the request of the Foreign Office and the Colonial Office. They considered it 'undesirable' until 'a final settlement has been reached with the Turkish Government in regard to the delimitation of the Turco-Iraq frontier in the Mosul Area'.

AIR 5/476: File S.15327 – RAF Control in Mesopotamia, 1921–3.

AIR 10/1115: Iraq Command Report, October 1922–April 1924 (AVM Sir John Salmond, 3 April 1924).

AIR 10/1319: Iraq Command Report, April 1924–November 1926 (AVM J.F.A. Higgins, 19 November 1926).

AIR 10/1845: Report on the Operations in Southern Kurdistan against Sheikh Mahmud, October 1930–May 1931 (C.Ll. Bullock, April 1932).

AIR 20/10207: Report on RAF Operations in Iraq from 1 February to 1 October 1922 (Air Cdre A.E. Borton, 31 March 1923).

Borton, Amyas: 'The Use of Aircraft in Small Wars', *Journal of the Royal United Service Institution*, Vol. LXV, February–November 1920.

Bowyer, Chaz: *RAF Operations, 1918–1938* (Kimber, London, 1988).

Cox, Jafna L.: 'A Splendid Training Ground: The Importance to the Royal Air Force of its Role in Iraq, 1919–32', *Journal of Imperial and Commonwealth History*, Vol. XIII, No. 2, January 1985.

Hamlin, John: *Flat Out: The Story of 30 Squadron, Royal Air Force* (Air-Britain, Tunbridge Wells, 2002).

House of Commons: *Hansard* (16 December 1919, Col. 1276W).

Jones, Ira: *An Air Fighter's Scrapbook* (Greenhill Books, London, 1990 – originally published in 1938).

Omissi, David: *Air Power and Colonial Control – The Royal Air Force, 1919–1939* (Manchester University Press, Manchester, 1990).

Salmond, Sir John: 'The Air Force in Iraq', *Journal of the Royal United Service Institution*, Vol. LXX, February–November 1925.

Sturtivant, Ray & Gordon Page: *The DH4/DH9 File* (Air-Britain, Tunbridge Wells, 1999).

Vincent, S.F.: *Flying Fever* (Jarrolds, London, 1972).

WO 374/7499: Captain S.S. Bond MC.

WO 374/45681: Captain R.K. Makant MC & Bar.

Chapter 6: Imperial Links – The Cape Flight

AIR 2/299: File 695962/26 – Publicity on Return of RAF Cape Flight, 1926.

AIR 2/299: File 730800/26 – Publication of Report on RAF Cape Flight, 1926.

AIR 10/1297: Report on the Cairo–Cape Flight carried out between 1st March and 21st June 1926 (Air Publication 1271, Air Ministry, April 1927).

Burge, C.G.: *Complete Book of Aviation* (Pitman, London, 1935).

Coningham, A.: Report on the Cairo–Kano Flight carried out between 27th October and 19th November 1925 (Air Publication 1202, Air Ministry, March 1926).

Flight magazine: 'Return of the Cape Flight', 24 June 1926.

House of Commons: *Hansard* (12 March 1925, Cols 1677–8; 25 February 1926, Cols 773–4).

Kinkead, S.M.: RAF Cape Flight Ground Party (& Draft AOC Letter to Air Ministry), August 1926 (Kinkead file, Fleet Air Arm Museum, Yeovilton).

Press report: *The Times* (31 October 1925).

Pulford, C.W.H.: 'The Royal Air Force Flight from Cairo to the Cape', *Journal of the Royal United Service Institution*, Vol. LXXII, February–November 1927.

Robertson, F.A. de V.: 'Return of the Cape Flight', *Flight* magazine, 24 June 1926.

Chapter 7: High Speed Flight – The Whitehall View

AIR 2/1215: File S.25597 – High Speed Seaplane Flight: Formation at Felixstowe, 1926–31.

AIR 5/508: File S.25008 – Participation of RAF Personnel in Schneider Cup Races, 1925–9.

AIR 5/525: File 749304/27 – Policy and Press Questions regarding 1927 Schneider Cup Race, 1927.

AIR 5/526: File 767659/27 – Organisation of RAF Flight for 1927 Schneider Cup Race, 1927–8.

AIR 5/529: File S.25997 – Schneider Cup Race, 1927 (General File), 1927.

AIR 5/530: File S.26233 – Organisation and Administration of High Speed Flight, Felixstowe, 1926–8.

AIR 19/126: Schneider Trophy Contest, 1927–9.

AVIA 19/313: Report ref. F/A/68 – MAEE: Notes on the Schneider Cup Race, 1927.

Andrews, C.F. & E.B. Morgan: *Supermarine Aircraft since 1914* (Putnam, London, 1981).

Baker, Anne: *From Biplane to Spitfire – The Life of ACM Sir Geoffrey Salmond* (Pen & Sword, Barnsley, 2003).

Flight magazine: 'Souvenir Number – The Schneider Trophy Contest', 6 September 1929.

James, Derek N.: *Gloster Aircraft since 1917* (2nd edition, Putnam, London, 1987).

James, Derek N.: *Schneider Trophy Aircraft 1913–1931* (Putnam, London, 1981).

Kinsey, Gordon: *Seaplanes – Felixstowe* (revised edition, Terence Dalton, Lavenham, 1985).

Chapter 8: High Speed Flight – The Pilot's View

Coombes, Lawrence: Text of Schneider Trophy Illustrated Talk (State Library of Victoria: Coombes Archive, MS13357, Series 9/Sequence 11).

Schofield, H.M.: *The High Speed and Other Flights* (John Hamilton, London, 1932).

Shipley, Edwin: *The Green Eagles of Calshot* (privately printed, 1992).

Chapter 9: Victory at Venice

Barker, Ralph: *The Schneider Trophy Races* (2nd edition, Airlife, Shrewsbury, 1981).

Eves, Edward: *The Schneider Trophy Story* (Airlife, Shrewsbury, 2001).

Moldon, David (ed.): *The Schneider Trophy Contest, 1913–1931, 50th Anniversary* (Schneider 81, Winchester, 1981).

Mondey, David: *The Schneider Trophy* (Robert Hale, London, 1975).

Press reports: 21 September–25 October 1927, Kinkead Presentation Album (Durrant's Press Agency, 1927).

Smith, Alan: *Schneider Trophy – Diamond Jubilee: Looking Back Sixty Years* (Waterfront Publications, Poole, 1991).

Templewood, Viscount (Sir Samuel Hoare): *Empire of the Air – The Advent of the Air Age, 1922–1929* (Collins, London, 1957).

Van Geffen, Colin: *The Story of the Schneider Trophy Air Races* (narrated by Alina Jenkins, audio book, Scarecrow Productions, 2009 – based on the author's illustrated presentations of the history of the contest, and available via 07801-817928).

Wilson, Charles & William Reader: *Men and Machines – A History of D. Napier & Son, Engineers, Ltd, 1808–1958* (Weidenfeld and Nicolson, London, 1958).

Chapter 10: Reactions to the Race

AIR 2/323: File S.26568 – Future Policy after 1927 Schneider Trophy Race, 1927–9.

AIR 2/1215: File S.25597 – High Speed Seaplane Flight: Formation at Felixstowe, 1926–31.

AIR 5/529: File S.25997 – Schneider Cup Race, 1927 (General File), 1927.

AIR 19/126: Schneider Trophy Contest, 1927–9.

Press reports: 21 September–25 October 1927, Kinkead Presentation Album (Durrant's Press Agency, 1927).

Chapter 11: Disaster in the Solent

AIR 28/120: Operations Record Book, covering RAF Calshot, 1928.

Biard, H.C.: *Wings* (Hurst & Blackett, London, 1934).

Biard, H.C.: 'The Spitfire's Ancestors' (interview) (BBC Sound Archive, Catalogue no. 892659; Reference no. 23782(1), 18 September 1957). I am grateful to Colin van Geffen for alerting me to this recording.

House of Commons: *Hansard* (12 March 1928, Cols 1533–1666).

Kenworthy, J.M.: *Sailors, Statesmen – and Others: An Autobiography* (Rich & Cowan, London, 1933); Obituary, *The Times*, 9 October 1953.

Press reports: *Birmingham Gazette, Daily Telegraph* (25 October 1927); *Daily Express, Daily Sketch, Daily Telegraph, Morning Post, Hampshire Advertiser and Southampton Times, Southern Daily Echo, The Times* (6–13 March 1928).

Shelton, John: *Schneider Trophy to Spitfire: The Design Career of R.J. Mitchell* (Haynes Publishing, Yeovil, 2008).

Chapter 12: An End and an Aftermath

ADM 116/2712: Case no. 2555 – Schneider Trophy Races, 1929–31.

AIR 2/1215: File S.25597 – High Speed Seaplane Flight: Formation at Felixstowe, 1926–31.

AIR 10/1449: SD(33)1 – RAF Report on Flying Accidents during January–June 1928.

AIR 19/126: Schneider Trophy Contest, 1927–9: Speech by Sir Samuel Hoare at the Birmingham Conservative Club, press released on 23 March 1928.

Air of Authority – A History of RAF Organisation· including Service records of senior officers (http://www.rafweb.org/Cdrs_Alp_ind.htm).

Baker, Hazel: Correspondence with the Author, 1999.

Coombes, Lawrence: Text of Schneider Trophy Illustrated Talk (State Library of Victoria: Coombes Archive, MS13357, Series 9/Sequence 11).

Drummond, Maldwin: Correspondence with the Author, 2009.

Etherington, William Charles: Interview with Alexander McKee, 8 March 1980, via Hazel Baker.

Housman, Laurence (ed.): *War Letters of Fallen Englishmen* (Gollancz, London, 1930).

Jones, Ira: *An Air Fighter's Scrapbook* (Greenhill Books, London, 1990 – originally published in 1938).

Jones, Ira: *Tiger Squadron – The Story of 74 Squadron RAF in Two World Wars* (W.H. Allen, London, 1954).

Kinkead file, Fleet Air Arm Museum, Yeovilton: Letters of condolence to Mrs Helen Kinkead, 1928.

Kirkpatrick, David: Correspondence with the Author, 2010.

McKee, Alexander: *Into the Blue – Great Mysteries of Aviation*, Ch. 5, 'The High Speed Flyer' (Souvenir Press, London, 1981); Letter, *Southern Daily Echo*, 26 February 1980.

McKinstry, Leo: *Spitfire – Portrait of a Legend* (John Murray, London, 2007).

Mitchell, Gordon: *R.J. Mitchell – Schooldays to Spitfire* (revised edn, privately published, 1997).

Owen, William Richard: Diary entries, March 1928 (courtesy of Jonathan Falconer). A fitter with the High Speed Flight who also looked after Kink's car, Owen noted that N221 had 'Crashed from 50ft full out ab[ou]t 340mph (?) flying towards sun'. Following the two-day RAF Court of Inquiry, he added incredulously: 'Major Cooper on Court found accident due to stalling whilst landing?'

Press reports: *Hampshire Advertiser and Southampton Times* (17 & 31 March 1928); *Southern Daily Echo* (14–17 March, 28 March & 20 April 1928).

Index

(Bold entries in brackets refer to
image numbers in the plates sections)

259

260

Mitchell, John, **(29)** 75–6; awarded DSO, 75

Mitchell, Reginald Joseph, **(39, 40)** xvii, 192, 202, 257; death, 224; designs Sea Lion II, 141; designs S4, 118, 141; designs S5, 155; designs S6A, S6B and Spitfire, 184, 224; tail flutter, 232; views on safety, 204; witnesses Kink's death, 217–19

Mitylene, 6, 21

Mondey, David, 183–4, 256

Mongalla, 121–3, 127, 130, 132, 136

Monro, Charles, 12–13

Mooltan, 139

Moon, Thomas Henry, **(49)** 171, 193

Moorslede, 29, 34

Morcourt, 61

Morecambe Bay, 198

Moreuil, 52

Morlancourt, 59

Morgan, Herbert Glyn Rhys, 235–6

Morning Post, 153, 173, 180, 191, 214–15, 249

Moscow, 65, 90–1, 97

Mosul, 102, 104, 109, 111, 113, 116, 255

Murmansk, 71

Mussolini, Benito, 169, 177, 191, 234

Nairobi, 130, 132, 136, 227

Napier engines (D. Napier & Son), 118, 124, 127, 139, 141, 150, 155–6, 174–5, 183–5, 188, 192, 200, 202, 209, 225, 256; Kinkead Memorial, 251

Naples, 137–8, 141, 217

N'dola, 128, 133

Needles, 137

Nestos, River, 14, 21, 23

Netley Castle, 163

New Forest, xiv–xv, 207

New Zealand, xii, 48

Nicholas II, 71

Nieuport, 28, 40, 44, 52, 237

Nieuport and General Aircraft Company, 142

Nigeria, 119–20, 124

Nile, River, 121–3, 131–2, 134

Nimule, 121–3, 128, 131–3, 136

Nœux-lès-Auxi, 56, 68, 245

Northern Rhodesia, 128, 133–4

Northolt Aerodrome, 125

Novocherkassk, 92, 94

Novorossiysk, 72–4, 76, 93–4

Nyasaland, 132

Observer, 176

Olinoye, 81

Olynyk, Frank, 36, 237

Omissi, David, 102–4, 255

Orel, 83, 97

Orlebar, Augustus Henry, 231–3; Kinkead Memorial, 251

Orr, Robert Seton Scott, 54–5, 60–1

Orrmont, Arthur, 87, 98, 251, 254

Orwell, River, 163

Ostend, 15, 27–8, 42–3, 145–6

Owen, William Richard, 257

Palapwe Road, 134

Palestine, 8, 103

parachutes, 35, 42, 59, 102, 203–4, 253; lives saved, 234–5

Passchendaele, 31–4, 36, 38, 40, 235, 237

Pattenden, Harry, 2–3

Payne, James Humphrey Allen, 4–5

Payne, William Labat, 125, 138

Pemberton-Billing, Noel, xviii

Péronne, 48

Perrin, Harold Ernest, 201; views on loss of N221, 219, 226, 249

Persia, 102, 111, 114, 116–17

Peschanoye, 86

Peskovatka, 81, 238

Petrograd, 71

Philbrick, Revd. Gary, xviii

Pishder tribe, 110

Pixton, Howard, 140

Poelcapelle, 32, 37, 237

Poland, 77

Polygon Wood, 32, 34, 36

porpoising, 158, 212

Port Said, 99, 139

Port Sudan, 121

Portland, 164

Portsmouth, 6, 12, 216, 222

Portsmouth Group, 164

Poulainville, 56, 61, 245

Pretoria, 128, 133–5

Prévost, Maurice, 140

Princess, 104

Proyart, 62

Pugh, Cecil, 4

Pulford, Conway Walter Heath, Cape Flight, 120–1, 124–38, 255; death, 233–4; Kinkead Memorial, 251

Pyramids, 134

Quinnell, John Charles ('Paddy'), 223–4

Rania, 106–8, 110

Ransome, Edward, 225

Rawlinson, Henry Seymour, 48